International Economic Negotiation: Models versus Reality

The International Institute for Applied Systems Analysis

is an interdisciplinary, nongovernmental research institution founded in 1972 by leading scientific organizations in 12 countries. Situated near Vienna, in the center of Europe, IIASA has been for more than two decades producing valuable scientific research on economic, technological, and environmental issues.

IIASA was one of the first international institutes to systematically study global issues of environment, technology, and development. IIASA's Governing Council states that the Institute's goal is: *to conduct international and interdisciplinary scientific studies to provide timely and relevant information and options, addressing critical issues of global environmental, economic, and social change, for the benefit of the public, the scientific community, and national and international institutions.* Research is organized around three central themes:

– Environment and Natural Resources;
– Energy and Technology;
– Population and Society.

The Institute now has national member organizations in the following countries:

Austria
The Austrian Academy of Sciences

Bulgaria*
The Bulgarian Committee for IIASA

Finland
The Finnish Committee for IIASA

Germany**
The Association for the Advancement
of IIASA

Hungary
The Hungarian Committee for Applied
Systems Analysis

Japan
The Japan Committee for IIASA

Kazakhstan*
The Ministry of Science –
The Academy of Sciences

Netherlands
The Netherlands Organization for
Scientific Research (NWO)

Norway
The Research Council of Norway

Poland
The Polish Academy of Sciences

Russian Federation
The Russian Academy of Sciences

Slovak Republic*
The Slovak Committee for IIASA

Sweden
The Swedish Council for Planning and
Coordination of Research (FRN)

Ukraine*
The Ukrainian Academy of Sciences

United States of America
The US Committee for IIASA

*Associate member
**Affiliate

International Economic Negotiation: Models versus Reality

Victor Kremenyuk and Gunnar Sjöstedt, editors

A Book Prepared by the Processes of International Negotiations (PIN) Project at the International Institute for Applied Systems Analysis (IIASA)

Edward Elgar
Cheltenham, UK • Northampton, MA, USA

International Institute for Applied Systems Analysis
Laxenburg, Austria

Published by
Edward Elgar Publishing Limited
Glensanda House
Montpellier Parade
Cheltenham
Glos GL50 1UA
UK

Edward Elgar Publishing, Inc.
136 West Street
Suite 202
Northampton
Massachusetts 01060
USA

$K 3941$
$.I 58$
2000

A catalogue record for this book
is available from the British Library

Library of Congress Cataloguing in Publication Data
International economic negotiations : models versus reality / Victor Kremenyuk and Gunnar Sjöstedt.
    "A book prepared by the Processes of International Negotiations (PIN)
  Project at the International Institute for Applied Systems Analysis (IIASA)."
    A collection of 15 papers prepared by an international group of researchers.
    Includes bibliographical references and index.
    1. Foreign trade regulation. 2. Investments, Foreign—Law and legislation.
  3. Negotiation. 4. Negotiation—Case studies. 5. Diplomacy. 6.
  Diplomacy—Case studies. I. Kremeniuk, Viktor Aleksandrovich. II. Sjöstedt,
  Gunnar. III. Process of International Negotiation Project.

    K3941 .I58 2000
    341.7'54—dc21   00-020552

ISBN 1 84064 167 3

Printed and bound in Great Britain by Biddles Ltd, www.biddles.co.uk

Contents

Figures

Tables

Preface

This is the seventh volume in the series of books prepared by the Processes of International Negotiation (PIN) Project at the International Institute for Applied Systems Analysis (IIASA) since 1991. Beginning with *International Negotiation: Analysis, Approaches, Issues* (V. Kremenyuk, ed.), this series included: *International Environmental Negotiations* (G. Sjöstedt, ed.); *Culture and Negotiation* (G.O. Faure and J. Rubin, eds); *International Multilateral Negotiations* (I.W. Zartman, ed.); and *Negotiating International Regimes* (B. Spector, G. Sjöstedt, and I.W. Zartman, eds). The most recent book compiled by the PIN Project, currently in press, is *Power and Negotiations* (jointly edited by I.W. Zartman and the late J.Z. Rubin). The present book on international economic negotiations thus continues this productive study of international negotiation in a typical manner for PIN: theoretical framework, case studies, and analysis.

One recurrent theme of the PIN program has been to assess the extent to which the issue area addressed in a negotiation influences how this process evolves and what challenges parties at the table must confront. Hence, one underlying issue is the extent to which typical, or structural, issue properties cause exceptions to the propositions of general negotiation theory. In addition to economic issues, highlighted in this book, PIN projects have already analyzed environmental and nuclear issues from this particular perspective.

Why economic negotiation? Obviously, this volume concentrates on a special type of negotiation, taking, as a basis of analysis, the subject area of negotiation – economic issues – and trying to identify its specific features and processes. The rationale for this focus is that the world economy uses negotiation extensively as a tool of economic advancement, and that this negotiation discusses figures: prices, dividends, tariffs, interest rates, etc. This gives the study of economic negotiations both a sense of urgency and a means of evaluation.

The focus on economic issues in international negotiation is timely for several reasons. First, due to the continued internationalization of national economies, countries increasingly place economic issues on the agenda of international negotiations. Second, economic issues are expected to be handled in a special and exceptionally rational way at the national as well as at the international level because decision makers are strongly influenced by the explicit and implicit recommendations of economic theory. Third, if this hypothesis about theory-driven, and in that sense rational, negotiator performance proves wrong, international economic relations may become far more conflictual and complex in the future than may have been anticipated from an assessment of prevalent economic theories. If this turns out to be the case, decision makers will increasingly call for measures to facilitate economic negotiation, which in turn requires a better understanding of the special circumstances of international economic cooperation as seen in a negotiation perspective. This is, in brief, the primary impetus for the present PIN book project on international economic negotiation.

Why "models versus reality?" It is well understood that in economic negotiation, as in all negotiations, or in any other area of human activity, theory and practice do not always go together. The task of the study is, first, to identify what type of theoretical approaches may be suggested as tools for analysis and then to demonstrate their applicability. The approach chosen is to juxtapose models of ideal negotiation (from both economic and negotiation perspectives) and what happens in reality. Only after that do we try to analyze the possibility of improving the current state of international economic negotiation.

As a result, the book consists of three main parts: a theoretical framework based on two interdependent approaches – economic theory and negotiation analysis; a group of case studies distributed among trade, business investment, finance, and macroeconomic issues; and an analytical section containing, as usual, lessons for both theory and practice. Thus, the book is clearly designed for both scholars and practitioners, students and teachers of negotiation, as well as business communities heavily engaged in international deals. It should not be regarded as a textbook, but as a serious academic attempt to bring a new vision to age-old problems which, we hope, will prove helpful to all those concerned.

Victor A. Kremenyuk
Gunnar Sjöstedt

Acknowledgments

This book is part of a series of studies conceived and coordinated by the PIN Steering Committee, an international group of researchers representing different approaches to the study of negotiation. The members are: Rudolf Avenhaus, University of the German Armed Forces (Munich); Guy Olivier Faure, Sorbonne University (Paris); Victor Kremenyuk, Academy of Sciences of Russia (Moscow); Winfried Lang, Austrian Ministry of Foreign Affairs and University of Vienna; Gunnar Sjöstedt, Swedish Institute of International Affairs (Stockholm); and I. William Zartman, Johns Hopkins University (Washington, DC).

The members of the interdisciplinary PIN Steering Committee represent, *inter alia*, games theory and systems analysis, modern history, political economy, political science, and sociology. The committee also represents theory as well as practice in the area of international negotiation. As in the present book, this international profile has guided the choice of PIN book projects.

Each PIN project is coordinated by one or more committee members, but the whole committee is engaged in the undertaking. In the current work, Professor I. William Zartman was of particularly great help and support to the project coordinators. We are also grateful for the support we have received from the large network of negotiation researchers associated with the PIN program. Some members of the network have contributed chapters to the book; others have offered constructive critiques on individual draft chapters.

The project coordinators owe very special thanks to Ulrike Neudeck, the resident project assistant at IIASA. Ms. Neudeck carried out the indispensable executive functions of this project at IIASA, coordinated the work of the project coordinators, and managed the laborious work of including changes in the manuscript. She also organized the meetings of the editorial committee as well as a large conference in which all the chapter authors took part.

We are also grateful for the support we have received from the present director of IIASA, Gordon MacDonald. Lilo Roggenland of IIASA's Publications Department produced the camera-ready copy, and Ewa Delpos designed the figures. The head of the Publications Department, Eryl Maedel, gave valuable assistance to the coordinators in the latest stages of the project. Margaret MacDonald copyedited the manuscript, polishing the prose to create a more coherent style and detecting and correcting inconsistencies and errors in the various chapters.

Moscow and Stockholm, 10 May 1999
Victor Kremenyuk
Gunnar Sjöstedt
Project Coordinators

Contributors

Anders Ahnlid is director in the Department for International Trade Policy, Ministry for Foreign Affairs, Stockholm, Sweden. During his 1991–1995 posting in Geneva he was the service negotiator for the Nordic countries in the Uruguay Round and for Sweden in the World Trade Organization. From 1995 to 1998 he represented Sweden in the OECD. He is currently conducting research in the field of international political economy, *inter alia* within the project "Multilateral Co-operation in Transition: Threat or Opportunity?" under the auspices of the Swedish Institute of International Affairs.

Richard A. DeFelice is a licensing manager in Lucent Technologies Inc.'s Intellectual Property Business, where he negotiates patent and technology licensing agreements in the Asia-Pacific Region. He joined Lucent from AT&T when the company was formed as a result of AT&T's divestiture of its systems and technology businesses. Previously, he negotiated intellectual property agreements in Europe and North America and worked for seven years as a product reliability and test engineer in AT&T's semiconductor business. Mr DeFelice has several patents pending in technology areas that include semiconductor processing, IC packaging, telecommunications systems, and consumer electronics.

Guy Olivier Faure is associate professor of sociology at the Sorbonne University, Paris, where he teaches international negotiation. His major research interests are in business negotiations, especially with China and Asian countries, focusing on strategies and cultural issues. He also is concerned with developing interdisciplinary approaches, and engages in consulting and training activities. Among his most recent publications are chapters in several of the PIN studies, as well as in the following edited volumes: *Processes of International Negotiations*, *Evolutionary Systems Design: Policy-Making under Complexity*, and *Conflits et Négociations dans le Commerce International: L'Uruguay Round*. Together with the late Jeffrey Z. Rubin, he edited *Culture and Negotiation*, the third volume in the PIN series.

Geoffrey Fink works in the venture capital field in London, following several years as a consultant with McKinsey & Company and previous work in the investment banking field. He holds a BA (summa cum laude) in political science from Yale University, an MALD from the Fletcher School of Law and Diplomacy, and a JD (magna cum laude) from Harvard Law School, where he studied in the Program on Negotiation. A multicultural/multiparty negotiation teaching case based on the EuroDisney scenario is available from the Program on Negotiation.

Annie M. Finn is an associate lawyer in the Litigation Department of the law firm of Fasken Campbell Godfrey in Toronto, Canada. Her broad civil litigation practice emphasizes corporate/commercial litigation, specifically competition law, wrongful dismissal cases, contractual/commercial disputes, and class-action proceedings. She served as an assistant to Gilbert Winham, a member of the Dispute Settlement Panel established under Chapter 19 of the Canada–US Free Trade Agreement and coauthored another paper with Mr Winham on the topic of accession to NAFTA. Ms Finn previously taught English at Fudan University, Shanghai, PRC.

Robert E. Kerwin is an independent consultant in electronics technology, intellectual property management, and quality management practices. In February 1994, he retired from AT&T as general manager of the Intellectual Property Division; he had previously served as AT&T's manager of corporate quality. Prior to that he had 22 years of experience in research and development at AT&T Bell Laboratories. Dr Kerwin holds 15 patents on microelectronics materials and processes, and has published 15 papers and four book chapters on microelectronics technology and quality management principles.

Victor Kremenyuk is deputy director of the Institute for USA and Canada Studies, Russian Academy of Sciences, Moscow. He is also a research associate at IIASA. His areas of interest are international conflict resolution, crisis management, foreign policy, and the negotiation process. He has published more than 100 works in Russian and other languages, and edited the first volume published by the PIN Program, *International Negotiation: Analysis, Approaches, Issues.*

Czesław Mesjasz teaches at the Cracow University of Economics and the Jagiellonian University, Cracow, Poland. His areas of interest include management, conflict and negotiation theory and practice, systems theory, peace research, financial negotiation, and contracting. In 1992–1994, he was a visiting research fellow at the Centre for Peace and Conflict Research in Copenhagen. He is the author of some 120 papers, conference papers, and book chapters, and has recently completed his "habilitation" thesis on bank–company contract negotiation. His book *Bankers and Generals: Finance and*

Security in East–West Relations from Perestroika to NATO Enlargement will be published by Ashgate Publishing Company in 2000.

Robert Neugeboren is a lecturer on economics at Harvard University, where he teaches a course in applied game theory. He has been a visiting research fellow at the Center for Ethics, Rationality and Society at the University of Chicago and a research consultant to the Consensus Building Institute in Cambridge, Massachusetts. His research focuses on the application of game theory and other formal models to processes of international cooperation.

John S. Odell is professor of international relations at the University of Southern California. A political scientist, he has also worked for a year at the office of the US Trade Representative and served as editor of *International Organization*. He is the author, coauthor, or coeditor of *US International Monetary Policy, Anti-Protection: Changing Forces in US Trade Politics*, and *International Trade Policies: Gains from Exchange between Economics and Political Science*, respectively.

Bright E. Okogu received his BSc and MSc degrees in economics from the London School of Economics, and a doctorate in economics from the University of Oxford, UK. He is a senior economist at the International Monetary Fund. Previously, he served as a market analyst in the Economics and Finance Department of the Organization of Petroleum Exporting Countries (OPEC), Vienna, Austria, and as senior operations officer at the OPEC Fund, also in Vienna. He has published almost 50 journal articles and book chapters. They include: "Marketing Dynamism: An Econometric Study of the Oil Pricing Policies of Selected OPEC Members," *Energy Economics* **13**(3), 1991; *Africa and Economic Structural Adjustment: Case Studies of Ghana, Nigeria, and Zambia*, OPEC Fund, 1992; "Issues in Petroleum Product Pricing in Nigeria," (Oxford) *Journal of African Economies* **4**(3), 1995; and "Petroleum Product Taxation and the Distribution of the Economic Rent in Traded Oil: Implications for the Market," *Journal of Energy Finance and Development* **1**(1), 1996.

Akilagpa Sawyerr, currently director of research, Association of African Universities, was previously vice-chancellor of the University of Ghana. Trained as a lawyer, and for many years lecturer and professor of law at the Universities of Ghana, Dar es Salaam, and Papua New Guinea, Professor Sawyerr was chief negotiator for the government of Ghana in the renegotiation of the VALCO Agreement. Professor Sawyerr spent the academic year 1992/93 as visiting scholar, Program on Negotiation, Harvard Law School, and Fulbright senior African research fellow, Fletcher School of Law and Diplomacy, Tufts University, working on his papers on the VALCO negotiations. He has published extensively on law, political economy, and higher education policy.

Gunnar Sjöstedt is senior research fellow at the Swedish Institute of International Affairs and also associate professor of political science at the University of Stockholm. His research work is concerned with processes of international cooperation and consultations in which negotiations represent an important element. He has studied the OECD as a communication system and the external role of the European community, as well as the transformation of the international trade regime incorporated in GATT and its external relations. He is the editor of *International Environmental Negotiations* and the co-editor of *Negotiating International Regimes*, the second and fourth books, respectively, in the PIN series.

Maria G. Vlasova focuses her research on topics of international economic integration, business negotiations, and crisis management. She is the author of various publications on international negotiations, transitional economics, and business values. In 1996, she was a visiting research fellow at Harvard University. She holds a PhD in economics and politics, and an MA in organizational development and international affairs. In addition to her research work, Dr Vlasova works as a consultant on business strategy, corporate affairs, and brand development for multinational corporations in Russia and Western Europe.

Lynn Wagner has attended and analyzed UN environmental negotiations for the *Earth Negotiations Bulletin* since 1994. She received her PhD from the Johns Hopkins University's Paul H. Nitze School of Advanced International Studies, where she studied international negotiation theory and international economics.

Gilbert R. Winham is professor of political science at Dalhousie University in Halifax, Nova Scotia, Canada. His interests include international negotiation and diplomatic practice, and he specializes in international commercial policy and trade negotiations. He has extensive experience in training government officers in negotiation methods through simulation exercises. His recent books include *International Trade and the Tokyo Round Negotiation*, *Trading with Canada: The Canada–US Free Trade Agreement*, and *The Halifax G-7 Summit: Issues on the Table* (with Sylvia Ostry).

I. William Zartman is Jacob Blaustein Professor of Conflict Resolution and International Organization at the Nitze School of Advanced International Studies of Johns Hopkins University. He is the author of *The Practical Negotiator*, *The 50% Solution*, and *Ripe for Resolution*, editor of *The Negotiation Process* and *Positive Sum*, among other books, and the coeditor of *Power and Negotiation*, the most recent book in the PIN series. He is organizer of the Washington Interest in Negotiations (WIN) Group and was distinguished fellow at the US Institute of Peace.

PIN Steering Committee:
Rudolf Avenhaus (Germany)
Guy Olivier Faure (France)
Victor Kremenyuk (Russia)
Winfried Lang†(Austria)
Gunnar Sjöstedt (Sweden)
I. William Zartman (USA)

Part I

Introduction

The overall aim of this project is to identify and assess what may be typical, or special, about international negotiations on economic issues. These negotiations are talks concerning the creation, distribution, and/or management of flows of material resources such as goods, services, currencies, or financial assets, whose value can be expressed in monetary terms. The main question addressed in the study is if, and how, the widespread perception of the qualities of economic issues may condition negotiating parties to deal with them differently than they do with other topics such as, for instance, territorial, military, or environmental questions. For example, does economic negotiation exhibit recurrent, special process features? Or do parties typically find it comparatively easy to reach an agreement in international economic talks? Are win–win solutions relatively more attainable when economic issues are negotiated than they are when other issue areas are deliberated in international talks?

One motive for this project is the suspicion that economic issues may have special intrinsic qualities influencing how they are handled at the negotiation table. One may, for instance, suspect that because economic issues always have a monetary value, this may facilitate interparty communication. Another justification for the study is that economics textbooks predict, and ordain, what rational decisions should be made in specific choice situations, such as in a negotiation. If negotiators follow the advice offered by economic theory, all parties concerned will supposedly gain in the long run, as the outcome of their talks will stimulate economic growth. If all parties perform in line with the recommendations of economic theory, they are supposed to find a mutually acceptable win–win solution to a negotiation problem. Therefore, the question should be raised if economic issues are not negotiated more rationally than other issues and lead relatively easily to value creation.

However, diplomats or businessmen who have been personally involved in economic negotiations like to testify that it would be highly naive to believe that negotiating parties perform as predicted by economic theory. For instance, governments have often been anxious to create, and sustain, agreements with other governments that are exceedingly costly from an economic-theoretical point of view to protect home markets or to bolster the international competitiveness of national companies, to promote national security, or simply to assert their sovereignty. If this latter view is correct, international economic deals should not be explained in terms of economic theory only, but also by drawing upon our knowledge about negotiation processes. Perhaps economic theory is no more relevant for economic negotiations than academic theories about deadly quarrels are for negotiations to prevent or arrest a war among states. Maybe international economic negotiations should best be analyzed without any attempt to introduce a theory-oriented issue analysis.

In the present study, a selection of cases of international economic negotiations will be investigated and systematically compared. The selected cases represent various combinations of the categories of actors involved in economic negotiations: private companies, governments and international organizations. The negotiations studied have concerned the main types of economic issues: trade between states and companies, direct investment, joint ventures, monetary relations, financial and macroeconomic questions.

The primary questions addressed with the help of the case studies are, first, to what extent economic theory is helpful in explaining the process and outcomes of international economic negotiations and, second, to what degree negotiation analysis is instrumental in achieving the same research objectives. A third, and synthesizing, research task is to identify properties characterizing international economic negotiations, regardless of whether these attributes are preferably expressed in terms of economic or negotiation theory.

The ultimate objective of the study is to draw lessons for further research from current practices of economic negotiation. The ambition is that the lessons learned will eventually also become useful for practice: that they may help to facilitate future negotiations over economic matters. Many analysts fear that economic relations risk becoming increasingly contentious in the near future. Somewhat paradoxically, this possible development would occur partly because economic issues now seem to acquire more importance compared to military-security concerns, particularly among industrialized countries. The alleged reason is that the Cold War and its risks of military confrontation forced the economic great powers to be extremely prudent when they were confronting each other over economic issues. These constraints have now disappeared. It is possible that in the longer term the economic great powers will tend to become more assertive in their mutual dealings. Thus, looking into the future, it is essential to certify that the main instrument of dispute settlement and conflict resolution in the economic area can be facilitated to the greatest extent possible.

Chapter 1

International Economic Negotiation: Research Tasks and Approaches

Victor Kremenyuk, Gunnar Sjöstedt, and I. William Zartman

1.1   Introduction

At first glance, the picture of international negotiations in the economic area gives the impression of a highly fragmented and chaotic activity where thousands of actors – banks, companies, government agencies, individuals – daily make deals that then establish prices on goods and services, interest rates on loans and credits, and thus set the conditions for the functioning of world markets. Different types of talks take place, involving various kinds of negotiators: bilateral and multilateral, company-to-company, government-to-government, and government-to-company; well established and institutionalized negotiations, such as World Trade Organization (WTO) talks or sessions of the United Nations Conference on Trade and Development, and sporadic, "one-shot" meetings, sometimes with a wide agenda of "economic cooperation" and sometimes with only one single item on the agenda. In some sense, the whole world market is one big negotiation, since there is no other way to make deals on the market than with the help of bargaining.

However, the world market exists within the constraints of international political realities. Although most economic negotiations involve private companies dealing with customers, contractors, or financial institutions, governments also have economic affairs that must be settled through negotiation. Economic transactions conducted in the world markets have a cumulative effect with a direct relation to national wealth, power, and security. For example, a successful negotiation resulting in an acceptable price for an important commodity may strengthen or weaken the economy of whole Third World nations, or may sometimes ruin them. An appropriate strategy of negotiation may give a nation a prosperous economy, while a poor strategy will destroy its competitiveness.

One of the most spectacular examples in the postwar history of important economic negotiations was the struggle between the Organization of Petroleum Exporting Countries (OPEC) and the major consumers of their product in the West. A successful negotiation strategy permitted OPEC to attain leverage from the Arab–Israeli "Yom Kippur" War in October 1973 and to change the price of oil through the threat of embargo. Another lesson is, however, that in the longer term changing conditions in world energy markets nullified OPEC's "victory." At the same time as international markets are conditioned by political realities, the latter are, in turn, influenced by economic developments.

Generally speaking, economic performance is one of the key indicators of the power of nations. Therefore, each government pays significant attention to the problems of safeguarding its economic positions and avoiding losses, and finding ways of optimizing the performance of its economic policies. Since the criteria of economic performance today include, together with the technological and financial base, currency exchange rate, investment in research and development, and a sound foreign economic policy, both governments and private companies have to pay great attention to negotiation on these issues as a tool to promote their interests and power in the world. This understanding of the role of international economic negotiation adds a significant political constraint to it and turns it into one of the important spheres of national policy. At the same time a question has to be raised regarding the extent to which national positions in international economic negotiations are constrained by market conditions.

1.2   Political Realities of International Economic Deals

Before this century, governments in the West were not particularly engaged in economic negotiations. These were regarded as a sphere of private interest where governments could play an auxiliary, supporting role but should not perform as direct participants (Kennedy, 1987). The situation changed significantly at the end of the nineteenth and the beginning of the twentieth century. A large part of the world was then divided among several major empires: British, French, German, Russian, Portuguese, Turkish, and Austro-Hungarian. The markets were protected by their respective national legislations, and companies were encouraged to subordinate their business interests to political purposes. Control over colonial economies and trading routes was regarded as an integral part of the conditions for national power. Monopolization of markets became an important objective. Individual companies of colonial powers ceased to operate freely without governmental support. In contrast, the only nonimperial great power of that time, the United States, was anxious to proclaim an Open Door policy wherever possible, first of all in China, in order to help US exporters to gain access to overseas markets. Other "newcomers," such as Japan, were, however, eager to pursue a "spheres of influence" policy, hoping to provide their economies with adequate markets abroad.

The political and military struggle about world markets contributed to producing major political crises in world politics that gave birth first to World War I and then to World War II. These wars had different political and ideological causes, but essentially, under the cover of ideological and other logos, the new contenders in world politics tried to open the rigid colonial system for freer competition. This purpose was declared by the "14 points" stated in 1918 by US President Woodrow Wilson (although it was never realized) and was reiterated in 1941 by the Atlantic Charter worked out by the United States and Britain. No wonder that as the victory of the Allies became clear in 1944, one of the first things to discuss and decide, even prior to the UN Charter, was the future organization of the world economy and world markets – the topic of the Allied Conference in Bretton Woods that created the World Bank and the International Monetary Fund (IMF).

Thus, national governments have retained the role of principal actors in international economic relations. However, after World War II governments monopolized the area of foreign trade and finance only in the communist countries. Nevertheless, also in countries with market economies, governments have developed policies of managed trade and have built up international regimes around such institutions as the IMF, the WTO (previously the General Agreement on Tariffs and Trade [GATT]), or various commodity agreements.

Governmental control over the foreign operations of national companies may be explained by the fact that economic issues have often been regarded through the prism of international power politics, which is the area of government responsibility. The Cold War (1947–1989) has only played the role of a major booster to this trend and has introduced such new elements of the international economy as embargoes, lists of prohibited items, economic warfare, and the like. But, even without ideological conflict in international relations, the idea of using foreign economic ties for political purposes has recurrently overshadowed the nineteenth century "free trade" philosophy and has colored "national strategic" thinking in the second half of the twentieth century in spite of free trade rhetoric and liberal, international regimes.

In the area of economic relations, governments often take the role of protector of national companies. This happens not only when there is a relationship across different types of political systems, as in the cases of centrally planned market economies or developed/less-developed economies, but also in deals struck by close allies with very similar economies: Japan–United States, European Union (EU)–United States, as well as among the members of the EU. In almost all these cases governments often interfere strongly under the pretext of a "national security" interest, or some other claimed motive for exception to the liberal international "rules of the game."

Now, what is the correlation between governmental interference and the process of negotiation concerning economic matters? First of all, as seen in a long-term perspective and in comparison with the norm of "commercial secrecy," which was typical of liberal thinking in the nineteenth century, economic negotiations have become highly transparent. The negotiation process has changed significantly and acquired a more formalized and bureaucratic mode, particularly when governments are involved. The attitudes toward this evolution are somewhat split in the business and academic communities. While there are still ultraliberal groups that regard government interference as something unacceptable (this was largely the position of Ross Perot, presidential candidate in the US election in 1992), others try to use it actively to seek both market penetration and additional security. These interests have acquired a still greater significance with the creation of the Export-Import Bank (Eximbank) and Overseas Private Investment Corporation in the United States and similar agencies in other countries that actually play the role of financial guarantors to individuals and companies trying to make deals in some "troubled waters."

Second, different economies perform differently and contribute, in this way, to power imbalances. For some time it has been fashionable to speak about Japan and Germany as economic giants and political dwarfs (though it is still remains to be seen what "dwarfs" they are), but this trivial observation simply sheds additional light on the problem of imbalance between economic weight and political influence in international relations. As to negotiation, such imbalances may actively interfere in the relations between normally friendly countries and sometimes bring them either to the edge of "trade war" or to other types of serious political controversy. Under these conditions the normal positive conditions for win–win solutions to negotiation problems will be undermined. Usually, a political power balance cannot coexist for a long time with an economic imbalance, and in the past this state of affairs always led to conflicts and sometimes war between contenders and countries defending the status quo. Although existing international regimes can be helpful in coping with such problems of imbalance, they cannot be trusted to eliminate them altogether.

Third, flows of money and resources uncontrolled by state authorities bring national economies close to one another and hence significantly influence policy considerations. The case of US–Chinese trade may be cited as an example. Quick growth of the annual trade between the two nations, to more than US$20 billion, has created a certain interdependence between them that has affected the US position on human rights in China. Here, again, is a case when economic relations play a feedback role in political events.

Fourth, controversies and conflicts have appeared between individual companies and government agencies regarding the conduct of economic negotiation. Since governments often had strong political prescriptions regarding the type of negotiating partner (e.g., lists of those nations where human rights abuses exclude the option of free trade), type of goods (e.g., proscriptive practices for special types of prohibited items: drugs, precious metals, strategic materials, weapons), and type of services (e.g., limits on the transfer of know-how due to security considerations), they caused problems for companies engaged in these areas. Besides, restrictive business practices contradict the whole idea of free trade and lead to certain difficulties in working out a reasonable and consistent national policy – particularly in defending this position in a negotiation. This type of inconsistency is, hence, built into the international economic policies of many countries. Management of international economic affairs and liberalization often go hand in hand in national policies, which may cause domestic friction between governments and private companies. Protectionism and other forms of state control over international economic transactions may produce political clashes because the intention to boost the economy in the short term will lead to the opposite effect in the longer term.

International interdependence counterbalances governmental interference in international economic deals. Due to the unequal distribution of resources necessary to sustain the modern economy and to unequal economic performance, a kind of division of labor has developed among nations with regard to their roles in international economic relations. In a given industry countries tend to be exporters or importers, and in the global financial system some are creditors and others are debtors. Economic interdependence is driven by doctrines of free trade and liberalization, although some governments have opted for relative autarky. Currently, world interdependence also manifests itself as political, cultural and ideological ties, human contacts, and business arrangements, as well as the development of science and research. Complex interdependence has acquired a universal nature. A vast majority of nations share such goals as the avoidance of nuclear or conventional war, respect for human rights and democratic institutions, social justice, and the preservation of the natural environment. These common values provide a strong basis for the coherence of international organization and international law.

World interdependence has recurrent effects on foreign policy making. First is the ethic of the lifeboat: "Don't rock it," because it may capsize and all will suffer. Second is the development of mutual interests: the safest world is the one where you don't have enemies. No security measures, taken individually or collectively, may provide a better guarantee of peace than the absence of enemies. The critical interests of an individual nation include the respect for the vital interests of other nations. Third is respect for international law as a universal code of conduct. Fourth, global issues bring nations closer in their search for the solution of their individual problems.

Increased interdependence has a direct relevance to international economic relations. Its "code of conduct" has been developed over many years and is in the process of further perfection. It reflects the long-term solidity of world markets and quasi-institutionalized patterns of relations among commercial partners. Reliable and predictable deals have become a norm of business conduct that daily reproduces itself as a mutually beneficial process. In economic negotiations, predictability and reliability are often valued more than promising risks.

These circumstances put their own strong imprint on international economic negotiation. Negotiators must respect the constraints of interdependence when developing strategies and making choices. They have to calculate their moves following Axelrod's theory of cooperation: they are forced to cooperate, starting from the simplest "tit for tat" exchanges and then moving to a much more advanced level of cooperation when the interests of both sides become largely integrated (Axelrod, 1984). This process may carry them along as far as the development of joint projects, creation of joint ventures, mergers of corporations, creation of common markets, and, at the highest level, movement toward multinational entities such as the EU.

The rapid growth of transnational and multinational companies (TNCs and MNCs) in the last decades has affected the development of interdependence and the position of the state in international politics. On many occasions intracompany transfers avoid public control. To some extent, this evolution has strained national government–company relations, since the creation of MNCs or TNCs was sometimes regarded as the illegal avoidance of government control and circumvention of what previously were straightforward export-import operations.

Interdependence has, hence, brought nations closer to one another and increasingly integrated them, especially in a number of regional settings. Rising interdependence has placed an imprint on negotiation strategies, has changed the psychological climate of negotiations, and has in the final analysis affected their outcome. Again, as an example, one may turn to US–Japanese economic ties, which generally bring a large multibillion surplus to the Japanese. This situation has created political problems in the United States, where the administration is recurrently accused of being incapable of defending US business interests. But in any US–Japanese confrontation over the asymmetrical results of their economic deals, political and security joint interests predominate and therefore constrain the need to correct an economic imbalance. A similar situation is discernible in intra-EU relations, where the German economic thrust is not merely tolerated, but is actually regarded by other leading nations such as the United Kingdom and France as a benefit shared by all of Europe.

Political realities are important elements of the general background conditions for international economic negotiations. These circumstances represent very different impacts on negotiations. On the one hand, it may be a political reality that economic negotiations must be seen as instruments of preserving or enhancing the power position of a nation in world politics. From this perspective economic issues stand out as one kind of security issue rather than as constituting a category of their own. On the other hand, complex interdependence in the world system offers a perspective pointing in a different direction. One may speculate that interdependence constrains governments to seek cooperative solutions to economic negotiation problems in line with the predictions and prescriptions of economic theories. This conjecture indicates that international negotiation on economic issues may, after all, have typical or special features.

1.3   Economic Theory as an Approach to the Study of International Economic Negotiation

One hypothesis of this study claims that economic issues are treated in a special – or typical – way in international negotiation because they have intrinsic qualities differing from those of other issues. Due to the lack of solid information in the literature, speculation is needed to specify these inherent issue properties and their significance. For example, one may conjecture that the exchange of offers and requests at the negotiation table is facilitated because typical economic stakes, such as tariffs or quotas, can easily be expressed quantitatively in exact numbers. In the search for viable solutions to distributive conflicts, reaching compromises will probably also be considerably easier when negotiating parties can calculate the consequences of various proposals for a negotiated solution with clarity and exactness. However, economic theory suggests another approach, preferable to speculation, to establish hypotheses about what may be special or typical for international economic negotiation.

Economic issues represent a research area where prescriptive theories have become especially strong and significant. Students of economics are trained to use theory not only to analyze and understand economic relationships and problems but also to apply in practice, be it in business firms, government offices or international organizations such as the WTO, the IMF, or the World Bank. Professional economists have, indeed, been able to attain the role of privileged advisors to "the Prince" that has usually been denied representatives of other social sciences (Coats, 1981; Pechman, 1989). If they are honored, the policy recommendations contained in economic theory should produce a distinct treatment of economic issues in decision processes, including in negotiation. Hence, one approach to assessing what may be typical or special for international economic negotiation is to analyze the extent to which policymakers and analysts behave in line with the prescriptions of economic theory.

Needless to say, there is nothing like one, single, homogeneous economic theory. Economics is an old science with a vast agenda, covering a large number of different subjects and representing a great variety of analytical approaches. This study focuses particularly on the so-called neoclassical theory applied to international economic issues (Gomes, 1990). It treats free trade theory as representative because it shares a number of critical characteristics typical of neoclassical theories pertaining to international economic relations generally. One basic premise of the general neoclassical theory is that economic actors, be they individuals, firms or national governments, have access to sufficient market information and make rational choices based on calculations of marginal utility and costs of the alternatives considered. From a technical point of view the theories considered here are constructed in a similar fashion. On the basis of a list of constraining assumptions, explanatory specifications are given about interaction effects of key variables, for example the interplay of demand and supply on different kinds of markets, such as free competition, oligopoly, or monopoly. Conjecture closely links explanation to prediction in economic theories. One example is free trade theory stipulating that economic actors have a self-interest in dismantling trade barriers at home as well as in other countries because they realize that they should concentrate their export efforts on products where they have a comparative advantage (McCord, 1970).

The economic theories examined here also have an explicit normative foundation: their principal task is to promote world welfare growth to the highest extent possible. To this normative guideline economic theory links a number of theoretical principles explaining how rational economic actors should behave in order to realize that overarching aim of economic activities (Arrow, 1996). For instance, the theory prescribes that resources should be used as efficiently as possible; another guideline is that existing obstacles to the free exchange of goods and services should be eliminated (Tumlir, 1985).

Free trade theory ordains that when a government is engaged in negotiating away tariffs or other trade obstacles it should not regard its own offers of reductions as sacrifices, since elimination of trade obstacles enhances economic growth. If company A is successful in the competition game, this is obviously good because it generates a profit, which, in turn, represents a contribution to economic growth. If, on the other hand, company B is unable to make a profit year after year it will not survive, but will leave room for competitors that are more efficient or produce more useful products. The disappearance of company B from the market may represent a disagreeable experience for its stockholders and employees. However, according to economic theory the important thing is that company B makes its last contribution to the national economy when it vanishes under the pressure of market forces, because it contributes to enhancing the efficiency of the national as well as the global economy. Likewise, the theory explains that although national decision makers should try to avoid large deficits in their balance of payments, they should not strive to build up payment surpluses either. Exceedingly large economic reserves represent an ineffective employment of resources (Gomes, 1990).

There is evidence that these and other, similar, recommendations derived from economic textbooks do, in fact, often serve as policy guidelines. For instance, the summary references to free trade theory that can be found in the charter of the WTO serve as a normative as well as an epistemic basis for the international trade regime (Bagwell, 1997). A large literature points out that the IMF and the World Bank have similarly been guided by neoclassical economic theory in their financial and monetary operations (Arneberg, 1996). Typical examples are the so-called conditional loans that the IMF grants to developing countries in order to help them cope with temporary external disequilibria. The conditions set by IMF do not follow from its desire to generate a profit on its loans, but from the instructions of neoclassical economic theory, which commands that a deficit in the budget of the state cannot be permitted to expand when that country has a growing deficit in its balance of payments.

Thus, the key concepts of economic theory are coupled in such a way that causal relationships between them are identified and explained. These explanations include causation between factors that, from a decision-making perspective, may be interpreted as linkages between policy objectives and policy means. The theory, and the policy recommendations, are underpinned by a number of principal norms spelling out a need to expand the world economy and to keep it in balance. The theory also contains prescriptions representing conclusions derived from accumulated scientific knowledge about economic circumstances and relationships; it explains how economic decision makers should perform in recurrent choice situations related to economic problems. Theory-driven prescriptions not only have strong normative and cognitive underpinnings, but they are also precise and relevant in recurrent decision situations. Both the authority and the relevance of the policy prescriptions have been further enhanced by their inclusion in various formal international regimes in the economic area.

1.3.1 The influence of economic theory on policy decisions

However, it has also been well established in the literature that economic actors do not always follow the prescriptions of the neoclassical theory. For example, already in the early 1960s Cyert and March demonstrated how intraorganizational factors and coalitions influence business firms to set prices different from those predicted by price theory (Cyert and March, 1992). This and other studies have indicated the need for a behavioral theory of the firm, for which Cyert and March laid such an inspiring foundation.

There is a vast literature on market failures. Descriptions of international negotiations concerning commercial matters demonstrate that measures undertaken in order to liberalize the national economy (e.g., tariff reductions) are often described as sacrifices or concessions, although neoclassical theory clearly explains that they are gains in the sense that they will promote economic growth. Free riding is only one explanation given in the literature as to why in particular choice situations national governments would prefer to disregard institutionalized rules of the game based on economic theory. However, the limitations of neoclassical theories are not necessarily incidental, as they often follow fairly distinct and recurrent patterns. These patterns have, in fact, been expressed in economic theories coexisting with the dominant neoclassical theory. For example, in the area of international trade these differing ideas have been labeled theories of managed or strategic trade. To some extent these theories challenge and compete with free trade theory and particularly have a different outlook on the role of governments and state authorities with respect to international trade: state intervention may be necessary to achieve important societal objectives other than economic welfare and growth. However, in reality theories giving support to the ideas of managed trade should primarily be regarded as supplements to neoclassical theories. The theories of managed trade pertain to the large volumes of international trade that for various reasons consistently fall outside the application domain of free trade theory. In reality only a minor part (not more than 30%) of the goods traded between different countries are considered to be systematically exchanged on a genuinely free market.

Various categories of goods may be identified that for various reasons are partly or completely outside the sphere of free trade in the neoclassical sense (Bhagwati, 1988; Howse, 1995; Lieberman, 1988). For example, temperate agricultural goods were the subjects of liberalization negotiations in the Uruguay Round, but will still continue to represent managed trade for the foreseeable future. Many tropical products and other similar commodities are partly managed by means of commodity agreements. The earlier system for managed trade in textiles, the Multi-Fiber Agreement, is in the process of being phased out as a result of the Uruguay Round. However, textiles remain a relatively protected sector through the help of "gray" trade policy measures, such as voluntary export restraints (VERs).

Arms and defense material are essentially not covered by WTO rules. Instead, trade in arms is controlled by individual government agencies. There is a private, uncontrolled international market for many types of weapon systems, particularly light arms. This trade is, however, also partly managed in the sense that governments try to restrict or stop it because it is illegal. In addition to illicit trade in weapons, there are international black markets for products that most governments have banned, such as drugs, and for trade in living beings, such as slaves or certain animals. Governments try to control trade in such prohibited goods as far as possible, sometimes in cooperation with one another.

Regional free trade areas and customs unions are not necessarily forbidden by the international trade regime. There is a WTO article stipulating under what conditions regional economic integration may be permitted. However, basically a free trade area is a fundamental contradiction to one of the pillars of the global free trade system, that of nondiscrimination. As seen in a longer time perspective, continental economic unions such as the EU or the recently established North American Free Trade Agreement (NAFTA) risk breaking down the global free trade system into a host of competing regional blocs.

Gray-area measures represent a particular form of import restrictions established mostly by the larger industrialized countries. They have been directed against particular targeted countries and are hence strongly discriminatory. Therefore, they are clearly contrary to the spirit as well as the letter of WTO. They are called gray because the government imposing them makes an effort to make them look legal. Two well-known categories of gray-area measures have been VERs and orderly market arrangements.

The historical evidence clearly shows that governmental noninterference does not automatically lead to free and competitive international markets. Secret cartels and other forms of intercompany agreements are examples of methods companies can employ in order to control international markets or escape government regulations. Cartels and other forms of company collusion represent restrictive business practices. Internal transactions of TNCs sometimes also violate the working of free market forces. A considerable portion of transborder economic exchange in the world consists in reality of internal transactions of large TNCs. Many firms operating at the global level have opted for a corporate, vertical integration strategy. Perhaps as much as 25% of total world trade consists of transborder transactions within the same company (Gray, 1985; Barrat-Brown, 1993; Bhagwati and Hudec, 1996).

State intervention in international transactions is, hence, frequent and may be due to various circumstances. There are, however, a few broad recurrent motives for state intervention in the area of international commerce. Domestic policy considerations may influence a government to undertake protectionist measures; for example, a government may bow to the lobbying activities of an interest group striving to preserve employment in a particular geographical area.

Sometimes, state intervention in economic flows (e.g., quantitative import restrictions) represents a direct response to international developments rather than being motivated by domestic policy concerns. One example is a need to react to a mounting imbalance in the national economy caused by external disturbances such as a monetary crisis. Concerns about national strategic capabilities or other security considerations have also made governments intervene in the economy, contrary to the policy predictions contained in free trade theory. Sanctions represent a special case in this regard: the use of asymmetrical interdependence to put pressure on another country for political reasons.

Thus, governments have a number of motives not to abide by the prescriptions of neoclassical theory. Some of these motives are incidental or irrational in the sense that governments act contrary to their own economic interests due to political considerations. However, most of the motives referred to above mean that governments find it to be in their best interest to act differently than the way neoclassical theory prescribes. Sometimes, these motives are related to something akin to crisis management in the sense that a government feels it has to employ exceptional methods in an exceptional situation, for instance to avoid "an attack" on the national currency by the market. It is, however, conceivable that governments may also choose deliberately to ignore neoclassical prescriptions as part of a long-term strategy.

The role and significance of economic theory in international negotiation have here been looked at through a window of analysis represented by trade theory. This approach seems acceptable because the purpose of the theoretical analysis has not been to undertake a comprehensive overview and assessment, but to identify general functions that economic theory may have in international negotiation. It is with this particular consideration in mind that trade theory has been considered representative of economic theory generally.

This study formulates several general questions regarding the role of neoclassical economic theory in understanding international negotiation on trade and other economic issues. First and foremost, are negotiators oriented toward objectives defined by economic theory? A critical test would be, for instance, if negotiators demonstrate that they prefer the long-term benefits predicted by economic theory (e.g., economic growth) to short-term gains by means of policy measures proscribed by economic theory.

A second important question is whether or not parties perform rationally, as prescribed by economic theory, in order to attain declared economic objectives acknowledged by economic theory. One test would be if parties undertake the necessary calculations to be achieve declared economic objectives. For example, a government would fail to meet the theory's criteria if it let its position in a negotiation be determined by domestic political considerations, for example, by a will to preserve a company in a particular region. Another test would be if a government combines the rhetoric of neoclassical norms with interventionist policies in preparing for a negotiation.

The third issue is if negotiators pursuing objectives inconsistent with neoclassical theory still demonstrate that their policies are constrained by those economic ideas. A fourth question is if negotiators who entirely repudiate neoclassical theory in carrying out a negotiation use a competing set of ideas, such as managed trade, as a frame of reference.

1.4 Negotiation Theory as an Approach to Economic Conflict Resolution[1]

In a negotiatory perspective, as in economics, free competition is the essence of the dynamics which in negotiations can best be termed political because they involve power. Negotiations, as one of the basic modes of decision making (Zartman, 1978, 1987a), take place when there is no decision rule, no authority, and no set price for the exchange of goods and services. In other words, negotiations are required when parties are "sovereign" and independent actors subject to no higher authority (at least in the area under discussion), when the only mechanism for making a decision is unanimity among equal parties (and hence each has a veto), and when the terms of trade among the various items to be exchanged or divided remain to be set. In such a case, price is set not by the free movement of forces of supply and demand as in a market economy, or by authoritative fiat as in a controlled economy, but essentially by various dimensions of what can simply be called demand, including power, interest, and the value of alternatives. Hence, it is not simply the fixed value and availability of the item in question that determine its price, but its evaluation by the competing parties and their attempts to change and to resist change in these evaluations.

In political negotiation, as opposed to economic forces and policies, the essential element to an agreement, and therefore the essential dynamic, derives from the fact that the outcome must satisfy the values and interests of each party – a fungible set of criteria that each side will try to inflect in the process of negotiation. If it does not, the party will walk away from agreement. These demand criteria leave the determination of outcomes in the hands of the parties and their subjective evaluations, not in the hidden hand of market forces. Thus, negotiated outcomes do not gravitate to some externally defined equilibrium.

On the other hand, these values do not come in infinite increments that can be portrayed on smooth curves. Instead, they come in lumpy and bumpy clumps, making outcomes a matter of selection rather than intersection (Valavanis, 1958). However heuristically seductive, indifference and demand curves do not depict the bargaining situation. In addition, the values are not by nature measurable by some common quantitative standard; they include a number of discrete components whose individual natures would be lost if they were aggregated into one value, even if a common unit could be found. The values of the components of demand are very much in the hands of the parties, and therefore manipulable. The existence of various forms of demand alone deprives the negotiation mechanism of other aspects that give economic theory its directness (even if not simplicity) and its straightforwardness (which some would even call determinism). As a result, rather than a process of combining fixed positions, negotiation is a process of identifying and choosing specifics out of a situation of uncertainties.

Before proceeding further, it should be noted that confrontation between economic and negotiation theory is in part a false debate. Negotiation theory, such as it is, is not developed to the same point as economic theory. There are attempts at a theory of negotiation (some of the best of which are conveniently collected in Young, 1975) and there is a good deal of useful conceptualization, but it has scarcely attained the level of rigor and comprehensiveness found in economic theory. However, much of the generalized, conceptual, or theoretical work that has been done on negotiation owes much to economics. Bilateral monopoly, game theory, comparative advantage and pricemaking/taking in trade, and many others are areas that have contributed to negotiation theory – in some cases before there was any field called negotiation. Since the reach of economic claims on knowledge is long, it is hard to separate the two fields in order to make a comparison.

Yet the confrontation is not meaningless. On the one hand, "economics" is used here narrowly (as already indicated in the previous discussion) to refer to market forces and theories of price determination, and not to the whole area of human activity on which economists might comment. It is also used to refer to a category of issues, including trade and finance, selected for study so as to provide a more coherent set of cases. The distinction between these two overlapping uses is clear enough in the discussion. On the other hand, the following discussion attempts to summarize and restate a generalized conceptualization (or theoretical elements) of negotiation in a way that emphasizes its basic characteristics and distinguishes it from economic attempts at theorization. It will do so using conceptual terms that permit contrasts with market explanations. This includes a characterization of the basic mechanism as demand driven, an enumeration of analytical and operational assumptions, and an identification of process elements.

1.4.1   Demands and assumptions

There are six dimensions of demand: pure demand, opportunity demand, demand intensity, relative demand, demand power, and opportunity power. Although these are dimensions or aspects of the same concept, it is only in image or heuristically that they can be combined to produce a single figure. Negotiators do combine them in their minds, much as a voter combines many attributes of competing candidates into a "score" that determines which one will receive the vote. Computers and analysis, however, have not yet reached that level of sophistication. The components require discrete discussion because they are meaningful separately.

The intrinsic value of the items to each of the parties ("pure demand") is the inherent "price" to be paid for them in the absence of other considerations. The higher the pure demand, the higher the price the party will be willing to pay for the item or, in other words, the amount of other similarly valued items it will be willing to trade for the item. The values that parties assign to traded items determine for each party how much to give and therefore how much to get in exchange.

The value and attainability of alternative outcomes or security points to each party ("opportunity demand") also have an effect on the terms of trade. Value is determined not only by intrinsic worth to the parties, but also by the distance between that value and the value of alternatives or the security point. The closer or the more valued attainable alternatives are, the less the party will be willing to pay for the negotiated item; the greater the distance between the two values and the greater the difficulty in obtaining the best alternative, the more the party will pay, all other dimensions being equal. Because of this effect, value determines power. Absolute power in negotiation can be expressed as the reciprocal of the distance between the party's security point and the other's offer, and relative power – which is what counts – as the ratio between the two parties' relative power. This basic figure is then modified by various other elements of demand and power.

The degree of each party's need for a solution ("demand intensity") also contributes to the final demand total. Even though the intrinsic value of an item may be high, the price the party will be willing to pay will be lower if its need for the item is low, and higher if the need for the item is high. Need is a highly subjective item and does not imply any "basic needs" theory, but rather a broader notion of the ability to do without.

The acceptability level (or justice) of each party's demands in relation to the others ("relative demand") adds a new dimension to demand. While the previous dimensions were intrapersonal, the price a party is willing to pay is also affected by interpersonal comparisons, and particularly by justice or equality-related comparisons, indicating lines of principle or declivities in demand that serve as limits – albeit movable – on the actions of the parties. These considerations produce a "bottom line," beyond the usual sense of a reservation price based on intrinsic value, security point, and need. Parties judge the fairness, and hence the acceptability, of a price or quantity in terms of what the other party gives or gets.

The ability of each party to present more attractive alternatives to the other ("demand power") is the most basic of the two ways each party has to bring the other to agreement. Parties can always try to improve their offers, either by raising them in fact or by convincing the other that they are more valuable than they first appeared. Negotiation is persuasion, that is, the effort to show either that the other party's demand elements are actually lower than it had initially perceived them to be or that the value of the items is actually higher.

The ability of each party to weaken the other's alternative outcomes ("opportunity power") is the second way of bringing the other to agreement. By lowering the security point, a party plays on the other's opportunity demand, increasing the attractiveness of the current offer. The two power dimensions are defined in terms of abilities, in consonance with the classic definition of power as the ability to move the other party in an intended direction (Tawney, 1931; Simon, 1953; Dahl, 1957; Thibaut and Kelley, 1959). This conceptualization identifies power with alternatives or security points. As long as the parties alone are the counterpoise to each other, power, justice, interest, and value remain the sole determinants of outcome (Zartman *et al.*, 1996).

Power is not absent from economic analyses of negotiation, despite claims to the contrary (Nash, 1950; Young, 1975). But it is written into the givens of the situation in terms of some single variable: preferences in game theory (Brams, 1985), strike costs in bargaining theory (Zeuthen, 1930), or reservation price in pricing theory (Lax and Sebenius, 1986). In negotiation analysis, it is what happens outside of the matrices and charts that is interesting, that is, the actions by which a party intends to inflect the other's behavior, values or preferences, or in other words power (Zartman and Rubin, 1999). At the opening of negotiations, the demands of the parties as posed do not coincide or overlap; if they did, there would be no negotiation, only a discovery expedition. The actions of the parties to move those lines, points, and zones so that they meet is the business of negotiation. It is accomplished through the use of demand and opportunity power, by presenting the other with more attractive alternatives, and by rendering its current alternatives less attractive. In so doing, it manipulates all four other dimensions of demand: the intrinsic values of the item, the value of its security point, the intensity or need of that value, and the threshold of acceptability. Their interaction in turn operates under a number of generally accepted principles that govern practice and frame analysis.

Rationality Assumption. Both sides have the same rationality, in that each chooses its preferred outcome over all others, and both possess the same knowledge about the bargaining processes, the conditions that determine how they unfold, and the outcomes they produce, although neither has good information about the other's preferences and power and both have an incentive for keeping the other in a state of imperfect information.

Positive-Sum Assumption. Since the parties pick their preferred outcomes, they will not accept a negotiated outcome unless it is better than (preferable to) their individual security points, the outcomes that each could achieve without negotiation.[2] Thus, each party continually negotiates against its own and the other's security point, as the reference points of negotiation (Zeuthen, 1930; Iklé and Leites, 1962). Economists term a similar concept the reservation value or price, psychologists the resistance front, and game theorists the threat point. Security points give value to outcomes, both proposed and eventual, beyond the outcome's intrinsic value; the greater the (positive) gap between the security point and the proposed outcome, the more willing a party will be to pay for that outcome. Therefore, if a party's security point rises, reducing the gap, it will be willing to pay less for an agreement and its position will be tougher, and the reverse if the security point falls. This assumption relates to the opportunity element of demand.

The concept of the security point is clear, but empirically, security points are both ambiguous and flexible. They are ambiguous because a party can refer to many things within the same definition: the best alternative to a negotiated agreement (BATNA; Fisher and Ury, 1991); what the parties had before the negotiations (status quo point); what they expect to get without negotiation; what they expect to get from a competing negotiation; what someone else got in another, similar negotiation; and so on. Security point is not simply the prenegotiation payoff, but a continually updated and manipulable referent. It is flexible because it can be altered by the other party's efforts, thus altering the value of the offers themselves. The security point therefore reflects demand and opportunity power.

Distribution Assumption. Since negotiation is joint decision making in which the parties have to satisfy their own interests before they lift their vetoes, they are interested in the best solution for all only to the extent it contains and guarantees the best solution for themselves. That outcome may incidentally be the most efficient solution, but it may also have to be an inefficient solution. Whether efficiency is obtained in a particular case is an empirical question, not a theoretical requirement of a solution. Negotiation has everything to do with distribution and nothing to do with efficiency (Young, 1989). Negotiatory concerns and processes are not the opposite of efficiency; efficiency simply is of no concern to them, in the same way as utility is independent of beauty. A solution to a conflict (problem) that is efficient is of no interest if it is not satisfying to all the negotiating parties, and a solution that is just and satisfying is acceptable even if it is not efficient. It may actually take inefficiency to achieve justice (equivalence) and satisfaction.

There are plenty of good and bad reasons why a negotiation might produce an agreement that is not efficient or optimal: good (rational) reasons such as the aim of one party to limit the other's gains or to make relative gains of its own, or the uncertainty of both parties about the appropriate items to include in the agreement to produce the optimal outcome and how to bring them in; and bad reasons such as ignorance, spite, blindness, or distraction, among others. In fact, the only reason why any party would be interested in efficiency would be to maximize its own and the other party's shares of an outcome drawn from limited resources. The only reason a party cares about the other party's shares at all is to provide an outcome that is sufficiently satisfying that the other party will sign and observe it, or, in other words, to create an agreement that will allow the first party to get its payoff. If the two parties cannot find enough in the current outcome to satisfy their separate interests, they will need to find ways to expand the pie (the items of exchange and/or division) to accommodate them.

Equivalence Assumption. The parties tend not to accept a negotiated outcome unless it is equivalent to that achieved by other parties (Keohane and Nye, 1986), since the parties are equal through their veto power over any outcome. Thus each party continually negotiates against the other party, as a second reference point of negotiation tied to relative demand. The other party's outcomes give value to one's own, beyond its intrinsic value. Empirically, equivalence too is ambiguous and flexible. It may refer to absolute outcomes, or relative improvements (new gains), or avoided losses, or counterweights to responsibilities, or compensatory benefits, the latter two being equalizers rather than equalities (Stein and Pauly, 1993; Zartman *et al.*, 1996). It too is flexible because it is based on subjective evaluations, and so can be altered.

Reciprocity Assumption. Since the parties consider themselves equal and look for an equal outcome, they expect process equality or a requirement for such equality, in other words, that concessions will be reciprocated (Larson, 1988). Not to reciprocate is considered worse than bad faith; it gives a clear signal that surrender, not negotiation, is the other party's goal in the process (Bartos, 1978). As a dynamic form of equivalence, the empirical application of reciprocity too is ambiguous and flexible. Although it does not indicate that concessions must be of equal magnitude, disproportional magnitude can ultimately lead to questions over whether there has been any reciprocation at all. Similarly, magnitudes (and therefore concessions at all) are subjective and their value varies by party.

As in economic theory and practice, these assumptions do not obtain perfectly in an imperfect world, but they represent a normative behavioral consensus that does govern practice and expectations in a general way and provide a limitation on the determination of outcomes by unilateral power. If the assumptions are not upheld during negotiations, the process is likely to break down and outcomes (agreements) are aborted.

1.4.2 Process and dynamics

In addition to these consensus assumptions, there are several alternative dimensions of interaction that shape the course of the negotiation process. As in many decision modes, process affects, if not determines, outcome. Once power, interest, and value become countervailing elements and parties retain the option of preventing a decision by not joining it, the situation has process implications. Three considerations shape the process to be followed and therefore the type of outcome to be achieved: the tactical dilemma, the interpersonal orientation, and the methodological direction. In none of these dimensional choices is the independent variable established as yet: since it is not known what determines the selection of one path over another or even what kind of parameter is involved, this study proposes a number of parameters for verification. It will be one of the challenges of the following case studies to compare and test various explanations for the choice of one type of process over another.

The negotiation process is ruled by a paradox, referred to as the Toughness or Negotiator's Dilemma, that makes it characteristically indeterminate and, for all its objective characteristics, ultimately subjectively based (Zartman, 1978; Lax and Sebenius, 1986). The dilemma states that the tougher negotiators behave, the more likely they are to gain a larger part of the outcome but the less likely they are to achieve any outcome (agreement) at all, whereas the softer they behave, the more likely they are to reach agreement but the less likely they are to get a large part of the agreed outcome. While one might imagine an equilibrium point in this situation obtainable through a mixed strategy, it is at best unstable and at worst unreal, and so serves very little as a frame of reference or doctrine for negotiators. Repeated efforts from different disciplines to establish a normative foundation for negotiations (Braithwaite, 1955; Barry, 1963; Nicolson, 1963) have not resolved the Dilemma, and some might say have been a total failure. Yet the interaction of toughness and softness is a major parameter for analysis and a key determinant of outcomes (Edgeworth, 1961; Bartos, 1974, 1978, 1987; Cross, 1969).

A two-purpose concession strategy (to reach and to attract the other party) gives rise to a number of different patterns as an answer to the Toughness Dilemma: tough to demand and soft to reward, soft to attract and tough to punish (Axelrod, 1984), soft to establish a bargaining zone and tough to clinch an agreement (Zartman and Rubin, 1999), and perhaps others. Each depends on a different intervening variable (the first on a Chicken Dilemma Game (CDG) perception, the second on a Prisoners' Dilemma Game (PDG) perception, the third on the relative perceived aggregate power of the parties, and so on). As a process of interacting strategies, matching (softness leads to softness, toughness leads to toughness) and mismatching (softness leads to toughness, toughness leads to softness) yield different results and depend on whether deadlock is preferred to bad agreement, as in a PDG, or vice versa, as in a CDG, respectively.

The process is also dominated by two different types of interpersonal orientation related to different outcomes (Nicolson, 1963; Walton and McKersie, 1965/1991; Rubin and Brown, 1975; Lax and Sebenius, 1986). Competitive parties that see the preferred outcomes as zero sum engage in value-taking or distributive behavior in which they negotiate against each other to get the optimal portion of the final sum. Cooperative parties that see the preferred outcome as positive sum, in which the agreement generates new goods, negotiate with each other in value-making or integrative behavior. Paradoxically perhaps, integrative bargaining does not preclude distributive bargaining, since the value that is newly created must then be distributed among the parties. Even more paradoxically, distributive bargaining does not preclude integrative outcomes, since even with hard-nosed distribution, the parties might both be better off with the end of the conflict.

This distinction in outcomes also separates negotiation from most economic theories on the subject, which focus on distributive bargaining alone. In this they are not entirely wrong, since, as seen, distribution is the primary aim in negotiation and is present whether the behavior is primarily distributive alone or integrative. Yet integrative bargaining is often the key to the whole process and a solution to the Negotiator's Dilemma, in that it can both enable agreement between parties and assure a larger share to each party. While earlier work assumed interpersonal orientation to be a fixed psychological trait, current studies are beginning to identify indicators of the type of outcome the party will consider possible, the interpersonal orientation it will adopt, or the type of behavior it will pursue (Boyer, 1996; Wagner, 1998).

It is intuitively obvious that merely indicating the existence of a Pareto optimal outcome somewhere out there is not sufficient to make the parties arrive at that point in their negotiations (Nash, 1950). If it were not so, negotiation would be mostly an integrative exercise of collaborative discovery. The very behavioral problem that economists have studied – distribution under bilateral monopoly – keeps parties from reaching the optimal outcome they have identified. To reach that optimal outcome, parties first have to see or find it, and then follow a process that will lead them there.

There are two components to any agreement and hence to the process that establishes it: the formula or framework that defines it and the details that govern distribution.[3] Every negotiation takes place within an overarching framework or formula that sets out the items to be covered and exchanged, the sense of justice governing that exchange, the contract zone delimiting the general dimensions of the traded items, and the general nature of the contract. If the negotiations take place under an already-established formula, this phase will be brief, often amounting to an acknowledgment (even implicit) of the framework. But if the negotiations are not just one in a recognized series or class, much time and effort will have to be spent in negotiating the formula itself. Negotiations over trade regimes, monetary systems, and "new series" in more detailed bargaining are formula focused.

The second phase deals with the distributive details, optimally implementing the general terms established by the formula. Negotiations over prices, joint venture terms, currency exchange rates, labor contracts, or licensing agreements, among others, tend to be distributive. While logically and optimally formula negotiations will come first so as to direct the subsequent bargaining deductively, the sequence may be reversed or mixed, so that the formula is built inductively from the details. The formula phase is cooperative and integrative by nature, the detail phase conflictual and distributive. As a result, the order in which they are taken will affect the nature of the agreement: negotiations that begin by establishing a formula will tend to produce a more integrative or positive-sum result, whereas negotiations in the reverse order will tend to be more nearly zero sum and distributive. Of course, the second phase (whichever it is) can override the initial spirit established by the first phase, so the tendency is not absolute.

Thus, there are two related components of methodological sequencing: the two parts to the agreement (formula and detail) and the order in which they are taken up in the actual bargaining. The latter breaks down into three types (Walton and McKersie, 1965/1991; Wagner, 1998; Hopmann, 1996; Zartman, 1978):

Deductive Negotiation. Joint determination of the outcome clearly best fits the various assumptions and, beyond that, the general spirit of maximizing payoffs. Since negotiation involves a mixture of cooperative and conflicting interests, giving rise to the Negotiator's Dilemma, it is not simply a matter of cooperatively discovering or inventing the largest pie, but of competitively determining respective shares of it. Even a pie so large that substantive demands for shares could be satisfied would not eliminate the procedural conflict inherent in the process. Thus, joint determination of outcomes involves a cooperative, unstructured, trial-and-error process of integrative negotiation, framing, formulation, and determination of appropriate references of justice, followed or accompanied by a competitive process of applying the formula to details and of manipulating security points as referents.

Single overarching concepts often constitute the grand formula under which negotiations are conducted. A comprehensive ban on whaling, applied equally to all, or a comprehensive ban on the use and production of chemical weapons, or a worldwide 50% reduction in chlorofluorocarbons provide examples. In economic matters, the 16 parallel free trade zones that linked the African members of the

Euro-African Association to the European Community (EC) under the Yaoundé Conventions, or the free trade area comprising Canada, the United States, and Mexico under the NAFTA agreement, are examples. In all these cases, the overarching formula is accompanied by both applications and derogations in detail. Since negotiation frequently involves taking back in detail what one gave away in principle (Freeman, 1997), pure integrative negotiation may be as much of an idealization as a pure market economy.

Constructed Negotiation. Because of the Reciprocity Assumption and the other assumptions, the formula may be constructed through tradeoffs based on terms of trade and compound equality rather than on a single principle of simple equality. The Equivalence Assumption is important to this procedure, as one party's traded item is roughly equated to the other's. The actual process may be a one-step linkage of one item to another to constitute the formula for agreement, or it may involve a multistep ratcheting process until a satisfactory equivalence is achieved. At the same time as the parties are looking for satisfactory terms of trade, they continue to keep open the possibility of working on each other's security points.

Simple tradeoffs were the basis for the Southwest African security settlement of 1988, when the withdrawal of South African troops from Namibia was traded against the withdrawal of Cuban troops from Angola, and of UN Security Council Resolution 242, on which subsequent Middle East peace processes were based, which posited an exchange of security for territory. A more complex process is illustrated by the 21-meeting Norwegian mediation process between Palestinians and Israelis throughout 1993. The Israelis could open with a demand for an end to the intifada, to which the Palestinians could respond, "Not till you've given me land," to which the Israelis could reply, "Not till you've given me a guaranteed limitation on your appetite for land, through recognition of Israel," to which the Palestinians could answer, "Not till you've given me recognition, too." The deal was closed on mutual recognition plus autonomy in exchange for an end to rebellion. Yet this was neither a single set of tradeoffs nor an agreed overarching principle (Corbin, 1994; Zartman, 1997).

Inductive Negotiation. There are still negotiations carried out by concession/convergence, despite the difficulty of maximizing the payoffs to both parties using this procedure. Concessions are exchanged from inflated opening positions for two conflicting purposes: to reach the other party's zone of agreement and to attract the other party to the first party's point of agreement. Both sides seek an agreement above their respective security points, and so invite efforts of the other to lower its security point and efforts of their own to maintain (or sometimes raise) theirs. In this way, the parties establish agreement on individual points located somewhere between their two openers, and so cobble together a formula inductively. That formula may have very little coherence, may even be contradictory among its items, and so may be fragile.

Concessionary behavior frequently occurs toward the end of a long set of negotiations, when the parties have exhausted both their solid reasons and their effective power to move the other, and no other option is left but to inch toward the middle and split the difference (Tracy, 1978; Bartos, 1978). Concessionary negotiation, however, does not always end up in the middle, as negotiators of the Israeli border disengagement agreements with Syria and Egypt in 1974–1975 (Rubin, 1981; Saunders and Albin, 1993), or negotiators of the Tokyo Round of the GATT talks (Winham, 1986), or negotiators of US–Soviet arms control agreements (Bunn, 1992) know. Deviations from the middle occur because the various patterns have been used effectively as power to move the other party in an intended direction, based on the strength of the desire for an agreement relative to its payoffs (in costs and benefits) and to the value of its security point.

In sum, the way in which parties reach an agreement determines to a large extent the agreement that they reach. No more than in economic theory do the ideal assumptions of negotiation theory determine outcomes in the activity to which they apply. Instead, they must be combined with the reality of alternative processes to explain how outcomes are created and hence what those outcomes are. These outcomes may not be efficient in economic terms, in that goods and services are employed wastefully. They may not even be Pareto optimal, in bargaining terms, in that the parties' individual and joint gains may not be maximized. Indeed, one or both parties' goals may quite specifically be that the outcome not be efficient or not be optimal, or both. Demand and power, at the background of assumptions and expressed in process, explain the outcome. Most of the studies in this volume, examining the source of power in negotiations, support the importance of alternatives and security points as the single most important variable, consistent with the demand dimensions initially indicated.

Each of these process models gives rise to hypotheses that specify in more detailed ways how process affects the outcome, often depending on various intervening variables. A number of hypotheses have already been presented above in regard to the Toughness Dilemma. Some of these are illustrated in Ahnlid's study of Uruguay Round negotiations, in Kerwin and DeFelice's study of intellectual property license negotiations, in Vlasova's study of the Commonwealth of Independent States (CIS) common market, and in Zartman and Wagner's study of European exchange rate negotiations.

In regard to the interpersonal orientations, preliminary evidence suggests that a party will see an integrative situation and aim at a positive-sum outcome if the basic assumptions of the process are deemed to have been respected in the previous period, or if its gains are inherently and positively tied to gains by the other party;

if not, the party will aim at distributive bargaining. Odell's study of US–Japanese trade negotiations and Winham and Finn's study of NAFTA negotiations examine these and related hypotheses. Obviously, it takes two (or more) to make a positive sum, so mixed orientations will give rise to negotiation's most perplexing situation, Nicolson's Dilemma: What happens when a Shopkeeper (integrative negotiator) meets a Warrior (distributive bargainer)? No clear or even hypothetical answers are available, either analytically or prescriptively. Initial indications are that the Warrior wins (Kritek, 1994), as examined in detail in Faure's study of joint ventures in China. However, there are means to help a Warrior concede to reach agreement (Ury, 1991), some of which are presented in Okogu's study of structural adjustment negotiations in Nigeria.

In regard to methodological sequencing, parties will obviously bargain inductively within a contract zone when a formula already exists. Kerwin and DeFelice's study of licensing, Faure's and Fink's studies of foreign investment, and Zartman and Wagner's study of exchange rate negotiations are examples. When a formula does not exist – the more interesting situation – the parties will negotiate deductively if they are both integrative negotiators (determined by the previous hypotheses), if there is a salient issue or cluster of issues that lends itself to formulation, or if there is a perceived aggregate power asymmetry. Vlasova uses a former Soviet case, Sawyerr uses a Ghanaian case, and Winham and Finn use a North American case to illustrate related hypotheses. These hypotheses provide many explanatory relations to pursue.

The overall objective of the project requires that case study authors look at their respective negotiation through two sets of analytical lenses simultaneously. A principal question is to what extent economic theory may constrain, or lead, parties to behave in a way that influences negotiation behavior, possibly to such an extent that negotiation theory must be supplemented or modified. The design of the project should, however, not be understood as a competition between negotiation and economic theory. A more realistic expectation is that insights from the two theoretical perspectives may be combined and, hence, lead to mutual enrichment for practice and for analysis.

Notes

[1] I am most grateful for the comments of John Odell and my PIN colleagues on previous drafts.

[2] There are also Negative-Sum negotiations, in which one party seeks to impose damage on the other whatever the cost, but this category is small and exceptional.

[3] There is also a prior phase of diagnosis that, though important, is not germane to the present discussion (Zartman and Berman, 1982; Stein, 1992).

Part II

Case Studies

The focus of this study is on negotiations on *economic issues*. The principal questions raised in the study are, first, if international, economic negotiations have certain features distinguishing them from negotiations on other issues and, second, if these idiosyncratic properties of economic negotiations mean that they are better interpreted with the help of issue-specific analytical frameworks – economic theory – than negotiation theory. The project has, however, not been framed as a competition between negotiation and economic theory respectively. The basic theoretical question is how negotiation and economic theory should best be combined in order to attain an understanding of international economic negotiations that is as comprehensive as possible. However, this analysis also entails an evaluation of the relative usefulness of each of the two approaches in different research contexts and for different types of research purposes.

The strategy selected to deal with these analytical issues can be described as a theory-driven comparative assessment of empirical cases. The cases are actual historical cases of economic negotiations that have all taken place during the last decades. The selection of cases reflects the many different faces that an economic issue put on the negotiation table may have. Hence, the following subcategories of economic issues are included in the study: *foreign direct investments, macroeconomic issues, financial and monetary issues,* and *trade questions* pertaining to both goods and services.

International, economic negotiations are dealt with by different types of actors; *national governments, private business companies* and *international organizations*. Governments and companies negotiate between themselves in some of the cases, whereas in others a company is at one side of the table and a government at the other. In several cases international organizations are key players. Thus, international economic negotiations have been conducted in different contexts, which has also been considered in the selection of cases. Some of the negotiations were two-party encounters, whereas others were pluri- or multilateral in character. The negotiations on NAFTA included three parties, whereas around 100 countries were involved in the negotiations on a services agreement in the Uruguay Round. Some of the case negotiations were conducted directly between the parties, whereas others unfolded within the context of an international regime or organization constraining some actors and supporting others.

The authors of the case studies were instructed to search for evidence in "their" negotiation supporting the proposition that its outcome could be understood by negotiation or economic theory, as these two bodies of knowledge are interpreted in the Introduction.

The section of case studies is organized in four subsections. The first of these addresses three cases related to foreign direct investment. One of these – a company–government encounter concerning the creation of a Disney park outside

Paris – interlinks two great industrialized countries, the United States and France. The second case involves European companies negotiating joint ventures with the Chinese authorities. The third case pertains to the confrontation between a large American company renegotiating the terms of a foreign direct investment in Ghana.

One case, constituting a section by itself, deals with negotiation on macroeconomic issues: domestic negotiations for the purpose of restructuring the Nigerian economy under the pressure of external economic disequilibria.

The section on financial and monetary issues contains two cases. One concerns recurrent debt rescheduling negotiations between the Polish government and the so-called London Club of private financial institutions. The other involves European Community negotiations regarding the relative values of member nations' currencies.

Five different cases of trade negotiations have been studied in this project. One of the cases refers to bilateral company-to-company negotiations concerning the licensing of intellectual property rights involving AT&T and other firms. Another case pertains to the recurrent trade negotiations between two of the greatest commercial powers, the United States and Japan. The three other cases were all conducted between national governments in different geographical and political contexts. The negotiations on trade in services in the Uruguay Round is a case of a truly global encounter taking place within the context of a well-established international organization, GATT/WTO. The other two cases are regional in character and were supported by much weaker international institutions. One case is the creation of NAFTA on the North American continent and the other negotiations between former members of the Soviet Union in order to establish a system of cooperation and integration.

Section 1

Direct Investment

Chapter 2

Negotiation Between the French Government and the Walt Disney Company Regarding Creation of Euro Disney

Geoffrey Fink

2.1 Introduction

This case study analyzes the negotiations between the Walt Disney Company and the French government that resulted in the 1992 opening of the Euro Disney theme park outside of Paris. In assessing the outcome of these negotiations, we will consider not only the immediate agreement reached by the parties, but also the development and initial operation of the project, to obtain an accurate view of the overall results.

This case has many of the elements of a paradigmatic modern international public–private economic negotiation. It involves a sophisticated global company, the government of a world power, a long-term, multibillion dollar investment project, and, helpful for our purposes, the glaring eye of the public media, which followed the entire course of the negotiation. Unfortunately, however, neither of the parties involved proved willing to discuss the negotiations with the author. This case therefore focuses on the tactics and outcomes of the negotiations rather than on their processes.

Given the identity of the actors and the nature of the negotiation, one might assume that this case demonstrates the power of economic theories as the best prognosticators of outcome in this sort of economic negotiation. Alternatively, the student of negotiation, considering the relative power, interests, and concerns of the parties, might confidently predict that negotiation theory offers key insights into the results of the case. In fact, this chapter will argue that neither of our imaginary advocates is entirely correct. This case indicates that negotiation theory maintains much more validity in a negotiation of this type, set in an international context, than does neoclassical economic theory, although the insights of the former can be usefully supplemented by certain alternative economic theories. Thus, both sets of theories are necessary if one is to obtain the fullest, most accurate, explanation of this type of international negotiation.

This case study begins with a chronological narration of Disney's decision to develop Euro Disney, the subsequent negotiation of the project's Master Agreement, the controversy surrounding the park's development, and the difficulties encountered in the initial period of operation. The study will then consider the ability of economic theories to explain the overall outcome of these negotiations, and lastly examine whether negotiation theories can do any better. As this case is written from a practitioner's perspective, with the belief that it contains some extremely valuable lessons for international business negotiators, the analytical sections also focus strongly on such lessons and the pitfalls of which they warn. None of these insights are particularly original; however, the fact that so many of them nonetheless arose in a negotiation between two extremely sophisticated parties indicates that this case has value for all practitioners in this field.

2.2   Narrative

2.2.1   Disney's international operations and the decision to develop Euro Disneyland

The Walt Disney Company is one of the world's leading entertainment companies. Theme parks and resorts are the most important of Disney's three principal businesses. International operations have acquired an increasing importance to the company, with the share of total revenue attributable to international business rising from 10% in 1987 to 17% in the 1993 fiscal year (Walt Disney Company, 1993, Annual Report:54). While all three of Disney's business segments are active overseas, the company's most visible foreign venture until the mid-1980s was Tokyo Disneyland. The park was built by Disney but is owned by a Japanese investment group, Oriental Land, from whom Disney receives licensing and management fees.

Tokyo Disneyland is an entirely American experience. The park has been described as a "world that envelops visitors in not one, but two fantasies – of a dreamy, simplified America, and of a land of flying elephants, talking mice and magical castles" (Greenhouse, 1991b). This American experience is apparently exactly what the Japanese wanted, since after an initially slow start the park did extraordinarily well. Disney rapidly came to regret its earlier decision to invest in the park on a licensing rather than a direct basis, and felt assured that its parks' success could travel.

By the mid-1980s, following Tokyo Disneyland's opening, the company had been flooded with "inquiries, invitations or flat offers of cash inducements" from over 200 locations, on four continents, hoping to be the site of future Disney investment (Mikelbank, 1991). With Disney parks firmly established in both the United States and Japan, expanding into Europe appeared to be the logical step for the company's parks and resorts division. Thus, in 1984 Disney decided to study the feasibility of a European Disney resort. Jim Cora, a Disney executive who played a key role in the development of Tokyo Disneyland, was assigned to head a project team given that task. The team came quite rapidly to the conclusion that a European Disneyland was not only feasible but also potentially very lucrative, and the focus of the company's efforts soon shifted to finding an appropriate site for the project.

2.2.2   Disney's decision to invest in France

Over 240 potential park locations were suggested to the company by European governments attracted by Disney's promise of 12,000 direct jobs and a further 48,000 persons to be employed in ancillary services (Aziz, 1992). The choices soon narrowed to Barcelona, a location to the east of London, or Marne-la-Vallée, 21 miles east of Paris. London's antiquated infrastructure and Britain's labyrinthine planning system, which would have made a nightmare of any transport upgrade and land acquisitions, resulted in the English location's rapid elimination from consideration (Waller, 1992).

The French site was extremely attractive to Disney based on both population and visitor figures (Chermont and Rayon, 1989). This prime location in the "heart of Europe" gives the Marne-la-Vallée site access to a much larger market than that of any other Disney park, as shown in *Table 2.1*. Moreover, the site's location, combined with Europe's high population density and France's excellent road, rail, and air transportation networks, resulted in the Marne-la-Vallée site having the largest number of nearby potential guests of any Disney park. *Table 2.2* shows a comparison.

Another highly advantageous characteristic of the French site was that it was one of the largest available land areas contiguous to a major European capital. The potential site stretched over 4,800 acres of flat potato-and-beet farmland, an area

Table 2.1. National population and park visitors.

	Number of Disney parks	Population (million)	Approximate attendance (thousand)
Europe	1[a]	337	11,000
US	3[b]	240	39,400
Japan	1	120	13,500

[a] A second park was scheduled to open in 1996 at Euro Disneyland; after an initial postponement, the project was being re-examined in 1999.
[b] Not including the Disney–MGM theme park.
Source: Euro Disney.

Table 2.2. Potential visitors.

Number of people (million) living within	Euro Disneyland	Walt Disney World	Disneyland
2-hour drive	17	6	16
4-hour drive	41	12	18
6-hour drive	109	13	22

Source: Euro Disney.

one-fifth the size of Paris itself. The French government, moreover, had made clear its interest in the employment and revenues that the Disney project would bring to the area and its willingness to cooperate extensively with the company.

According to several sources, Disney decided virtually immediately that it would choose the Marne-la-Vallée site (Woodyard, 1992). The company then used the same negotiating tactic that it used in California when choosing a site for its second California park, where it pitted Anaheim against Long Beach in a battle for concessions.

In order to increase the pressure on the French government, Disney sought to make Barcelona appear a more attractive location than it actually was. Barcelona's principal advantage was its weather, which is far more similar to Florida's or California's climes than the French site's. Paris is known for its inclement weather, and the company repeatedly noted this while pointedly neglecting to mention that "in designing Tokyo Disneyland, the Disney design and engineering teams acquired solid experience in adapting the parks to harsh weather conditions [which now] pose no major obstacles to 'imagineers'" (Chermont and Rayon, 1989:26). In retrospect, perhaps Disney should have paid the weather as much attention from a substantive point of view as it did from a tactical negotiation one.

Disney also pointed out that of three large amusement parks that had recently opened in France, "all have fallen flat and two have been forced into bankruptcy" (Greenhouse, 1991a). Again, this claim ignored the tremendous difference in scope, scale, experience, and reputation that existed between those parks and the

Euro Disneyland proposal, which was unique in Europe. In contrast, Barcelona's relatively poor transportation system and the absence of the availability of large, flat tracts of land were rarely mentioned by Disney during the period in which the company was negotiating with both the French and Spanish governments (Greenhouse, 1991a).

The French government, meanwhile, was being extremely responsive to Disney's investment-related requests. While Barcelona is the capital of the semi-autonomous Catalan region of Spain, the French site was located in one of the five *ville nouvelle* ("new city") development zones in the Paris region. Thus, while any proposals relating to the Spanish site would presumably have to go through local, regional, and national reviews, the *villes nouvelles'* regional development authorities reported to the national level and had jurisdiction over zoning and planning superseding that of overlapping local governments. These authorities are known as *Établissements Public d'Aménagement* (EPA), and the EPA for the Disney area was EPAMarne. The critical land acquisition and use issues would thus be dealt with far more expeditiously in France than at the Spanish site. The French also satisfied one of Disney's major criteria by promising to expropriate all of the land Disney wanted for its development, as well as making preliminary promises to upgrade the area's transportation infrastructure.

An initial letter of understanding between Disney and the French government was signed on 18 December 1985 by French Prime Minister Laurent Fabius and Michael Eisner, Disney chairman and chief executive officer (CEO). That the French prime minister himself signed the letter is an indication of the importance of this project to the government, which dealt with it on a virtually intergovernmental, rather than public–private, level.

Having established its serious interest in the Marne-la-Vallée site, but also raising a supposedly strong alternative in terms of the allegedly very attractive location in Spain, the company began 15 months of intense negotiations with the French side.

2.2.3   Parties' interests and resulting issues

A summary of the two parties' key interests is set out below and illustrated in *Table 2.3*.

Disney's concerns were relatively clear. The company believed that Marne-la-Vallée was clearly the most desirable site for its project. Disney therefore viewed its interests in the ensuing negotiations as primarily financial, involving ways to maximize the marginal benefits obtainable from the French side. Though marginal in the sense that they were secondary to Disney's principal interest in establishing the park at Marne-la-Vallée, they should not be taken to be insignificant in financial terms.

Table 2.3. Parties' interests and issues.

Disney	France
Favorable land purchase terms	Development of Paris's eastern suburbs
Financing scheme minimizing Disney's initial capital investment	Decreasing unemployment through the 60,000 jobs anticipated from the project
Agreement structure maximizing Disney's share of upside potential	Stimulus to the languishing construction industry
Tax concessions	Revenue for French suppliers during both the construction and operational phases
Government-financed upgrades to the area's transportation infrastructure	Improvement of France's balance of payments through enhanced tourism
	Showcase project demonstrating that France was dynamic, ready, and able to compete successfully for foreign direct investment

The Euro Disneyland project, as planned, involved a tremendous investment. The first of the several development phases, Phase 1A, alone represented an investment of FF14.9 billion (Chermont and Rayon, 1989:6). The size of the project meant that the effect of any concessions that the company could obtain from the government would be multiplied manyfold as compared to their effect on any other international investment project undertaken in France's recent history, with the sole exception of the Euro Tunnel.

The French had a distinct set of benefits they sought to gain from the project, and these ranged from the political to the economic. In contrast with Disney's interests, those of the French government were joint rather than several. All of these interests would be satisfied to some degree were an agreement to be reached, and none would be met if the French government failed to attract Disney to Marne-la-Vallée. France's interests were thus much less subject to disaggregation and individual analysis than were Disney's, given that they all depended on the same operative condition: obtaining the Disney investment. The French national government team therefore went into the negotiations with an essentially unconditional mandate to woo Disney.

2.2.4   Negotiating structure established

Disney had different negotiating teams dealing with each of the various French parties. These teams were all operating under the aegis of the External Relations Department (ERD), which had a central coordination role. There was an overall ERD team, led by Jim Cora, who subsequently became president of Disneyland International, and Lee Lanselle, who was later named Director of Worldwide Project

Development and Coordination for Disney International, which, aided by the input of the other teams, dealt with the top French interministerial team. This first group was given orders to "play hardball." Neither Eisner nor Disney President Frank Wells, who was overseeing the project, was willing to concede many points to the French. Neither man wanted a repeat of the Japanese deal (Resener, 1992).

On the French side, Disney initially began talks with the Ministry of International Trade. It soon became apparent, however, that there were five principal French parties whose interests were intimately affected by the project. These were the French government; the Île-de-France region; the Department of Seine-et-Marne; the five *communes*, or towns, within whose bounds the project area lay; and the Paris Regional Transit Authority, or RATP. Because the discussions involved various topics under the different and overlapping ministries responsible for the different parties, the government appointed an interministerial delegate to act as intermediary in the substantive negotiations between Disney and all of the French parties other than the RATP. The delegate became the "point man" for the national government as well as the local and regional governments.

The interministerial delegate had the authority to deal with all issues, other than land use and planning, involving the parties he represented. These two issues fell under the purview of EPAMarne. As EPAMarne was also a national government body, having it as a third party with whom these issues had to be negotiated did not impede the negotiation process to any great extent.

The degree of national involvement in the Disney project was so extensive that shortly after the initial stage of negotiations ended, EPAMarne, which was originally a standard *ville nouvelle* EPA, was dissolved and replaced with EPAFrance. This new agency had the same responsibilities as its predecessor, but was specifically created and staffed for the Euro Disney project.

The French negotiating structure was therefore composed of the interministerial delegate's team, with the broadest authority, the EPA team dealing with land use issues, and the RATP representatives discussing Paris-area commuting issues.

2.2.5 The Master Agreement

The main round of negotiations culminated in *The Agreement on the Creation and the Operation of Euro Disneyland in France* (the "Master Agreement"), signed on 24 March 1987, between Eisner and Jacques Chirac, the conservative politician who had replaced Fabius as Prime Minister (Chermont and Rayon, 1989:23). This contract, as its name implies, is the overall legal document governing the Disney investment. It legally binds the two Euro Disney holding companies, Euro Disneyland S.A. and Euro Disneyland SNC, the French government, and a number of regional and local government bodies.

The negotiations took over a year to complete, not only because of a change of government in France, but also because of the novelty of this sort of agreement to both parties. Although the French state had considerable experience in managing relations with businesses, the nature and degree of the public–private partnership involved in the Euro Disneyland project were unique. Similarly, while Disney was certainly familiar with complex contracts it, too, had only limited experience with managing the degree of public–private cooperation involved in this project. As Disney General Counsel Stephen Juge stated, "[Euro Disneyland's Master Agreement is] very much unlike Anaheim or Florida or Japan where the basic legal framework is private ... . The main way in which Euro Disneyland differs from our other parks is that the overall framework of the project is based on a 30-year agreement with the French government" (Chermont and Rayon, 1989).

2.2.6   Land issues

As discussed previously, one of the key issues in the Master Agreement negotiations concerned the tremendous amount of land that Disney would need. Most of the real estate was privately owned farmland that the government had promised in preliminary talks to help acquire. Under the terms of the Agreement the French government was to use its eminent domain powers, referred to in this context as a *projet d'interet general* (PIG), to allow Disney to bypass what would otherwise have certainly been difficult negotiations with a multitude of small landowners, each of who would have known that by holding out he could put the whole project in jeopardy. According to Juge, Disney was able to convince the French government to utilize the PIG provision on a previously unheard-of scale.

Moreover, the government set a fixed square meter sale price to Disney of FF11.10, which was relatively expensive for farmland but very inexpensive for developed use, plus the cost of any necessary secondary infrastructure work and the operating expenses of EPAFrance. As one would expect, the farmers whose land was to be expropriated erupted into a storm of protest upon learning of these terms, especially when they discovered that the government would pay them compensation of only FF4 per square meter, thereby realizing an instant profit of almost 200%. As the EPAs had full jurisdiction over the land issues the farmers had no say in this part of the negotiations, particularly as, contrary to French law, the mayors of the five communes were not consulted before the sale was made. The government negotiated in secret and presented the locals with a *fait accompli* (Aziz, 1992).

As the entire area on which Disney holds a purchase option is zoned as a *zone d'aménagement différé* (ZAD), it allows for progressive development with land purchases at the preset price in successive stages over a 20-year period. These provisions amounted to a tremendous subsidy from the government to Disney, as they allow the company to purchase land at essentially agricultural rates, develop it, and then resell or rent it at market rates. Disney was therefore basically guaranteed a risk-free profit on its extensive planned range of development activities.

These real estate provisions were particularly important in view of the fact that Disney, unbeknownst to most, intended "to make the Marne-la-Vallée region ... both a resort area and a permanent place of residence ..." by creating an entire planned community. In the long term Euro Disneyland was envisioned much more as a vast real estate development than as a mere theme park.

In return for these significant benefits Disney accepted limited constraints on development. While the Master Agreement incorporated specific official approval of the Phase 1 program of development, it only provided general approval of the overall master plan and the detailed plans for future development phases. The initiation of each subsequent phase is therefore conditional on approval from EPAFrance.

A major result of this requirement for independent approval of each subsequent development stage was to create a stronger degree of instrumentalism in Disney's underlying interests (Lax and Sebenius, 1991a). Through the agreement reached on this issue the government was able to influence virtually all of the other issues embodied in the Master Agreement. Disney could hardly seek to force entirely one-sided terms on other issues, as this ZAD approval requirement made the tremendously important peripheral development program much more dependent on repeated dealing with the government. This may well be a reason why these initial negotiations went as smoothly as they did. Each side realized that this structure made relationship interests far more important than they would otherwise have been, particularly as some of the legal provisions of the Master Agreement made Disney much less dependent than typical investors on French goodwill.

2.2.7   Legal issues

On a local level, Disney received some important legal concessions from the French. Disney was exempted from normal, and potentially "exceedingly complex," zoning regulations, and was subject only to the technical oversight of EPAFrance.

Going much further, the Master Agreement also granted Disney full control of any activity within a six-mile radius of the park, including decision-making powers over zoning and traffic control as well as the responsibility for maintaining public order. Critics complained that this gave Euro Disneyland the same status as a duchy or principality (Roth, 1992). The newspaper *Le Monde Diplomatique*, in an article headlined "France's Gifts to Euro Disney," equated the company's position under this legal framework to that of sole administrative agent of what is in effect a major city (Azocar, 1992).

2.2.8   Investment structuring and financing issues

Disney was able to obtain extraordinarily favorable financing terms on the project, gaining a 49% interest in Euro Disney for a mere US$160 million, or under 4% of the project's total investment capital. Under the Master Agreement other investors were to provide US$1.2 billion in equity, the French government would provide a low-interest US$960 million loan, and banks would loan another US$1.6 billion. The remaining US$400 million needed would come from special partnerships formed to buy properties and lease them back. John Forsgren, Euro Disney's chief financial officer, boasted that few companies other than Disney could even dream of arranging a similar financing package.

This is the area of the Master Agreement where Disney made the most substantial concessions in return for what are admittedly exceptional terms. The company assented to a linkage of the availability of funds from the Caisse des Dépôts, the government lending agency, to successful raising of equity by the two holding companies and to the degree of construction completed according to a predetermined schedule. Moreover, Disney's compensation for the duration of the 30-year park management contract was subordinated to the repayment of the Caisse and private loans, and the Walt Disney Company guaranteed certain borrowings of the various Euro Disney companies.

The Master Agreement required that the Walt Disney Company organize and manage two owner, or holding, companies: Euro Disneyland S.A. and Euro Disneyland SNC. The agreement limited the Walt Disney Company to a 49% stake in these two companies, and required that, until 1992, the companies encourage EC nationals to hold majority interests. Disney chose to hold the maximum share allowable in Euro Disneyland SCA, which is the development and operation management company, but limited its stake in Euro Disneyland SNC, the financing company, to 17% for tax reasons. *Figure 2.1* shows the resulting structure.

Last, a certain percentage of Disney's management fees from Euro Disneyland is performance based, coming from incentive fees based on the growth rate of the park's cash flows. The park's success will also impact Disney's revenues as a result of the company's decision to hold a 49% equity stake in Euro Disneyland SCA (Chermont and Rayon, 1989:7). Thus, both short- and long-term revenues will depend on how successfully the project is run.

In addition to the direct financing benefits, Disney negotiators obtained what *Le Monde Diplomatique* described as "exceptional tax benefits, beginning with a reduction in purchase taxes from 18.6% down to 7%, an exceptional feat in France." The government also gave Disney the right to depreciate Magic Kingdom assets on an accelerated 10-year basis rather than the usual 20-year basis. This had the effect of substantially reducing accounting profits, and therefore taxes, in the initial 10-year period.

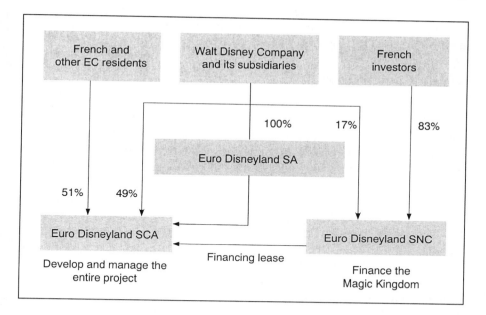

Figure 2.1. Euro Disney financing structure. Source: Euro Disney.

2.2.9   Infrastructure issues

A willingness to invest in infrastructure improvement, particularly for transportation, was another incentive that the French government used to draw Disney to Marne-la-Vallée. As visitors are the lifeblood of any entertainment venture, and commuter access is crucial to successful suburban development, this aspect of the negotiations impacted both Disney's park and peripheral development programs.

The RATP agreed to extend the Paris Regional Express Railway network to a new station that it would build at the Magic Kingdom's main gate, making the park a half-hour ride from the center of Paris and greatly increasing accessibility from throughout the greater Paris metropolitan area. An indemnity agreement was included whereby Disney would compensate the RATP should the number of riders on the new line prove insufficient to cover its operating costs. In an innovative provision, any indemnity paid must be used by the RATP to promote Euro Disneyland.

Two major highway interchanges from the large A4 expressway, 22 miles of roadway, 20 bridges, and transportation canals were also to be built by the government pursuant to the agreement. Alongside this new transportation grid, the government agreed to build a power grid to bring the necessary electricity to the development site. The total cost of the government's infrastructure work was estimated at US$400 million (Azocar, 1992).

2.2.10   Cultural issues

The last major area covered by the Master Agreement, and the one that certainly attracted the most attention and probably the most emotional reactions, was that of the park's cultural context. Responding to concerns characterizing Mickey Mouse as a "Trojan mouse of American cultural imperialism" (Whitcher, 1992), Disney agreed in the Master Agreement that Euro Disneyland's Magic Kingdom would feature European cultural themes and would include at the least one attraction depicting European civilization. Disney's approach to this issue during these initial negotiations was extremely flexible and accommodating, with Disney's CEO, Robert Fitzpatrick declaring, "We will make all the adjustments necessary for the perfect harmonization of 'Euro Disneyland in France' with the culture and aspirations of the French people" (Cottrell, 1991).

As the French language is integral to French culture, the Master Agreement included "fairly precise guidelines" dealing with this "potentially prickly" issue. These provided that French was to be the "official" language of the park, used in signs and some attractions, although other languages could be used on a "complementary basis," e.g., for subtitling. While Disney was, overall, very accommodating on cultural issues at this stage, it did draw the line at renaming "famous attractions," insisting on the inclusion of a clause stating that "translation from English is not necessary for the names of famous attractions." Somewhat surprisingly, however, the company agreed to change the names of certain of its best-known characters. A Canadian newspaper described the somewhat strange result of this agreement:

> Cinderella became Cendrillon easily enough. Similarly Snow White is now Blanche-Neige, Sleeping Beauty is La Belle au Bois Dormant, and Mickey Mouse becomes plain Mickey (pronounced Mee-kay), although for some reason Donald Duck remains just that, and Pinocchio gets to keep his Neapolitan handle. But Goofy becomes Dingo. Goofy, eh? [Mostyn, 1992]

In sum, the Master Agreement included agreements on both some very precise cultural issues and on some very general principles regarding culture.

2.2.11   Disney's responsibilities

Disney, of course, provided the French side with the expected benefits in return for the many concessions enumerated above. These included making available, under license, the Disney name and other intellectual properties, building and opening the Magic Kingdom theme park, managing the park for a 30-year period during which time much of its compensation, as discussed earlier, would be tied to shareholder returns, and using its "best efforts" to carry out the peripheral development plan. In addition to these relatively standard terms, Disney also agreed to use French and other EC contractors and suppliers for 60% to 90% of each category of costs. Local food and beverage products would also be given preference and French and other EC companies would be given "priority consideration as participants in park attractions" (Chermont and Rayon, 1989:48–49).

2.2.12   From Master Agreement to park opening

The signing of the Master Agreement represented a successful close to the first stage of the Euro Disney project. Years of careful preparation and negotiation had produced a comprehensive framework for one of the largest foreign investment projects in France's recent history. Both the national government and Disney must have been understandably satisfied at the time with an agreement that, overall, appeared reasonably fair and mutually beneficial.

The first indication that the development of Euro Disney might not follow the course anticipated by the main parties came soon after the signing of the Master Agreement, during a press conference held to promote the upcoming public offering of Euro Disney SCA shares. Staged on the steps of the beautiful Greek-revival Paris Bourse (stock exchange) building, the event was intended to be a magic Disney moment giving a glimpse of what could be expected of the Euro Disney park. The podium was decorated with pictures of favorite cartoon characters, while a troupe of Disney dancers performed for the crowd. Disney chairman Eisner, Euro Disney CEO Fitzpatrick, and other senior company officials arrived in cars driven by cast members dressed up as Mickey, Goofy, and other characters. An observer recounts what happened next:

> Fitzpatrick walked out into the sunlight. Then Eisner. Then the real stars of the hour: Mickey, Minnie, Donald, Goofy, Pluto.
> Splat.
> An egg.
> Splat splat.
> Ketchup. Tomatoes.
> Up there onstage, at noon, in front of the television cameras, top executives of a giant corporation and costumed animals with enormous heads scurried for cover behind pillars. Out on the street, demonstrators carried placards saying "Mickey, Go Home."
> And that was how it began. [Mikelbank, 1991]

The demonstrators, a mere dozen young communists protesting what they described as the government's unwarranted concessions to the company, nevertheless were able very effectively to destroy Euro Disney's earliest public "magic moment."

This unexpected spectacle was but the first event in a pattern of attacks on Disney and management errors that dogged the park's development and first two years of operation. Many of these problems resulted, either directly or indirectly, from the positions taken and agreements reached in the Master Agreement negotiations. We will now consider two such consequences of the earlier negotiations: first, how Disney became the target of sharp attacks on cultural grounds, and second, the operational mistakes resulting from Disney's and the government's attitude during the negotiations.

2.2.13   Disney and the decline of French culture

As construction on Euro Disney progressed, France's "popular intellectuals" seized upon the project as a vehicle for decrying what they saw as the ongoing American onslaught against traditional French culture, and they did so with a vengeance. Ariane Mnouchkine, a writer and theater director, made the much-publicized reference to Euro Disney as a "cultural Chernobyl," while a column by French Academy member Jean Cau in the leading conservative daily *Le Figaro* discussed "this horror of cardboard, plastic, atrocious colors, solidified chewing gum constructions and idiotic folk stories that come straight out of cartoon books for obese Americans. It is going to wipe out millions of children ... mutilate their imaginations." Taking criticism to an extreme, Jacques Juillard, a writer for the weekly *Nouvel Observateur*, claimed "I wish with all my heart for an uprising in May 1992 that will set Disneyland afire!"

Euro Disney was not the root cause of the outcry, of course, but simply served as a focal point around which French discontent at the growing encroachment of American culture could crystallize. The French have always had a mixed relationship with America, and this is particularly true in the cultural realm. The French intelligentsia's attack on Euro Disney as a proxy for exported American culture came about less because they saw corporate America forcing itself upon traditional France than because the past 15 years have seen France adopt Americana all too easily. Any observer of France cannot help but be struck by the extent to which the French, most particularly the youth segment, have welcomed American styles and habits into their lives. In that respect one of the most insightful comments made in the course of the debate over the project was that of Jacqueline Remy in *l'Express*, who argued that "at the core, America gives us the same effects as ice cream: it makes us sick, but we keep asking for it" (Weil, 1992).

As the project drove toward completion, it became apparent that Disney was taking full advantage of the relative vagueness of the cultural provisions of the

Master Agreement in order to keep the park as similar to its American and Japanese siblings as possible. The project's degree of "Europeanization" has been described as "modest, even notional" (Cottrell, 1991), and the company appears to have made very limited concessions to European culture. The company's claims to the contrary ring somewhat hollow: Disney cites the fact that Sleeping Beauty's castle was designed to look more whimsical and fairy-tale like than those on other parks, given the proximity of the chateaux of the Loire valley, as a "cultural concession." Disney also notes that, in compliance with the terms of the Master Agreement, a Jules Verne exhibit was included as the centerpiece of Discoveryland, but this hardly struck critics as a wholesale adoption of French culture.

These two changes aside, Disney's description of how the park fulfills the admittedly vague promise of cultural sensitivity is even more ephemeral. Disney points out "that certain of Walt Disney's 'fabulous creations,' such as Snow White, Pinocchio and Dumbo, have their origins in 'European tales and legends,' and so are enjoying ... 'return to their roots'" (Cottrell, 1991).

Even the area of language, which Disney believed to have been quite comprehensively addressed in the Master Agreement, created new controversy and amply demonstrated the difficulties that may result when parties to an agreement come from different backgrounds and read different subtexts into an agreement. As discussed previously, the Master Agreement had been drafted to state that while French would be the official language of the park, other languages could be used on a "complementary basis" and for naming "famous attractions." Agreement on the names of major Disney characters was worked out at that time on a case-by-case basis.

Given this background, Disney officials were surprised to be contacted in 1991 by the Délégation sur la Langue, a branch of the French Prime Minister's office that monitors use of the French language. Jean-Claude Amboise, spokesperson for the Délégation, explained that the government wanted Disney to translate the names of various attractions such as "Frontierland, Fantasyland, Big Thunder Mountain, and Pirates of the Caribbean" into French. When Disney replied that these were "famous attractions," which therefore fell under the Master Agreement's exemption, Amboise answered with a display of the Cartesian logic for which the French are so well known: he claimed that the exemption did not apply because "what's famous in the United States is not necessarily the case in France or Europe" (Lever, 1992). Disney ended up accepting the government's offer to negotiate attraction names on a case-by-case basis, and was ultimately able to convince the government that in order to ensure a "true" Disney experience most of the attractions should keep their original names (Lever, 1992).

Aside from the realm of language and one or two actual physical park elements, Disney appeared to feel that it could largely afford to ignore the criticisms of those both within and outside the government who were calling for a truly *Euro* Disneyland. Indeed, Fitzpatrick admitted as much when he described Euro Disney as "a synergy of our other parks, taking from our best" (Mikelbank, 1991). Disney, in fact, seemed to be doing this quite deliberately, as it appears that the company had, whether by careful analysis or instinct, decided that visitors would want an American experience. If, as this author believes, Disney had decided this in the earliest stages of project planning, then its public stance during the negotiation of the Master Agreement was certainly somewhat misleading. Michael Eisner, chairman of Disney, set the tone for the company's answer to critics by saying, "If they bring their children to Disneyland, they'll have a good time." Statements of this kind did little to dampen opposition to Euro Disney.

However, as the project neared completion, the view that Euro Disney was the harbinger of the destruction of traditional France was rapidly put into perspective even by "intellectuals." Political commentator Jean-François Revel wrote in *Le Point* that France's "cultural prophets" should stop contemplating their "media-driven navels and turning a tearful eye towards Euro Disney ... . If French culture, or European culture, can be crushed by Mickey Mouse, or more precisely by Mickey's geographic relocation, it means that this culture is disconcertingly fragile."

Although the cultural debate would almost certainly have occurred regardless of Disney's reaction, the company's apparent surprise and lack of coherent response to the charges being leveled against it did nothing to help protect Disney's all-important public image. Throughout the initial stages of the project, Disney appeared to view culture and its potential impact on Disney's image more as a political and public relations issue than as a substantive interest. While the ultimate effects of this controversy were not extreme, the company undoubtedly suffered some very undesirable public relations effects from its lack of understanding of what the culture issue actually represented to the French and its failure to treat it accordingly.

2.2.14   Initial operations

The Euro Disney theme park opened to great fanfare on 21 April 1992. The opening ceremonies were broadcast live to 30 countries, where audiences had their first opportunity to admire Disney's most elaborate park to date. The profusion of international stars drew attention away from the fact that there were no senior French government officials in attendance, and visitors were awed by the magic that Disney had created on what had been potato fields a mere five years earlier.

The park's operations began on a mixed note. While attendance met Disney's initial projections, management noticed several disturbing facts quite rapidly. Visits by the French were running at approximately 12% below the anticipated rate of 50%; hotel occupancy, at 57%, was below Disney's 80–85% benchmark; and merchandising was not doing nearly as well as expected. These problems persisted throughout the first year of operations, and while the park met its annual goal of 11 million visitors during each of the first two years it sustained a loss of FF188 million for the 1991–1992 fiscal year, which leapt to FF4,750 million for 1992–1993. These terrible financial results made it very obvious that the company had engaged in some serious miscalculations in its initial plans and methods, with resultingly negative bottom-line impact on all parties involved.

The project's poor initial financial results can be attributed in large part to a misunderstanding of the European market. Disney maintains that those losses were due to the park's having been opened at the low point of a pan-European recession, but upon closer examination it appears that many of the problems leading to the losses would likely have occurred regardless of the economic climate.

Recognizing that serious steps had to be taken to stem the tide of red ink, Disney moved to reorganize Euro Disney's management. On 11 April 1993, Disney named Philippe Bourguignon, a 45-year-old Frenchman, to succeed Fitzpatrick as CEO and chairman of Euro Disney. The new management initiated significant changes in relatively short order, as a wide range of operational issues were revisited and modified to better match consumer expectations.

The combination of new policies and cost reductions did not prevent further huge losses for 1993 and early 1994, and in early 1994 there were concerns that the losses incurred by the project were so high that they would lead to the park's closing. Euro Disney's losses meant that the project's creditors could not be paid out of earnings, as planned. Formal negotiations between Euro Disney and its creditors, organized into a committee, were therefore undertaken in early 1994. On 14 March 1994, Disney, Euro Disney, and the creditors' committee announced a financial restructuring plan calling for a reduction of the project's outstanding bank debt from FF16 to 10 billion. This was to be accomplished by a combination of actions. The banks would forgive interest and lengthen bond maturity; Disney would give up its contractual royalty payments for five years and accept reduced payments for a further five years; and both Disney and the banks would invest additional capital.

The head of the Banque Nationale de Paris, lead commercial bank to the project, stated that "the sharing of the restructuring effort between Walt Disney and the banks seems appropriate to the interests held by the various parties." Disney, abandoning its earlier stance, would in effect fund 60% of the restructuring by injecting FF4.3 billion into the project.

These negotiations, like those culminating in the Master Agreement, prove that Disney can be a formidable negotiator when dealing with familiar issues in a controlled setting. In fact, Disney's strong position in these restructuring negotiations was in part due to the careful financial safeguards that it had negotiated as part of the Master Agreement and loan agreements. In these circumstances, Disney's experience and strength could be used to their full advantage

Disney was able to use a combination of mutual concessions, coalition-building with the French government – a powerful partner with vested interests in a favorable outcome, and a legally strong walk-away option to shift a substantial portion of the costs of its initial mistakes onto the project's creditors and shareholders. As in the Master Agreement negotiations, Disney was able to achieve virtually all of the goals it had set for the negotiations. But as with the Master Agreement, only time will determine the ultimate results of these negotiations.[1]

2.3   Economic Theories

2.3.1   Neoclassical market behavior theory

Given that the Euro Disney project involved two highly sophisticated parties negotiating an investment agreement it would seem fertile ground for application of the neoclassical economic theory of market behavior. "Neoclassical economic theory assumes that individual preferences are exogenous, ordered, and stable ... [and that] individuals make independent rational choices to maximize their utility." While the applicability of this *homo œconomicus* model to the "real" world has been questioned, the main parties to this case would seem to display many of the model's characteristics.

Both Disney and the French government were sophisticated actors with tremendous resources at their disposal, endowing them with the potential to execute careful analysis of the situation. The negotiation occurred in a market setting that, albeit not perfect, had the potential for relatively efficient and accurate exchange of information. Although the parties were very different sorts of organizations, they were each tremendously powerful in their own right and there was therefore no major inherent power disparity between them, an important factor given that "... power remains outside the corpus of neoclassical theory." Both parties were well-organized hierarchies, implying that the result of their analyses would be transmitted to the senior decision makers in each organization, and that the decisions reached would then be implemented in a consistent fashion by subordinates. In sum, both the company and the government in this situation appear to satisfy the rational-actor model that lies at the core of neoclassical economic theory.

The theory would therefore suggest that, being "consistent maximizers," each party would behave in a predictable, utility-maximizing fashion. This suggestion is further reinforced by the fact that this case involves a free-market contract willingly entered into by each party, given that forming contracts was one of the two particular types of activities (the other being war) to which neoclassical economic analysis was originally conceived as being applicable.

As was described in the above chronology, such was not the case. Both parties were ultimately surprised by at least some of the outcomes of the agreement, and neither came close to optimizing its benefits from the negotiation – although, over-all, the negotiations must be evaluated as very successful. Why the discrepancy between theory and practice? Neoclassical economic theory posits rational actors seeking to maximize individual gain. As has been noted, "... *rationality* in the model rests on the assumption that preferences are consistently ordered, *maximiza-tion* on the assumption that choices 'reveal' preferences, and *individuality* on the assumption that all acts are evaluated in terms of their anticipated consequences for the self." All three of these assumptions proved false in the Euro Disney case, and while some or all of these elements may be missing from any economic negotia-tion, the chance that they will be absent is greater in international negotiations than in domestic ones.

2.3.2 Identification of interests: maximization

Obvious though it may seem, this element bears emphasizing. The most funda-mental requirement for a rational, efficient agreement is the ability of the parties involved to determine their interests in the negotiation in question. If such inter-ests, or preferences, are not clear to the parties themselves, then it is only by chance that parties will make choices that will maximize the fulfillment of their underlying interests. In this case, both parties fell short in this key area, and this failure made the achievement of an optimal outcome virtually impossible.

Disney focused entirely on financial and control issues in its negotiations, ap-parently never consciously recognizing that it had a strong interest in maintaining its sterling public image. This oversight did not come about because Disney sud-denly decided that it no longer cared about its public persona; rather, the company simply did not contemplate the possibility that this would even become an issue. All of its prior experience led the company to this conclusion, but in assuming that precedents set in one (or two, including Japan) areas of the world would have full validity in a new area – Europe – Disney made a classic international misstep.

Disney was a company genuinely accustomed to being loved by the public. Local leaders had always welcomed Disney developments as well-managed attrac-tions that would draw tourists into the area economy while the general public, raised on Disney characters, was typically delighted to have such wholesome family en-tertainment available. This friendly public image was one of which the company was very protective, and which had never been challenged on any significant scale. It appears that Disney officials did not even contemplate, in negotiating the Master Agreement, that Euro Disney would receive anything less than a traditional warm welcome. Had the company identified the protection of its carefully crafted image as an interest in the project's negotiation, it would almost certainly not have treated cultural questions as relative "throwaways."

The national government similarly failed to enter into the negotiations with an accurate picture of its overall interests. While there was a tremendous number of benefits that jointly constituted the government's interest in obtaining the project, it seems that the government was almost overwhelmed by them. Rather than methodically analyzing each of its interests, the government simply focused on the overall goal of attracting the investment. The government's attention was therefore directed at "beating" the other prospective sites and convincing Disney to choose Marne-la-Vallée. Disney's ongoing reminders that other allegedly desirable sites were more than willing to accommodate the company certainly reinforced this focus, as did the fact that the French government had previously, and publicly, signed a letter of interest regarding the project. Thus, the government negotiators' focus was on securing the project, and they appeared to give little consideration to building safeguards into the Agreement to protect against the eventuality that the project not be as successful as anticipated.

These two examples are typical of the risk, which is likely to arise in international settings, of parties' failing to recognize important interests. That Disney, an experienced global operator, would feel comfortable assuming that the most important issues in European projects would essentially exactly mirror those in American and Japanese ventures is indicative of the strength of the tendency to rely on past experience in judging which interests are important. While such experience can certainly be a useful reference, one cannot afford to let it be the sole guide when faced with an entirely new environment. The French government's mistake, meanwhile, is one that may typically arise in the context of foreign direct investment projects. With the increasing globalization of finance and capital movements there is ever more competition for investment funds, and governments seeking to become the recipients of such funds risk becoming fixated on "winning" the investment contest without considering in detail why they want to do so, i.e., their underlying interests.

2.3.3 Prioritization of interests: rationality

It was obviously impossible for the parties to try to maximize interests of whose existence they were not consciously aware. However, even in cases where very definite interests were being pursued, the two parties were in very different positions in terms of their ability to prioritize, or order, their interests.

The French government seems to have been the weaker actor as concerns ordering interests, presumably because the varied, and predominantly political, nature of its interests made such an evaluation difficult. Whereas Disney had the objective criterion of projected returns by which to evaluate its various financial interests, the

French side did not have any comparable yardstick. Although both economic and negotiation theory claim that "seemingly intangible tradeoffs can also be dealt with in analogous ways [to those used for tangible factors]" (Lax and Sebenius, 1991b), it would have taken a significant degree of "analytical introspection" by the French side to produce a ranking of any real value. Moreover, the number of parties involved on the French side, all of whom had congruent but not identical interests, would certainly have made this task even more difficult.

Thus, while the French negotiators may have been able to get a very general "sense of the order of magnitude of the value" of their various options, this sense would have been much less useful than Disney's far more precise analysis. The government's inability to quantify, and therefore to prioritize, its interests left it unable to calculate which interests it should press in its search for an optimal package. This problem compounded what has been described as a typical French problem wherein French negotiators "cannot ... compromise their maximalist proposal and hence end up having to 'cave in' and accept a worse deal than they could have made" simply in order to avoid having to walk away from the deal altogether.

Thus, even in the setting of an economic negotiation where, in theory, all interests, financial or otherwise, should be quantifiable and therefore subject to rank-ordering, this case suggests that such rigorous analysis may not occur in practice. Even sophisticated, resource-rich parties, such as the French national government, will simply not engage in the complex process of comparatively valuing interests that are not expressed in a common currency. Given that the consistent ordering of preferences is a fundamental requirement for the functioning of the Rationality Assumption upon which neoclassical economic analysis depends, such analysis will obviously be largely unproductive in the absence of effective ordering.

2.3.4 Accurate evaluation costs and benefits: individuality

The final element necessary for neoclassical economic analysis to have provided an accurate guide to the parties' actions is an accurate evaluation of the costs and benefits inherent to each interest, so that the net impact of its fulfillment may be calculated. Such a calculation is crucial if actors are to behave as the rational egotists upon whose actions neoclassical theory is premised. As with the previous two elements, however, neither Disney nor the French government fulfilled this condition.

Cost/benefit calculations, as with any market balancing mechanism, require accurate information if they are to produce the correct optimal result. Neither Disney nor the French government was able to predict accurately the outcomes of the initial negotiations because each was working with flawed data. The reasons that erroneous information was used, and that those errors were not caught, contain a significant lesson for anyone involved in international economic negotiations.

Throughout the negotiations Disney had shown a great deal of self-confidence. Whether demanding substantial concessions from the government or dismissing the attacks of the cultural elite, the company exhibited "a certain corporate smugness, that the French critics of Euro Disneyland find annoying ... [CEO Fitzpatrick's] greatest fear, he says confidently [before the park was opened], 'is that we may be too successful.' The park, he notes, can handle only 50,000 visitors a day" (Mikelbank, 1991). This self-assurance, presumably based on prior experience, led Disney to adopt the view that it did not need to reassess existing policies and procedures for use in the context of the Euro Disney project. It also served to intimidate outside parties who might otherwise have questioned what Disney was doing. This internal certainty and external timidity combined to foreclose any possibility that analysis would be carried out with valid data.

There have been claims that while Disney accurately predicted attendance at Euro Disney, its overall financial projections were unrealistic from the start: "Everyone in the US knew [the projections for the project] were hyped ... [but] Disney was a magic name," said one analyst. Based on Disney's past successes, Americans were very reluctant to question the company's projections, and when Europeans did dare to raise questions they were ridiculed by the Disney staff. For example, in 1990 Fitzpatrick was quoted in *Business Week* as saying, "We're seeing Cartesian skepticism meeting American can-do-ism." Rather than admitting that local parties might have useful insights into the nature of this new market, Disney steadfastly based its scenarios on past successes and optimism for the future. Thus, for example, when the question of whether Europeans would stand in line in the winter was raised in a strategy meeting, a former Disney executive says that the immediate response was, "'The Japanese do.' No one said, 'The Japanese are different.'" Of course, these differences subsequently became all too obvious.

The impact that Disney's attitude had on the initial negotiations is clear: the company's projections for the venture were unquestioningly accepted as the basis for negotiations by both sides, with the result that no cross-checking occurred. Each group had the ongoing potential during these negotiations to take action to avoid this mistake, yet neither did. Somewhat ironically, in retrospect it is clear that had either side done so, both would have benefited in the longer term.

While Disney's reliance on its optimistic figures is understandable, if not legitimate, the French government's compliance is surprising. The probable reasons for the government's passivity are twofold. One must remember that the French government was using this project as a showpiece and symbol of what could be accomplished through investment in "modern" France. The first explanation for the government's acquiescence was therefore probably that the government feared looking unsophisticated or inexperienced to the company, an appearance that would run directly counter to the image it was seeking to project. The government did in fact have very little experience negotiating projects of this type, but so would most other national governments in its position.

Although the French government employs some very capable functionaries, a project like Euro Disney was virtually unheard of and government representatives would have required considerable training and explanation to be in a position to challenge Disney's figures. For this to take place the negotiators would have had to admit to their superiors that they did not feel qualified to assess the Disney proposal – certainly a difficult admission to make – and the government would have had to delay the negotiations while the necessary institutional knowledge was acquired. While this second course of action would certainly have been wiser in the longer term than the first option of doing nothing, it would also have required much more effort to carry out. A third option would have been for the government to turn to an outside party, such as an investment bank or a consulting firm, to verify the Disney data, but doing so runs very much against the grain of French statism, under which the government is loath to admit that anything lies beyond its competence. Thus, of the three options available to government negotiators, by far the easiest from both a personal and institutional point of view was simply accepting Disney's figures.

The second reason for the government's failure to challenge Disney resulted from the competitive nature of the negotiations. Disney, we recall, had set up the process so that various potential sites were in competition with one another, even though it had reportedly settled on Marne-la-Vallée early on. In the initial negotiations the French government saw itself as being in competition with Spain and England, and thus did not want to appear obstreperous for fear of losing the project altogether. Of course, the result of this was that the government relied on Disney's information when negotiating the costs and benefits of the projects. By accepting Disney's figures, the government worked with an overly optimistic projection of potential benefits, and was therefore willing to incur higher costs than it objectively should have.

The reason that this twofold "silencing effect" is more likely to arise in an international setting relates to the greater chances that one or both parties will be dealing with issues or using methods that are relatively unfamiliar. In such cases, there is often a natural tendency to choose the path of least resistance and accept the other side's information at face value, rather than taking the more difficult courses of admitting ignorance or acquiring the knowledge to evaluate the information in question appropriately. That tendency will be exacerbated in competitive situations, which are common when a party, either public or private, is seeking to attract foreign direct investment. Working on the basis of incorrect data, neither Disney nor the French government could hope to carry out the rational cost/benefit analysis required to satisfy the individuality assumption of neoclassical economics.

2.4   Alternative Economic Models

The dictates of the neoclassical market theory model did not and, given the circumstances, could not have predicted the decisions of the actors in the Euro Disney negotiations. None of the model's three key assumptions were satisfied by either Disney or the government. As Kremenyuk, Sjöstedt, and Zartman point out in the Introduction, however, even in "pure" economic transactions, such as those in the arena of international trade, the neoclassical free market model often does not pertain. Thus, it was perhaps too much to expect the Euro Disney negotiations to hew to the neoclassical model and, to judge the overall applicability of economic models, we should consider the explanatory power of some of the alternative models. These seek to explain motives that drive actors in a different direction from the dictates of market theory. To the extent that these motives are acknowledged and studied by economic theory, they are appropriately classed within the category of economic explanations.

2.5   The Influence of Domestic Politics

It has been recognized that the nature of democratic systems is such that government and politicians alike may be driven to take certain actions for the sake of re-election rather than for reasons of optimal efficiency. In the Euro Disney negotiations, the area of culture is one in which attention to domestic politics guided one side's actions in an ostensibly nonrational but actually appropriate direction, while the other side's inattention to political sensibilities had unwelcome but predictable results.

As described above, the development of Euro Disney triggered a veritable onslaught by the French media and intellectuals against the project. Yet all of the critics' vitriol was directed at Disney, while the national government, which had courted the project in the first place, escaped virtually unscathed. The clearest explanation for this outcome involves the extent to which each of the two parties considered domestic politics while negotiating the cultural component of the Master Agreement.

Given the amount of money at issue in the Master Agreement negotiations, the French government directed what appeared to be an inordinate amount of attention to the cultural component of the talks. While Disney received tremendous concessions in other areas, it was an object of amusement to certain observers that the same government that willingly granted the project a nearly US$1 billion loan would expend efforts discussing what Snow White should be called in French. Any "rational" assessment would seem to suggest that the government had inverted its priorities.

The government's actions, however, become not merely understandable but indeed logical if domestic politics are considered. The government was undoubtedly aware that the project's development would trigger at least a certain degree of cultural resistance, even if they did not anticipate the ferocity of the attacks that resulted. Officials also must have known that, if the media had a basis on which to portray the government as responsible for the cultural "selling-out" of France, the effect on most voters would probably be much greater than any reaction that would result from a debate over the financing terms offered to Disney.

Thus, by devoting the attention necessary to building both specific guarantees and general statements of principle regarding culture into the Master Agreement, the government was subsequently able to frame the issue as one where it had taken all measures possible to safeguard French culture, while Disney appeared to be the one not complying with the terms of the Agreement. From the government's viewpoint, therefore, domestic political concerns framed the agreement that it reached and the eventual result thereof.

Disney's failure to consider the influence of domestic politics cost it dearly in terms of public relations, and contains a sobering lesson for the international economic negotiator; namely, that domestic politics can hold surprising concerns and focus on unexpected issues. Despite Disney's international sophistication, it appears to have been caught largely unawares by the cultural attacks. While such surprises can occur in any negotiating context, they are more prevalent in international negotiations due to cultural unfamiliarity. Thus, ex-Euro Disney CEO Fitzpatrick, discussing a lesson painfully learned, opined that "Americans have difficulty understanding a system with a national academy to govern use of the language, and a ministry on language that reports to the president." The Euro Disney case thus supports the validity of domestic politics as a rational explanation for negotiators' actions, and also demonstrates the potential costs of failing to consider such concerns.

2.5.1 The concern with image and appearances

A second concern that rationalizes seemingly irrational economic decisions is that of parties' attention to their external image. This in turn ties into both tactical and strategic power issues.

Again, one must look beyond market efficiency to explain the rationality of the government's decisions. The neoclassical economist, studying the Euro Disney investment, would analyze the various financing costs, subsidies, and other economic benefits granted by the government and compare them to the anticipated benefits, both direct (from the project) and indirect (from the multiplier effect), of the investment in order to obtain a projected return that should serve as a rational guide to decision making. Assuming that the return was marginal at best, the economist would question the government's conclusion of the Master Agreement, This analysis, however, would miss what were undoubtedly some of the most important motivating factors for the French government.

The government was determined to make this project a showpiece, and as such it bore a significance far beyond its economic return. Various analysts have recognized in the French a "fascination with grandiose, elegant themes rather than feasible projects." These projects, from Haussmann's boulevards through the Eiffel Tower to Mitterrand's 1980s projects of the new Opera and City Library, all have a significance far beyond their economic impact. Each in turn served to show the world that France was at the forefront of progress and development in a given area, be it urban design, engineering, or arts and literature. While it may initially sound absurd to compare a mouse-inhabited amusement park with these other achievements, in its own way Euro Disney was very much part of this lineage of projects. By the mid-1980s the changes sweeping international business and the globalization of economic competition were already well underway, and the French government knew that it had a poor international image as a site for foreign direct investment. It was entirely in keeping with the French mindset and prior practice to seek out the biggest foreign investment project being contemplated in Europe, successfully woo it, and then hold the results out for the world to see.

Whether or not the particular project was economically sensible for the government was almost secondary; what was of primary importance was that the project be won. If that required massive government loans and subsidies, so be it, as long as the result was a project that was a world model. Understanding these motivations requires journeying quite a distance from the neoclassical economist's position, but once they are recognized, they do provide a foundation of reason to the government's actions.

2.6   Negotiation Theories

This case study bears out Kremenyuk *et al.*'s observation in the introductory chapter that in many international negotiations market forces will not drive parties' strategies and decision making. Having seen that neoclassical market economic theory is of limited value in understanding the Euro Disney negotiations or predicting their outcome, although other economic theories are helpful, we now put negotiation theories to the test.

2.6.1 The power of alternatives

One of the traditional elements of negotiation analysis is evaluating parties' alternatives. In this case, considering each parties' alternatives – actual and portrayed – suggests the outcomes that did in fact occur, confirming the validity of this analysis.

From the very beginning, Disney sought to strengthen its apparent alternatives by downplaying the strengths of Marne-la-Vallée and stressing those of competing sites. Negotiation theorists would predict that this tactic would result in a stronger negotiating position for Disney in the Master Agreement negotiations (Lax and Sebenius, 1991b).

France, on the other hand, had a rather poor BATNA (best alternative to a negotiated agreement) and could do little to dissimulate it. Through its strong upfront commitment, discussed below, the government made it clear that it very much wanted the project and that it had no fallback investment opportunity. The government's security point was very low, and Disney therefore knew that it would be relatively simple to negotiate an outcome that would distribute the financial rewards largely in its favor, while still coming in above the government's BATNA. This situation should, according to negotiation theory, strengthen Disney's position and conversely result in a relatively low level of negotiating power for the French government (Fisher and Ury, 1981).

The combined effect of Disney's effective maneuvering to portray a strong BATNA and the government's undeniably weak BATNA would, under traditional negotiation analysis, be expected to produce an agreement in which the distribution favored the company. As we saw in the narrative, that is indeed what occurred. Disney received a financial package that met virtually all of its desires, at considerable expense to the government. It must be noted that this does not mean that the government did not also achieve its desired outcome, i.e., obtaining the investment sought. However, it did so at significant cost, and it is this allocation of financial benefits and burdens that is accurately predicted by negotiation analysis.

2.6.2 The dual nature of commitment

Another important element of negotiation analysis is the role of commitment. Commitment, in the context of negotiations, is a double-edged sword. While in moderation it is a positive force, giving parties a stake in the process and keeping them from walking away too easily, in excess it can act as a set of blinders, tying parties to a process when they would be better served by abandoning it (Fisher, 1991).

In its enthusiasm for Euro Disney, the French government made major public commitments at an early stage of the process. The government visibly attributed significant importance to the project by having the prime minister sign the initial letter of understanding between France and Disney. Had the government not followed through on this commitment, it would not only have suffered a humiliating loss of credibility, but might also have reinforced the very stereotype it was seeking to shed: that of a bureaucratic, internationally uncompetitive economy.

The degree and visibility of France's commitment would lead one to predict that in subsequent negotiations the government might give short shrift to the other elements of its negotiation. Overall, this prediction appears to be borne out by the facts. The government did in fact "sell out" other interests, such as equity for the farmers whose land was being expropriated and security for the loans it was making, in order to help guarantee the success of the project. While in certain areas, such as the cultural debate, the government did not defend Disney, it is telling that none of these situations went to the core of the project or threatened the potential for its long-term profitability, much less its very existence. Thus, negotiation theory's prediction that France's initial commitments would weaken its subsequent negotiating position appears to be borne out in all of the later negotiations that impacted key areas of the project.

2.6.3   The need to define interests

Without repeating the entire earlier discussion regarding identification of interests, it should be noted that this is as important for negotiation theory as for economic theory. As Kremenyuk *et al.* note in the introductory chapter, the Rationality Assumption is one of the generally accepted epistemic principles governing negotiation practice and analysis. However, we argued above that it is impossible to carry out effective economic analysis if interests are not accurately defined, and the same holds true for negotiation analysis. While negotiation theory does not say that it is impossible to conclude an agreement if one is not aware of one's interests, it does suggest that the outcome will be suboptimal because it will be impossible to quantitatively assess tradeoffs.

Recapitulating the example used in the economic discussion, this certainly seems to have been the case in respect to the outcome of Disney's culture-focused negotiation. The weakness of its outcome in this area is in stark contrast to the outcome of the financial negotiations in which Disney had a strong understanding of its interests. Since the same negotiating team worked out both parts of the Agreement, the best apparent explanation for the significant difference in quality of outcomes is that the company thoroughly understood its interests in one case but did not in the other. The company did extremely well in negotiating the issues regarding which it understood its preferred outcome, and was caught by surprise with regard to those for which it did not. The earlier assertion that such a discrepancy is particularly likely to arise in an international setting is equally applicable when considering the question of interest identification in the context of negotiation theory.

2.6.4   The fallacy of unitary, rational actors

A final element of negotiation theory to be considered is the question of intraparty divisions, or the fallacy of the oft-held view of actors as unitary. The French government presented a unified facade when negotiating with Disney. The establishment of the interministerial delegate's office for "one-stop shopping" considerably facilitated the negotiation process, but at the same time must certainly have served to give the French government the appearance of a monolithic entity. Disney spoke to delegates who, with the considerable authority of the prime minister behind them, were able to exert command in virtually any area of the government, including areas such as local land development that were not normally even within the national government's purview.

The negotiation theorist, being well attuned to the importance of understanding whether parties are truly monolithic, would expect to see divisions in this unified faade appearing at later stages of the process as different parties within the government act to promote the interests of their branch as well as those of the government as a whole (Fisher, 1980). That Disney held no such expectation was demonstrated by its surprise when the language dispute arose on the initiative of the Délégation sur la Langue, and then again when government labor inspectors subsequently backed employees in a work dispute.

The facts of the case thus bore out the prediction of negotiation theory in this area. Large, complex actors such as governments are virtually never unitary actors, and negotiating counterparts who have viewed them as such will probably react with surprise and dismay when the divisions become apparent.

2.6.5   Conclusions on negotiation theory

In conclusion, various basic tools used by negotiation analysts do in fact have considerable validity in predicting the outcome of this case study. A constructive negotiation was carried out, and the final outcomes on the various items at issue were in accordance with the predictions of negotiation theory. Both the Master Agreement and the subsequent financial restructuring accord were reached as the results of multiple tradeoffs, and each party ended up with an agreement that exceeded its security point. In this respect the negotiations must be termed successful for both parties, bearing in mind that success must be gauged in relation to the parties' initial BATNAs, and not to the project's ultimate financial results.

That the negotiations can be considered to have been successful for both sides despite the various mistakes made by each is probably attributable in large part to the fact that this was a joint project rather than a one-time, zero-sum negotiation. Both Disney and the government almost certainly realized that pushing the other too far toward its security point would have been counterproductive given the long-term, interdependent nature of the project. Foreign direct investment negotiations may differ from other international economic negotiations in this respect, in that the interdependence of the parties is carried to an extreme.

2.7   Conclusions

The Euro Disney case suggests that in complex international economic negotiations involving multiple, differing issues, negotiation theory may well have greater explanatory power than traditional economic theory. Particularly in international settings, neoclassical market theory will perform poorly in explaining the actions and outcomes of this kind of negotiation because the parties, no matter how sophisticated, will typically lack the degree of analytical clarity necessary to act as the rational, independent utility-maximizers upon whom the theory is premised. On the other hand, to the extent that economic theory seeks to recognize and explain some of the most common factors that drive entities not to behave as suggested by neoclassical thought, it does provide some accurate insights into the processes and outcomes of such negotiations.

Negotiation theory generally seems to perform better in predicting the course that such international negotiations will follow. The principles of negotiation theory appear less subject to disruption in an international setting, and in fact seem to maintain as much of their analytical validity in a situation such as Euro Disney as in a purely national negotiation.

The Euro Disney case is also useful in that it demonstrates that despite the relevance of negotiation frameworks in predicting and explaining outcomes of international negotiations, parties who are skilled negotiators in a domestic context may nevertheless find unexpected pitfalls in an international setting. Misunderstood interests, false perceptions, and miscommunications are but a few of the traps that await a negotiator in his or her first foray into a new milieu, and past successes in different settings may only serve to increase the risk that a mistake will be made. This case study may therefore serve to heighten negotiators' appreciation of both the usefulness of their skills in analyzing international negotiations and of the increased caution they must exercise when actually operating in such an environment.

Note

[1] Editors' note: The change in management, as well as the restructuring package, have in the meantime improved both Euro Disney's image and its financial situation. Now known as Disneyland Paris, the park became Europe's most popular tourist attraction in 1997, drawing some 12.5 million visitors in both 1997 and 1998.

Chapter 3

Negotiation on Joint Ventures in China

Guy Olivier Faure

One day the hen said to the pig:

"Let's start a joint venture!"
"OK, but what should we produce?"
"Food! We will set up a restaurant."
"Fine!"

Then the hen went to the bank to obtain financial support.
The banker asked several questions:

"What do you intend to sell?"
"Food."
"What kind of food?"
"Omelet with bacon."
"How will you get the ingredients?"
"I will provide the eggs. The pig will provide the bacon."

3.1 Introduction

The creation of a joint venture is probably among the most widespread and complex negotiations that exists nowadays, and paradoxically one of the least studied or understood. The negotiation of a joint venture in a context such as China further adds to the complexity and mystery. It is such a process, a tale full of sound and fury, that this chapter will examine. Two companies, one European and one Chinese, endeavor to build a common project that integrates multiple dimensions: economic and human, organizational and cultural. This diversity makes it a typical form of joint venture negotiation.

The main objective of the study is to identify the fundamental rationales governing the negotiation process. To serve this purpose, a case is first presented, and then its most significant aspects are analyzed along two different lines: one economic, and the other pertaining to negotiation theory embedded in an organizational and human framework.

The case study is based on interviews, complemented by analysis based on both research and practice. The technology involved is purposely not made very explicit; company names and places have been modified for reasons of confidentiality. The focus of the study is directed toward the interaction itself, and the technical aspects are presented only when necessary for the understanding of the whole negotiation.

The chapter is divided into three parts: an introduction to joint ventures in China that sets the context and presents the main characteristics of this type of investment; the description of the case, drawn from a real situation, with special emphasis on the process itself; and an analysis aimed at clarifying the economic dimension, then expanding on other dimensions to provide an explanation of the final outcome that is as relevant as possible to reality.

3.2   Joint Ventures and China

The evolution of economics confronts the observer with new forms of organization that answer to new logical systems and demonstrate the increasing degree of integration of the international economy. In the domain of strategic corporate alliances, the joint venture concept is remarkable for the rapidity with which it developed, its ubiquity, and its innovative design. A joint venture can be considered a hybrid form of organization that resulted from both a market coordination rationale and a hierarchical rationale.

The market implies the contract as a basic tool for autonomous interaction between a corporation and its external partners in the areas of supplies, use of licences, or franchising agreements. Hierarchical coordination establishes dependency relations of a holding-subsidiary type between the founding companies. The joint venture borrows from the two formulas, autonomy and dependence, in managing a complex balance between two or more partners within a new organizational structure.

From a strictly economic viewpoint, the rationale for a joint venture is that it achieves an optimum balance between various constraints such as internal control or management of complex know-how (Hennart, 1988). Recent international developments in corporate theories tend to emphasize two criteria for decision making and for choosing among such strategic alternate options as licensing, franchising, contractual joint venture, equity joint venture, or acquisition: the levels of risk and of control on the main parameters of activity (Williamson, 1981; Collins and Dorley, 1992).

The definition of the term "joint venture" remains the topic of numerous debates. Dupont (1991) observes that, in everyday language, the term covers multiple forms of contracts such as licensing and technology transfer, as well as sharing research and development expenditure or setting up a common organization. However, "joint venture" now tends to be defined in more precise terms. Three minimum criteria must be met:

- A commonality of objectives, means, risks, and rewards for the parent organizations.
- The creation of a distinct entity with a legal and financial structure.
- The intention to set the foundations of a durable organization.

3.2.1   Development of joint ventures in China

Under the "four modernizations" program – in agriculture, industry, science and technology, and defense – China decided to become a major industrial nation. To achieve this goal, China broke away from a policy of minimizing imports to a new strategy that consisted of seeking for help and cooperation from foreign firms. In 1979 the country promulgated its first joint venture regulations as one of the basic instruments of the "open door" policy. As underlined by Stewart and Carver (1997), until that time borrowing money or making a profit had been anathema, and this new policy was viewed as a major ideological shift.

Joint ventures first appeared in China that same year, only six in the whole country. By 1 January 1998, 292,345 had been officially approved. During 1979–1997, foreign direct investment amounted to US$562.3 billion; for 1993 alone, the total amount contracted was US$110.85 billion (Li, 1994). Joint venture activity produces one quarter of China's total imports and exports. The main areas in which joint ventures have developed are light industry, electronics, and textiles.

Two types of joint ventures operate in the Chinese market: the contractual joint venture (CJV) and the equity joint venture (EJV). The CJV is a limited liability entity or business partnership in which both the Chinese and the foreign parties contribute cash, buildings, equipment, materials, industrial and intellectual property rights, land rights, labor, resources, and services. Neither party is forced to assign a monetary value to its investment contribution, and no maximum or minimum investment is required. The CJV provides great flexibility regarding structure of the assets, organization, and management. It can be quickly developed and the foreign investor can recover the registered capital during the life of the contract.

The other type of joint venture, the EJV, is a limited liability corporation jointly funded and operated by each party. Risks, profits, and assets remaining upon expiration of the venture are shared according to the percentage of equity held by each party. To start an EJV, the parties must follow a complicated process to obtain State Planning Commission approval after a feasibility study. Then the parties negotiate the contract itself and submit the agreement to the Ministry of Foreign Economic Relations and Trade (MOFERT) for approval. Each party's investment contribution can take the form of cash, buildings, equipment, materials, or industrial and intellectual property rights, as well as land use rights. Labor is not a permissible contribution. The foreign party must contribute a minimum 25% of the equity. Preferential tax treatment is given for some years after the joint venture starts making a profit.

The third type of investment in China, the wholly foreign-owned enterprise, involves all the risks and difficulties linked to setting up autonomously on the Chinese market. Thus, this option remains far less popular than the joint venture formulas.

3.2.2   Rationale for joint ventures in China

One of the new values that China has emphasized in its liberalizing economic policy concerns material gains and profit making through individual initiative. The new slogan "getting rich is glorious" found deep resonance at all social levels. The moral legitimation was that the prosperity of some would subsequently bring advantages to others as well. In addition, this viewpoint fits tidily into traditional Chinese culture, for, according to an old saying: "When you get to the top, even your chicken and your dogs go to heaven" (Shapiro *et al.*, 1991). Moreover, Chinese industry and the entire economy should benefit considerably from the development of the joint venture sector. When parent companies have been able to position the joint venture according to their own corporate strategy, and have clarified their respective motivations, they can seek ways to complement each other.

Selling on the Chinese market is one of the major reasons why a Western company commits itself, whereas obtaining modern technology, export opportunities, and foreign exchange are usually considered good reasons for a Chinese organization to involve itself in the creation of a joint venture. The two ambitions are far from incompatible, but they arise from approaches and logical systems that may be substantially different. To complement each other in the general task the future partners want to undertake, the foreign company, in addition to sophisticated technology, brings equipment and expertise, financial investments, its experience on the international market, its reputation, its management skills, and its logistics. The Chinese company contributes buildings, rights to use land, labor, its knowledge of and experience in the Chinese market and distribution channels, and its expertise in dealing with high officials, bureaucracy, and local authorities. Such complementarity in the respective contributions of each party is an absolute necessity both to ensure the relevance of the common approach and to secure some long-run stability for the joint venture.

When these conditions are met, what are the realistic chances of success for the joint venture? In China, EJVs are often viewed as the most challenging form of cooperation because the shared responsibility involves not only the risk of the investment, but also the day-to-day management of the venture with its uncertainties and complexity. Chinese authorities tend to be overoptimistic on the proportion of successful joint ventures. If one turns from China's official figures to several Western surveys, the results are less encouraging. In a study concerning 34 joint ventures in Shenzhen, a special economic zone with an exceptional number of business facilities, Henley and Mee-Kau (1991) observe that half of them do not meet their profit targets, and that a third are operating with a foreign exchange deficit. According to Goldenberg (1988), out of 4,000 US and Japanese joint ventures only a third are profitable in local currency, and another third is clearly losing money.

Another critical challenge for joint venture management is to ensure that people of different cultures can work together successfully within a complex bureaucratic environment. Other major obstacles may be delays in plant construction due to administrative difficulties or shortages of raw materials, and a labor force that is less skilled than expected. A study carried out in Tianjin at Otis Elevator shows that the average time to build a comparable elevator is 215 hours in France, 250 hours in Japan, and 1,400 hours in Tianjin (Mayer *et al.*, 1991). In addition, the quality of Chinese components may be too low to meet international standards, and the transportation system may prove inadequate, thus hindering regular distribution of the product.

3.2.3 The foreign partners

Foreign direct investment in EJVs during 1979–1986 amounted to US$3.86 billion. Hong Kong and Macao alone accounted for 70% of this total, followed by the United States (9.3%), Japan (7.3%), and Germany (2.8%). If one considers the number of projects the distribution remains similar (Campbell, 1989), with Hong Kong and Macao accounting for 76.7%, the United States for 7.9%, and Japan for 7.2%. Large EJVs are a form of investment specific to China, especially in construction projects. Japan has a dominant position in property development, the United States in the oil sector, and together they dominate the market in electrical and electronic products. By region, the location of joint ventures shows a strong

concentration in the coastal provinces, where foreign companies can find better facilities, especially those related to transportation. Most of the joint ventures are
set up to last 10 to 15 years, but the term can be notably longer, in particular if
the amount of capital investment is very high and therefore takes longer to be recovered. In terms of equity split, the average foreign contribution for the period
1979–1986 amounted to 43.4% (Campbell, 1989). The current trend for Western
partners is to seek a clear majority.

3.2.4   Creating a joint venture in China

The Chinese context offers a number of characteristics that lead a foreign operator to devise a very specific approach (Faure-Bouteiller, 1998). Setting up a joint
venture in China means experiencing in a single activity a microcosm of all the
observable difficulties displayed by this country, be they economic, financial, legal, cultural, or organizational. It is a long and complicated process that can be
divided into four stages, each one underlaid by a particular rationale: preliminary
investigation, prenegotiation, negotiation, and implementation.

The preliminary investigation covers the initial approach to the Chinese market.
The aims are to become more familiar with market characteristics, to assess market
potential, to select an area, to develop a network of contracts with companies, public administration, and influential people, and then to find a possible partner. This
exploratory stage is mainly a phase for collecting information before acting.

The prenegotiation phase includes making the first contacts with the Chinese
company that could be a partner, assessing the compatibility of the two parties'
objectives, ascertaining if they have common views on market strategy, conducting
the feasibility study, and signing a letter of intent. Such a document is not legally
binding, but instead aims at showing the commitment of each party to carry on
with the process as far as possible. As a consequence, the parties normally stop any
parallel negotiation with other potential partners.

When the feasibility study has been approved by the appropriate authorities, the
full negotiation can take place. At this stage the parties discuss everything necessary to set up and operate the future joint venture, such as the rights and obligations
of each party, as well as the respective contributions of capital, technology, expertise, and other resources. The negotiation also addresses issues concerning the
management of the joint venture, its decision-making structure, its policy for personnel management, and the conditions for its termination. At this stage the parties
also explore such issues as domestic and export pricing of the future products for
sale. This phase is rather complex, because it may deal with more than 50 issues,
involve a large number of negotiators, last for a long time by Western standards
(sometimes up to eight years), and be subject to multiple unexpected events.

The last stage of the whole process concerns the implementation of the agreement. It would be logical to think that negotiations are now over, but this is usually not the case. At this stage, surprises crop up on a daily basis because, for instance, the working conditions or supplies of raw materials may undergo dramatic, unforeseen external changes. It is an illusion to believe that one can simply rely on the written contract, and numerous renegotiations may take place.

3.2.5 The contractual framework for joint ventures in China

When the law on joint ventures was promulgated in September 1979, China had almost no economic legislation. As Shapiro *et al.* (1991) stress, there was no law on registration of industrial and commercial enterprises, notarization of documents, trademark registration and protection, or contracts. The "Law of the PRC on Chinese-Foreign Joint Ventures" was the first in this new legal corpus and demonstrated the concern and interest of the Chinese authorities in such types of activities. In the 1980s, it was followed by a number of regulations intended to complete the legal framework necessary to reassure foreigners that they could venture into the Chinese system of production with reasonable chances of success.

Those laws mainly concerned protection of resources and profits and limited liability, as well as a number of practical issues. They included the 25% minimum foreign investment, the Chinese partner's right to appoint the chairman, the repatriation of profit, taxation, the duration of the joint venture, technology transfer, and arbitration of disputes. The point was not just to reassure foreigners, but especially to encourage technology transfer and the manufacture of products for export. In 1983 a set of "Regulations for the Implementation of the Law on Joint Ventures Using Chinese and Foreign Investment" was passed. It concerned mainly the geographical and industrial sectors in which joint ventures would be permitted, technology transfer, the use of land sites and the corresponding fees, preferential treatment in customs duties and taxes, requirements to maintain a balance in foreign exchange, and the duration of the joint venture (normally from 10 to 30 years).

In 1985 China issued the "Foreign Economic Contract Law" and the "Accounting Regulations of Joint Ventures," which were followed in 1986 by the "Regulations on Problems of Foreign Exchange Balances of Joint Ventures" to answer to the difficulties met by foreign investors. As mentioned by Shapiro *et al.* (1991), priority in supply of raw materials and energy provided only vague insurance; foreigners were subject to higher prices for land and materials than their Chinese competitors, and to ever-expanding taxes. Thus, earning a profit was not an obvious outcome, especially if the joint venture did not have the autonomy to decide upon its production level and whom to hire.

In October 1986, the "22 Articles for the Encouragement of Foreign Investment" were issued, offering additional facilities mainly to enterprises manufacturing export products or operating with advanced technology. These regulations included provisions concerning the enterprises' autonomy in setting their own production and operational plans, as well as greater management autonomy on recruitment and discharge of personnel; reduction in labor charges, land use fees, and customs duties; reduction of or exemption from taxes; guarantees of at least partial energy supply, transportation, and communication equipment; and permission to adjust foreign exchange across joint venture enterprises.

This apparatus of laws and regulations has contributed considerably to reducing the weakness of the Chinese legal system and, as a consequence, to overcoming the reservations of Western investors regarding involvement in joint ventures. However, these laws fall far short of eliminating all uncertainties, especially in relation to how the authorities interpret and enforce the laws. Laws are still often incomplete and decrees to put them into practice can take years to be issued. Furthermore, there are regulations called "internal laws" that are not accessible to foreigners, but can be used in matters concerning them directly (Bret, 1992). Some memoranda written to enforce a regulation simply contradict these rules. In the domain of customs duties, for example, it is not unusual to receive a refusal based on a simple memo that opposes an international agreement. As Deslandres and Deschandol (1986) emphasize, informal limits in terms of freedom of action are much narrower than official limits. Like the market economy in China, the law is still in an embryonic stage and its weakness adds to the strictly economic risk.

The Chinese authorities, on their side, strongly criticize a number of current practices as being counterproductive with regard to the general purpose that joint ventures should serve the national economy. These include tax evasion by foreign investors, supply of outdated equipment instead of state-of-the-art technology, and artificially increased prices of imported raw materials and decreased prices for exported products, which result in little or no profit for the joint venture but bring money into the foreign parent company. But all the evil does not come from the foreigners: some Chinese enterprises and individuals, after transferring their funds to foreign countries – usually Hong Kong – come back to invest in China to benefit from preferential policies reserved for foreigners (*China Daily*, Business Weekly, 6 December 1992).

3.3   The Technicom versus Shanghai Eastern Wind Case

The development of the Chinese market, increasing competition, the growth in consumer buying power, and the evolution of consumption subject the products offered to quality requirements that were previously very unusual. Moreover, the need for foreign exchange prompted China to enter the export market, and consequently to raise quality standards.

These requirements led to the establishment of numerous joint ventures that manufacture products for direct consumption and include a certain level of technology. The case presented here, in which a Chinese enterprise negotiated with a European multinational company, is a typical illustration of such a new trend. The number of issues at stake, their interconnections, the great variety of institutional and individual actors and of cultures involved throughout the process make it a complex negotiation, because it gives rise to different rationales corresponding to dimensions of distinct natures. Although an impressive number of business negotiations of all types are currently taking place with foreigners in China, only very few publications provide detailed accounts of the bargaining processes involved (Mann, 1989; Pye, 1982; Deslandres and Deschandol, 1986; Hakam and Chan, 1990; Webber, 1989; Shapiro *et al.*, 1991).

Negotiations with West European companies take place within a historical, political, and economic context that the Chinese culture takes into account far more than most Western cultures would. Such a view has a definite influence on the relations that people develop. The economic, but not military, power of Europe distinguishes it in China's eyes from the American trading partner; its technological capability and the absence of common borders also sets it apart from the Russian partner. Lastly, the absence of recent contentious matters linked to wars of a quasi-colonial style gives a special place to Europe when compared with the Japanese counterpart. It is in such a context that, after what the Chinese call "liberation" and Western languages term "the 1949 revolution," trade relations between China and Europe developed.

3.3.1   The broad economic context: Chinese–European trade relations

No matter what external events occurred, Western Europe has always maintained trade relations with China. Even in the first years of the communist regime, when Soviet influence was at its peak, Western Europe still managed to account for 15% of China's total trade. In the Chinese political framework, Western Europe was perceived as an "intermediate zone" able to play the role of an ally to balance the world domination by the two superpowers. In 1975, China and the EC as such decided to establish diplomatic links. This new step was followed by the negotiation of an economic agreement, the "1978 European Community–China Trade Agreement." Its main features were a commitment to promote and intensify trade between the two partners; most favored nation treatment on duties, regulations, taxes and formalities; and attempts to balance Sino-EC trade and promote exchanges. From the Chinese viewpoint, business relations must abide by three principles, "equality, mutual benefit, and friendly cooperation," which are defined as the basis for action.

After the signing of the 1978 agreement, EC imports and exports steadily increased. Within five years their total value doubled. Of the three major trading blocs, the EC, with a total comparable to that of the United States, was far behind Japan. In 1979, a textile agreement highly favorable to China was signed, and that same year China also became entitled to benefit under the European Community General System of Preferences Scheme. Among EC members, Germany was the most important trading partner, accounting for over a third of all trade.

In 1985 the EC and China concluded a new "Trade and Economic Co-operation Agreement," reflecting a mutual desire for enhancing economic ties. Cooperation included areas such as industry and mining, agriculture and agro-industry, science and technology, energy, transport and communication, environmental protection, cooperation in Third World countries, etc. The forms of economic cooperation were also mentioned: joint production and joint ventures, common exploitation of resources, technology transfer, technical assistance including the training of staff, etc. The joint venture form explicitly cited corresponds to an already established practice. The point was to support its development because, in the eyes of the Chinese authorities, this was a preferred mechanism for carrying on with the open door policy to modernize the economy of the country.

3.3.2   The case

The Chinese market for consumer products containing mid-level technology is already a large and promising one if one takes into consideration the growing buying power in urban areas and the population's adherence to the Western model of consumption. One of the major problems China has to confront in the industrial domain is that of quality. The current level of domestic production does not enable companies to export as much as they would like to, and even leads to strong dissatisfaction at the national level, leaving a large portion of the market to foreign competitors.

One of the solutions considered, importing the components and assembling them locally, did not bring the expected results. Quality and service problems remained as acute as before; in addition, because the products were distributed under famous brand names, they provided a rather negative image of those brands. Setting up joint ventures could be viewed as the best option for simultaneously raising the quality of the products and keeping production costs low. "Technicom" is a multinational company of European origin that operates in a great variety of domains, among them light technology equipment. The company enjoys a good international reputation and operates in Asia from its Hong Kong base, where it set up a holding company, Technicom Asia Pacific Holding. To enter the Chinese market, Technicom contemplated the possibility of organizing such structures as EJVs, and sought Chinese partners likely to assimilate its basic technology and production management methods quickly.

Technicom contacted the MOFERT, which investigated various possibilities. After discussing the issue with its Shanghai branch, the ministry suggested that Technicom contact a state-owned company, the "Shanghai Eastern Wind Factory," which had a strong national reputation for technical expertise. The local MOFERT bureau actively supported the idea of setting up such a joint venture, which would bring investment not only of cash, but also of technology. Moreover, the enterprise would bring a positive image, because Technicom enjoyed a good reputation, and the Shanghai area is careful about its own reputation for quality products.

Technicom thereupon invited high-ranking officials from MOFERT, technical experts from the technical bureaus, and local authorities to visit its European headquarters. The purpose of the trip for the Chinese side was to make sure that Technicom could provide the most advanced technology for the future joint venture. China's national policy is to search systematically for the most up-to-date technology in this field, and the Chinese delegation had to give its approval before accepting Technicom as the right potential partner. The officials stayed two weeks, whereas the Chinese technical experts stayed another two weeks to assess product quality, as well as the efficiency of the production line and of the factory as a whole. The final outcome of this visit was official approval that enabled both parties to go ahead with the project.

Initiated by the Shanghai branch of the MOFERT, the first contacts took place in Shenzhen, a special economic zone near Hong Kong. The first round of discussions focused on each party's contribution to the joint venture capital, allocation of management responsibilities in the joint venture, and technology transfer. After three days of hard discussions, with the local MOFERT branch acting as mediator, the parties reached no agreement.

Following two months of silence, the parties met again with a list of 10 issues to talk over. A week of negotiation enabled the parties to find common ground on only half of these issues, and the parties separated in the belief that nothing more could be done. They viewed the situation as hopeless and all participants concluded that there was no point in meeting again.

Then a third party entered the process: the "Shanghai Bureau for High Technologies." It managed to convince both parties to return to the negotiating table. The discussion began again, tense and exhausting. Each side tended to impose its own vision of the project, ignoring that of the other. But from time to time after the working meetings, negotiators met for dinner to restore a friendly personal relationship.

At the end of this new round of discussions, the parties reached an "agreement in principle" on the following issues:

- Form of cooperation: an EJV.
- Distribution of the contribution between the two parent companies: Technicom 51%, Eastern Wind 49%.
- Technicom's right to choose the general manager in charge of production.
- Technology transfer.
- The amount of cash needed by the joint venture to start operations.

The parties wrote and signed a letter of intent stating those points, and then organized a final banquet to celebrate the successful end of that phase.

In China, financial experts from both sides began meeting on a regular basis to conduct a feasibility study. The work done led to three versions of the study, one for each side and one sent to the MOFERT to seek its formal approval. After some time Beijing gave its approval for the second phase of the negotiation to start.

These negotiations discussed four contracts: the articles of association, the joint venture contract, technology transfer, and equipment supply. On the Shanghai Eastern Wind side, around 30 people took part in the negotiation at various times, according to the expertise needed for the topic under discussion. Whatever the issue, the Chinese team never included fewer than 10 people. On the European side, four people carried out all the negotiations: the general manager of the Technicom holding for the Asia Pacific region; the designated general manager of the future joint venture, a lawyer, and a Chinese assistant.

Negotiations were carried out in English and in Chinese through interpretation. In fact, interpretation played a very important role in the negotiation, because the parties displayed highly contrasting cultural views. To gain an advantage, each side indulged in role playing, sometimes overacting. All members of the European delegation participated rather freely, intervening in the discussion at any time, and occasionally raising diverging opinions that could not be missed by their Chinese counterparts. On the Chinese side, a leader with a strong sense of organization and discipline coordinated the discussion. Technical experts only spoke when asked to do so. The members of the group never argued among themselves in front of the other party. If a real problem arose, they met in a separate room to work together and clear up the issue. On most issues, especially strategic ones, the head of the delegation, the only member to know the intentions of the authorities, usually imposed his views. Unless the point under discussion was highly technical there was no real debate, and the leader always had the final word. The Chinese side tried by all means to get the negotiations to take place in Shanghai, on their home ground. Technicom preferred Beijing, where it had an office. Finally, the parties agreed to hold the discussions alternatively in Shanghai and in Beijing.

3.3.3   Articles of association

The negotiation focused mainly on principles. There were many issues to be discussed, such as the name of the joint venture, its location, the capital contribution, equipment, technology transfer, the organization of the joint venture, its decision-making and management structure, the arbitration court, and the duration of the venture. Numbers and details were deferred to the next stage. For two months, both parties met for two-week periods; in between, each delegation returned to its headquarters to evaluate the current state of the process and to prepare for the next round. Negotiations remained tough, but there was noticeable and constant progress.

To show their commitment to the project, both sides decided on a 25-year duration for the joint venture. The equity split, a major issue in the power balance, was 51% for Technicom and 49% for Shanghai Eastern Wind. The participants also decided how long the management would remain in the hands of Europeans. This was both a power issue and a crucial financial issue, because one foreigner can cost as much as 50 Chinese. If production worked as planned, Chinese executives would take over after a certain period that would differ according to the type of skills involved. Technicom would always choose the general manager, the technical manager, and the quality control manager. A Chinese citizen would take over as financial manager after completing training and assisting the foreign financial manager for four years. The arbitration court chosen was in Stockholm, one of the few places outside China that the Chinese could accept. Technicom would provide two new production lines and a secondary line, whereas Shanghai Eastern Wind would bring an additional secondary line to the joint venture. Technicom was required to provide the most advanced technology and the corresponding expertise to the best of its ability. These negotiations led to a final document 10 pages long.

3.3.4   Joint venture contract

During this stage, the parties discussed issues pertaining to capital contribution as well as all matters concerning the setup of the joint venture in its various aspects. The talks no longer focused on principles, but on details. The many points to be dealt with included each contribution and its timing, each piece of equipment, and the banks in which to establish accounts. This was a delicate and difficult phase, because the purpose was to arrive at a valuation of assets, such as buildings and land rights, based on rather arbitrary criteria. With regard to this type of issue, the parties' interests were in direct conflict, and the goal appeared to be to confront the other party, rather than to confront the market together.

All of the participants doubted that the negotiation would ever lead anywhere and became somewhat discouraged. The Chinese party preferred to play a game of attrition, while Europeans sometimes succumbed to outbursts of anger and made threats. The process could be viewed as a continuous fight with upheavals, mutual hatred, and insults from the European side. However, the Chinese interpreter did not translate the harsh words and the insults, even when asked by the European side to do so. Thus, neither side went too far in the eyes of the other and at the end of the day both parties still agreed to shake hands when they left the negotiating table.

Over a period of a year, the parties again met for two-week periods, then returned to their headquarters to assess the current status and prepare the next stage. Finally, the negotiators made arrangements regarding each sensitive issue, sometimes finding rather creative solutions. For instance, on the contribution in cash for both sides, Technicom definitively refused any offer lower than 30% from the Chinese partner; however, a government regulation did not allow the Chinese company to go beyond 15%. Shanghai Eastern Wind managed the difficulty by accepting 30% and then manipulating the oversight process in such a way that the MOFERT representatives sent to check the whole contract returned to Beijing without having checked that part of the contract. On other occasions, Shanghai Eastern Wind resorted to the threat of having MOFERT veto the entire project to obtain final concessions from the European party. The resulting document was 50 pages long, including 10 pages of appendix. It went as far as possible into details, because the negotiators designed it as an umbrella to protect them from anticipated future storms.

3.3.5   Technology transfer

Shanghai Eastern Wind viewed the industrial cooperation contract as the most crucial issue. It concerned such topics as the type of technology to be transferred, its scope, the corresponding amount of money, how the technology would be transferred (through documents, training, or on the production line), and when the transfer would take place. It also covered the kind of training that would be most appropriate, what staff categories would be involved, how many people, for how long, with which goals, and, last but not least, who would cover the costs. Alternative approaches included bringing in visiting experts from Europe or trainers from Hong Kong, or sending Chinese staff abroad. If the latter alternative were chosen, should the training take place in Europe, or Singapore? The most sensitive issue was the technology itself, with many related points such as the production line equipment, its manufacture and installation, the production volume to be expected, the yearly plans until the production line reached its full capacity, and the standards to apply for testing the equipment.

The technology transfer was negotiated simultaneously with the joint venture contract and encountered the same difficulties. More than a month was needed to come to an agreement. The final document concerning this topic was 25 pages long, with another 25 pages of appendix.

The number of Chinese to be sent abroad for training gave rise to hefty arguments. Technicom wanted the Chinese staff to be trained in Singapore, whereas Shanghai Eastern Wind insisted on having them sent to Europe. The conflict reignited over the number of Chinese to be trained. Finally, the parties reached an agreement that 24 people would be sent to Europe. Then Technicom raised a new point: to make the courses truly useful, they required a score of 600 on the Test of English as a Foreign Language (TOEFL) to admit Chinese into the training program. Since there were probably no Chinese who could meet this condition, the endemic conflict erupted in a new area. After a while, Technicom gave up the idea of resorting to the TOEFL and the Chinese side agreed to organize evening classes that would train their people in English. Eventually, when it became obvious that nothing could be achieved without concessions from both sides, the parties overcame one obstacle after another through discussion.

3.3.6   Equipment supply

In connection with the supply of equipment, the participants discussed the type of machines provided by Technicom, their quantity, their characteristics, the other equipment necessary, the delivery conditions, and spare parts. Two issues led to an especially tense discussion: pricing and conditions of payment and delivery. The Chinese were very concerned about getting the most up-to-date technology, and formulated all kinds of questions. Technicom engineers give answers that often seemed unintelligible to the Chinese, and incomprehension fed suspicion. Two rounds lasting a total of 20 days were necessary to clarify the technical aspects. The entire discussion was carried out in Shanghai. It led to a 15-page document with a 40-page appendix.

Pricing was an even hotter issue. To deal with this matter, Technicom took an unusual stance, bringing no less than 13 people to the negotiation table instead of the usual team of 4. Shanghai Eastern Wind called on experts from the import/export corporation dealing with their products to stand on its side. These experts were very familiar with the international market. The discussion became very difficult over this thorny point, and sometimes went on for 18 continuous hours without any result. The head of the Technicom delegation had to meet a deadline for returning to Europe. The Chinese happened to know about it and started running out the clock. The conflict escalated and each side left, threatening the other side. It took some time to cool down the whole situation.

Then, another problem arose, bringing the negotiation to the verge of collapse. Technicom sold not merely equipment, but a whole system. Some of its components were made by a third party, an American company. The Chinese realized that the separate cost of the components was 20% to 30% higher than they would themselves pay if they were to buy them directly. But there was no room for any concession because Technicom already made no profit on those components, for which it obviously paid a much higher price than did the Chinese. This led to another deadlock, more painful than ever. The Chinese side did not believe what Technicom said and systematically checked the information provided in the United States, in Europe, and with its own administration. Finally, convinced that Technicom had told the truth, the Chinese offered to buy those components by themselves in order to get out of the stalemate situation. The purchasing department of Technicom strongly objected to this proposal. This led to an internal deadlock within Technicom. Eventually the general director of Technicom Europe settled the conflict by accepting the Chinese suggestion.

After having come across quite a few of these unexpected obstacles, the two sides reached an overall agreement. The president of Technicom Consumer Products came to Shanghai to sign the contract, which was written in two original versions, one Chinese, one English. The wording was slightly different to enable the Chinese side to obtain final approval more easily from the administrative authority in Beijing. From English into Chinese the translation could be considered as accurate, but the Chinese version left more space for ambiguity. A final banquet closed the ceremony in a friendly atmosphere punctuated by a number of toasts.

MOFERT had to give its final approval within two months. Obtaining this approval was typically the job of the Chinese partner and Shanghai Eastern Wind knew very well how to deal with the bureaucracy. But the task did not appear easy, for some of Technicom's requirements were too high with regard to what was usually accepted, or were simply unusual compared to what the authorities considered "international practice." The head of the Technicom delegation went to Beijing to provide explanations, as in former times foreign ambassadors did at the Court of Emperor Qianlong. By doing so, he "gave face" to the officials and obtained their agreement. The following day, Shanghai Eastern Wind organized a banquet to associate those officials with the "success of the negotiation."

The whole negotiation, with its deadlocks and intermissions between the different stages of the process, lasted three years. If we now consider the interactions between the two parties during the entire process, alternations between cooperative and conflictual attitudes were numerous. The negotiation was carried out article after article. In the cooperative sequences, both parties managed to exchange advantages through mutual concessions costing the giver less than they would benefit the receiver. Personal relations helped only in small matters. As soon as there was a significant cost involved, only solid concessions could overcome deadlocks. In this case money also talked.

When an issue threatened to become too much of an obstacle with no obvious way to clear it, the negotiators left it aside. Gradually a group of sensitive issues accumulated and there came a time where they had to be dealt with. But at that moment something new had modified some of the basic conditions of the game: the mayor of Shanghai had met the head of the Technicom delegation and they had agreed on a date for the signing of the contract. Although not legally binding, such a deadline contributed strongly to the progress of the negotiation. Time, energy, and money already spent by both sides (US$1.5 million, according to Technicom) facilitated concessions. As a matter of fact, most of the concessions still to be made cost very little compared to what had already been spent. Threats by both sides to break away had, by then, almost no credibility. It even happened that the other party stated "We know that it is not possible for you to break away. After all you have already spent, you would not like it to be for nothing!" or "What would your boss say to you if you come back to him with no result?" These arguments ultimately made sense to both parties.

Table 3.1 summarizes the negotiation process.

3.4 Analysis

Developing analytical thoughts about this case requires scrutinizing the facts with the help of conceptual instruments adapted to the study of joint venture negotiations. To serve this purpose, the theoretical tools available to researchers will be reviewed first. Thereafter, the study will identify the major variables governing the negotiation process and analyze their individual roles to show how and to what extent they pertained and influenced the final outcome. Finally, conclusions will be drawn from the observations made to reassess what could be defined as a global optimum for the outcome, and the way to reach it.

3.4.1 Theoretical approaches to joint venture negotiations

If one considers the basic knowledge that has been attained in the domain of joint venture negotiations, there is no such thing as a specific theory. There are theoretical approaches to joint ventures as a whole, but paradoxically, even though the negotiations leading to the establishment of the joint venture constitute one of the most crucial points governing its efficiency and even survival, research efforts have shown only little concern for that aspect. The main difficulty that the joint venture has to confront, its instability (Harrigan, 1988), can be resolved to a large degree at the stage where cooperation is established. The Lorange and Roos model (1987) clearly expresses this. The authors show the existing relationship between factors

Table 3.1. Process summary.

Phase	Activity
Prenegotiation	MOFERT/Technicom preliminary contacts Shanghai Eastern Wind joins Visit to Technicom's European headquarters Chinese official approval
Negotiation: Phase I	First round of negotiation. Shenzhen (3 days) Exploratory discussions (capital contributions, management responsibilities, technology transfer) *Deadlock* (2 months) Second round of negotiation (1 week) Disagreement on 5 out of 10 issues *Total breakoff* Shanghai Bureau for High Technology mediates Third round of negotiation Agreement on principle Letter of intent signed Feasibility study MOFERT approval
Negotiation: Phase II (Four contracts to be discussed)	Articles of association (2 months) (Joint venture duration, equity split, choice of the manager and top management, location of the Arbitration Court, etc.) Joint venture contract (1 year) (Cash contributions, valuation of assets, equipments, timing for contributions, etc.) MOFERT approval Technology transfer (1 month) (Type of technology, scope, training, production volume, year plans, etc.) *Conflict and deadlock on the TOEFL issue* Equipment supply (20 days) (Types of machines, quantity, characteristics, pricing, delivery conditions, etc.) *Deadlock on pricing* *Open crisis on valuation of components* Exchange of threats Local mayor meets Technicom delegation head Agreement on a final deadline Global agreement signed (two original versions) Technicom, then Eastern Wind, meet with MOFERT Final MOFERT approval

that influence the setup of the joint venture and its performance, considering the latter as a dependent variable.

One of the major themes common to all research on joint ventures is complexity. To some extent, such a negotiation is to usual business negotiation what the Uruguay Round is to the purchase of a secondhand car. In addition, it is complexity concerning a bilaterally oriented negotiation, whereas the few existing works in this domain, such as Zartman's (1994), mainly characterize complexity by the number of actors or parties creating situations in which multilateral logical systems prevail.

Insights from the Chinese context within which the negotiation takes place, types of Chinese negotiators involved in the process, and influential cultural factors operate as an "invisible great wall" as analyzed by Fang (1999), Faure and Chen (1997), Lang (1998), Li (1999), and Tung (1982). The descriptive analytic approach exemplified by Faure (1998), Hakam and Chan (1990), Li (1994), and Weiss (1987), seeks to present an account of the process built from issues negotiated, individual players involved, and conditions under which the actions take place. Strategic implications are drawn from the observations made.

A second type of approach, more oriented toward consulting, is presented by Lewis (1990), who refers to Fisher and Ury's (1981) analytical tools, and applies them to selected negotiations on alliances and joint ventures. The work yields a number of recommendations aimed at strengthening the integrative aspect of the process and, as a consequence, reducing the risk of future instability of the joint venture. From a similar perspective, Shapiro *et al.* (1991) draw conclusions concerning the most influential variables on the negotiation process from their own experience as negotiators in China. They also convey their view of Chinese negotiators' behavior, analyze the reasons for it, and finally suggest guidelines for Western negotiators to reduce misunderstandings and enhance their effectiveness. Campbell (1989), basing his work on a field study of 30 EJVs in China, offers observations of practical use on various important issues such as time, Chinese negotiating style, and negotiating teams. The author then derives a set of guidelines for the foreign negotiator, addressing both the process itself and the context of the negotiation.

With similar intentions, authors such as Blackman (1997), De Keijzer (1992), Eiteman (1990), Fischer (1993), Kearney (1987), Kindel (1990), Neunuebel (1995), Tay (1995), and Wagner (1993) draw upon their experience as negotiators or on their own observations to offer useful advice for the practitioner operating in China. Gray and Yan (1992) offer a structural approach to joint venture formation and provide a framework for examining the factors that create instability and performance decline, and as a consequence, a process of renegotiation.

An approach of a more abstract and deductive character resorts to game theory to suggest a framework designed to secure the partners' cooperation and to ensure the joint venture's success. The authors, Gulati *et al.* (1994), work from hypotheses derived from interviews with managers of this type of venture. The explanatory variable on which they base their research is the type of vision that each partner in the alliance brings over, the respective gains made by each side, and the type of commitment subsequently produced.

3.4.2   Application to the case: Economic analysis

A negotiation is a mixed activity that can be understood from two different perspectives: substance and process. Negotiation analysis applies mainly to the process, whereas the economic approach focuses on the content. When the negotiation concerns tangible issues, economic analysis seems especially relevant. If such a choice is kept open in terms of perspectives, one of the basic questions that can be raised addresses the heuristic value of each of the related theories. What do we learn while applying economic theory to the joint venture type of negotiation, or to the logical systems developed by the actors? Does economic analysis provide a suitable explanation of the actual outcome, in light of the complexity of these negotiations? Given what is supposed to be its strong point – its predictive capacity – does such a theory operate as a true predictor of parties' behaviors, and of the final outcome?

Economic analysis performs better when applied to the reasons for setting up a joint venture than to the negotiation of the setup. However, if applied to the negotiation phase itself, it raises the problem of the conflicting rationales at work or, at least, of the divergence between the rationale of one party and that of the whole negotiation. Each party has a number of objectives to reach with a strategy dominated by a competitive mode. If we now consider negotiation as a joint decision-making system, that system operates on the basis of a global logic that is mostly cooperative. Such a mismatch, underlined by scholars such as Bartos (1978), makes the economic approach awkward to implement because of the initial choice that must be made of how best to describe the phenomenon studied: the negotiators striving to maximizing their individual gains, or the negotiation as a system that provides a potential for an optimum.

A process theory based on the construction of a convergent concessions dynamic, such as that formulated by Pen (1952), avoids this difficulty but raises another type of problem. For instance, how can the negotiation create the concept of "ophelimity," which encompasses the satisfaction the negotiator draws from the attainment of an outcome, and the "propensity to fight," which is the highest level of risk that a negotiator is willing to accept? Because there is no clear way to apply it to real-life situations, such a deductive approach remains merely hypothetical.

Cross (1969) suggested a way to escape this impasse by constructing the negotiation system as a problem of resource distribution. To be relevant and practicable,
this concept implies that what will be shared must be a finite quantity that is homogeneous and can be divided. In fact, the case studied incorporates nonmeasurable
and indivisible values such as concern with face or status, the negotiators' reputation among their constituents, and the friendliness or occasional animosity that
showed through at some stages of the negotiation.

The selection of a small number of issues regarded as the most influential on
the outcome may allow an approach to a Nash solution – a formal optimum. However, in addition to being an approximation, this formal optimum is based on the
hypothesis that the possible payoffs are transparent. What is observed in the Tech-
nicom/Eastern Wind negotiation is precisely the absence of this transparency, for
various reasons such as the role of the "secrecy" culture related to the existing Chinese political system. Thus, the implementation of such an approach is far from
being realistic.

On some issues, fair information sharing prevails in terms of the consequences
of various possible choices for each party such as equity split, cash payments, or
supply of some equipment. In these cases, what can be observed is an attempt by
both parties to manipulate the basis data of the model to obtain higher gains. Such
a practice considerably lowers the predictive capability of the model, if it does not
nullify it.

To be rationally applied, the economic approach has to be based on an accurate
cost/benefit analysis that neither side finds easy to manage. For instance, Technicom found it impossible to assess the true cost of some concessions, such as
financing training for the employees. Joint ventures suffer from high staff turnover,
and as soon as they are trained, Chinese executives, who know the high demand
for executives in joint ventures, might look for a better-paid position in another
company. In the same way, it was extremely difficult for Shanghai Eastern Wind
to assess the real benefits of technology transfer, for instance because of the many
remaining uncertainties regarding the ability of the Chinese to learn quickly and to
make efficient use of the equipment.

Another important point in such a long-lasting negotiation is the learning effect
produced by the process itself. For both sides, going through years of discussion
develops greater cultural intimacy and a better personal understanding that is not
without bearing upon the final outcome of the negotiation but that cannot easily be
incorporated in a monorationale approach based exclusively on utility functions.
One can only suggest, as Young (1975) did, the absolute necessity of being able to
express the expected values of that type of complex outcome on a multidimensional
payoff space, but the tool has still to be worked out.

It is very difficult, as well as probably highly unrealistic, to try to evaluate the ideal economic outcome of a negotiation as expected by each of the parties, especially in a country where the main issues are far from being strictly economic, and where historical, political, and organizational constraints, as well as culture, are determinant categories for action (Faure *et al.*, 1998). Thus, to build weighted utility functions, or to calculate a Pareto optimum or a Nash solution, would make only little sense in a normative context in which actors have multidimensional cognitive frames and aim at reaching multiple, even relatively conflicting, objectives. If there is one place where the aphorism "business is business" does not apply, it is China. Going from the company to the bureaus may mean the will to follow the legal procedure, but may also mean abandoning the economic rationale for complying with political requirements. Conflicting priorities within the same party may undermine the usefulness of the economic model.

As a matter of fact, these field observations make approaches with a strong economic focus, such as institutional theory (North, 1990), much more practical. Such an approach aims at describing and explaining economic performance by combining a theory of human behavior with a theory of transaction costs. The integration of the cost of economic exchange differentiates this approach from neoclassical theories. The exchange process entails considerable costs that compete with production costs, especially concerning information and its collection, measuring the valuable attributes of what is being exchanged, protecting rights, and enforcing agreements. In the case of a complex negotiation focused on an issue such as technology transfer or establishment of a joint venture, costs may reach quite an amazing level. If, in addition, cultural obstacles crop up, costs may rise again.

In the Technicom/Eastern Wind negotiation, the actors spontaneously demonstrated the relevance of this approach through their statements and behavior. Especially toward the end of the process, they emphasized elements such as time, energy, and money already spent, which are typical transaction costs, to restart the convergence dynamics, even though agreement had not been achieved. Considering the outcome of the Technicom/Eastern Wind venture, the net gains from the negotiation equaled the gross gains, which are the standard gains in the Walrasian model under the assumptions of instantaneous exchange and individuals fully informed about their exchange commodity and the terms of trade, minus the costs of enforcing the agreement, and minus the losses resulting from imperfect monitoring of that agreement.

When the parties to the negotiation can affect the flow of income from an asset such as the joint venture and, in addition, the income is not fully predictable, it becomes even costlier to determine whether the flow is what it should be. Negotiated issues such as the joint venture's power structure, decision-making processes, and arbitration increase the transaction costs and do not greatly reduce either the degree of uncertainty affecting the economic result of the venture or the need for more policing and controls. The institutional constraints built through the negotiation tend to reduce the uncertainties to a tolerable level, and the transaction costs reflect the price of reaching this level. In that sense negotiation can be viewed as a process of institutionalization, and fitted into a property rights approach (Chen, 1995; Furubotn and Pejovich, 1974). The difficulty arises because with institutional theory, whatever its relevance to joint venture negotiations, it is extremely problematic to assess the transaction costs for both parties because of limited access to information and because of the multiple nature of the costs involved. Another difficulty lies in the fact that the general pattern of negotiation has to be implemented in a cultural setting where people are constrained by bonding, norms of conduct, rituals, beliefs, and cognitive biases that make the real transaction much more complex, uncertain, and unpredictable as to its final outcome. In this respect, the context within which the transaction develops is definitely a major element of the game.

If there is any place where the maxim of the optimistic negotiator, "Do not take no for an answer," has to be turned into "Do not take yes for an answer," it is again China. Thus, this type of situational context must not be taken as the background of the story, a distant scene, but as an active constituent, the basic referent, and the system for organizing meaning. Starting from this context, the point is to analyze the role of the main variables influencing the negotiation process, their mutual relations, and the way their rationales combine. Lastly, the quality of a negotiation must not be assessed simply on the basis of the content of the written agreement, but primarily by taking into account the real consequences of the agreement – in this case the setting up of the joint venture and its performance.

3.4.3 Application to the case: The economic rationale within diverging expectations

The basic question to raise is the ontological one: Why a joint venture? What motivates people to adopt a form of organization that carries with it so many constraints and exposes it to so much risk? Why not resort to the market, or be satisfied with limited property rights? The answer is, among others, provided by transaction cost theory (Williamson, 1979). The main reason for setting up an economic institution such as a joint venture lies in the minimization of production and transaction costs. Production costs are reduced by combining high-performing Western technology with low-cost labor. Minimizing transaction costs is tightly connected with the rights of property and control that benefit both partners, and allow close and low-cost control by creating "mutual hostages" (Kogut, 1988). Such a situation tends to promote a new value, forbearance, supported by the trust built during the development of the relationship as well as by the role of networks of obligations operating on a broader scale.

On occasion, practitioners may find this view somehow theoretical and prefer to seek another explanation more closely connected with their field experience. An alternative answer consists of considering the choice of the joint venture formula not as a way to minimize costs but as a means to maximize profit in a given situation. It is called "strategic" behavior and has its maximum relevance within a limited period of time. In view of the overall international economic situation and the uncertainty prevailing on the Chinese market, the intention of the European parent company tends to coincide with the first approach, but the position of the Chinese counterpart may favor the strategic option. "Same bed, different dreams," says a Chinese proverb. Shared explicit objectives do not exclude long-term diverging intentions. The various actors in the negotiation all seem to have obviously different interests. The Chinese authorities are primarily concerned with job creation, especially with millions of farmers leaving the countryside for the cities; next, with raising Chinese technology to the level of international standards; then, with enhancing the company's productivity; then, with exporting to obtain the foreign exchange necessary to finance technology transfers; and finally, with modernizing its economic infrastructure. Decision makers in public administration consider the distribution of economic activity among the provinces, as well as the development of technical know-how and managerial skills as additional priorities. For the Chinese enterprise, the first goal is to make quick money and to benefit from advantages to which it was not entitled as a state-owned company.

The Western company has other ambitions that are, in turn, quite different from what the Chinese partner imagines, such as making money at China's expense. To the Chinese, most of its objectives appear "not clear" or "easily changing for unknown reasons." In fact, the Western company wants, first, to secure a position on the Chinese market to be able to take advantage of future opportunities and potentialities. For a major Western company, it is becoming increasingly unthinkable to have no presence in a market that corresponds to one-quarter of the world population. In addition to access to new markets, to low production costs, and to the possibility of sourcing their most basic supplies, China offers economies of scale in production and distribution. In this case, the type of product to be manufactured by the joint venture belongs to the category of consumer goods with a medium level of technology. Technicom believed that it would easily find customers on the Chinese market provided the official authorities did not directly interfere to protect state enterprises from competition for which they had never been prepared.

This may be viewed as a rather idealistic picture. In fact, Western companies performing technology transfer within a joint venture setting confront a number of problems that make the final outcome contrast strongly with what they expected. A former US ambassador to China, Winston Lord, in a speech delivered in 1986, summarized in a few words the acuteness of the ensuing problem: "Many business people are frustrated by high costs, price gouging, tight foreign-exchange controls, limited access to the Chinese market, bureaucratic foot dragging, lack of qualified local personnel, and unpredictability" (Mathur and Chen, 1987). Thus, added to the intrinsic instability of the joint venture are the various vicissitudes stemming from the Chinese context.

The operating performance of a joint venture is tightly linked to the adjustment level achieved prior to the setup, that is, the very complex negotiation aimed at giving it birth. Inadequate negotiation at this level often accounts for subsequent failures. A United Nations agency specialized in this domain has identified no fewer than 142 issues to be negotiated, which can be classified into 18 categories (Dupont, 1991). The number of issues, their interrelationships, and their mutual influences make any prediction concerning the final outcome of the negotiation highly questionable. In addition, it is extremely difficult to derive from the content of the agreement any reliable assumption on how well the joint venture will actually perform.

Among the 50 or more issues usually negotiated in a joint venture agreement, three of them have a prominent role from the economic viewpoint: pricing of products, technology transfer, and valuation of contributions. Pricing is a hot issue, but not because of conflicting interests. In fact, both sides understand very well that the venture cannot be designed in such a way that it loses money, and also that the benefit is tightly limited by the demand and by the availability of competitive products. But a total misunderstanding arises regarding these two limitations. The Chinese side does not does not fully understand how Western accounting practices work, and how the European side interprets and extrapolates from cost structures.

Technology transfer raises another type of problem that has no obvious solution. The Chinese have an almost pathological concern with obtaining the most advanced technology, even if their equipment does not enable them to use it properly. They always tend to suspect that the foreign partner is trying to get rid of outdated equipment at their expense. Such an attitude elicits a strong demand for technical information during the negotiation and may turn it into a long-lasting free training seminar. An additional constraint makes it even more difficult to devise any solution. The more sophisticated the technology, the higher the fees to be paid. Whatever the technical interest of the equipment, the Chinese are not prepared to pay that cost.

The valuation of both sides' contributions is a highly critical issue, in particular because China does not use Western valuation procedures. Contributions that are not made in hard cash, such as buildings and land-use rights, are subject to quite arbitrary valuation with no clear economic justification. If, as is often the case, these are the only Chinese contributions to capitalization, they can be overvalued exorbitantly.

Among the other issues usually negotiated in a joint venture agreement, some may also have a substantial economic impact on the final outcome. They include the feasibility study, and the training of Chinese staff and workers. If the chairman of the joint venture is Chinese, the general manager and the top executives are often foreigners. Their salaries, extremely high by Chinese standards, raise similar expectations among the local executives and deprive the joint venture of a significant part of its foreign exchange. On the other hand, the very length of the negotiation, accounting for years, with travel and housing for the Europeans, as well as the amount of time they must concern themselves with the project in their own company, has quite a high monetary cost that many Western companies simply do not think to integrate in the overall costs at the very beginning of the negotiation. While engaging in a joint venture negotiation, Western negotiators seldom imagine that they are only at the very start of a process that may sometimes last for almost a decade, whether the cause be the overall political situation, the slowness of decision-making processes, the succession of cultural misunderstandings, or the consequences of the Chinese resorting to long-term negotiation tactics such as attrition or squashing (Faure, 1998).

3.4.4   The nonmonetary costs

In addition to monetary costs, nonmonetary costs that relate to other dimensions have to be taken into account in the assessment of the negotiation. The negotiators must consider the costs linked to their personal lives, and the company must include organizational costs in the final balance sheet. The success or failure of a negotiation influences the negotiators' reputations and their future careers. Even if signing an agreement requires the will of at least two parties, not reaching any agreement is often viewed as resulting from the negotiators' inability to achieve what they were assigned to do. However, this agreement cannot be obtained at any cost, be this cost financial or related to the negotiator's face in the eyes of the other party. There is a face cost rationale that finds its paramount expression in the Chinese culture (Bond, 1986). In many cases a deadlock or a breakoff is a better outcome than a loss of face. If feelings of real humiliation arise at some stage of the negotiation, it becomes imperative for the so-called victim to regain face. Usually this requires the implementation of distributive or coercive tactics that distract the parties from the search for an optimum agreement.

The negotiator must also endure costs of a psychological nature. Getting into the analytical categories of the other party – for the Chinese side, following lengthy demonstrations of Western logic; for the European side, listening to holistic and metaphorical Chinese approaches – is always tedious. However, these exercises also have an adaptive value because, at least, they enable everyone to communicate with their counterparts. The cultural dislocation that foreigners in China must constantly endure within the sphere of the negotiation requires considerable psychological effort. However, if such an effort is not made, misunderstandings and cognitive dissonance would increase and play a very harmful role in the negotiation progress.

The organizational costs that the Western company has to bear are mainly linked to the complexity of the decision-making system when it expands from the enterprise itself to the Chinese administrative structure. The length of the process, the slowness, and the lack of formal rules means that no one is certain about the criteria that will be used in making a decision. The opacity of the administrative structure and the internal conflicts within the bureaucracy make all decision-making mechanisms uncertain and unstable. As a consequence, it is difficult to benefit as much as could be expected from previous experience.

The perception of time also has consequences in terms of costs. As stressed by Campbell (1989:56), "the Chinese concept of time is radically different from that of the West. Time demonstrates commitment." The longer a discussion is made to last on one point, the more important this point is understood to be for the discussant. To "save time" means to lose seriousness. Time is not just an equivalent of money; when too much time is required, it is also a cost in terms of missed opportunities, such as learning through the actual operation of the joint venture and lack of availability for other projects.

Among the main factors influencing the negotiation process one can distinguish the general suspicion that often prevails in the Chinese mind, the complexity of the task, the unbalanced security point structure, the mismatch of tactics used by the two sides, the deadlocks, and the role of the interpreter. It is quite usual for negotiations in China to start in an atmosphere of suspicion. Cultural traits or attitudes elicited by circumstances, and distrust, are among the basic characteristics of an interaction with foreigners (Shapiro *et al.*, 1991). The Chinese tend to look systematically for a hidden motive behind each action, and to add their own interpretation to any signal, any move, any silence. Ascribing Machiavellian intentions that the counterpart may never have had strongly contributes to creating an atmosphere unpropitious to openings, risk-taking, and straightforward cooperation.

The complexity of the task operates as a multiplying factor with regard to distrust. A global view and understanding of the negotiation are extremely hard to attain because of the number and variety of the issues. It is accordingly difficult to perceive what is at stake behind the demands and to foresee the consequences of each possible move. Because of the lack of a clear vision of the global outcome, suspicion perpetuates itself, impelling the actors toward greater stubbornness and bringing the system toward greater paralysis.

The security points of both parties perceptibly influence the course of the negotiation, especially the shifts from integrative to distributive orientation. In phase 1 of the process costs and risks incurred by both parties are low and relatively equivalent. It is an exploratory phase that, even if it leads to no agreement, will be viewed as a testing exercise for both companies, a learning process providing experience in a new domain. For example, Technicom learned from the Chinese administrative procedures and from the cultural context; the Shanghai Eastern Wind negotiators had an interesting stay abroad with the result that, even if the negotiation had failed, their activities would not be useless from the viewpoint of learning through experience, although what they gained is hard to assess precisely.

The rationale of phase 2 is drastically different. The longer the negotiation process continued, the higher the related costs became, with very little compensation if a final agreement were not reached. The US$1.5 million already spent by Technicom according to its own calculations illustrates the relevance of the transaction cost approach and demonstrates that the company had no alternative solution to striking a deal. Technicom had to achieve an agreement, even at a high price, or otherwise incur dramatic losses.

Eastern Wind did not really have a security point, because the negotiation took place on its home ground and this considerably reduced the company's expenses. In addition, whatever might have happened at the end, Eastern Wind gained substantial technical knowledge that increased proportionally with the length of the negotiation. In this respect, Eastern Wind resolved for itself the basic Negotiator's Dilemma of maximizing gains but reducing the chances of an agreement, because in both cases it would achieve gains. Eastern Wind was inclined to prolong the negotiation and even to risk a breakoff by the other side, whereas it was in Technicom's interest to accelerate the concession-making process. This situational asymmetry between the parties threw the negotiation system out of balance, prevented the possibility of turning it into a true joint problem-solving approach, and gave rise to a number of painful deadlocks.

The choice of tactics used by the two parties and their explosive interactions reinforced difficulties at the process level. The Chinese readily resorted to attrition tactics, a gradual wearing down that the Europeans found very uncomfortable to cope with (Faure, 1995b). Unable to implement proper countertactics, the Technicom negotiators expressed their frustration through outbursts of anger – verbal aggressions that did not help to put the process back on the right track. The combination of these clashes produced a number of deadlocks, and overcoming them imposed costs.

The price of escaping a deadlock can be paid in various domains: economic, psychological, social, or even political. According to the nature and the extent of the deadlock, negotiators have applied leverage at four points, bearing respectively on the context, the relationship, the substance of the negotiation, and the overall structure. Getting out of a deadlock by means of the context consists of modifying the atmosphere of the negotiation by organizing recreational activities, sightseeing, tours, dinners, or banquets. Playing on the relationship is intended to appeal directly to individual participants through greetings and gifts (silk cloth, ties, fans, lacquerware, cloisonné items, pens, calendars, notebooks, etc.). Participants can act on the very substance of the negotiation through concessions, adding issues, or withdrawing thorny points. Playing on the structure of the negotiation usually means introducing a third party to act as a mediator and, by doing so, to allow openings that the parties would never accept under other conditions. This is a procedure of conflict resolution typical of the traditional Chinese culture that still applies today (Chen and Faure, 1995; Wall and Blum, 1991). In the case presented, the Chinese public administration took on this job as a measure of last resort.

In this type of negotiation, where neither side speaks the other's language, the interpreter plays an important role. The function fulfilled is much more than mere translation and results in true mediation. The interpreter puts a personal imprint on messages by shaping them on the basis of his or her own understanding, leaving some points out, reducing the level of antagonism in the exchanges by using moderate language, helping the relationship by amplifying the positive aspects, and sometimes influencing the whole process simply by making mistakes in the translation. The role of the interpreter goes beyond managing the relationship between the parties with the related manipulations that can be carried out; it extends to drafting the text of the agreement in both languages. Here the interpreter can display great talent in the management of the ambiguity that words may carry.

3.4.5   The game and the way to play

In the Chinese perception of negotiation, the zero-sum game vision often prevails (Faure, 1995b). This is probably a consequence of an economy of scarcity, a rural tradition, and a culture of equality within which everybody should stay at the same level. It noticeably leads to turning a game with an a priori strong integrative potential into a highly distributive game at the level of implementation. Benefits do not initially derive from the market, but should be gained at the partner's expense. On the other hand, any concession to the foreign party can be immediately perceived as a gain at the expense of China. Many Chinese negotiators view the very concept of "mutual gains" as a fallacious construction aimed at misleading them.

The idea of a joint venture implies that the parties will eventually play the same game, but the negotiation needed to set it up foreshadows to some extent the relational style between the partners once the firm begins operating, and that may produce considerable setbacks. A general understanding of the game presupposes an exercise of decoding the overall situation. The Chinese assume that the foreign party came to make money at China's expense, and the goal is to manage in such a way that China gets something in return. Such an attitude, which corresponds to the culture of suspicion, leads the parties to fight against each other, instead of fighting for the benefit of the joint venture. In addition, a joint venture type of negotiation, lengthy and complex as it is, still does not enable the negotiators to modify the formula of the agreement substantially because the agenda is almost fixed from the start. The general framework is always the same, and the list of issues to be discussed does not really depend on the parties. Only priorities may change, as well as the cost of concessions. If the general philosophy of the joint venture is integrative, the operating structure of the negotiation is widely distributive. As a matter of fact, the negotiation design impels parties to discuss the issues at stake sequentially. Thus, tradeoffs between issues are quite problematic to consider because of the inherent risk of reopening discussion on a point that had previously been secured, sometimes after substantial effort, and because it is important not to encourage the other party to rediscuss all issues that might produce an additional benefit.

If the rules of the game do not depend greatly upon the will of the foreign party, under certain circumstances they can be changed during the negotiation process by the administrative authorities, a highly powerful third party that can intervene at any time on such issues as priorities, or how to interpret formal rules.

To believe that the negotiation has brought no regular benefits during the whole process is a way of losing face, a situation difficult for the Chinese party to stand. The point is not to counterbalance gains and losses, advantages and concessions, but not to lose anything in the game (Faure, 1999).

The two parties have sharply divergent views of the initial situation. The foreign company comes to do business, to discuss a project, and to explore a potential range of mutual interests for which it may be possible to mobilize common resources. The Chinese side sees the foreign company coming to China as being in the position of demanding something. It will have to produce the first offers and take the final steps to come to an agreement. The Chinese attitude becomes mainly defensive and does not leave much space for innovation and risk taking.

Official principles such as "equality" and "mutual benefit" are seldom put into practice in the negotiation itself because of the existing asymmetry between the parties. The basic Chinese assumption, that foreign companies will first try to get rid of their obsolete equipment and technology, leads the local party to launch a process of unending questions that express their distrust and annoy the foreign side, reinforcing the defensive and static potential of the game. The economic and managerial asymmetry results from the difference between the levels of development of the two companies. In the Chinese view, the foreign company is rich and must contribute accordingly. Fairness is regarded strictly as an implementation of the needs rule, and the resources must be distributed to meet the requirements of the party with the most important needs.

Even the corporate culture of each company does not help much in building a common understanding of the future joint venture. The two partners are far from understanding the very concept of "company" in the same way. As a matter of fact, in the current economic system, dominated by state-owned enterprises, the latter is reduced to one or several plants or a grouping of workshops with some sort of coordination among them. The whole activity is focused on production. Even if basic management functions, such as marketing, finance, human resources, and research and development, now exist as structural subunits in the organization chart, they are rarely performed as they are in the West. The Chinese company is just the level at which decisions made at the administrative and political levels are carried out (Chen, 1995).

The final question about the game concerns when it is over. Here again visions differ between the parties. For the Western company, once the contract has been signed the purpose shifts simply to implementing it. For the Chinese side, a signature at the bottom of the contract does not bring an end to discussions, but must be viewed as one episode in a much lengthier process. Nowhere as much as in China does the concept of renegotiation reach its full meaning.

3.5 Conclusion

As shown in this case, which is typical of many negotiations in China, the rationale of the game is not one-dimensional, and the key factors that govern the agreement are not all economic. The joint venture is an organization of a new type, differing from traditional organizations in its purpose, culture, and mode of operation. In the context of a socialist, centrally planned economy where public administration and Communist Party are assimilated, the joint venture, with its capitalist goals, appears as an oxymoron. This aspect adds considerably to the other obstacles linked to its dual nature. This is why the negotiation aimed at setting up the venture plays a crucial role. What is left out, neglected, or poorly dealt with at this stage will appear again in the form of major problems for the actual functioning of the joint venture. The negotiation governs not only the existence of the venture and its operating efficiency, but also its organizational character, because it foreshadows the relationships within the joint venture.

Each phase of the negotiation develops along a particular logic and exhibits the working of distinct key factors. In the prenegotiation phase, motivation, commitment of each one of the parties, compatibility of objectives, and strategic outlook are the main variables. These operate as background factors, predating the negotiation process itself, and are not substantially modified by that process.

By contrast, in the negotiation phase, although the agenda is relatively fixed a priori, each party's priorities are different and the order in which the issues at stake will be discussed is totally open. One of the key points influencing the course of that stage is not just what each of the parties will bring in terms of tangible contributions, but the assessment of their willingness to contribute in proportion to their own resources. This judgment is important for the Chinese side because it will govern the quality of the process.

The Western company did not come to China either to lose money or to give birth to a competitor. As a consequence, it will restrict its contribution in capital and in technology transfer. But at the same time, the company runs the risk of turning a cooperative relationship, viewed as a joint effort toward a common goal, into an antagonistic relationship – a zero-sum game. The Chinese enterprise may appear to be more concerned with getting foreign exchange and facilities by means of the joint venture than with thinking about the future in managerial terms.

Cultural aspects play a complex part and are often poorly controlled. National and ethnic cultures elicit different perceptions of the very nature of the game going on (Faure and Rubin, 1993). They also originate in misunderstandings throughout the process, misapprehensions that may lead to mutual *"procès d'intention,"* giving rise to a conflictual spiral. Organizational cultures also emphasize difficulties because they express diverging values. The organizational culture of the Western company is often powerful and rather market driven. That of the Chinese enterprise is much weaker and rather bureaucratic or techno-bureaucratic. Negotiators' cultures are also very dissimilar in the behaviors they generate. Western negotiators are individualistic and often make quick decisions on their own. The Chinese negotiators are more collectively oriented and risk averse, and tend to resort to committee opinion. Lastly, professional cultures, which often are the true bridge in negotiations, do not always play that assigned role because meetings of the two sides may involve experts of different types, such as engineers with managers, lawyers with engineers, or salesmen with engineers.

One of the most efficient solutions for cultural problems is to use the negotiation as an active learning process. As negotiations in China often last a very long time, compared to the amount of time a Western negotiator spends negotiating in the West, it is possible to turn what initially appears as a major drawback into an advantage. It is also an opportunity to work on building trust – a factor as essential to the positive conclusion of the negotiation as the reputation of the Western product or the projected demand for it.

The asymmetrical perception of the initial situation – the idea that the Western company is wealthy and the Chinese enterprise is not – leads to a pattern of concession making along a reciprocity principle that does not assume any equivalence between the terms of exchange. Obligations are viewed as different, and depend upon the status of the parties. Here again, the economic rationale is affected by sociocultural values.

Finally, the role of information may be decisive for several reasons. It may be scarce, or poorly processed in the company, or collected and organized in a way that is useless in managerial terms. This may occur because an obsession with secrecy still prevails in the company (Li, 1994), or because all the participants think primarily of protecting themselves, or because the first loyalty is to the politico-administrative authority. These factors slow down the negotiation progress, make the atmosphere more oppressive, and do not lead the process to integrative ends.

Acknowledgments

Among the people who helped me in various ways to write this chapter, I would especially like to mention Cai Li Juan, and also Indru Advani, Hubert Bazin, Claude Bret, Chen Derong, Michel Chevet, Bertrand Cristau, Olivier Dauchez, Gérard Deleens, Axel Detz, Dominique Devinat, Fang Wuling, Jean-Marc Giraud, Huang Zhen, Michel Hue, Philippe Jullian, Alain Langlois, Hélène Lefrère, Li Zhaoxi, Olivier Monange, Jean-Charles Riccio, Michel Rozay, Aldo Salvador, Song Yunxin, Bernard Terminet Schuppon, Bruno Villette, Wilfried Vanhonacker, Yan Lan, and Zhou Yuan.

Chapter 4

Renegotiation of the VALCO Agreement in Ghana: Contribution to a Theoretical Interpretation

Akilagpa Sawyerr

4.1   Introduction

In 1962 the government of Ghana concluded an agreement with a consortium of two US aluminium transnationals, Kaiser Aluminum and Chemical Corporation (now Maxxam) and Reynolds Metals Corporation, for the establishment in Ghana of a hydroelectric power generating facility and an aluminium smelter. Under the agreement, known as the VALCO Agreement, the bulk of the power to be generated by the power plant was to be sold to the Volta Aluminium Company Ltd. (VALCO). The government constructed and, through the Volta River Authority (VRA), a parastatal set up for the purpose, operated the power generation facility (which included a dam and a transmission grid), while the Kaiser/Reynolds consortium, through its subsidiary VALCO, built and ran the aluminium smelter. By mid-1967 the project was in operation.

The main features of the VALCO Agreement included:

- A guarantee to supply, on average, more than 60% of total energy produced by VRA to VALCO, at a fixed price of 2.625 mills (one mill = US$0.001) per kilowatt/hour (kW/h).
- A special fiscal package that gave VALCO, among other things, a fixed income tax rate, as well as exemption from taxes on dividends and power use and from the exchange control regulations, in addition to the usual pioneer industry reliefs.
- Freedom for VALCO to import alumina (the principal raw material for aluminium production) duty free, thereby removing one of the initial attractions of the scheme for Ghana – the prospect for the creation of an integrated aluminium industry on the basis of the large local supplies of bauxite and cheap energy.

In addition, VALCO was virtually insulated from local control by reason of a fixed 30-year term for the Master Agreement with an option for 20 more, without provision for review; a guarantee against nationalization; unrestricted access to compulsory international arbitration; and a "frozen law" provision, which made VALCO subject to the law of Ghana as it stood on 22 January 1962, prohibiting future legislative or administrative action that would affect its status or operation.

These extensive and very special privileges had been granted, and justified, in the expectation that the Volta River Project would accelerate the industrialization and development of the country. By the end of the 1970s, however, the perception had grown, both in Ghana and internationally, that while the benefits to Ghana had not materialized, at any rate to the extent expected, VALCO's shareholders were doing very well out of it. Effectively shielded from local economic and social hardships, they were making substantial profits out of the national economy.

In particular, VALCO was paying what was reckoned to be one of the lowest arms-length power prices paid by any aluminium smelter in the world, especially after the oil price increases of the 1970s. Nor had it paid any income or other taxes, despite 12 years of obvious profitability – its books showed over US$100 million in undistributed profits by the end of 1982 (apart from considerable shareholder gains from the tolling arrangement, discovered in the course of the negotiations). Moreover, unwilling themselves to help integrate aluminium production within Ghana by putting in an alumina plant to process local bauxite to feed their smelter, the shareholders were generally believed to be obstructing attempts to attract others to do so (Graham, 1982). Well-founded or not, these beliefs shaped the popular perception of VALCO and the agreement. Finally, the agreement's purported restraints on the sovereign powers of the state became increasingly offensive to national sensibilities, even as the full extent of the social and environmental side-effects of the Volta River Project became clearer.

When at the end of 1981 a *coup d'état* brought a military regime with a populist and anti-imperialist posture to power, matters were quickly brought to a head. Reflecting the general mood of popular disenchantment with the VALCO Agreement, the new government decided that the agreement needed fundamental restructuring to remove VALCO from its extremely privileged position. The government therefore called for a restructuring of the relationships established by the agreement to remove the special privileges enjoyed by VALCO and its shareholders, and to increase the smelter's contribution to the national development effort. VALCO accepted the invitation and talks started in February 1983. The result of two years of hard negotiation was the rewriting of key aspects of the agreement.

As will quickly become obvious, the negotiations involved the restructuring of an investment agreement, essentially by getting a powerful party, in this case the foreign investor, to give up part of its considerable advantages under the agreement in order to make the arrangement more balanced in altered circumstances. Furthermore, they provide an interesting case study of parties adopting sharply contrasting approaches to negotiation, and of resolving the resulting problems largely through insistence by one side on principled negotiation. This chapter will, therefore, concentrate on an examination of the negotiation process itself in order to highlight aspects helpful to our general understanding of negotiation theory and practice as applied to investment relations between a transnational company and an underdeveloped country.

4.2 The Renegotiation

The negotiations covered all the major aspects of the agreement, including the supply and price of power, income and other taxes and duties, the price paid for services rendered by VALCO to the shareholders, the frozen law provision, exemptions from the exchange control regulations, government participation in the equity of VALCO, and pollution control. To facilitate our analysis of the negotiation process, however, we focus on the negotiation of the price paid by VALCO for VRA power. Not only was this acknowledged by both sides as the central issue in the negotiations, but, as will become clear, the mood and pattern of the negotiations also turned largely on the positions adopted by the two sides at different stages on the power rate question. Moreover, the cut and thrust of the power rate negotiation highlights such issues of theory and practice as the Negotiator's Dilemma, principled negotiations, negative commitment, ripeness, the impact of off-the-table factors, and the identification and prioritization of interests (Tsikata, 1990; Faber, 1990; Graham, 1982).

4.3   The Process

The negotiation process itself was divided into two distinct phases on either side of a five-month breakdown. The first phase consisted of three rounds of talks held between February and May 1983. This phase was characterized by mounting distrust and contention, culminating in the breakdown. The second phase lasted from January to December 1984, and was conducted in a much more cooperative mode, steady progress being made through hard-headed, sometimes fierce negotiations. The reasons for the difference between the phases will become clear as the story unfolds.

The negotiating styles of the two sides, especially during the first phase of the negotiations, reflected a marked contrast in concept and approach. While Ghana favored the separate treatment of issues within stated principles, at least to begin with, VALCO tended to lump issues together and push for tradeoffs of packages.

4.3.1   Starting premises and approach

Ghana's starting premise was that in the circumstances of the 1980s, and after over a decade of highly profitable operation, VALCO should be able to operate profitably without the special privileges, and to make a more positive contribution to national development, especially in the area of national revenue. The government therefore proposed at the outset that VALCO pay for power at a rate set by reference to the weighted average price paid by aluminium smelters throughout the world, and be liable to taxation to the same extent as comparable commercial and industrial undertakings in Ghana. A third matter related to the amount of power guaranteed to VALCO. Ghana argued that the allocation guaranteed VALCO in 1962 was based on what was later found to have been an overestimation of the long-run firm energy capability of the dam. It was therefore necessary to adjust VALCO's guaranteed power to reflect the actual capability. In an opening "Position Paper" and subsequent presentations, Ghana outlined the principles underlying each of its proposals – on the power rate, guaranteed power, taxation issues, exchange control, tolling charges, etc. – and invited a response from VALCO. As explained by Ghana,

> ... the purpose of discussing each major element of the proposals separately is to establish it on a rational basis. This is not to ignore the obvious fact that each element is but part of a package. Thus as we make progress with the separate elements, the nature of the package becomes clearer, and adjustments in the total package become possible and meaningful.

The essence of VALCO's quite different approach is captured in this excerpt from its initial response to Ghana's opening position:

We believe that the negotiations should attempt to mutually arrive at an overall formula whereby the profits of the operations of VALCO are computed and shared in a manner that results in a fair and reasonable return to VALCO, VRA and the people of Ghana.

As the VALCO "pie" was limited in size, it was further said, the critical issues related to the proportions in which it was to be shared between VALCO and government. In this view, as elaborated in the course of the first phase of the negotiations, the principal consideration in any final settlement was to be VALCO's bottom line, protected as far as possible from what one would consider normal commercial risks.

This difference in the approaches of the two sides proved crucial to the tone and course of the first phase, as much of that phase turned out to be essentially a contest over which approach would shape the negotiations. It was the resolution of this contest through the breakdown of the talks that set the scene for the more cooperative second phase.

4.3.2 The power rate negotiation

On the specific matter of negotiating the power rate, Ghana took an early decision to concentrate on improving the power rate, not only because it was the most obvious symbol of the unbalanced relationship between the parties, but also because, as an up-front charge, it was fairly easy to monitor. The maxim was: "A power dollar is better than a tax dollar." VALCO, too, acknowledged the centrality of the power rate because of its importance as a major cost item as well as its easier creditability for US tax purposes. This is as far as agreement went, because the parties differed markedly in their approach to the settlement of the issue and their expectations of the outcome.

Ghana put forward the principle that:

The basic rate [to be paid by VALCO] should bear a reasonable relation to an average price of power delivered to aluminium smelters around the world. On the assumption that the VALCO smelter is of average efficiency, VALCO could be expected to pay such a rate while remaining profitable in circumstances that might themselves be considered normal ... Once we have determined what such a price should be, we can then look at ways of making exceptional arrangements for times when the industry or VALCO are ... facing exceptional difficulties.

The weighted average price at the time was, by Ghana's calculation, 22 mills per kW/h, a figure that, according to the proposal, was to be "suitably indexed."

The averaging process underlying this principle involved listing and assessing all the aluminium smelters in the world: their operating capacities, current and projected, and the rates they paid for energy. It also involved the careful compilation of the exchange rates of all relevant currencies to facilitate the translation of all power prices into US dollars. All this information was made available to VALCO as part of the documentation in support of the Ghana proposal.

VALCO's initial reaction was to counterpropose an increase of the rate from 5 to 8 mills, without linking the proposed figure to any principle. Taken with the rest of the package, this was seen by Ghana as placing the country in a worse position overall than under the agreement that was being negotiated. Ghana refused to begin horse-trading at this stage, insisting that the applicable principles be agreed upon first. When all effort in that direction failed, Ghana called for the adjournment of the talks to give VALCO a chance to reconsider its position and come back for "meaningful negotiations."

This appears to have had some effect, since during the next round of talks VALCO took issue with the proposed method for calculating the weighted average world price, putting forward an alternative averaging concept that yielded figures ranging from 8.1 to 15.5 mills. By the end of the round Ghana felt that broad agreement had been reached on a principle for determining the base power rate, namely, the principle of relating the rate to the world average. What remained in contention were the assumptions underlying the calculation of the average. Also outstanding were disagreements over VALCO's insistence on indexing the agreed base rate to its profitability from year to year, the effective date of any new rate, and Ghana's proposal for a periodic review of the agreed rate. As these were eminently negotiable issues, the next round promised progress.

The positive omens for the next round were strengthened by the drastic devaluation of Ghana's currency, the cedi, in April 1983, from ¢2.75 = US$1 to about ¢30 = US$1. The significance of this development to the negotiations was that it resulted in a dramatic reduction in VALCO's local costs and an increase in its profitability. From the very beginning of the negotiations VALCO had complained that, as a result of the overvaluation of the cedi, it received less in cedis from the Bank of Ghana for the dollars it brought in to cover its local costs than it would have obtained on the parallel ("black") market. This difference it described sarcastically as an "exchange rate tax," one of the reasons it could not afford to pay more for energy. Indeed, using figures supplied by VALCO, Ghana estimated that had the devaluation occurred in 1982 it would have saved VALCO over US$26 million on its labor costs alone. Again, assuming a full four-potline operation, VALCO's after-tax income in 1983 could rise by an extra US$14 million. By removing this "exchange rate tax," the 1983 devaluation removed one of VALCO's main objections to a power price increase.

The Ghana team was, therefore, taken completely by surprise when, early in the third round, VALCO repudiated the averaging principle and the progress made in the previous round, observing that, "We should get away from averages and consider VALCO's profitability." Despite their shock, the Ghana team continued to press for the general acceptance of the principle of averaging, which would yield a "base power rate." By this time Ghana had gone beyond bare averaging by spelling out the elements of a formula for an "operational power rate." The formula was to be constructed as follows: to take care of VALCO's expressed concern about the impact of low metal prices on its profitability, the base rate was to be indexed to the price of metal; and to deal with the impact of allegedly unreliable energy supplies, the base rate was to be further adjusted according to the amount of energy made available to VALCO. But Ghana insisted that all these matters, important as they were, had to be kept separate from the determination of the base rate that would be payable in conditions of reasonable metal prices and normal energy supplies.

As VALCO hardened its position against the principle of averaging as a basis for fixing the base rate, and kept harping on the health of its bottom line, Ghana's chief negotiator called the two leaders of the VALCO team aside for a lengthy private consultation at which he gave the further assurance that, provided an appropriate power rate could be agreed, Ghana was prepared to consider adjustments to its tax proposals. This was subsequently put into writing.

When all this proved of no avail, Ghana refused to engage in serious discussion of any other issues until VALCO clarified its position on the power rate. In the end, and after much foot-dragging, VALCO put in a proposal of 12.5 mills. But as before, this was unrelated to any principle and was so hedged about with qualifications that, under existing and foreseeable conditions, the proposal gave Ghana no more than it had under the existing agreement – this in spite of the windfall given VALCO by the removal of the "exchange rate tax."

4.3.3 Collapse

Ghana promptly terminated the talks and declared the collapse of the negotiations. It would have no further part in the farce of talking at cross-purposes on the fundamental issues. It nevertheless left its last proposals on the table, informing VALCO that talks could only be resumed if the company put in proposals that Ghana considered indicative of an intention to engage in productive negotiations.

Within a week of the breakdown, VRA informed VALCO that as a result of the extremely low level of water in the dam it was cutting off the supply of energy to VALCO until the lake was restored to its normal operating level. This brought VALCO's production to a halt. It must be stated that VRA's action was perfectly legitimate under the *force majeure* provision in the agreement. Indeed, VALCO had already had to shut down two of its four operational potlines before the start of talks, and the whole country was under a regime of scheduled blackouts. What was important here was the timing of the shutdown and the definitiveness it gave to the collapse of the talks.

4.3.4 Revival

Early in July, the deputy managing director of VALCO called a press conference at which he expressed regret at the breakdown of the talks. Acknowledging that the power price paid by VALCO was unfair, he stated that VALCO was taking a fresh look at the major issues at stake, and hoped that, with effort on all sides, progress would be made. In September 1984 VALCO put forward a comprehensive set of proposals on all the main issues in the negotiations. Though the specifics were not fully aligned with Ghana's proposals, there was enough convergence on the under-lying principles to make further discussion meaningful. Of particular interest was the proposal on power, which stated that: "VALCO's base power rate would bear a close relationship to the average price of power delivered to smelters around the world which is estimated at 15 US mills per kW/h in mid-1983," and was to be adjusted in accordance with the supply of power to VALCO and the price of pri-mary aluminium. Similarly, on all the main issues the proposal sought to establish linkages with Ghana's position of principle.

Following a series of informal meetings at which Ghana obtained clarification of VALCO's position and satisfied itself that VALCO was ready for serious talks, the negotiations were resumed in January 1984. After a tentative start, the resumed talks proceeded in an atmosphere quite unlike that which had prevailed before the breakdown. With broad agreement on the principles for determining the power rate and other key issues, the discussion tended to concentrate on the development of formulas for operationalizing the principles, the determination of what further in-formation was needed, the elaboration and application of appropriate methods for assessing such information, and the checking and comparison of figures and other data. For this and other technical work the parties increasingly resorted to work-ing groups, with plenary sessions used for breaking deadlocks and clarifying the mandate of the working groups. The focus shifted more and more to narrowing gaps between the sides, and exploring and developing options. The emerging ele-ments began to be combined and traded off internally *within packages*, so that each side would proffer proposals on, say, all the financial issues – the power rate, the tolling charge, income, dividend, and interest taxes, and import duty – as a package. From this stage, the talks moved inexorably to the exchange of concessions on the key components of the competing packages, leading, finally, to the conclusion and initialing of an agreement on all the main issues on 10 July 1984.

4.4 Final Agreement

After a series of extended and surprisingly controversial drafting sessions, the final agreement was approved by the government, VRA, the shareholders, the various lenders, and others whose approval was required, and signed on 30 January 1985.

The final settlement provided for a base power rate of 17 mills per kW/h. By means of a complex formula this was indexed to the price of aluminium on the London Metal Exchange and adjusted by reference to the amount of energy made available to VALCO, subject to a minimum price of 10 mills per kW/h. Other elements of the package included:

- A reduction in the amount of energy guaranteed to VALCO by 15–17%, thereby increasing the amount available to Ghana for domestic use or export to higher-paying customers.
- The alteration of the tolling charge formula to increase the chances of VALCO dealing with its shareholders on the basis of arms-length pricing of services and supplies.
- The raising of the income tax rate from 40% to 46%, and the introduction of interest and dividend taxes.
- The replacement of the frozen law provision by one applying the current law of Ghana "and applicable rules of international law."
- The improvement of the prospects for an integrated aluminium industry by the reservation of power to introduce alumina duty under stated conditions.
- Substantial relaxation of exchange control restrictions on repatriation of VALCO profits by the shareholders.
- The introduction of a quinquennial review provision.

An intangible but very important outcome of the settlement was a vast improvement in relations between the shareholders and government, and in the overall atmosphere surrounding the VALCO operation. More tangibly, estimates of the total revenue gain to Ghana as a result of the changes, in a year of normal aluminium prices and full supply of energy to VALCO, ranged from US$23 million to US$43 million. Indeed, a study conducted for the government in 1988 showed that over the period January 1985 to October 1988 VALCO had paid VRA in excess of US$69 million more for power than it would have paid under the old agreement. This is apart from the extra revenue the government obtained from the sale of the energy saved as a result of the reduction of VALCO's guaranteed power, or more generally, from the new taxes.

At least as significant as these revenue gains was that once VALCO got back to full production, and made up the losses incurred during the shutdown, its profit position became very healthy. Indeed, aided by very high aluminium prices on the world market, VALCO recorded its highest annual profit ever in 1988, despite paying the new power rate and increased taxes. All this would suggest that despite, or because of, the contentiousness of the initial stages of the negotiations the final settlement must have struck about the right balance.

4.5   Economic Theories

The story of the renegotiation of the VALCO Agreement as told above has had to be greatly simplified for the purposes of this discussion. But it still presents some of the most interesting aspects of the negotiation and constitutes a basis for examining the relative value of neoclassical economic theory and negotiation theory in the explanation of international economic negotiations.

As the theory underlying neoclassical economic analysis deals primarily with macro-level aggregates, on the one hand, and, on the other, the "average" individual or organization, its utility as a basis for analyzing the process or predicting the outcome of a particular international economic negotiation must be limited. Potentially productive, though, is its assumption of rational choices made by economic actors aware of their interests and options, and acting in pursuit of those interests in competition with others acting similarly. The following analysis draws on some of its insights in examining the principal facts in the case.

4.5.1   Access to information

Given the financial strength, the sophistication, and the industry experience of VALCO's shareholders, and the official resources available to Ghana, access to essential information should not normally be a problem in a negotiation of this magnitude. As it turned out, VALCO had access to the bulk of the information needed to form sound judgments about all the matters under negotiation – from the history of the project and the details of its operation, to company and general aluminium industry information. While the same cannot be said about Ghana at the start of the negotiations, its negotiators made up any deficit fairly quickly. This was done partly through the use of expert consultants to gather information on a vast scale before the commencement of the talks and throughout the negotiations. The other source was VALCO itself, which, in response to written interrogatories administered in the course of the talks, supplied very detailed company and industry information. Thus both sides had or quickly acquired the bulk of the information needed for making informed decisions in pursuit of their economic and other interests in the negotiation. The critical issues for the application of economic theory to the analysis of the negotiations, therefore, relate less to access to information than to the identification and prioritization of interests by the parties, and the accuracy of their evaluation of the costs and benefits of alternative positions.

4.5.2 Identification and prioritization of interests

As to identification and prioritization of interests, Ghana, as already noted, opted for revenue maximization, primarily on the basis of an increase of the power rate and a reduction of VALCO's guaranteed energy supply. This meant giving lower priority to important concerns such as the integration of the aluminium industry, participation in VALCO's equity, and rigorous pollution control of smelter operations. At the same time it recognized the national interest in keeping VALCO as a baseload user of VRA energy, employer of labor, and net foreign exchange contributor. Therefore, both in framing its positions and in holding itself ready to consider evidence from VALCO about the impact of the various proposals on its profitability, Ghana took into account the need for VALCO to remain internationally competitive.

I cannot speak with equal certainty about how successful and consistent VALCO was in identifying and prioritizing its interests. But for the shareholders of VALCO, the principal concerns would surely have been to maintain the high profitability and total shareholder control of the company, and to secure the long-term stability of the investment by maintaining the relative insulation of the project while shielding it from public controversy by establishing a good corporate image in Ghana. What came across the table, especially in the first phase, however, was a single-minded concern for protecting the company's bottom line by preserving the advantages obtained under the old agreement. It is true that world aluminium prices at the time were not such as would dispose any aluminium producer to accept any increases in its costs with equanimity. In this sense VALCO's hard-line position would seem consistent with the dictates of basic economics. But it is not clear what conception of economic rationality accounts for VALCO's initial failure to see, and act on the basis, that its interest in a healthy bottom line could be secured at a level far below that of the proposals it was insisting on, especially after the April 1983 devaluation of the cedi. By not taking adequate account of the desperate economic situation of Ghana, the grave discontent over the one-sidedness of the agreement as it operated at the time, and any sense of "objective" justice other than that of acquired rights, VALCO was unable to maintain a credible negotiating position. Clearly, neither the course of the negotiations nor the outcome can be adequately explained by reference to economic theories alone. Too many of the determining factors lay outside the simple logic of the market.

4.6   Negotiation Theories

The analysis of the negotiations from the perspective of negotiation theory appears more productive, providing support for several of its better-known propositions, clarifying others, and generally yielding useful insights.

4.6.1   "Principled negotiation/firm flexibility"

The approach adopted by Ghana conforms remarkably well to the prescriptions of principled negotiation – the presentation of a principle of decision and the insistence on dealing at that level in the first instance, combined with a readiness to consider modifications necessary to accommodate the legitimate interests of all parties (in this case, indexation, adjustment, etc.): "hard on principle, soft on modalities." It also fits with Pruitt's notion of "firm flexibility": firm as to basic interests, flexible as to proposals (Pruitt, 1991:42).

On the other hand, VALCO may have paid the price of adopting a different approach. In the first place, by not separating its interests – in a profitable venture – from the positions it started with – minimal give on the power rate and other financial matters – it was unable to take advantage of the flexibility that resulted from the alteration of its bottom line by the massive devaluation of the cedi early in the negotiation. Second, by not grounding its positions firmly on principle, it had difficulty in dealing rationally and flexibly with the apparent clash between the logic of the averaging principle and the maintenance of its bottom line. In consequence, after it had rejected averaging in phase one, when compelled to adopt it in phase two VALCO seemed not to have any principled basis for defending its interests, and might have given away more than necessary.

4.6.2   The force of objective criteria

Ghana's development and insistence on the concept of the weighted average price as a basis for negotiating a power price under normal conditions was critical not only to the course of the negotiation but also to its outcome. It left VALCO little room for representing Ghana's position as arbitrary or unreasonable, and put the company very much on the defensive in trying to hold on to its "contractual rights." Moreover, it is difficult to think of any other concept that would have had the simplicity, robustness, and moral weight to sustain a threefold increase in the power rate, given the relationship of the parties and the conditions of the aluminium industry at the time.

Another striking feature was the consistency lent to Ghana's power rate proposal by this insistence on principle. At the end of two years of hard negotiation,

the agreed base power rate was 17 mills, compared to the 22 mills originally proposed by Ghana. When it is considered that, as a result of the closure of many
high-cost smelters in 1983 and concessions on the categories of smelters included,
the weighted average power price, as calculated by Ghana and incorporated in its
proposals by March 1984, had dropped to 18 mills, the robustness of the proposal
is quite remarkable.

4.6.3   The Negotiator's Dilemma

In negotiating terms, the devaluation of the cedi and the consequent elimination of
the exchange rate tax could be considered to have increased the chances for a win–
win situation by enlarging the VALCO "pie." At the same time, though, it placed
VALCO on the horns of the Negotiator's Dilemma: to insist on the maximum gain
and reduce the chances of agreement, or to soften its position and improve the
chances of a negotiated settlement. VALCO chose the horn of plenty, and paid
quite a price.

   What considerations influenced VALCO's choice? For a start, since the devaluation "windfall" had not been conceded to it at the negotiating table, the company
probably saw no point in making any concession for it – why "pay" for something obtained "free"? On this view, far from seeing the removal of the exchange
rate tax as weakening its case against paying a higher price for power, and, in any
event, making a negotiated settlement easier by enlarging the "pie," VALCO saw
it as weakening Ghana's bargaining position. The result was that VALCO lost all
interest in the averaging principle, and repudiated it in the disastrous third round.

   In further explanation of VALCO's reaction, note might be taken of VALCO's
complaint that by the third round its move from 5 through 10 to 12 mills had not
been reciprocated by Ghana, which had maintained its proposal at 22 mills from the
start. Clearly VALCO did not see Ghana's agreement to explore the indexation and
adjustment issues as a concession consistent with principle, perhaps because the
"concession" had been in the Ghana position paper from the start. This reflected a
failure to appreciate the implications of Ghana's posture of principled negotiation,
which posited that as long as correct application of the agreed principle yielded a
22 mill rate, there was no reason to alter that figure before the stage of concession
trading within and between packages had been reached. Again, by looking for
reciprocation only in movements in the base rate, thereby ignoring concessions
in other areas that could mean quite substantial reductions in the operational rate,
VALCO, in a sense, misapplied the Reciprocity Assumption.

4.6.4   Negative commitment and the use of pressure

The tactical significance of the breakdown of the talks and the shutdown of VALCO should be noted. In the first place, the timing of the curtailment of power supply to VALCO and the uncertainty about when, or in the circumstances whether, it would be restored, gave Ghana considerable leverage in the waiting game.

Second, it is important to note that Ghana did not act in a fit of anger or pique. The measures it took were carefully considered and the consequences assessed in advance against the possibility of the talks going the way they did in the third round. Ghana's positions on all the main issues had been so crafted as to be defensible before the international community, the aluminium industry, and international financial circles at any time. Apart from ascertaining that its package would reduce but not eliminate VALCO's competitiveness, Ghana also satisfied itself that Kaiser, the principal shareholder of VALCO, would not lightly walk away from a subsidiary that was still the lowest-cost supplier of primary metal to its fabricating plant in the United States and to its customers elsewhere, especially in view of the shutdown of most of its smelters in other parts of the world.

It is worth emphasizing that Ghana was not pressing for acceptance of its proposed principle, much less its specific power rate proposal. Its concern was to ensure that the parties joined issue on the basis of principle.

A fourth aspect of Ghana's actions was the confirmation that Ghana was not prepared to settle at any price. As the packages on offer and in prospect were little better than the status quo, Ghana's BATNA was a unilateral imposition of the most reasonable package consistent with its basic interests, obviously at the risk of litigation by VALCO and its shareholders. This outcome, though not the preferred option, had been under consideration from before the initiation of the negotiations. In any event, for reasons already given, litigation by VALCO was considered an unlikely outcome.

Finally, the measures, as well as the barely concealed threat of unilateral action, can be seen as a vigorous exercise in "negative commitment." It indicated decisively that while Ghana was prepared to accommodate the legitimate concerns of VALCO, it would not deal otherwise than on principle. It would not accept VALCO's bottom line as the yardstick for determining outcomes, nor would it be bullied into accepting a deal that denied its basic interests. At the same time, the last proposals were not withdrawn but left on the table.

This tactic had the effect of compelling VALCO to confront the real choices and settle down to serious principled negotiation. Given the common interest of all parties in a negotiated, rather than a unilateral, settlement the tactic can, thus, be said to have been effective and successful.

4.6.5 Integrative negotiation/joint determination of outcomes

The contrast between the two phases of the negotiations sheds some light on the value as well as the limitations of integrative negotiation and joint determination of outcomes as ideal types. From the very start VALCO sought to introduce the form of joint problem solving through the use of working groups, even though neither side was at that stage dealing with the substantive issues in a problem-solving manner. In view of the gap between the parties on both basic principles and specific proposals, Ghana rejected this suggestion, insisting that working groups were best used for technical discussions or the development of options within broadly agreed parameters. Thus, the first three rounds of talks took the form mainly of plenary sessions, and, in substance, were an increasingly bitter struggle over guiding principles.

In contrast to this, the fourth and fifth rounds made extensive use of working groups to undertake technical tasks, narrow the gaps between the sides, and develop options. As the talks progressed the overall negotiating atmosphere became increasingly informal and cooperative, though both sides remained hard headed in the actual negotiation. Once the principles of decision on the main issues had been settled, and the positions of the parties had converged as far as argumentation and persuasion could take them – but not before – the talks moved steadily through a problem-solving stage into a concessionary negotiation mode. The final stages of the negotiations saw the rapid convergence of the two sets of positions through the exchange of concessions on the key components of the competing packages, culminating in the conclusion of an agreement.

4.6.6 Ripeness

Finally, a word about the notion of "ripeness." This can be seen as providing an overarching explanation of the course of the negotiations. With the benefit of hindsight, it can be said that neither the relationship of the parties, particularly the history of easy VALCO victories in previous power rate negotiations with the VRA, nor the dynamics of the exchanges at the negotiating table had set the scene by May 1983 for the negotiation of an outcome acceptable to both sides, especially Ghana. The situation was simply not "ripe" for a negotiated settlement. It took a combination of factors external to the negotiations – the devaluation of the Ghana cedi and improvements in world aluminium price projections, on the positive side, and the collapse of the talks and the shutdown of VALCO on the negative side, among others – to restore momentum and create conditions for more cooperative negotiations and a successful settlement.

A weakness of the notion of ripeness as a practical tool for negotiators is that the ripeness of a situation for a negotiated resolution can only be definitively determined ex post facto. Nevertheless, the concept can help in the characterization of the dynamics of a negotiation as it evolves. Where parties are aware of the notion and test evolving trends for ripeness, there is greater likelihood that they can read the signs and anticipate the kind of impasse faced in the third round, and more consciously manipulate the off-the-table factors that alone hold the key, in most cases, to breaking the deadlock and making the situation ripe.

4.7 Conclusion

The first conclusion from this analysis of the renegotiation of the VALCO Agreement is that economic theory by itself is inadequate to the task of analyzing and explaining complex international economic negotiations. This is hardly surprising because, apart from market considerations, the negotiating context takes in factors of history and political power balances, as well as micro factors such as the personality and disposition of key parties to the negotiation, and the degree of technical preparation and skill.

On the other hand, this case study confirms such key propositions of negotiation theory as the force of objective criteria, and sheds light on the limitations of such notions as ripeness and joint problem solving in a situation of widely divergent starting positions.

But perhaps its most significant contribution will be to our appreciation of the strengths and limitations of the concept of principled negotiation. It demonstrates beyond doubt the critical value of the concept not only as a theoretical construct, but also as an operational guide. In this case it proved of value not simply to the party applying it, but actually to both sides in helping to secure an outcome that, in the end, was hailed even by VALCO – an outcome that could probably not have been attained any other way.

It is necessary and instructive, however, to specify some of the main conditions for the successful execution of principled negotiation in this case. The first of these would be the basic fairness of the proposed principle – asking an international company to pay for a key service at the rate paid on average by similar companies worldwide, subject to allowances for special handicaps arising from local circumstances. The second would be the technical soundness of the method for applying that principle, especially in relation to the compilation and analysis of the list of smelters and their characteristics. Third, throughout the negotiations Ghana made explicit its openness to accommodating the basic interests of VALCO, demonstrating this by the early fleshing out of the indexation and adjustment dimensions of its proposal. All these together laid a good basis for the cooperative exploration of options.

Significantly, although the main elements were present by the end of the first round, and one side was anxious to proceed on the basis of principled problem solving throughout, it took the shock of the collapse of the talks and the firm demonstration of Ghana's refusal to deal otherwise than on principle to create the conditions for successful principled negotiation.

Finally, this case study lends support to the proposition that in international economic negotiations, a party's economic and technical weakness need not always translate into a negative outcome.

Section 2

Macroeconomic Issues

Chapter 5

Understanding Nigeria's Economic Reform Experience: An Application of Negotiation Theory

*Bright E. Okogu**

5.1   Introduction

Neoclassical economic theory has made a strong comeback in developing countries since the 1980s, when most of them pursued a mixed economy strategy and a few, such as Angola, Ethiopia, Mozambique, and Nicaragua, officially had a central planning system. During that decade, several of them adopted economic reform packages in the form of structural adjustment programs (SAP) fashioned by the IMF and the World Bank. This trend was further deepened from 1989 on when the central planning approach to economic management collapsed with the demise of the former Soviet Union and socialist Eastern Europe, and these countries subsequently adopted market orthodoxies. Together with developing countries, these nations are currently undergoing economic reforms based on free market doctrines.

The adoption of an SAP has become a prerequisite for obtaining credit on the international financial market, or for rescheduling existing debts and gaining

*This paper was written while the author was on the staff of OPEC.

entitlement to debt relief packages such as the Brady plan, the World Bank's special program of assistance, and the Toronto and Trinidad initiatives. At the center of these reforms are the conditionality policies aimed at opening up the economy and imposing monetary and fiscal discipline. These measures are considered capable of bringing about internal and external equilibrium. However, the adoption of these policies, almost without exception, has resulted in a drastic depreciation of the exchange rate of the countries in question, along with rising unemployment and inflation, resulting in severe hardship on the population, especially in the short-to-medium term.

Current scholarship on the subject of structural adjustment has reached a consensus on the need for these reforms: a situation of persistent disequilibrium is clearly unsustainable. There is, however, less agreement on the method, pace, policy mix, and conditionality (see, for example, the criticisms by UNECA, 1989). For instance, there is considerable doubt whether developing countries that have a weak export base and depend heavily on intermediate imported inputs can benefit much from a policy of devaluation that is meant to promote exports. In other words, do the conditions exist in these countries for a fulfillment of the Marshall–Lerner elasticity condition? On the sociopolitical front, these policies carry considerable risk (Cooper, 1971), as experience from adjusting countries – from Algeria to Venezuela, from Russia to Zambia – continues to show. Invariably, these countries have been forced to deviate from the pure market path. The presumption that the market, as a unique social institution, will always tend to equilibrium is challenged by the evidence; therefore, we must use alternative theories, such as negotiation theory, to try to understand the dynamics of the underlying complex interactions. The reality is that the economy is operating away from classical saddle-point equilibrium, as the government tries to strike a balance between the theoretically ideal set of policies and what is acceptable to interested social forces at home.

In order to study the subject, this chapter draws on the paradigm and experience of SAP in Nigeria, with special (but not exclusive) focus on exchange rate management. An offshoot of the Nigerian case study is that it provides an opportunity to observe the practice of negotiation under a highly centralized military government. Is the process necessarily easier under such a system? The continued depreciation of the Nigerian currency – the naira – under the program has resulted in great hardship for the population; yet the value of the naira is still significantly higher than the "equilibrium" level dictated by the free market, and the level that multilateral credit institutions would like to see. In trying to strike a balance between the two positions, the government has had to listen to the contending interest groups, both domestic and foreign. As often happens in such a situation, in an attempt to please everyone, the government has succeeded in alienating most groups. For example, a majority of ordinary Nigerians are unhappy because the effective exchange rate for them is the parallel market rate, which is much lower than the official rate; multi-lateral institutions and creditors, on the other hand, are unhappy because they point out that the official rate is too high relative to the free market rate.

A number of specific questions arise at this point. How did the system come to settle at such an obvious state of economic disequilibrium? Is economic theory a reliable predictor of real life behavior? How does the government of a less developed country enlist the support of its people in implementing a program it has agreed to with foreign creditors and which must bring so much hardship to them? How have the different interest groups and positions been placated so far in the face of their clear dissatisfaction with the existing situation? Do alternative theories, such as negotiation theory, provide a better explanation of the outcome of complex economic problems?

The rest of the chapter will be devoted to answering these and related questions. First, though, we analyze the theory and practice of the SAP in Nigeria (Section 5.2), while Section 5.3 touches on the exchange rate system, with a view to bringing out the predictions of economic theory vis-à-vis the "correct" exchange rate. A comparative analysis of the official and market-predicted rates sets the scene for Section 5.4, which looks at the process of negotiation between the Nigerian government and creditor institutions on the one hand, and on the other hand, between the government and social groups in Nigeria to whom it tried to sell the program. Section 5.5 concludes the study.

5.2 Theory and Practice of the SAP in Nigeria

The necessity for the adoption of a program of economic reforms in Nigeria became indisputable by the mid-1980s, following clear signs of serious structural imbalances in the system. The world oil market had become weak since 1981, leading to a substantial rise in the deficits in the foreign account. Foreign reserves, which had been in a relatively healthy state in 1979 and 1980, had become depleted to the extent that, by 1982, they were only enough to cover one month of imports. By the end of 1983, the foreign debt stood at about $18.54 billion, with a debt–export ratio of 170.8%.

At the theoretical level, the roots of the Nigerian economic difficulty can be traced to the effect of the Dutch Disease syndrome, where a booming oil sector created a new set of unsustainable relative prices between the traded and nontraded sectors of the economy (see, among others, Corden, 1981; Corden and Neary, 1982; Neary and Van Wijnbergen, 1986; Benjamin *et al.*, 1986). The basic mechanism of the model is as follows: the booming (oil) sector results in a spending effect that pushes up all domestic prices. However, the price of the traded goods sector is determined by the equivalent world price of this good and the nominal exchange rate. Thus, it cannot rise beyond the world price level because of competition from imports.

On the other hand, the price of the nontraded goods sector is not similarly constrained; it will rise to whatever level is determined by the domestic demand–supply interactions, since these goods are not traded internationally. You cannot import a haircut, for instance! This relatively higher increase in the price of the nontraded sector is equivalent to a rise in the exchange rate of the local currency. The traded goods sector becomes uncompetitive as relatively cheaper imports flood in, thus leading to deficits in the trade balance. At the same time, local entrepreneurs find it more profitable to shift resources away from the traded goods sector to the nontraded goods sector and/or trading activities related to importation. Further, if the proceeds from the booming sector are not sterilized, the domestic money supply increases at an even faster rate, leading to even more domestic demand for both traded and nontraded goods, and thus exacerbating the initial currency appreciation.

In the Nigerian experience, all of these influences were evident. The oil boom started in earnest in the early 1970s, and reached a peak in 1979/80 during the second oil price shock. Prior to this period, agriculture had dominated the economy in terms of its contribution to gross domestic product (GDP), employment, and foreign exchange earnings. Since then, the situation has changed. The agricultural sector in particular has suffered a serious reversal as a diversion of resources to trading activities and petty contracts, as well as rural-urban migration, took their toll. Similarly, the naira appreciated in real terms against major world currencies during the same period, making imports cheap and attractive.

It was against this background that Nigeria adopted the SAP in 1986. The conditions underlying the program constitute the building blocks of the reform policies as practiced in all countries undergoing such a restructuring exercise. These are trade liberalization, a freely functioning foreign exchange market, the phase-out of state subsidies, reduced government intervention in the economy, and fiscal discipline leading to an eventual elimination of budget deficits.

The theoretical justification for trade liberalization and a free foreign exchange market stems from the commonly accepted notion of the superiority of free trade to autarky. Whatever seems to facilitate the process, such as free access to international media of exchange, should be judged superior to other alternatives. The third requirement centers on the need for efficient allocation and use of resources as dictated by the price mechanism, while the last two conditions arise from the belief that the state should concentrate on providing an enabling environment for business that is run and dominated by the private sector. In other words, the government should limit itself to providing and maintaining necessary infrastructure – roads, water, electricity, some basic level of health and education – as well as security, law and order, and so on. Obviously, this is an extreme representation of the true position as, admittedly, there are varying degrees of free market arrangements. The individual in this stylized society is assumed to know best and, in pursuing his own best interests, will also therefore maximize society's interests. According to this dictum, a government adopting this minimalist approach will be better able to balance its books.

It is easy to see the monetarist orthodoxy underlying the SAP as currently practiced. The role of monetary and fiscal policies under the program is also, predictably, expected to be minimalist. Friedman (1968), for example, denies any long-term benefit of a deliberate monetary expansion, and rational expectationists (Lucas, 1975; Sargent, 1998; Barro, 1977; among others) explicitly argue that such a policy can only be inflationary without yielding any benefits of real output growth.

A related matter is that the internal and external disequilibrium symptomatic of the adjusting economies – domestic and foreign debt – could be reduced or eliminated as a result of implementing these policies. The underlying theory behind the debt issue, which is really a result of persistent deficit in the external account, is well covered in the international economics literature. The absorption approach to the balance of payments, for example, sees this imbalance as arising from a situation where the domestic aggregate demand of an economy (absorption) is greater than its real productive capacity (see Alexander, 1952). Thus, a squeeze on domestic consumption would release resources for meeting such debt obligations.

The debate between monetarists and competing schools of thought is well known in the literature, and it is not our intention to address the subject in this paper. Abstracting from the dialectics regarding the position of this doctrine vis-à-vis others, there are doubts, at both the theoretical and policy levels, as to whether a wholesale application of these policies to developing countries is capable of producing the expected results, given the structural peculiarities of their economies.

An example of this problem can be seen in the issue of devaluation, which is normally expected to result in an improved trade balance, working through the medium of import and export elasticities. The underlying theory of a freely floating exchange rate system is that it will eliminate excess demand and supply through appropriate adjustments in the "price" of the currency. Having found its equilibrium level, the exchange rate would ensure an efficient allocation of scarce resources as indicated by the principle of "willingness to pay." We have argued elsewhere (Okogu, 1992) that "willingness to pay" very often translates into "ability to pay," meaning that those who can afford to bid for foreign exchange at the free market rate may not necessarily be those that will use it efficiently in the development sense. This is exacerbated by the very skewed income distribution in many developing countries, which makes it possible for mostly the rich to bid for scarce foreign currency and use it to import luxuries.

The expected efficiency is manifested in increased exports and reduced imports of goods and services, increased investment and, consequently, output, as well as a reduction in transaction costs (bureaucratic allocation of foreign exchange with its attendant potential for abuse, queues, and so on). According to this approach, the anticipated result, subject to certain assumptions about elasticities, is an improvement in the balance of payments – irrespective of whether the analysis is based on the traditional elasticities approach, the absorption approach, or the monetary approach to the balance of payments (Marshall, 1924; Lerner, 1944; Harberger, 1950; Alexander, 1952; Frenkel and Johnson, 1976).

The reality is that the so-called Marshall–Lerner elasticity criterion is not always met for these countries. The export sector is usually weak, because it is dominated by agriculture and raw materials with highly volatile international prices; there is a high import content in the input mix of the industrial and commercial sector; the marginal propensity to import is quite high, and so on. These factors have commonly been identified in the literature as contributing to the failure of adjustment policies (see, among others, Cooper, 1971; Krugman and Taylor, 1978; Porter and Ranney, 1982; Osagie, 1986; Ajayi, 1986; Okogu, 1987, 1992).

In its own adjustment program, Nigeria adopted most of the conditions indicated earlier. Trade was largely liberalized except in the case of certain grains, wheat, and a few other items. Manufacturers were required to buy increasing amounts of their raw materials locally, as in the case of the breweries, which substituted local grains for imported barley. In many cases, though, manufacturers were forced not by the government, but by the deteriorating exchange rate, to look inward. In connection with export policy, the guidelines have oscillated over the years between allowing exporters to keep all of their foreign exchange earnings and making it mandatory for them to return such earnings to the country.

The naira was allowed to float when the two-tier exchange rate system was introduced in September 1986, with government transactions occurring at the more favorable exchange rate. Although it was a free market in theory, the government intervened from time to time in order to prevent the exchange rate from exceeding some unstated bound. For example, at the sixth weekly auction, the government intervened when the naira fell below N5=$1 for the first time, accusing the authorized banks of "bidding too highly." The next open intervention came on 12 February 1987, this time because the value of the currency was too high, at N3=$1. On this occasion, the government fixed the exchange rate at N3.50=$1. Initially, the Central Bank of Nigeria (CBN) made $50 million available per week. This was soon raised to $75 million, as demand far outstripped supply. By July 1987, the rates in the two windows were allowed to converge at N3.54=$1. The value of the naira has continued to deteriorate since then, reaching an official rate of about N22=$1 in 1993 and staying at that level until it was abolished in 1999.

Since 1986, several developments have taken place that are worth mentioning. First, starting in 1988, the government issued a number of licences to nonbank agents for the operation of bureaux de change. Second, various nonbank financial institutions (many of them owned by established banks or their senior officers), which took deposits and specialized in short-term business financing, came into existence. The number of commercial and merchant banking institutions rose from just a handful in 1986 to over 120 in 1993. This banking explosion can be attributed to the flawed operation of the foreign exchange market. There was a wide spread between the official exchange rate on the one hand, and both the bureau and parallel market rates on the other, thus creating huge opportunities for arbitrage. As of the end of 1993, for example, the bureau/parallel market rate commanded a 100% premium over the official rate. The gap has widened further since then. Buying and selling foreign exchange came to form the core of banking business in Nigeria.

The 1994 budget introduced new controls, including outlawing parallel market operations and prohibiting bureaux de change and banks from foreign exchange dealings in their own right. Instead, they were to become agents of the CBN, earning only a small commission on such transactions. Because of these changes, some of the banks ran into difficulties, resulting in the liquidation of unviable ones.

Regarding the other three conditions, the government has sold off many of its holdings in flour mills, cement factories, insurance companies, hotels, distilleries, and so on since the issue of Privatization Decree number 25 of 1988. Similarly, it has made significant strides since 1994 in phasing out subsidies, particularly in the contentious area of petroleum product pricing. The deficit in the government account remains large, however, because of other problems in the economy.

5.3 Exchange Rate Behavior Under SAP

The operation of the foreign exchange market is the core of the adjustment program in Nigeria, and exchange rate behavior has become the barometer by which the public has measured the success or failure of the whole program. Consequently, the sharp decline of the naira exchange rate since the inception of the program in 1986 (from N1=$1.50 in 1985 to about N85=$1 in 1998) has caused great tension in the Nigerian society. Using elements of negotiation theory, we shall analyze the dynamics of how Nigeria has maintained such a contentious system over the years in its diverse social setting, and how the contending social groups have been mollified. In order to situate the discussion properly within that theory, however, we must first take a closer look at the behavior of the official exchange rate, and its deviation from the level dictated by pure market theory.

The demand for foreign currency in the formal sector depends on the domestic money supply, because this will determine effective demand for foreign exchange.

In the same vein, the demand for foreign exchange is derived demand; it depends on the value of required imports of goods and services. The equilibrium in the money sector is:

$$M^d = M^s, \tag{5.1}$$

where M^d and M^s represent the demand for, and supply of money respectively. But M^d is a function of income Y; price P; and the interest rate R. Thus,

$$M^d = M^d(Y, P, R) = M^s. \tag{5.2}$$

A tight monetary policy, for example, in the form of a higher central bank discount rate or contractionary open market operations, will have the effect of reducing the money supply as market agents adjust their portfolios. This will reduce the effective demand for foreign exchange and, ceteris paribus, strengthen the value of the local currency. In general terms, the demand for foreign currency is cast as a function of the exchange rate and volume of imports M, as well as of the domestic money supply situation. On the other hand, the supply, which is under the control and monopoly of the central bank, is also a function of the "price" (exchange rate E) and availability of foreign currency F. The inverse relationship between demand and price is obvious, but the relationship between supply and price does not have the usual positive coefficient because the motivation of the CBN is not necessarily to maximize its naira earnings per dollar sold. Indeed, it is clear that it sometimes operates with a view to protecting the value of the naira. It should, however, be noted that the negative relationship between current supply and the exchange rate is a weak one because the government faces a very tight constraint in this respect.

Finally, the current supply of foreign exchange depends on the lagged exchange rate, as the government is assumed to base today's decision on its experience in the previous period. This is analogous to the case of agricultural goods, where current output (supply) depends on the price in the last period when the planting decision was taken. In the present case, the government's objective is to prevent the exchange rate from moving beyond some predetermined policy band – an objective that it tries to achieve by varying the supply of foreign currency, subject to availability (in the case of increasing supplies). Thus the equations are as follows:

$$Qd = a - bE + cM + dY - eR \tag{5.3}$$

$$Qs = f - gE_{t-1} + hF. \tag{5.4}$$

At equilibrium, the market-clearing exchange rate is determined by equating demand to supply in order to produce a single first-order difference equation, that is,

$$gE_{t-1} - bE_t = f - a + hF_t - cM_t - dY_t + eR_t. \tag{5.5}$$

Rearranging terms, we have

$$
\begin{aligned}
E_t &= \frac{(gE_{t-1} + f - a - hF_t + cM_t + dY_t - eR_t)}{b} \\
&= \frac{g}{b}(E_{t-1}) + \frac{1}{b}(a - f + cM_t - hF_t + dY_t - eR_t).
\end{aligned}
\tag{5.6}
$$

Equation 5.6 is the dynamic (intertemporal) equilibrium exchange rate path of the above model, and shows the nature of the relationship between the current exchange rate and determining variables. The parameters b and g denote the slopes of the demand and supply curves respectively, with $g/b > 1$ because the foreign exchange supply curve is inelastic relative to demand, reflecting the scarcity of this resource. Similarly, $a - f$ represents the intercept, while c, h, d, e are parameters reflecting the link between the equilibrium exchange rate and the relevant variables.

From the above, it is clear that the exchange rate at any point in time is a function of the amount of foreign currency earned by the government (supply factor), the demand for imports, the GDP, and domestic interest rates (demand factors). Also of implicit importance are the elasticities underlying the coefficients, such as the proportion of export earnings the government decides to put up for sale (itself determined by many factors, including the debt situation); as well as domestic monetary, fiscal and trade policies. It is not central to our purpose in this chapter to assess the relative strengths of the variables identified above, for example, through regression estimates. Rather, we are more interested in obtaining indications of what the pure per-period market-determined equilibrium exchange rate would be in the absence of intervention, so as to provide a basis for comparison with actual rates.

Because we lack reliable parameter values, the equilibrium exchange rate in equation (5.6) cannot be calculated directly. Instead, we take the parallel market/bureau rates as proxy, since they provide the closest representation of a free market at which the forces implied in equation (5.6) play themselves out. These are presented in *Table 5.1*, along with the official rates, the demand for and supply of foreign exchange. It can be seen that the "pure" market equilibrium exchange rate, as approximated by the parallel market rate, differs substantially from the official ("negotiated") rate; the system has persistently failed to produce a convergence between the official and parallel/interbank rates over the years, thereby violating one of the conditions of the reform package. Economic theory thus appears to be a poor predictor of reality. How is the difference to be explained?

Table 5.1. Market rates, 1989–1993.

Period	Supply (US$)	Demand (US$)	Official rate (N per $)	Parallel market rate (N per $)	Spread (%)
1989 Q1	128.70	597.83	7.40	10.51	42.03
1989 Q2	161.60	1308.80	7.48	10.58	41.44
1989 Q3	254.87	1960.87	7.25	10.30	42.07
1989 Q4	254.17	1911.60	7.51	10.66	41.94
1990 Q1	253.33	1642.10	7.90	9.48	20.00
1990 Q2	196.23	1267.07	7.94	9.53	20.03
1990 Q3	197.43	1615.40	7.96	9.55	19.97
1990 Q4	235.03	2207.63	8.34	10.02	20.14
1991 Q1	308.93	866.57	9.43	12.99	37.75
1991 Q2	253.33	729.50	9.47	13.05	37.80
1991 Q3	252.43	755.57	10.95	15.09	37.81
1991 Q4	238.10	799.13	9.87	13.60	37.79
1992 Q1	387.90	839.63	12.49	18.23	45.96
1992 Q2	313.67	936.62	18.57	19.44	4.68
1992 Q3	518.23	1248.82	18.85	20.81	10.40
1992 Q4	473.67	1414.27	19.59	22.84	16.59
1993 Q1	n.a	n.a	22.28	28.19	26.53
1993 Q2	n.a	n.a	22.22	34.86	56.89
1993 Q3	n.a	n.a	21.89	37.65	72.00
1993 Q4	n.a	n.a	21.89	43.91	100.59

Source: Central Bank of Nigeria, Lagos.

5.4 Bridging the Gap Between Theory and Reality: The Role of Negotiations

The SAP has been a source of tremendous tension in Nigerian society – between the government and the governed, between different social classes, and between the government and the country's international creditors. The Bretton Woods institutions are displeased with the government on grounds that the measures taken so far have not gone far enough. For example, they have long expressed the wish to see a convergence between official and free market exchange rates as a prelude to further devaluation. This section seeks to explain the role of negotiations in reaching the present "equilibrium" between the government and multilateral institutions on the one hand, and between the government and Nigerians on the other.

5.4.1 Vertical negotiation: Nigerian government versus the IMF/World Bank

Negotiation theory seeks to provide an understanding of the dynamics by which corporate entities, such as the state, reach an agreement with other entities in economic, political or security matters, and of the process of reconciling and/or satisfying the competing or opposing domestic interest groups that may be affected by the outcome. In its simplest form, international negotiations can be seen as a two-party, one-issue game – each party, in most cases, consisting of many interest groups. The task facing the policymaker in such a situation can be seen at two levels: the domestic level and the international level (see, for example, Putnam, 1988). The former involves reconciling the positions of the diverse domestic constituencies and coming up with a common position that then forms the basis of negotiation at the second – international – level with other sovereign entities.

The main issue at stake in the negotiation of Nigeria's adjustment was whether the government would accept the conditions (exchange rate liberalization/devaluation, removal of subsidies, trade liberalization, and a tightening of monetary and fiscal policies) laid out by the IMF. From the government's point of view, it was clear that fulfilling these conditions carried enormous political risks; moreover, it did not want to be seen as giving in to such demands, because this would amount to surrendering some of its sovereignty. By 1986, the oil price collapse had shown how vulnerable Nigeria was, and creditors knew it only too well. Foreign exchange reserves were low, and new lines of credit were needed to continue to feed the import-dependent economy. The new government also needed to sustain the wave of popular support it was then enjoying.

The creditors, as represented by the Bretton Woods institutions, had a clear objective: to fulfill their historical mandate. However, they were very conscious that they were dealing with a sovereign state with veto power over the issues being negotiated. The efficacy of this veto is, however, limited because the adjusting country cannot hope to participate fully in the world economy unless it gets a clean bill of health from these institutions. The negotiation was an example of bilateral monopoly bargaining with a typical indeterminate outcome where the settlement point depends on the relative bargaining strengths of both parties and their ability to hold out, use threats, bluffs and counterbluffs, and so on. Unlike the typical distributive case, the outcome preferred by the creditor side in this instance was a win–win situation. The creditors did not seek to foist a policy on the country that might turn out to be more than it could handle; a country facing instability as a result of conditions imposed for adjustment is no good to anyone.

The strategy of the IMF, as usual, was to draw up tight conditions that the government had to meet, and at a rapid pace. It would help the process along by providing credit facilities as long as the reform was implemented as prescribed;

otherwise, it would withhold support and ask other creditors to do the same. It encouraged the government to get various interest groups involved as stakeholders so as to win their support. The Fund was, no doubt, aware that the government might not be able to meet the conditions or stick to the recommended pace, but it was a good point to start the negotiation.

The Nigerian government would have liked its debt rescheduling and other benefits to occur at minimum cost to the country, but this was clearly not possible and, in any case, it had come to recognize the objective fact that the economy needed reform. The government's strategy was to implement the reform, but at a pace that would not threaten the country's social and political stability. In this regard, a two-tier exchange rate system was to be maintained using the secure (though dwindling) oil revenues to finance it, thereby retaining some of the implicit subsidy. Further, it could always play the democracy card, as the reform program was cast as an integral part of the transition exercise. It could expect a sympathetic hearing from the international community, and the influential political class at home, eager for a return to civil rule, would support the program. The government certainly underestimated the extent of reform necessary, and how long it would take before results were felt. For example, the original SAP document set a 24-month time frame as the time required for the gains of SAP to materialize. It was in this frame of mind that the negotiation battle was joined in 1986, and both sides played on their knowledge of the other party's strengths and weaknesses.

In general, domestic differences can work either in favor of the country or against it in international negotiations, depending on the nature of the issue at stake. Mayer (1992), using the distinction first advanced by Walton and McKersie in 1965, distinguishes between *distributive* and *integrative* bargaining issues. A distributive bargaining strategy, sometimes known as competitive strategy (Dupont and Faure, 1991), is one where each party seeks to maximize its share of a given value, while an integrative strategy, also referred to as value-creating (Lax and Sebenius, 1986) or collaborative (Thomas, 1976), is one where both parties work toward creating joint value. In the former, domestic constraints can, in some cases, be a useful tool in the negotiating arsenal of a party: "Having one's hands tied can be quite useful in extracting concessions from an opponent in negotiation" (Mayer, 1992:796). In the latter, it can be a drawback, as the required room for flexibility is denied the negotiator. The application of these cases is relatively straightforward in most international bargaining processes; for example, during the EU–USA trade negotiations in the last days of the Uruguay Round GATT talks (November/December 1993) the United States, in order to extract value from its opponents, repeatedly cited pressure from Congress and its negotiating deadline.

In the case of a nation-state negotiating with multilateral institutions on issues of structural adjustment, the distinction is not quite so obvious; the negotiation contains a mixture of integrative and distributive elements. It is integrative in that a successful economic reform program will increase global welfare, transform the material conditions of the adjusting country and endow it with new prestige and power, while for the multilateral institutions such a success could be held up as an achievement – a fulfillment of one of their *raisons d'être*. Similarly, it is distributive to the extent that it could result in a transfer of resources from LDCs to creditor countries and multilateral financial institutions in the form of debt repayment, and so on. There is a pervasive belief in indebted developing countries – right or wrong – that a primary purpose of the ongoing economic reforms is to squeeze as much debt repayment as possible from them. This view has some logic, because under the absorption approach to the balance of payments, a devaluation is supposed to lead to a reduction in domestic absorption, thereby freeing resources for the external sector (see Alexander, 1952). However, the gains from the adjustment process, if it succeeds, are in the distant future; the present carries mostly hardship. The attitude of social groups regarding the program thus depends on their discount rate – how they value the stream of future gains relative to present comfort. Generally, the lower the income of an individual, ceteris paribus, the higher the discount rate (Fisher, 1930).

The exchange rate model presented in the previous section gives an indication of the exchange rate that the creditor side wanted to see as far as the devaluation requirement is concerned; it always argued for a quick convergence between the official and open market rates. Similarly, the immediate removal of subsidies for petroleum and other commodities was a recurrent theme, as this was seen as the key to balancing the public accounts. These conditions were unacceptable to the government, especially in terms of the timing, and it resisted by playing the threat-to-stability card.

In bilateral bargaining, it is common for both sides to use threats and counter-threats, bluffs and counterbluffs, to extract concessions from the other party. At the negotiating table with its creditors, the government utilized some of these instruments. For example, Nigeria threatened to limit its debt-service ratio unilaterally to about 20% in 1991 and again in 1992 when negotiations with creditors stalled – a threat that was soon actualized, as the country has fallen behind in its debt repayments since that time. Similarly, it tried to link the policy requirements of adjustment to the survival of the Nigerian state. In his 1992 budget speech, President Babangida, explaining to creditors why Nigeria deserved relief, stated that: "The Nation cannot survive, or engage in any other developmental activities, if indeed it pays out as much as [the estimated] $5.565 billion on debt service." This was at a time when the government was at an advanced stage of its program of transition to civilian rule, later aborted for reasons unrelated to the economic reform process. The government also dropped several hints regarding the need not to rock the democratization boat.

Similarly, the government pulled back at the last moment, many times, from removing the subsidy on petroleum products – a major policy disagreement between it and Bretton Woods institutions – arguing each time that the political atmosphere was not right. In fairness to the government, there had been riots or threats of strikes and civil disorder whenever it appeared that the policy might be implemented. Although the creditor institutions have never accepted the continued petroleum subsidies in Nigeria, the government has managed to extract concessions in the form of their tacit acquiescence by citing domestic opposition. On their part, the IMF/World Bank made it clear that Nigeria could not expect relief until it implemented the adjustment satisfactorily. As of July 1996, for example, the IMF had refused to approve Nigeria's medium-term economic program, and this took a toll on international confidence in the economy. However, the Nigerian government continued to hold out and to call the bluff of the IMF/World Bank up to a point, using its secure oil revenues as a buffer.

In the end, both sides had to make concessions. Nigeria has had to allow the interbank naira exchange rate to depreciate to levels that had been unthinkable just a few years before (in 1998, it was about N85 to the dollar), although the official rate, reserved for government transactions alone, stayed at N22 to the dollar (a concession by the creditor side). This also meant that the government had to allow those banks that survived primarily on a subsidized foreign exchange market to fail. In terms of the exchange rate equations given earlier, this implied a convergence between the theoretical equilibrium rate and the secondary rate at which most transactions take place. As for the petroleum products subsidy, the government has also gradually raised the price toward the level suggested by the adjustment conditions, although, once more, the IMF/World Bank argue that it has not gone high enough. Similarly, the public sector has continued to shed manpower, all in an attempt to rein in the budget deficit.

The negotiation is an ongoing process. There is still disagreement between Nigeria and the IMF, but the experience so far shows the process by which the present "equilibrium" was negotiated, and initial positions modified. Nigeria's structural adjustment has been carried out in fits and starts, each stage reflecting concessions and compromises in the negotiation between Nigeria and its creditors.

5.5   Horizontal Negotiation: Nigerian Government versus its Citizens

The outcome of most negotiations usually has differential effects on different groups; there are gainers and losers. In the case of Nigeria, for instance, the liberalized exchange rate market became a veritable source of unrequited profit. The few institutions (banks and the larger business houses) authorized to deal in this market were gainers, in contrast to the rest, which had to resort to the more expensive second window or parallel exchange market. In the traded goods sector, prices rose in naira terms, thus making it more attractive as compared to the nontraded sector; prices improved in favor of the rural sector relative to the urban (especially the urban poor) sector, thus redistributing wealth. These effects certainly consolidated opposition to the program; more so because even some of those groups that gained from it suffered in other ways as most key socioeconomic indicators in the society worsened.

It should be pointed out that although some groups stand to gain in this adjustment example, they are very small indeed. In principle, the gainers can compensate losers, thereby bringing about a Hicks-Kaldor Pareto improvement (Hicks, 1939; Kaldor, 1939), but it is unlikely that their gain in this instance will match the losses of the rest of society, at least in the short run. In any case, Scitovsky (1941) has long made the point that unless compensation actually takes place, the gain remains only potential, and so, virtually irrelevant. Such compensations are notoriously difficult to implement, not only because of the difficulty in identifying the groups, but also because not all of the gains of the favored group are strictly legal. The constraining influence of domestic interest groups on the negotiating process is thus likely to be very severe.

In the run-up to the adoption of SAP in Nigeria, the federal government launched a national debate on the desirability of such a policy. At issue was whether Nigeria should accept an extended structural adjustment facility worth some $2.5 billion from the multilateral financial institutions, along with the attendant requirements. This was expected to open the way for rescheduling the country's debt and for other creditors to extend similar dispensation to Nigeria. To this end, a national committee was set up to conduct public hearings. It sat in all the major Nigerian cities and received written and verbal submissions for and against the program.

At the end of the hearings, it was obvious that the nation had overwhelmingly rejected the adjustment package, and the government acknowledged the result. The popular objection to the program was based on the aversion to the conditions imposed, especially the one relating to the devaluation of the national currency. Besides, there appears to have been some confusion, because the popular understanding was that a rejection of the program implied a rejection of the conditions as well. The government went ahead to introduce the program anyway, claiming that its version was "home grown" and based on nationalistic considerations.

In negotiating with the domestic constituency, the government's initial position was probably not very different from that of the IMF/World Bank, except perhaps for the pace of implementation. The government was, however, apprehensive of the public's reaction to the expected hardship arising from the program. Rather than go ahead to introduce SAP directly, it let Nigerians believe that they were a part of the decision process by conducting an elaborate public debate. This act was seen as a concession by a military government not used to handling public policy through open debate. For its part, the public was implacably opposed to the program. Obviously, something had to give.

The government made concrete concessions in the form of choosing to introduce the reforms in small steps rather than at the pace recommended by the IMF. In this respect, the government intervened in the foreign exchange market from time to time when it felt that the rate of naira depreciation was too rapid, just as it approached the issue of subsidy phaseout in small steps. It let the public know that it was "resisting" the IMF by not going as far and as fast as the creditor side would have liked. The nonconvergence between the IMF-preferred exchange rate and the prevailing official level was constantly used as evidence by officials that the government was "with the people." This was clearly understood as a concession to the Nigerian public, although it is debatable how much it helped the process. On its part, the public grudgingly accepted the implementation of the various requirements, protesting every stage of the process and the attendant hardship. From time to time, the government increased the salaries and allowances of public servants, although never by enough to match the rate of inflation.

5.6 Issue Redefinition

Next, we turn to the question of how the government managed the conflicts and contradictions arising from the program and, in particular, the negotiating instruments used in the process. The Nigerian government relied on two principal tactics/instruments often employed by negotiators: issue redefinition and the use of strategic side payments.

This use of issue redefinition by policymakers in international negotiations is a common tactic. Economic issues can be redefined as security or strategic issues, a domestic policy issue can be redefined as a foreign policy issue (Ikenberry, 1988), just to gain the support of groups that would otherwise remain opposed to the policy. As noted by Friman (1993:391), "... this tactic entails efforts by policy makers to gain domestic support by persuading others that more inclusive policy concerns that affect core national values are at stake." In the Nigerian case, issue redefinition was geared toward achieving a twofold result. First, the (then) new military administration nurtured a notion of economic democracy, complete with what amounted to a national referendum. For this it got rave reviews, in the form of the rather curious phrase of being "the most democratic military government" in the country's history. Second, by accepting the popular verdict of rejecting the Fund's conditions, the administration pandered to the nationalistic instinct of Nigerians. In fairness to the government, it did not take the IMF loan, but there was nothing uniquely Nigerian about the policies introduced; they were exactly the same standard conditions usually proffered by the IMF. The nationalistic sentiments generated by the redefinition of the underlying issue did help in the initial takeoff of the program, even though it was not to last.

5.6.1   Strategic use of side payments to facilitate negotiations

Very often, negotiators find that to placate domestic interest groups opposed to their negotiating position they must make side payments to such groups. Such payments do not have to be in the form of cash, although they could conceivably be. More often than not, they take the form of material concessions on other issues of interest to the group in question. In this respect, Mayer (1992:806) cites an interesting example of President Nixon rewarding the US Joint Chiefs of Staff by agreeing to the production of a new Trident submarine with multiple warhead missiles in return for their support of the first Strategic Arms Limitation Treaty.

It should be noted that opportunities for side payments are not always so clearly defined. Sometimes, there are difficulties in identifying a companion issue acceptable to all members of the particular social group on which to base such a trade. As in most negotiation cases, the larger the number of individuals involved, the more dispersed they are, and the more diverse the members of the group are, the higher the transaction costs, thus making it more difficult to reach a consensus. A good analogy can be seen in the externality literature, where many individual landlords suffering from the pollution caused by a nearby factory try to reach an agreement with the factory owners. The high transaction costs implied by the large number of sufferers are commonly cited as a source of market failure preventing a negotiated outcome (see, for example, Coase, 1960). Presumably, in a democratic society, the elected representatives of these groups or relevant trade associations would represent their interests. A further drawback to the deployment of this tactic in domestic negotiations relates to the problem of the demonstration effect. Once a payment precedent is established, other interest groups that might otherwise not have taken a strong opposing position may be encouraged to do so in the expectation of gaining side payments as well.

At the international level, side payments are also sometimes used to persuade a negotiating opponent to grant concessions on other issues, whether or not they are related. A recent example was the Clinton administration's extension of China's most-favored-nation status in the spring of 1994, even though China had not fulfilled the human rights criteria set by the administration, and despite the well-publicized threat not to extend it unless the conditions were met. The consensus was that the United States had to give in on this matter in the expectation that it could then hope to get the support of China in the standoff with North Korea over the issue of suspected nuclear weapons development by that country. The manner of the resolution of the crisis provides another example of this kind of behavior. When an agreement was eventually reached between the United States and North Korea in October 1994, the latter was rewarded with diplomatic recognition and civil nuclear power plants to be built for it by the United States and its allies in return for halting its nuclear weapons program and submitting to international inspection and monitoring. Another example was the increase of aid to Israel by the United States during the 1990–1991 Gulf crisis in return for the former agreeing to stay out of the conflict.

An interesting question arises at this stage: do chief negotiators representing societies without formal democratic institutions have an easier time doing their job? In other words, are they subject to fewer pressures from domestic dissent than in democratic societies? The general line of thought in this regard is that the fragmentation of state power between the executive and legislative branches creates avenues for effective policy dissent and gridlock. By contrast, a regime enjoying concentrated power is thought to be less prone to this constraint. On the face of it, this would appear to be the case. A military government does not have to worry about electoral support; there is no legislative arm to be lobbied for a bill to be passed, and so on. This, however, is an erroneous conclusion. The concern of the Nigerian government regarding the implementation of SAP centered on how to enlist the support of various social groups, as well as satisfy international creditors. Domestic groups included, among others, the organized private sector, the bureaucracy, the intelligentsia, the police and armed forces (including retired but still influential generals), students and the rural sector. Obviously, these groups wield different types and amounts of influence on policy issues, but their views are watched closely.

A military regime, though all-powerful in theory, is weak by definition, precisely because of its illegitimate roots. Consequently, it is constantly seeking to legitimize itself by trying to build a consensus on issues that have the potential to derail it. It has long been acknowledged that the Nigerian business community and other influential civilians have, on occasion, played a direct or indirect role in bringing about a change of government through their interaction with military officers. Similarly, unrest in the universities, whether precipitated by students or their professors, has been a constant sore point for Nigerian military regimes since 1972, when the first student fatality occurred at the hands of riot police.

The most influential group outside government, as far as policy making is concerned, is the group of retired generals. They generally enjoy almost the same privileges as they did as serving officers, and they tend to maintain their contacts in the armed forces. They very often play leadership roles in their communities, and those who were in government usually end up as opinion leaders whose views are actively sought on a variety of national issues.

What has been the Nigerian experience in the use of side payment tactics to get these groups on board on the issue of structural adjustment? As stated earlier, the program opened up numerous opportunities for new business ventures, mostly in areas relating to finance and foreign exchange trading. From about 40 banks in 1985, the number of commercial and merchant banks at the end of 1993 stood at over 120, in addition to a good number of nonbank financial institutions. Starting from about 1987, the government authorized the issue of new licences in line with the ongoing economic liberalization. The immediate beneficiaries of this boom came not only from the ranks of established businessmen, but also from retired senior military officers and other public servants. In some cases, it was a partnership between them, with the military party usually being responsible for securing the licence. In a capitalist society such as Nigeria's, there is probably nothing wrong with this. However, it is hard to believe that the operation of the foreign exchange market in such a way that there was a persistent spread between the official and secondary windows (sometimes in excess of 100%) was purely coincidental.

The government introduced new guidelines in 1989, restricting the margin on foreign exchange trading to 1%. It is common knowledge in Nigeria that this was dutifully ignored by all banks. Banks customarily posted official buy–sell rates on billboards, but it was clearly understood that if a customer seriously wanted to buy foreign currency from them, it was at their own (under-the-counter) rate, usually the same as the secondary market rate. The function of commercial banks was soon transformed from that of financial intermediation in the traditional sense to one where their primary business was to trade on the spread between the two markets. In this regard, the *London Financial Times* (5 March 1992) noted that "... scores of recently formed small banks benefited from the wide margin between the official and parallel rates," and that "most of them would not survive a squeeze [of this spread]. Hence this group of banks, many of which have close links with government, has a vested interest in the status quo."

The World Bank generally recommends consensus building for these programs. Thus, the World Bank (1994) advises that "Political leaders must build a broad-based consensus on the need for reform so that adjustment programs are not derailed by powerful interest groups" (p. xii). By turning a blind eye to these failings of the program, the government took the easy way out; it did not convince these groups "on the need" for the program, but secured their support through side payments, which had the effect of undermining the whole program. This is not to ignore the separate issue of *state capacity* – the ability of states to implement official policy in the face of opposition from powerful interest groups. The Nigerian state is obviously weak in several respects, but some of the excesses in the operation of the foreign exchange market before the 1995 change cannot be explained by this factor alone; they bordered on state acquiescence.

Ironically, this constituted a major weakness of the program: most final users of foreign exchange could not obtain it, or they paid far more for it (to private banks) than the official rate, thus undermining one of the original objectives of the program. As a result, the government had difficulties securing a standby agreement with its creditors (see *Financial Times*, 5 March 1992). A related effect of this activity was that banks generated excess liquidity in the system, which they then used to support their bids at the auction. Banks, including new ones, were declaring unreasonably high profits; they were awash in naira, which were then quickly ploughed back into the foreign exchange trade. This was why the Central Bank, on a number of occasions, intervened in the market, on the grounds that the banks were "bidding too highly." In addition, it took steps on some of these occasions to mop up excess liquidity from the system by issuing banks with compulsory "stabilization securities" (estimated in 1994 to amount to about N28 billion).

Another element of side payments was in the area of privatization of state-owned companies – one of the key elements of the adjustment conditions. Some of the assets were sold off through open share offers; others, such as hotel groups, were sold en bloc. Again, it was the rich and influential groups that bought the bulk of these assets. As far as creditors were concerned, the Nigerian government appeared to have earned some credit with them by swiftly privatizing state assets. The apparent progress on this front was seen as a kind of concession, and convinced the multilateral institutions to be more patient on the failings related to the operation of other aspects of the program.

Petroleum product subsidies provide another illustration of implicit side payment. Following the price increase in October 1994, the price of gasoline in Nigeria rose to about 14 cents per liter (using the free market exchange rate), and still contained a large element of state subsidy. This compared with an average price of 76.5 cents per liter in the neighboring countries of Benin, Cameroon, Chad, and Niger. A clear opportunity for arbitrage thus existed, and this has resulted in cross-border smuggling of products. The usual argument for fuel subsidies is that the government wishes to protect the weaker sections of society from the effects of a high price for the product in question. However, this policy ended up creating (predictable) scarcity, resulting in the average consumer paying "black" market prices many times higher than the controlled price (Okogu, 1995, provides a detailed analysis of this issue). It is a measure of the frustration of workers in this respect that delegates to a national workshop in October 1993 organized by the umbrella trade union, the National Labour Congress, argued that, "We are already buying fuel at between N25 and N50. We would back any price increase if this will only ensure steady supply of products ... ."

The issue of petroleum subsidies is an emotional one in Nigeria, and it is true that the government's hands are tied somewhat, politically speaking. However, those powerful social groups, allegedly including senior public officials and security officers, enjoying huge profits from cross-border smuggling activities, are unlikely to want to see a phaseout of subsidies. The government is aware of these activities, and it is unlikely that state incapacity alone can explain the continued flourishing of this activity.

Lastly, the government made side payments to middle-rank officers in the armed forces and senior police officers in 1992, in the form of free new cars, at a cost to the nation of N500 million. Following public outcry, the government tried to explain it away in terms of a need to maintain professionalism in the forces, later adding that these officers would pay back the loans. It was also stated that these were the ranks "most vulnerable" to outside influences. The public was skeptical, and this appeared well founded, because two years later an investigation by the media showed that not only was repayment not occurring, but there was also apparently no administrative arrangement for it. It should be noted that this "gift" came about 20 months after the attempted coup of 1990. The term "settlement" crept into the Nigerian sociopolitical lexicon during the life of that administration, and roughly translates as "payoff." A person who has been "settled" is someone who has been paid off in cash or kind (for example, a government contract or appointment to public office) so as to secure his or her loyalty.

Finally, we offer a brief observation on the benefit–cost balance of the Nigerian experience of negotiation in respect to SAP, and the instruments employed in the process. Real, scarce national resources have been invested in the bargaining instruments, especially those relating to side payments. These include, among others, the inefficient deployment of foreign exchange to buy the loyalty of powerful groups. The World Bank estimated the cost of the indirect subsidy to banks, in the form of the spread between official and market rates, at $500 million in 1990 alone.

Have there been any benefits to the economy or society? The main benefit appears to have been the survival, and hence a semblance of political stability, of the regime that introduced the adjustment program. It is not our intention to trivialize the importance of political stability, as this unquantifiable factor is the bane of many an African economy. The apparent stability enabled the program of structural adjustment to be implemented in some form, but this has proved to be inadequate to turn the economy around. The cost of side payments, coupled with limited state capacity, seems to have placed a heavy burden on the Nigerian economy and society far in excess of the gains from negotiation, thus producing a suboptimal solution.

5.7 Conclusion

Negotiation theory provides an insight into the process by which complex economic and social issues are resolved. This chapter has explored the process by which the Nigerian government negotiated with the IMF on the one hand, and with its citizens on the other, during the adoption and implementation of an economic reform program in Nigeria. We have shown that the government made concessions to, and extracted concessions from, the other two parties in order to launch the reform. Although the outcome has left all sides dissatisfied so far, in the sense that the resulting half-measures have failed to transform the economy, the negotiation did allow the program to be implemented in some form. We have also identified the tactics and instruments deployed in the vertical and horizontal negotiation process. The limitation of state capacity, combined with the high cost of side payments, has led to the program itself being stunted. Among other things, government policy up to 1995 caused a huge spread to develop between the interbank and parallel market rates, which it allowed the authorized banks to cream off, thereby compromising the integrity of the entire program.

In addition, this chapter has addressed a related matter of theoretical interest, namely, whether an authoritarian government has an easier time in garnering domestic support than does a democratically elected one. The answer from the Nigerian paradigm suggests that, contrary to theoretical expectation, the absence of electoral legitimacy underlying such a regime forces it continually to seek accommodation with opposing groups. The government is therefore prone to compromising its policies. It cannot challenge its detractors by threatening to "go to the people" at an election. Consequently, it is forced to overcompensate in the form of side payments.

There continues to be serious opposition to the program. The way forward would appear to be to strengthen the implementational aspects of the program through an enhancement of state capacity. This would help to reduce the level of implicit "costs" in the form of side payments to social interest groups. Any step that enhances economic performance (such as debt reduction) and/or reduces the hardship on the most vulnerable groups in society would contribute in this respect. There is thus a role for the international creditor community. Finally, it would appear that a purposeful and honest government with a secure and popular base will be in the best position to fend off the challenge of self-seeking, powerful interest groups as it attempts to implement a beneficial program of adjustment. Even so, because of its contentious nature, such a public policy issue will still have to proceed through negotiation.

Section 3

Financial and Monetary Issues

Chapter 6

Reorganization of Commercial Debt: Negotiations between Poland and the London Club (1981–1994)

Czesław Mesjasz

6.1   Introduction

The history of negotiations on reorganization (reduction) of Poland's commercial debt provides a unique opportunity to study the impact of political factors on international multilateral financial negotiations. The peculiarity of the Polish case for practical and theoretical reasons stems from the fact that the negotiations on debt reduction were conducted during the period when the conflict of political interests between the government of Poland and the Western creditor governments was replaced by political cooperation. The evolution and interplay of economic and political concerns of three principal actors – Poland, commercial banks, and Western governments – provides specific empirical material for the study of domestic and international factors influencing the outcome of that particular kind of international negotiation.

Numerous limitations hamper studies of debt reduction negotiations, primarily the absence of any coherent theory and the lack of data, especially for the period 1981–1988. It is, however, possible to present how economic factors were influenced by other concerns in those negotiations. Economic models provide some solutions as well as analogies and metaphors that make it possible to produce descriptions, explanations, and sometimes prescriptions. The main aim of the study is to investigate the impact of the political concerns of all actors on the process and on the outcome of each stage of Poland's commercial debt negotiations in 1981–1994.

Our principal goal is to find a middle-of-the road position between two approaches. The first is represented by writings on neoclassical economics that apply mathematical models of conflict, negotiations, and bargaining in describing and explaining economic aspects of the process and outcome of negotiations over debt repayment and reduction (reorganization), e.g., Bulow and Rogoff (1988a, 1988b, 1989a, 1989b, 1990); Kaneko and Prokop (1993); and Wells (1993). The second approach, taken from political economy, is based on a less rigorous application of game models. Single play and repeated games are used as analogies and metaphors to depict the process and the character of conflict and negotiations. Within that approach attempts are made to describe and explain, or even to predict, the factors determining the process and the outcome of negotiations on debt reorganization – power, issue strength, coalition stability, etc. (see Lipson, 1986; Aggarwal and Allan, 1992).

6.2   An Overview of Theoretical Concepts

Neither neoclassical economic theory nor negotiation theory have so far yielded any comprehensive predictive and prescriptive models of negotiations on reorganization (reduction) of sovereign commercial debt. Some concepts applicable to that area deal with the following issues:

- Ability-to-pay and willingness-to-pay approaches (insolvency vs. illiquidity).
- The costs of default.
- Debt, investment and growth.
- Efficiency of the forms of debt reorganization.
- Organizational determinants of the debt reorganization process.

Strategic considerations accompanying negotiations on debt reorganization are connected with all the above issues. Because traditional concepts of solvency and liquidity are less useful in understanding problems of sovereign debt, some theoretical writings emphasize the willingness-to-pay nature of the problem. It can be put into several theoretical frameworks:

- Pure reputational analysis.
- Bargaining theoretical framework.
- Consequences of information asymmetry (Atkeson's contract-based approach, the signaling equilibrium approach, and the impact of third party actions on negotiations; Atkeson, 1991).

In pure reputational analysis the cost to a sovereign borrower of an unjustifiable debt repudiation is a loss of reputation, which denies access to future loans. An unjustifiable repudiation is one that occurs in the absence of a negative state of affairs in the borrowing country. An excusable default following an adverse shock does not result in a loss of reputation (see Eaton and Gersovitz, 1981; Grossman and Van Huyck, 1988). Some authors conclude that the typical pattern of foreign lending was a burst of lending followed by widespread defaults. Moreover, countries that defaulted were seldom punished by their creditors (Eichengreen and Lindert, 1989; Lindert and Morton, 1989). Advocates of opposing views have found empirical support for the prediction that previous defaults have a significant impact on the current terms of credit.

Several bargaining theory-based writings link conditions for debt repudiation with the process of debt rescheduling. Bulow and Rogoff (1989a, 1989b) argue that countries rarely announce outright repudiations of their debt or even permanent partial defaults. Their model uses a dynamic bargaining model proposed by Rubinstein (1982) to represent the ongoing process of rescheduling. The players in Bulow and Rogoff's model – a country and a consortium of unified banks – are completely rational, risk neutral, and fully informed, and fully anticipate the possibility of rescheduling. Although the model does not endogenize every element of the bargaining process, it still makes it possible to draw conclusions about the impact of an unanticipated interest rate rise, which, paradoxically, can also hurt the bargaining position of bank creditors.

Reputation models and bargaining models correspond to the issue of information asymmetry. In a model proposed by Atkeson (1991), capital flows among countries are constrained by two market imperfections. The first is moral hazard, where asymmetry exists between the actions of borrowers and the risk of repudiation. The moral hazard problem in a contracting economy in the model arises from the assumption that lenders cannot observe whether borrowers choose to invest or consume the proceeds of loans. The second impediment to contracting arises from the assumption that lenders cannot appeal to some third party to enforce repayment of loans.

In a model including asymmetric information about the type of government in the borrowing country (myopic or farsighted), Cole *et al.* (1989) study the issue of the voluntary resumption of lending to a country that has been in default. The main argument of their work is that the defaulting country need not be excluded from capital markets for a fixed period. If it can signal to lenders that the type of government has changed, it will be able to resume borrowing. Unexpected repayment (after the country's exclusion from capital markets) can be treated as such a signal.

A revised model of bargaining with asymmetric information has been used to analyze the effects of IMF loan policy on the bargaining process and equilibrium outcomes in debt negotiations (Wells, 1993). In some countries, the IMF has instituted a policy change required in the Brady Plan called "lending in arrears": disbursement of funds whether an agreement has been reached with creditors or not. It is shown that the IMF policy of no lending in arrears, according to which no loans are disbursed until an agreement is reached with creditors, has a very different effect on the outcome of the bargaining game than a policy of lending in arrears.

6.3   The Costs of Default

The costs of default should be distinguished from the penalty. "Penalty" means an action taken by lenders in response to default, with the intention of lowering the welfare of the defaulter. "Cost of default" in turn means any negative effect on the welfare of the borrower as a consequence of default – the costs of default are therefore larger than penalties (Arora, 1993).

Two penalties for debt repudiation may be identified: denial of access to credit markets and trade sanctions. The incentive for creditor banks to impose penalties may be small, especially if penalties also impose a cost on the creditors. Conflicts of interest between various creditors can make penalties less plausible as well. It is not yet clear whether temporary suspension of debt service imposes additional burdens on the debtor, although it means that the debt continues to grow at the rate of interest. Usually the debtor gains by postponing repayment indefinitely and will always choose to do so unless threatened with a penalty (Arora, 1993).

Writings in political economy make a new contribution by formalizing political constraints to standard models of lending. Some works deal with internal political situations and borrowing – government change, distribution of the costs of default or debt servicing within the debtor country, or the relationship between the structural characteristics of an economy and the likelihood of debt rescheduling (Arora, 1993). A general observation has been made that overborrowing emerges as a rational response to political uncertainty, even when the costs of default are high ex ante (Özler and Tabellini, 1991).

6.4   Debt, Investment, and Growth

Discussion of the impact of indebtedness on investment and growth concentrates upon the effects of the "debt overhang," which expresses a situation where a sovereign country has borrowed money from foreign banks and has not succeeded in fulfilling the scheduled repayments for some period. In the "debt vs. growth" discussion the debt overhang argument says that high external debt acts as a marginal tax on investment, since a fraction of the gain in output resulting from increased investment accrues to creditors in the form of debt repayment.

Theoretical views and empirical evidence on debt overhang are ambiguous. It is particularly difficult to prove whether slowdown in economic growth was caused by debt repayment or whether it happened beforehand. The ambiguity suggests the need for further empirical analysis to establish the direction of causal links and to understand the distortion to incentives imposed by a high level of debt (Arora, 1993).

6.5   Efficiency of the Forms of Debt Reorganization

In debt reorganization two kinds of actions can be discerned: debt relief (or forgiveness) and debt restructuring (or rescheduling). Agreement on debt relief reflects the recognition of an ability-to-pay problem. For creditors, debt relief should increase the chance of repayment while providing benefits for debtors. The objections to debt relief are based on the "precedence" problem and the free rider problem. The precedence problem arises when providing debt relief to one debtor undermines the banks' bargaining position toward other debtors. The increase in the market price of debt remaining after the relief leads to the free rider problem, which could be described with the n-person Prisoners' Dilemma analogy. Since holders of the debt receive a capital gain after such an operation, each creditor has an incentive to refrain from providing debt relief but gains if other creditors follow suit.

The discussion of the policy of debt reduction has been divided between an interventionist approach, which advocates external funding of debt reduction, and a market-based approach, which supports debt reduction through market mechanisms. Recent debt reduction schemes show that the banks and the IMF have taken a hybrid approach, in which creditors are offered a menu of new debt instruments, whose value is increased by additional resources.

6.6   General Determinants and Outcomes of Debt Negotiations

In studying the process of debt negotiations the following organizational aspects must be taken into account:

- Procedure of negotiations (stages).
- Overall strength of actors (power).
- Internal differentiation of actors.
- Distribution of information between actors.

Conciliation and the shift in distribution of costs and benefits between banks and debtors can be achieved in their negotiations by a recourse to norms and rules, one's own capabilities, and both state and nonstate allies, as well as through links to the future (Aggarwal, 1987:10).

Agreements on cooperation determine the costs of adjustment borne by banks and indebted countries. The models of economic theory provide only partial solutions to the problem of distribution of debt bargaining costs. Political economy offers more universal frameworks. Four "ideal-typical" outcomes from negotiations over the distribution of costs in debt negotiations were proposed by Aggarwal (1987:5–6):

- The debtor repudiates its obligations and the bank stops lending.
- The debtor imposes a moratorium on repayment, while the bank keeps it liquid by providing a temporary inflow of capital.
- The debtor concedes to bank demands for continued debt servicing under increasing adjustment pain without receiving additional credits.
- The bank and debtor compromise by rescheduling the existing debt, and new money is provided to the debtor, which follows adjustment policies designed to improve its ability to repay.

Experience from the debt reduction schemes of the late 1980s and the early 1990s shows that the collection of outcomes can be supplemented with debt forgiveness as a part of debt reorganization (reduction).

6.7   Conceptual Framework of Analysis

The complexity of debt reorganization negotiations and the fragmentary character of theoretical concepts based on economic theory and on negotiations analysis hamper any detailed analysis of empirical cases. To avoid those problems, the following analytical framework is proposed. The history of negotiations on reorganization (reduction) of Poland's commercial debt is divided into five periods, reflecting different economic and political circumstances inside and outside the country in the period 1981–1994. Historical data on debt negotiations in each period are then compared using a set of economic criteria stemming from debt negotiation models. The set of economic criteria includes:

- Reputational criteria of a borrower and their consequences.
- The impact of interest rate changes.
- Informational symmetry and/or asymmetry.
- The role of third party economic intervention – Western creditor governments and the IMF.
- Factors determining Poland's ability to pay (volume of exports, debt service burden, potential costs of default, penalties).
- Consequences for investment and growth.
- Efficiency of debt relief and reorganization:
  - Evaluation of the agreement.
  - Comparison with other agreements.
- Internal coherence of the London Club.

Political concerns relate to the following actors:

- Governments of Poland before and after 1989.
- The Solidarity trade union, which expressed the views of the majority of the Polish population before 1989.
- Lenders (commercial banks) – the London Club.
- Government lenders – the Paris Club.
- International financial institutions – the IMF, the World Bank, the Bank of International Settlement, and the European Bank for Reconstruction and Development – after 1991.

Political considerations take various factors into account. For Poland, they are:

- Internal stability (position of the government, social unrest).
- Human rights policy.
- Political will for reforms.

For Western governments and institutions, they are:

- Position of Western governments toward the political situation and reforms in Poland.
- Concerns about human rights in Poland.
- Influence of Western governments on international financial institutions.
- Security concerns of Western governments and organizations.
- Links with Western policy toward the developing countries.

The combination of all the above factors for each period leads to descriptions of high complexity, beyond the scope of this paper. To make the explanation simpler, yet productive, the following approach is proposed that allows us to use the case of Poland in a twofold way. First, it is possible to contrast theoretical economic concepts of debt reorganization negotiations with the reality of political influence. Second, it is also possible to demonstrate some ways in which "pure" economic models of debt reorganization negotiations can be enriched and made more compatible with empirical evidence.

6.8   History and Determinants of Negotiations

6.8.1   Period I: March 1981–December 1981

In March 1981 the Polish Trade Bank (Bank Handlowy) announced the country's inability to meet payments (interest and principal) on its loans due in the second quarter of 1981 and asked for refinancing (*Financial Times* [FT], 31 March 1981; *International Herald Tribune* [IHT], 3 April 1981; Cohen, 1986). Shortly after this announcement, Western banks withdrew several hundred million dollars in short-term deposits in Poland, creating one of the reasons for Poland's severe debt-servicing difficulties in 1981 (Zloch-Christy, 1987:105).

Economic reasons for that step were based purely on the ability to pay. However, the banks believed that, should Poland reform its economy, the country's potential would allow it to repay the debt. Total debt payments due for 1981 reached the level of US$10.1 billion, while the reserves at the end of 1980 shrank to US$574 million (World Debt Tables of the World Bank [WDT], 1993–1994). Since it remained outside the Bretton Woods institutions, Poland could not expect their involvement in solving its debt crisis. The economic situation was deteriorating and the internal situation was becoming unstable. A growing threat of Soviet intervention also cast a shadow on the Poland's position.

The negotiating position of the banks was chiefly determined by the fear of default, which could result from the economic crisis and the unstable internal situation in Poland. The anxiety of European and American banks was not solely due to their exposure in Poland. They felt secured against such a course of events (*Wall Street Journal*, 21 and 24 December 1981). In 1981, they instead feared to set a precedent that could cause a chain reaction, especially among highly indebted Latin American countries. Consequences for trade with Poland were not taken into account either; the Polish share in Western trade was marginal. In response to the declaration of payment suspension the banks canceled lending to Poland and began to withdraw their short-term deposits from Polish banks.

The situation of the banks was shaped by three additional economic factors: unequal exposure in Poland, with domination of European, mainly West German, banks; the high debt of Latin America; and the end of illusions about the "umbrella theory," according to which the USSR was expected to save its allies from any problems with debt repayment. In addition to uncertainty regarding developments in Poland, they also were not sufficiently informed about the overall economic and financial position of the country. Finally, coordination of their actions toward the indebted countries was at an early stage of development: 19 members of the banks' task force represented 460 institutions involved (*Zycie Gospodarcze* [ZG], 19 April 1981).

Negotiations on restructuring of Poland's commercial debt began in March 1981 and continued after the 27 April 1981 agreement on the official debt. Throughout 1981 purely economic and technical issues dominated the negotiations on commercial debt. The aim of the Polish negotiators was to refinance the US$3.1 billion falling due in 1981 (FT, 26 March 1981). During a meeting between the bank task force and Polish representatives in late April 1981 the banks were only willing to discuss the remaining three-quarters due (IHT, 29 April 1981). In addition to the disagreement on the first quarter payments, the banks' demand that Poland provide more economic information and implement a workable economic stabilization program blocked the negotiations (FT, 7 June 1981).

In May 1981, the bank task force rejected the Polish demand for renegotiating commercial debt on the same terms as the Paris Club agreement. Disagreements arose between European and American banks on the loans to the Polish copper industry made by two of the US institutions (IHT, 22 May 1981). At a meeting in Paris on 24–25 June 1981, the task force recommended that all but 5% of the US$2.4 billion owed in 1981 be rescheduled for 7.5 years with an interest rate of 1.75% over the London Interbank Offered Rate (LIBOR) and a 1% penalty charge. The American banks required the Polish government to take steps to increase exports and provide detailed information on the status of its debt owed to the Eastern Bloc countries. To achieve a final agreement, the negotiations were postponed until July (IHT, 26 June 1981). Representatives of 60 American banks met on 30 June 1981 and proposed that all agreements with Poland be postponed until the end of 1981, when the situation might become more stable (IHT, 1–2 July 1981).

Poland's response to the demands was initially negative. On 27 July 1981, a Polish government official accused the banks of being "uncooperative" (*Quarterly*

Economic Review of Poland, 1981). However, during a meeting in Vienna on 30 September–1 October 1981, Poland accepted the terms proposed by the banks on 22 July, and agreed to pay the remaining 1981 interest and 5% of the principal – some US$0.5 billion to be paid by the end of December 1981 (FT and IHT, 2 October 1981).

Due to decreasing exports and a worsening overall economic situation, Poland was not able to meet the demands. On 16 December 1981 (three days after the imposition of martial law), Polish authorities asked Western banks for a short-term loan of US$0.3 billion to help cover the interest due, but the banks rejected the request (Aggarwal and Allan, 1992).

The process and the outcome of the first stage of negotiations were predominantly determined by economic concerns. No settlement was reached because the debtor failed to come up with the necessary goodwill payments. Poland intended to solve the problems resulting from its inability to repay the debt. The banks wanted to prevent Poland's default and to minimize the resources offered to a country in deep structural crisis with limited ability to implement the economic reforms needed to promote the adjustment policy. In fact, the reforms planned for 1981 were of a very limited character. The banks did not consider any further loans to ease the actual position of the debtor. They were not concerned about trade with Poland or about the prospects of economic growth facilitating the repayment.

The impact of political factors on the process and on the outcome of negotiations in the first period was limited to three issues. First, the internal political situation undermined the position of Poland vis-à-vis the banks and negated any trust in the country's short-term payment ability. Second, instability undermined any prospects for fast reform, or at least sound adjustment policy. Third, Poland's prospects for regaining liquidity and long-term solvency were frustrated by political and ideological obstacles that made necessary reforms impossible. The banks could not expect improved payment conditions to influence future debt repayment.

6.8.2   Period II: January 1982–April 1984

Imposition of martial law on 13 December 1981 dramatically changed the context of debt negotiations. Economic sanctions were imposed on Poland, and on 11 January 1982, NATO members refused to reschedule official loans until martial law was lifted and the Polish government opened dialogue with the church and the Solidarity trade union (FT, 12 January 1982). The application to the IMF and the World Bank that Poland had officially submitted on 10 November became irrelevant for the time being.

Negotiations with commercial banks continued and a rescheduling agreement was signed on 6 April 1982 that reflected the conditions proposed on 22 July 1981 (see *Table 6.1*). In the meantime, on 16 March 1982, Poland repaid US$350 million – 100% of the interest on its 1981 obligations (Aggarwal, 1987).

Following the agreement both parties realized the need to begin rescheduling the nearly US$3.4 billion payments due in 1982. Poland asked to postpone payments of interest on the 1982 obligations and to receive new credit. As before, the banks did not want to reschedule interest payments to avoid setting an unwanted precedent – rescheduling of principal is accepted when interest payments are met (*New York Times* [NYT], 6 May 1982).

The second rescheduling agreement was signed in Vienna on 6 November 1982, on slightly more favorable conditions for Poland. It included not only the principal, but also interest. Poland agreed to repay 5% of the principal in 12 months (20 August and 20 November 1983). Banks agreed to delay repayments of US$1.1 billion interest until March 1983 (three installments: 19 November 1982, 20 December 1982, 20 March 1983), and to recycle 50% of that amount as trade credits (ZG, 14 November 1982).

As in 1982, negotiations between Poland and the commercial banks were conducted in two rounds. The first round began in mid-March 1983 and the final agreement was signed on 3 November 1983 in Luxembourg. The terms of the agreement included the repayment of the interest in three installments by the end of 1983 with 65% of that recycled in the form of short-term trade credits.

The agreements reached in the second period of negotiations did not satisfy Poland's economic demands. They allowed the country to postpone problems of liquidity but did not include any credits to enhance export capabilities, which were rapidly deteriorating in 1981–1983. It was apparent that the ability to repay future debt was not taken into account. The agreement achieved only one economic aim – preventing Poland from declaring default. It was of special importance at the time of the Latin American debt crisis, which broke out in August 1982.

The main political issue in the negotiations on the Polish debt immediately after martial law was introduced in December 1981 resulted from the determination of some American politicians to encourage banks to declare Poland in default. On 31 January 1982, the US government had to repay US$71 million that Poland owed to US banks under the Commodity Credit Corporation of the Department of Agriculture, but did not require the banks to declare Poland in default. By the end of the year, the total amount that the United States repaid to the banks rose to about US$340 million (*East–West*, 10 February 1982, p. 2).

This stirred up the discussion whether to declare Poland in default or to use debt repayment as a leverage. Defense Department representatives argued for maintaining a hard line and formally declaring Poland in default (NYT, 1 February 1982). On 8 February 1982, Senator Daniel Patrick Moynihan introduced legislation (not passed) in the US Senate to declare Poland in default (Aggarwal, 1987:70).

Table 6.1. Poland: Commercial debt restructuring agreements 1982–1989.

Date of signature	Consolidation period Beginning date	Length (months)	Amount restructured (%)	Amount restructured (US$ million)	Repayment terms (consolidated portion only) Maturity (years/months)	Grace period (years/months)	Interest[a] (margin)
April 1982	26.03.1981	9	95 principal	1,925	7/0	4/0	1 3/4
November 1982	01.01.1982	12	95 principal	2,225	7/6	4/0	1 3/4
November 1983	01.01.1983	12	95 principal	1,254	10/0	4/6	1 7/8
July 1984[b]	01.01.1984	48	95 principal	1,480	10/0	5/0	1 3/4
September 1986[c]	01.01.1986	24	95 principal	1,940	5/0	5/0	1 3/4
July 1988[d]	01.01.1988	72	100 principal	8,310	15/0	0/0	15/16
June 1989	01.05.1989	20	principal	206[e]			
October 1989	01.10.1989	3	interest	145[e]			

[a] Percentage points above LIBOR.
[b] Includes US$335 million in short-term trade credits.
[c] Covers debt rescheduled in 1982.
[d] MYRA. Also improved the terms of earlier agreements.
[e] Deferment: Short-term rollover of current maturities. Agreements in principle only.
Source: World Debt Tables 1992–1993, Vol. 1, p. 99; East–West, 29 November 1985, p. 3.

Similarly, Defense Secretary Caspar Weinberger encouraged US bankers to declare Poland in default, but the step was resisted by the bankers (*Los Angeles Times*, 4 July 1982).

Declaration of Poland's default was opposed not only by the bankers. Representatives of the US government executive branch, especially of the Treasury and State Departments, resisted it as well. Along with economic concerns they also wanted to preserve the possibility of using debt negotiations as political leverage to influence the Polish government's policy toward Solidarity. The West German government was also interested in maintaining economic and political ties with Poland. Under such circumstances the bankers could not yield to the pressure on default, but they could not neglect political considerations either (see Cohen, 1986).

Political influence on the banks' stance in negotiations was especially visible when conditions offered to Poland are compared with those given to Latin American debtors in the same period (see *Table 6.1*). In 1982 there was support from US government agencies, the Federal Reserve, and the European central banks following the Mexican debt crisis of August 1982. Terms given to Poland in 1983 – no additional funding and an interest rate 1/8% higher than that of the two previous agreements – were harder than those offered to Argentina, Brazil, and Mexico. The margin in the agreements signed with them in 1983 by private creditors was either higher than, or at least comparable to, that of Poland. However, in 1983 the three Latin American debtors received new loans from commercial banks: Argentina US$1.8 billion, Brazil US$4.8 billion, and Mexico US$5 billion. Poland had to settle its debts annually, while Mexico rescheduled its obligations on a multiyear basis (WDT, 1992–1993).

The reluctance of the banks was directly caused by pressure from Western governments. Indirect political influence was exerted in several ways. First, the banks reaffirmed that under current political circumstances Poland would not be able to increase exports and begin repaying its debt. Second, due to uncertainty and sanctions, the banks could not offer Poland any fresh loans, because guarantees from their governments were impossible to obtain. Third, decisions about lending taken by the banks purely on economic grounds would have been unacceptable to the Western governments demanding changes in Poland's internal policy, which regarded the Polish crisis as weakening the Soviet empire.

6.8.3 Period III: April 1984–July 1988

During talks held in Warsaw on 25–27 April 1984, delegates of Poland (Bank Handlowy and Ministry of Finance) and of commercial banks reached an initial agreement on rescheduling of Poland's debt due in 1984–1987. After consultation with all the banks, the agreement was signed on 13 July 1984 in London. It allowed Poland to reschedule 95% of the principal due in 1984–1987 so that it would be repaid over 10 years with 5 years' grace period (WDT, 1992–1993; see *Table 6.1*). Poland received some US$600 million in extra trade credits. Short-term credit of US$335 million was to be given toward the end of 1984 and the rest was an extension or recycling of existing trade credits with an initial interest rate 1–5/8% over LIBOR, to be decreased after 1 July 1987 to 1–3/4% over LIBOR (ZG, 13 May 1984). The four-year agreement was more favorable to Poland. It did not mean, however, that commercial banks had restored their confidence in the future of Poland's economy. It was a signal that after the worst period of the Latin American debt crisis, the Polish debt was not worth annual consideration.

A new round of negotiations began in June 1986 in a new economic and political context. On 12 June 1986, Poland rejoined the IMF, and on 27 June 1986 the World Bank. On 22 July 1986 the amnesty was declared and on 15 September 1986 all political prisoners were released. Membership in the Bretton Woods institutions could not bring Poland any immediate financial gains without an appropriate adjustment policy and economic reforms. The "seal of approval" of the IMF and political changes allowed Poland to negotiate debt rescheduling on more favorable and less politicized terms. In the meantime, the first official credits were given as well – a German credit of DM100 million in March 1986 (*East–West*, 27 March 1986, p. 5), and in June 1986, the British government agreed to provide a US$30 million revolving line for short-term business transactions (FT, 10 June 1986).

The agreement on commercial debt rescheduling was reached on 12 June 1986 and signed on 9 September 1986 (WDT, 1992–1993; Keesing's, October 1986, p. 34686). It concerned the debt due in 1986–1987 and stipulated that obligations of 1981–1982 would be rescheduled for the second time (see *Table 6.1*). The banks refused to grant Poland new financing. Due to the terms of the agreement, Poland rescinded any applications for new money.

In February 1987, a new round of talks began, parallel to negotiations with official creditors. The initial agreement was signed in July 1987 and the final deal was struck on 20 July 1988. The MYRA (Multiyear Rescheduling Agreement) concerned Poland's entire commercial debt, including payments rescheduled beforehand. The banks agreed to lower the interest rate and Poland was given a new short-term loan of US$1 billion (see *Table 6.1*). The agreement provided for other forms of debt restructuring – bonds or debt-for-equity swaps – that were not implemented (WDT, 1992–1993; ZG, 31 July 1988).

In the third period, the role of political factors was still significant, although it had gradually decreased since September 1986. In the agreement of 1984, political concerns, especially the pressure on the Polish government aimed at changing its human rights policy, stood in opposition to pure economic reasons, e.g., the payment capabilities of the debtor and the absence of new extra funds that were almost routinely offered to Latin American debtors in the subsequent rescheduling agreements.

The links between political concerns of Western governments and commercial debt rescheduling became decisive in 1986. The calendar of financial agreements to a large extent corresponded to the steps undertaken by the Polish authorities in changing their human rights policy. An important split among the Western countries occurred. The European governments preferred a more flexible approach in economic and financial negotiations. The US government changed its attitudes only slightly, still treating financial negotiations with Poland as an instrument of gaining concessions. During the vote on Polish membership in the IMF the US delegation abstained from voting and did not support loans for Poland in 1985 and in 1986 (*Economist*, 14 September 1985; *Wall Street Journal*, 23 May 1986).

Although the position of Poland in debt negotiations was weak, the Polish authorities attempted to exploit the differences between the official and commercial creditors. Polish leaders ceaselessly complained that Western governments conducted a policy of creating obstacles to debt repayment. After resuming talks with official creditors in 1985 and 1986, Poland tried to exploit the differences between commercial banks and government creditors by purposely giving preference in repayments to the former (FT, 8 January 1986).

6.8.4   Period IV: July 1988–June 1991

The limited economic reforms introduced by Poland's communist government in 1988 could not solve any of the country's problems. The reforms and then the "Round Table" talks conducted in the first half of 1989 were accompanied by attempts to ease the debt burden. In March 1989, Poland proposed to sign an interim agreement on repayment of the debt owed to the Paris Club. Poland had unilaterally suspended payments of principal and interest on public debt in February 1988, with tacit consent from the creditor governments.

Changes in Poland's economic and political situation in 1989 could not help but affect the commercial debt negotiations. Coincidentally, during the Round Table talks between the Polish government and Solidarity, on 10 March 1989, US Treasury Secretary Nicholas Brady announced the plan that was to bear his name. The plan embodied debt-service reduction along with rescheduling the principal and extending new money packages. It was not the first proposal of this kind, but there was an important difference between the Baker Plan and the Brady Plan. The former treated the debt crisis as a short-term liquidity problem that could be solved by new, more generous lending; the latter recognized the possible existence of a solvency problem that required debt relief, thereby increasing the chances of growth and eventually of repayment.

At the same time, immediately before and after the elections of 4 June 1989, far-reaching economic reforms in Poland became inevitable. Western assistance, including reduction of official and commercial debt, became an intrinsic element of the economic plans of the Solidarity government. It was expected that the London Club would agree to postpone payments of all interest on medium- and long-term lending due for 1989 and 1990, which would be followed by the negotiation of debt reduction along the lines of the Brady Plan (Government of Poland 1989; FT, 27 September 1989; *Rzeczpospolita*, 12 October 1989).

Poland's bargaining position changed dramatically in 1989–1990. Western assistance improved the country's position toward the banks. This assistance included short-term grants, World Bank loans, and a US$1 billion stabilization fund approved in December 1990 as well as the IMF loans – an SDR545 million (US$739.6 million), 13-month standby loan approved on 5 February 1990, which was succeeded on 18 April 1991 by an SDR1.224 billion (US$1.674 billion) Extended Financing Facility (IMF Annual Report, 1991). Complete suspension of payments to the Paris Club in 1990 and partial suspension of payments to the London Club temporarily eased the debt burden. In addition, Poland's surplus in convertible currencies increased to US$2.2 billion in 1990 (FT, 3 May 1991).

Negotiations on reorganization of commercial debt received another stimulus after the agreement on official debt reduction signed on 21 April 1991, when the Paris Club agreed to reduce 50% of the debt (*Rzeczpospolita*, 23 April 1991). After that the banks found themselves under strong pressure from the creditor governments to follow suit, especially when the necessity of achieving agreement with the London Club was made part of the Paris Club deal (WDT, 1991–1992:63). The response from the banks after the reduction of official debt left no doubt. On 22 April 1991, Horst Schulmann, director of the International Institute of Finance in Washington, representing the 150 biggest commercial banks, called upon the IMF and the World Bank to stop lending to such countries as Poland. His argument was that they had sufficient foreign reserves to pay back their debt, but used delay of interest payments in negotiations on debt reduction. He added that the agreement between Poland and the Paris Club was dangerous because it might create illusions among other debtor states. He also stressed that commercial banks, despite the pressure from governments, would not take similar steps (*Gazeta Wyborcza* [GW], 24 April 1991).

Negotiations between July 1988 and June 1991 did not bring any concrete results. After two agreements of deferment, signed in June and in October 1989, the talks between Poland and commercial bank creditors remained deadlocked. On 1 January 1990 Poland unilaterally suspended servicing of the medium- and short-term debt to commercial banks. Calls for 80% debt reductions made in June 1990 met with a reluctant response from commercial banks. Before discussing general proposals, the banks wanted Poland to pay a part of interest arrears (FT, 17 March 1991). At the beginning of May 1991, Poland offered to repay interest (FT, 3 May 1991). However, in June 1991 Poland announced its intentions to delay scheduled repayments and prolong negotiations with commercial creditors (*Economist*, 15 June 1991). Talks with the London Club broke off in June 1991 when Poland stopped repaying part of the interest on the medium- and long-term portions of the debt. Poland argued that transition to a market economy required a comprehensive reduction of the bank debt accumulated by the old communist regime – similar to the 50% writeoff granted Poland in March 1991 by the Paris Club (IHT, 30–31 January 1993). The impasse remained unresolved until the end of 1991. Before making any arrangements, the banks requested that Poland pay off US$250 million in interest arrears (estimated at some US$1.2 billion at the beginning of 1992; WDT, 1992–1993; UN/ECE Bulletin, 1993:104). Due to the deadlock in negotiations with commercial banks, and in the debt rescheduling and debt relief agreement with the Paris Club, Poland was excluded from international financial market and commercial banks reduced their exposure toward the country.

In the period under discussion Western and Polish political interests became more interrelated. After the agreement with the IMF and the announcement of reforms by Poland's communist government in 1988, the Western governments took a "wait-and-see" attitude. Such an approach diminished the role of political pressure on the banks and temporarily left the banks more room to maneuver in negotiations on the debt. With no fear of supporting the unwelcome government, the banks could put more stress on economic incentives aimed at guaranteeing future repayment – new money for Poland in 1988.

At the same time, links between debt restructuring and the internal policy of the Polish government also lost their meaning. Both the government and Solidarity agreed that the economy must be completely reformed. Therefore the use of private debt rescheduling lost its role in a linkage policy. New Western offers also became important, yet they were linked not only to political changes but also to economic reforms.

Due to political changes in 1989–1990, the banks found themselves under other political pressures. This time it was the desire of Western governments to secure a peaceful transition in Poland as well as implementation of reforms, including an adjustment policy guaranteeing the solution to the debt problems. The success of reforms in Poland was also viewed as a pattern for other countries in the region to follow.

The Brady Plan gave Poland a new source of pressure on the banks. Poland's wishes, however, went further than a typical Brady Plan approach. Its claims for reduction of the official debt stated that the reduction should be viewed as a kind of price paid by the West for elimination of communism. Such an approach was difficult to apply in negotiations with the banks; thus, it was stated several times that the communist government that was to blame for the debt crisis had acted against the will of the nation.

6.8.5   Period V: June 1991–October 1994

After the collapse of the debt negotiations, contacts between Poland and representatives of the London Club were very limited. In addition, a financial-political scandal involving Jan Sawicki, the chief Polish negotiator, which broke out in August 1991, contributed to the deadlock in the negotiations (FT, 23 August 1991). Two meetings held in 1992 were of a purely informational character. A delegation of commercial banks visited Warsaw in December 1992 to study the state of the Polish economy and evaluate the significance of a new letter of intent negotiated with the IMF in October–November 1992. After accepting the letter of intent, which led to unblocking some forms of Western assistance – the Paris Club reduction and the use of the stabilization fund – the London Club representatives declared their willingness to resume talks with Poland. Initially they complained that the Polish government neglected the issue of the private debt and delayed the negotiations. In the statement of 19 November 1992 they also stressed that Poland should not claim a very high reduction because the efforts could prove counterproductive. The statement was interpreted by the Polish officials purely as strengthening the bargaining position of the banks (GW, 20 and 21–22 November 1992). They stressed, however, that Poland could not expect to achieve a level of reduction comparable to the agreement signed with the Paris Club (GW, 12–13 December 1992).

After signing the letter of intent with the IMF Poland and the banks were ready to resume the talks. In January 1993 Poland nominated a new debt negotiator, Krzysztof Krowacki, and proposed new ideas on rescheduling and reduction of its US$12.1 billion debt to commercial banks. At the same time Poland decided to decrease repayment of interest on revolving credit to 20% (*Rzeczpospolita*, 12–13 March 1994).

According to the Polish Ministry of Finance, the negotiations were to be based on three principles. First, negotiations should be comprehensive and include principal and interest repayment. Second, the reduction should be comparable to the 50% agreed in 1991 with the Paris Club. Third, the debt payments to the London Club could not exceed the country's capabilities of repayment.

The first technical meeting took place in Vienna in February 1992. On 7 May 1993 the delegations met once again and on 20 May 1992 Poland resumed repayment of interest arrears (*Rzeczpospolita*, 12–13 March 1994). On 7 July 1993 the two parties met in Frankfurt for further discussions, especially concerning the outlook for foreign investment and for Polish export earnings. According to Krzysztof

Krowacki, the banks were divided between two groups. The first group, composed of European banks was interested in rapid solution. The other group was more afraid of creating an unwelcome precedent by accepting a Paris Club type of debt reduction (*East–West*, 19 July 1993, p. 4). In addition, the Polish debt was a subject of intense speculation caused by expectations connected with the debt reduction agreement. The Polish debt was traded more often than the debt of any other developing country – some 35% of the debt owed to 600 banks was retained by traders (Bank [Warsaw], No. 10, 1994).

On 21 July 1993, negotiations between Poland and London Club creditors were suspended indefinitely. The discussion was planned to last until 23 July 1993. The banks proposed a 28% reduction of the principal without considering the interest arrears. The suggested agreement would have cost Poland US$2.5 million at the beginning. Krzysztof Krowacki, the chief Polish negotiator, advised by the US merchant bank Kidder Peabody and the US law firm White and Case, said that the banks' proposal should correspond to the three principles (*East–West*, 27 July 1993, p. 6; *Rzeczpospolita*, 28 July 1993).

The talks were resumed in August 1993. In September the chairmanship of the bank task force was taken over by Dresdner Bank after Barclays had given up the chair in July 1993. Polish influence on the change remains unclear. According to the chief Polish negotiator, the change was necessary because German banks were vitally interested in achieving the agreement (see Krzysztof Krowacki in an interview with Bank [Warsaw], No. 10, 1994; GW, 8 September 1994).

In January 1994, the banks agreed to include interest in the reduction package. Finally, on 10 March 1994 Poland concluded an agreement with the London Club, which was initialed on 11 March 1994. In May 1994 Poland offered to buy back a part of its debt at a price between US$0.38 and US$0.41 (FT, 24 May 1994).

The procedure included some other steps when the Polish representative had to convince bankers to accept the agreement ("roadshow"). The deadline for the banks' decision passed on 29 June. The final agreement between Poland and 13 representatives of the London Club was signed on 14 September 1994 and came into effect on 27 October 1994.

The total amount of debt outstanding to the London Club, US$14 billion, comprised three elements:

- US$8.7 billion of main debt remaining from the 1970s; outstanding under the 1988 restructuring agreement (1988 RA).
- US$1.1 billion of revolving credits outstanding under the 1983 and 1984 revolving short-term trade agreements (1983/1984 RSTAs).
- US$4.2 billion of past due interest (PDI) that accrued from 1989–1994 (Ministry of Finance, Warsaw, Press Release, 14 September 1994).

Table 6.2. Creditor response to exchange options.

	1988 RA debt %		1983/1984 RSTA debt %
Cash buyback	24.20	Cash buyback	26.60
Discount bond	61.02	RSTA bond	74.40
Par bond	10.36		
Debt conversion bond	4.41		

Table 6.3. Forecast of debt repayment (London Club and Paris Club).

Year	Amount (US$ billion)
2005	4.0
2006	4.4
2007	4.8
2008	5.2
2009	2.9

Source: Małecki, 1994:27.

As shown in *Table 6.2*, creditors had the choice of exchanging old debt for cash or for new securities. Those opting for debt conversion bonds were also required to extend new money to Poland in the form of new money bonds. All PDI remaining after the cash buyback was to be converted into new PDI bonds.

The overall reduction was 49.2%, which was fully comparable with the Paris Club requirements for their second and last stage of debt reduction. Poland would have to bear the implementation cost, approximately US$1.9 billion. This expense would be financed from Poland's own reserves and from credits provided for this purpose by the IMF and the World Bank. This cost was fully within Poland's ability to finance.

More data are still needed to evaluate the benefits and costs of the agreement, or to build models that make it possible to analyze its consequences. Unless Poland's economic growth accelerates, the debt problem may seem merely postponed. Repayments of the commercial debt in the 1990s have been rather low – some US$400 million to US$500 million (*Gazeta Bankowa*, 19 March 1994). Although the precise amounts of repayments predicted have not been disclosed yet, some projections published by the Bank Handlowy in Warsaw show that future debt repayments will be quite challenging. *Table 6.3* presents these forecasts.

When compared with other debt reduction agreements, the Polish deal seems to be the most profitable. The agreement gave Poland a "break" in debt repayments, but its success is very much dependent on future economic growth. Several economic reasons support the deal. The most important one is Polish cooperation with the IMF and its implementation of economic shock therapy as well as the adjustment policy. Although Poland is not an important market at present, a shadow of the

Table 6.4. Total estimated percentage of commercial debt reduction.

Country	Reduced debt %
Mexico	31
Philippines	18
Venezuela	23
Uruguay	48
Brazil	35
Bulgaria	38
Poland	49.5

Source: GW, 8 September 1994, p. 15.

future of the increasing significance of trade with Poland also encouraged the banks to be more cooperative in their dealings. Finally, hitherto undisclosed prospects offered to banks by the Polish negotiators also played a significant role in achieving the deal. Other economic consequences of implementation of the scheme, such as the future prices of bonds, consequences of buybacks, etc., will have to be analyzed in detail to provide a sound answer.

Political factors in the fifth period were connected with the pressure exerted by the creditor governments on the banks directly through diplomatic channels, and indirectly through the Paris Club agreement and through side payments – the stabilization fund, grants, bilateral credits, and other forms of assistance. In addition, the governments helped Poland by ensuring coherence of the banks' position toward the debt. Political considerations were instrumental in eliminating the split between the European and American banks. According to Krzysztof Krowacki, the American banks, which had obtained most of the Polish debt on the secondary market, were reluctant to see any far-reaching debt reduction. They feared that the deal with Poland would create an unwelcome precedent for Latin American debtors (see *Table 6.4*). In addition, they were not much interested in future cooperation with Poland. The support given to Poland by the US administration and the US Congress reduced their reluctance (GW, 8 September 1994).

The European banks remained undecided. It was the role of the Polish negotiators and their advisors to convince the European, mainly German, banks to change their position. As a bargaining chip they probably used the prospects of future cooperation not only with Poland, but also with other countries of the region. Unfortunately, this part of negotiations and the role of diplomatic efforts in that field remains rather unclear (see interviews with Krzysztof Krowacki in Bank [Warsaw], No. 10, 1994; GW, 8 September 1994; *Warsaw Voice*, 6 November 1994).

The final stage of negotiations was conducted under conditions of decreasing direct political pressure from the creditor governments. Besides eliminating the divide between the American and European banks, it was reflected in indirect pressure connected with the Paris Club deal. What is even more important, the Paris Club agreement included a clause that Poland had to reach a debt restructuring agreement with the commercial banks before 31 March 1994 – the deadline for the subsequent stage of the reduction deal (see interview with Krzysztof Krowacki in GW, 8 September 1994).

Creditor governments also contributed to the success of the negotiations process by partially financing the consulting firms, Kidder Peabody, the US merchant bank, and the US law firm White and Case. The merits of the latter were especially praised by Krzysztof Krowacki (GW, 8 September 1994). It must be added that despite changes of government in the fifth period, the internal political situation in Poland did not influence the negotiation process.

6.9   Conclusions

The Polish case has shown two basic patterns of how political factors influence negotiations on commercial debt reorganization – negotiations that are always conducted between unequal partners (banks and creditor governments vs. debtor countries). First, divergent political interests of the creditor countries and of the debtor, and present and future economic links, are of secondary importance to the creditors. Second, corresponding interests of the creditor countries and of the debtor, and present and future economic interests, are important but not vital for the creditors. The first pattern dominated in 1981–1988 and the second in the period 1989–1994. These patterns of relations are not typical only for Poland. Several Latin American countries passed through similar changes in the 1980s. The specificity of the Polish case stems from the contrasts between interests as well as the role Poland played in the final period of the Cold War.

According to the first pattern, reflecting conflicting interests, Western political influence in the negotiations was used as a means to achieve political goals: keeping pressure on the Polish government, stimulating changes in the country, and influencing the political situation in the Eastern bloc. Under those circumstances only short-term economic interests of the creditors – governments and commercial banks – were taken into account. These consisted of avoiding Poland's default in the period of uncertainty caused by the Latin American debt crisis. Later, in 1986–1988, Western economic concerns were associated with the need to guarantee Poland's ability to secure minimal repayment.

Throughout the period 1982–1986 the economic results of negotiations differed substantially from the predictions of economic theory. The Western banks were not concerned with improving Poland's long-term repayment ability. They did not take concerns over repudiation, appropriate management of debt overhang, or optimization of rescheduling into account in the process. The Polish government, in turn, did not implement sufficient adjustment and market reforms to improve the economy. The concessions made by the banks and by Poland in those periods were needed to keep financial relations at a level that allowed debt rescheduling, thus leaving room for a possible variety of maneuvers by both parties.

In 1989–1994, Western political influence was used to support the political and economic goals of Poland and of the West itself: a stable process of successful market reforms. The history of the negotiations shows that under such circumstances economic aspects began to play a more significant role.

The political position of Polish governments also evolved with time. In the period of conflicting interests the communist government tried only to guarantee short-term liquidity, to find a balance between external economic pressure resulting from adjustment to demands for debt repayment, and to preserve social stability inside the country. Some efforts to exploit differences between the institutional positions between the banks and the creditor governments were used simply to minimize the repayment burden.

After 1989, the Polish Solidarity governments used two political instruments to exert pressure on the commercial creditors: links between positive response from the banks and the success of reforms, and the claims for a kind of post-Cold War "peace dividend" – a reward for Poland's role in demolishing the communist system.

Comparison of negotiations in both periods shows an interesting asymmetry in the private debt reorganization negotiations, in which the debtor country is always a weaker party. When political interests of creditor governments are in strong opposition to political interests of the debtor, their political concerns always prevail over their own economic interests, the interests of the banks, and the economic interests of the debtor. For private banks the dominance of political concerns is usually associated with an expectation of pressure and/or compensation from the governments.

When political interests of the creditors correspond to the political interests of the debtors, then the creditor governments prefer to seek a balance between their own short- and long-term economic concerns and the short- and long-term interests of the debtor. Such "economization" of relationships is rather natural, yet it can hypothetically lead to the situation where a stronger actor (banks) would be interested in exploiting their advantages, which stem from pure economic strength. The position taken by the commercial banks in their bargaining process with Poland after 1989 supports that conclusion. The long-term interests of the banks to a large extent contradicted the political interests of the Western states and had to be restrained by the direct and indirect influence of creditor governments. As a result, after opposing reduction of the Polish debt, the banks had to accept a measure that proved more favorable than reductions offered to other debtor countries (see *Table 6.2*). However, it is evident that such a situation will never be repeated. According to the agreements, the Polish commercial debt is nonreschedulable and will have to be repaid under any circumstances.

Chapter 7

Snake in the Tunnel: Monetary Negotiations in the European Union

I. William Zartman and Lynn Wagner

In 1992–1993, a series of collective actions were undertaken by the then 12 members of the EC to keep their currencies in line with each other, in a mechanism originally termed "the snake," as the Community (now a Union) moved reluctantly toward a common currency. In the end, EC members on 2 August 1993 finally abandoned a year of efforts to stay in line and greatly enlarged the band of permissible fluctuation (the girth of the "snake"), in order to keep the European Monetary System (EMS) alive.[1]

The two acts of this case can be taken as representative of the two boundaries on both the actions and the analysis contained in this collective study. Within the subject of economic negotiations, what is the impact of economic effects and of negotiation possibilities? Economics is often presented as a determinant element in action and analysis alike, whereas negotiation is frequently portrayed as a means of open-ended creativity that reponds only to its own process dynamics. As the EMS case shows, both are correct. Economic considerations – facts and relationships – constitute a part of reality, with which negotiations and other attempts at creativity must deal. Negotiation involves restructuring relations and perceptions of reality to create new outcomes. Successful, lasting outcomes must respect certain economic equilibrium factors. As the European experience shows, negotiators may be innovative in their attempts to achieve an equilibrium in ways other than the standard formulas. But such creations must be robust enough to change economic facts and relations (not an impossible task, but not an easy one), or else the economic forces will undo the political act and reimpose their own reality and relations.

7.1   The Snake

The exchange rate mechanism (ERM) of the EMS was created, in 1979, with the goal of limiting exchange rate fluctuations among countries in the EC. Less fluctuation would create greater predictability and less risk in transactions among participating members, which in turn should stimulate specialization in production, increase trade and investment between member countries, and thus increase welfare. Ultimately, these values would be maximized by a common currency, for which monetary stability was a necessary prelude.

The EMS countries adopted an adjustable peg system, whereby each currency could fluctuate by 2.25% (6% in the case of Portugal and Spain) on either side of a central established rate. Each currency also had a bilateral central rate with every other currency, with the same size band for permissible fluctuation. The central rates were set on the basis of currency values and economic conditions when the system was established, but could be readjusted as necessary. If the bilateral exchange rate were to fluctuate beyond the acceptable band, the two nations involved were expected to intervene jointly to maintain the rate by selling the strong currency to buy the weak, or readjust the central rate. In this way the central rate for the system would be maintained.

Some critics have argued that the EMS was in fact a system of one-sided pegs with the deutsche mark, just as the Bretton Woods system consisted of one-sided pegs with the US dollar. A cooperative multi- or bilateral peg system does not allow any one country to pursue an independent monetary policy because the shared rules of intervention would require that country to counter its policy with agreed-upon measures. The lead country in a system of one-sided pegs can have an independent monetary policy. Germany's anti-inflationary reputation is the reason why the other EC members accepted the de facto system; by law, remembering the German experience with inflation in the 1930s, the German central bank, the Bundesbank, must keep inflation under 2% and, unlike other European central banks, acts independently of elected officials (*Economist*, 5 December 1992, p. 81). By pegging to the deutsche mark, other countries were forced either to follow Germany's anti-inflationary monetary policies or to readjust their exchange rate with the deutsche mark.

During the 1992–1993 period, Germany underwent significant domestic economic changes, which affected the value of the deutsche mark in relation to other EMS currencies. Its monetary supply had grown as a result of its method of financing unification with East Germany. Rather than raising money through increased taxes to subsidize and revive the East German economy, Germany chose to borrow, which increased demand for goods and services and therefore raised prices. To combat the inflationary impact of this policy, the Bundesbank kept interest rates high. In a simple two-period model, the change in the nominal interest rate is equal to the change in the real interest rate plus the change in the expected rate of inflation (Sachs and Larraine, 1992, chapter 8); the rise in the latter dictated a high level in the nominal interest rate.

Because of Germany's role as the anchor of the EMS, pressures created by these changes were transferred from the mark – which many considered to be overvalued – to the other EMS currencies (*Economist*, 31 July 1993, p. 65). Thus, the other EMS members faced the choice of matching Germany's high interest rates or devaluing their own currency. In a simple model, the domestic interest rate equals the foreign interest rate plus the expected rate of change in the exchange rate; in reality, among other complications there are a number of different interest rates, giving a greater flexibility of responses. This relationship is driven by interest arbitrage, whereby investors make the choice between holding domestic or foreign financial instruments based on the return. But riding on this mechanism, which ties together the economies of sovereign states, is the role of the currency investor or speculator as both enforcer of the mechanism and profiteer from it.

Speculators buy and sell financial assets in order to make a profit by selling and buying (seconds or years) later, when prices have changed. Price differences are eliminated as a result of many speculators' acting independently, forming part of the process through which a market equilibrium – the point at which there is no pressure for prices to change – is reached. Investors' decisions are instantaneous and money crosses national borders just as quickly. These decisions automatically consider both exchange and interest rates in the search for the highest return. A higher return attracts funds, which will lead to a higher demand for interest-bearing assets denominated in that currency. Codeterminate with the demand for assets is the demand for currency to purchase those assets. Increased demand for currency causes a relative increase in the exchange rate, which will continue to increase until the real return is equivalent on interest-bearing assets across countries. Free capital mobility ensures that interest and exchange rates are mutually determined across countries. The rise in German interest rates, for example, meant that France and the other 10 EC members had either to raise their own interest rates, to devalue, to persuade the Germans to lower their interest rate, or to combine the three.

Thus, there should be no difference in behavior within any of the pairs of bilateral pegs, since it was these 66 bilateral pairs of "ribs" – or in reality the 11 important "ribs" involving Germany – that kept the snake together. Under the pressure of change, each of these relationships involved concessionary negotiations, with one party or the other giving in to its partner in order to maintain the relationship. The result, as in many cases, would produce a positive sum to the extent that it brought satisfaction to both sides over the maintenance of the EMS. In some – or even many – cases, that satisfaction would have to be considerable to outweigh the cost of the concession. If the reverse obtained and the cost of the concession outweighed the perceived short- or long-term benefits of the continuing relation, the negotiation would contravene the Positive-Sum and Equality Assumptions.

Another way of looking at the process would be to weigh the cost of the concession against expected costs and benefits of future negotiations, when the other party might be expected to make some concessions, producing an aggregated positive sum outcome on the basis of the Reciprocity Assumption. But if neither of these approaches produced a positive sum outcome in the short or long run, the Rationality Assumption would indicate that the party would not make the concession, or would not negotiate, or would not stay in the system.

The problem confronting authorities in the EC countries is therefore a challenge to integrative and constructive negotiation. It is a methodological challenge to constructive negotiation, since the alternatives are so few and so clear that it is difficult to see how complex tradeoffs and compound equality can be obtained. Here the complexity of the EU itself might provide an answer, by bringing innumerable items out of its vast array of competencies and issues into the monetary negotiations to counterbalance the necessary concessions. It appears, however, that this was not done, although more research may be needed to bring out the details.

Integrative negotiation would involve reframing the issues either to create a Homans–deCallières situation, where a positive sum was created by harmonizing the real interests of the parties through trading off items valued more by one than by the other for items valued inversely, or to provide a nonconcessionary response that would satisfy both sides and the external exigencies as well. Thus, either an integrative or a constructive negotiation would provide an alternative to the stark choices – indeed, imperatives – offered by the economic model.

7.2   The 1992 Crisis

The conjuncture of economic conditions and political events gave the crisis its dimensions and set the terms for the negotiations. European economic conditions outside of Germany did not call for high interest rates, which caused speculators to doubt that the other EC members would try to match Germany's high interest rates for long. France, in particular, wanted to cut its interest rates to stimulate growth, as lower interest rates would encourage investment and therefore economic expansion. But France's ability to act was limited by the German decisions, since in order to lower its interest rates, France would have to devalue the franc if Germany would not lower its own interest rates. The importance of the Franco–German axis in the EC and in the European unification process in general, at a crucial moment in that process, made this question one of crisis proportions and made the maintenance of the Franco–German – and above it, the European – relationship a benefit of weight, counterbalancing necessary concessions. The EC members had just negotiated the Maastricht Treaty at the end of 1991, which spelled out the process of European unification to begin at the end of the following year and stipulated that, to move on to a common currency – from an EMS to a European Monetary Union – EC members must have kept their currencies within the 2.25% range of the ERM without strain or devaluation for two years.

A specific high point of tension within that process was scheduled for 20 September 1992, when the French population was to vote in a referendum of ratification on the treaty. The outcome of the vote was very much up in the air. Already on 2 June a Danish referendum had rejected the treaty, causing the ecu (European currency unit, forerunner of the euro) loan market to collapse and the European currencies to fall to the lower limits of their acceptable band. If the unification process were to mean that France could not take its own measures to provide economic growth and improve welfare when it needed to, or if France's European partners – particularly Germany, the most important one – were not going to support such efforts, or indeed were to make them more difficult, then there would be little incentive for popular support for the Maastricht Treaty. Thereafter, whatever the outcome of the vote, pressures on the currency would continue, both as a result of domestic economic conditions and as a consequence of whatever ties – strengthened by a positive vote or weakened by a negative one – remained with the other countries and currencies of Europe.

Some analysts (Obstfeld, 1986; Eichengreen and Wyplosz, 1993; Riché and Wyplosz, 1993) have made the point that currencies can come under attack even when the economy is doing well. A self-fulfilling speculative attack can be made based on the impact of external events on market expectations, i.e., on the chance that the government will be forced to lower the exchange rate, enabling speculators to make their profit; such governments are termed "wet." Election periods and times of institutional testing provide such events, and the years of the Maastricht Treaty and referenda provide an empirical example (Chang, 1995). "Dry" government, on the other hand, will hold firm and repel the speculators.

The other members were in an even more vulnerable position. While they were less central to the process, since they were outside of the central axis, many of them – notably Italy, Spain, Great Britain, Ireland, and Portugal – were much weaker economically, and, of course, of that group, Italy was a major and original member of the EC and the United Kingdom was a later addition of great weight. Under pressure, on 4 September, Italy raised its interest rate, on the eve of the first meeting of the European finance ministers since the Danish rejection. The weekend meeting, held at Bath on 4–5 September 1992, began a pattern of "half articulated expectations by some countries that were deliberately ignored by others" (Norman and Barber, 1992). French Finance Minister Michel Sapin and British Chancellor of the Exchequer Norman Lamont would not contemplate devaluation. German Bundesbank president Helmut Schlesinger was under pressure to reduce interest rates, which he did not have statutory authority to do. Representatives finally agreed on a four-point statement reaffirming their opposition to currency realignment and noting a Bundesbank promise not to raise interest rates. Schlesinger distanced himself from the statement regarding alignment the next day. The meeting broke up in recriminations and indecision; the German minister let it be known to the British "with evidence but discretion" that a devaluation of the pound was in order because "the differences in competitivity have become unbearable"; the British minister retorted, "You are strangling us with your interest rates" (Israelewicz and Lazare, 1992a). Each side stuck to its guns.

Germany then broadened its strategy, as devaluation pressures on other European currencies continued. After meeting with Chancellor Helmut Kohl in Frankfurt on 11 September (Norman, 1992), Schlesinger agreed to a drop in the German interest rates in exchange for a general realignment of the European currencies, which he hoped to obtain on his planned weekend trip through Paris to Rome. The French president of the European Monetary Committee, Jean-Claude Trichet, did not call a committee meeting to consider this tradeoff, probably because of the very magnitude of the decision required to change radically the economic and monetary policy of five EC members and possibly because of the marginal position of the franc on the edge of the five just before the French referendum. Instead, he conducted the lira negotiations bilaterally with the other EMS members by telephone, precluding a general debate on the issue. The British did not move. The Italians believed that a 15% devaluation would be best but agreed to 7%. Sweden raised its interest rate to 500% per year, Ireland to 300%. The Bundesbank lowered its rates slightly (half a point off the discount rates and a quarter point on the Lombard rate that governs the German money market), and other European central banks followed suit.

As a result of the inconclusive week of 3–13 September the system blew apart. The lira devaluation rewarded the speculators, who then increased speculations on the value of the pound on Monday, 14 September. On Tuesday evening, sterling closed at its lowest point ever in the ERM. An unauthorized report quoting

Schlesinger's support for a more comprehensive realignment drove sterling through the ERM floor in after-hours trading. The next day, Britain attempted to support the pound by twice increasing interest rates, but the levels were indefensible and were ignored by speculators.

16 September was Black Wednesday, as the speculators attacked both the weakened lira and the pound. George Soros made a cool US$1 billion speculating on the pound. The Bundesbank alone spent DM60 billion buying up the weak pound and lira, the same amount as is usually spent on the euro money market in a year; the Bank of England has not yet announced how much it spent in the attempt to shore up the pound, but it borrowed US$14.5 billion worth of deutsche marks as part of the effort (Millman, 1995:190).[2] By the end of the day, the United Kingdom gave in, after raising interest rates from 10% to 12% and then 15% in the same day. Italy and Britain left the EMS and devalued; Spain remained in but devalued 5%, still within its permissible range. The European Monetary Committee met at midnight to accept the decisions. Speculators then turned to attack the franc, along with the Irish crown. If they too fell, the EMS would be destroyed.

The narrowness of the French vote of approval in the referendum of 20 September – 51% – was as much of an incitement to renewed speculation as a clear negative would have been. French policy the next day was quick and firm: no devaluation, no break in the bilateral franc–mark peg, no abandonment of the EMS. In constant contact with the Germans (which was not always easy because the top French authorities were in Washington for an IMF meeting), the French evoked the "worst-case scenario" or the German security point. "When they felt the Germans weakening, they suggested, very discreetly to be sure, the catastrophic consequences for Europe of a break in the Franco–German link. In case the negotiations failed, could Germany be the first officially to leave the EMS?" (Israelewicz and Lazare, 1992b). Nonetheless, the pressure of speculation continued to rise.

In the early morning of 23 September, as Spain and then Portugal and Ireland announced the imposition of currency controls, the Bank of France raised the interest rates only on its pension funds and issued a joint announcement with the Bundesbank in strongest terms reaffirming the franc–mark peg. Two days later, Chancellor Kohl reasserted the parity between the franc and the mark and the maintenance of the EMS, which the European foreign ministers confirmed in their meeting in Brussels on 28 September. The Franco–German statement of 23 September did not overcome the speculators' pressure until the end of the day on Wall Street, 11 o'clock that night in Europe. Full confidence was not restored until pressure had subsided completely at the end of the following month with the recovery of the FF160 billion used to maintain the franc–mark parity. In the operation, France won FF2 billion from the speculators.

The outcome of the bilateral consultations and internal policy discussion was to save the system without invoking any of the painful concessions on interest or exchange rates, relying only on a firm statement from the parties involved, plus a massive injection of funds to buy up the besieged currency. Since many economic effects are based on the ephemeral ingredient of confidence, the theoretical simplicity of the confidence-building measure could not hide its practically challenging nature. Yet confidence was restored in the franc and the franc–mark parity through a simple, if firm, declaration that made the massive backup buying of the weaker currency effective. It was an unusual case of integrative negotiation (except for the speculators), conducted through the use of firm statements to convey commitment (Schelling, 1960:23–28, 43–46) backed by "putting money where the mouth is," the economic equivalent of coercion (George *et al.*, 1971).

7.3   The 1993 Crisis

Yet the victory in the 1992 crisis was in the longer run ephemeral. France had successfully negotiated with Germany to win its agreement, trading off its satisfaction at maintenance of the EMS against the cost of concession on the exchange versus interest rate issue. But it did not negotiate any tradeoffs that altered the inexorable balance between the two rates; that is, essentially it negotiated the political but not the economic issue. The fundamental reasons for the 1992 crisis, the economic misalignments, remained largely unchanged (except for the pound and the lira, which were the subjects of specific economic measures that alleviated the strain, notably withdrawal from the EMS). Political rhetoric and expectations, backed momentarily by a shot of currency, had been manipulated to win the battle, but they bypassed the underlying economic realities, which again became targets of speculators' and governments' actions the following year. By the middle of 1993, speculators' pressures had increased again. France met its obligations by maintaining its high interest rates to match those of Germany, holding back inflation but provoking recession and unemployment. In mid-summer a French economic forecast pointed to prospects of a shrinking economy, triggering a new attack on the franc in the expectation that the Balladur government would not maintain high interest rates. Indeed, France would have preferred to cut its interest rates to stimulate growth, and was unable to do so as long as Germany retained its own high rate. The alternative for France was to devalue, and the salience of the alternative raised expectations and pressures from investors and speculators.

Speculators and officials alike looked to the last meeting of the Bundesbank before its summer recess, on 29 July 1993, for an indication of its support for the franc. This time, that support was not forthcoming. The French referendum was a year past and had been won, no matter how barely; the alternative to holding the line was Germany's preferred choice, a European realignment. The Bundesbank's decision was to trim its Lombard rate by half a point to 7.75% but to maintain its high discount rate at 6.75%, driving the Bank of France's rate to 10% to support the attractiveness of the franc and again raising pressure to crisis proportions (*Economist*, 17 July 1993, pp. 69–70; 31 July 1993, pp. 65–66). The currencies of Denmark, Spain, Portugal, and Belgium were also under pressure. Soros, who two days before the Bundesbank decision had announced that he would not speculate against the franc so as not to be accused of undermining the EMS and the EC, now announced that the ERM would be inoperative by Monday, killed by the selfish actions of the Bundesbank (*Le Figaro*, 26 July 1993; *International Herald Tribune*, 31 July 1993). The following day alone, Germany spent US$35 billion in buying up francs and other weaker currencies, the Banque de France incurred a FF180 billion deficit in foreign exchange holdings, and the European Monetary Committee went into emergency session over the weekend to take appropriate measures to save the EMS.

This time, both the decision and the process of arriving at it were different. Only the mechanism was the same: a weekend meeting (when the financial markets are closed) on 1–2 August 1993, this time at Brussels. There were nearly as many proposals as countries in attendance (*New York Times*, 2 August 1993; *Financial Times*, 17 August 1993; *Economist*, 7 August 1993, p. 24). Germany initially suggested widening all ERM bands to 6%. France objected, noting that such a change would not stop speculators, and it proposed that the mark drop out of the ERM and float on its own until German unification had been internally digested; the Netherlands was also proposed for temporary suspension. Spain proposed abandoning the ERM entirely. The Benelux countries, however, wanted to retain their currencies' tie to the mark. Portugal suggested a "fast track" monetary union between the mark and the franc, an idea that Germany dismissed as a joke. Belgium then proposed staying in the ERM with currency controls, which others rejected.

Attention then moved to a generalized float, whereby the value of all the currencies in the ERM would be determined by the open market, without any range restrictions. Germany, under pressure from Britain and the EC Commissioner for Monetary Affairs, opposed the suggestion. Attention then turned to a restricted float within wider bands than currently authorized. Out of a range of six possible responses concerning different-size bands of permissible exchange rate fluctuation, the European financial leaders chose to increase the girth of the snake sevenfold, from 2.25% to 15% above and below the current rate, following a French proposal that would provide wide enough bands to confuse speculators, leave room for a cut in French interest rates if necessary, and keep the ERM alive. In effect, they rejected both a costly defense of the status quo and abandon of the system to a free float and instead allowed greater latitude for a "nondevaluation." Schlesinger noted that the agreement made speculation riskier and reduced the need for the Bundes-bank to buy up francs and other weak currencies; this, plus the maintenance of the ERM, constituted the "considerable satisfaction" that the Bundesbank required to outweigh the cost of concession. (Germany and Holland, and eventually Bel-gium, agreed to use their strong currency position to remain within the original 2.25% band, an additional confidence-building measure that reduced the likelihood of a chain of widespread competitive devaluations). European currencies dropped immediately to or toward their lowest permissible rate against the mark, but then rebounded to precrisis levels. The loosening of the system allowed it to function within the previous limits.

The outcome of the negotiations attenuated the pressure against the European currencies by making profitable speculation more difficult and the costly measures to combat it less likely. The effective and permissible devaluation allowed weaker currency countries to lower their interest rates, although in fact only Spain did so (France made only two small cuts). It saved the EMS by making membership less difficult, rendering it less likely that members would have to leave if they could not play the game: it became easier to stay in the game. The real price of these measures was of a political nature. The likelihood of achieving a European Mon-etary Union with its common currency was put off for the time being. Notably, England could remain in the system, which benefited it, while staving off pressure to move on to a union, which – it felt – would harm it. The Franco–German axis weathered the crisis, although the underlying difference in the two economies left the questions of both national policy and sustained cooperation unanswered.

7.4   Analysis

The various measures adopted in both crises were different examples of integrative negotiation, avoiding the mechanical effects of the simple economic models. In economic terms, they had to do something to meet the pressures of change; in fact, they did something else. The measures adopted were of course economic, but they were such that they avoided sharp concession and created integrative outcomes. The 1992 response saved the system by forcefully reaffirming it; the 1993 response saved it by loosening it.

In both cases, there were losers to cooperation, notably the United Kingdom and Italy, which suspended their participation in the ERM (although they remained part of the decision mechanism in 1993). Thus, the refusal of concessions among the continuing players was made at the cost of other players who were forced out of the game. But these players were losers only in regard to their ERM member-ship; they did the best for themselves by going it alone, while the others did the best for themselves by cooperating. It was the cooperation of the others that made the dropouts' suspension a livable option, since the latter were always assured of something to return to when cooperation became more attractive to them. Since it was in the Ten's interest that the dropouts remain healthy, for eventual return, the Two were not strictly free riders. Thus, the Rationality, Positive Sum, and Equality Assumptions were maintained to result in a triage between those players who benefited from the integrative outcome in the 1992 round and those who did not and so dropped out. In the 1993 round, all met again within a loosened system from which all benefited. (Britain and Italy remained suspended at the end of 1995, awaiting better times.) The fact that players could drop out prevented the use of a veto and circumvented the Distributive Assumption.

In economic terms, the outcome was determined by the interplay of supply and demand of the various currencies. Interest rates and preemptive buying increased the supply to alleviate the pressure of speculators' demand. In fact, the negotiations, as expected, reduced that demand in other ways, essentially by asserting that it was fruitless. They also served to increase the measure of supply by manipulating motivations (demand power). The most important source of power – defined as an exercise by one party that produces movement by another (Zartman and Rubin, 1999) – as used by France in the most crucial moments of the crises was the threat of seeing the EMS collapse – the evocation of Germany's security point. This argument alone, repeated again and again, brought Germany to reaffirm the Franco–German axis and the franc–mark parity in 1992 and to seek an inventive way of reaffirming the axis without having to reaffirm the parity in 1993. In 1992, the French had the power to bring Germany in to help it live up to the politico-economic standard; in 1993, with some but not enough power to accomplish the feat again, they lowered the standard and then passed the test again. As an exercise of power, it was hard to beat and hard to avoid.

It would be incomplete to analyze the EMS negotiations as if they occurred on the international level alone. Each set of national decision makers was also negotiating within a national context, and could only do what that context permitted (Evans *et al.*, 1993). Such constraints were often used as commitments (Schelling, 1960), particularly useful in restoring confidence. French Premier Edouard Balladur threatened to resign if the franc was to be devalued, and Chancellor Kohl similarly staked his political position on his policy. British Prime Minister John Major also fought for his political position during the two crises, although with less clear commitments. These contexts both committed and constrained the actors, serving as elements of both power and weakness on opposite sides of the same coin.

All actors recognized the need for adjustment in the ERM, but wished others to bear the burden of it and make the necessary concessions. France wanted Germany to lower its interest rates but above all to support the franc, and Germany wanted

France to realign its exchange rate; both wanted to retain the Franco–German axis and, riding on it, the EU. Joint decision making – i.e., negotiation – was required to retain the system, in the absence of one country's bearing the burden alone. In 1992, the member states attempted to override the economic realities and the operative relationship of those realities with a joint statement of confidence, in a "self-fulfilling anti-speculative defense" negotiated between the two hubs of the axis, trading the relationship for a policy concession. In 1993, the states again faced the renewed realities of the EMS under attack, and again addressed its problems with an alternative to the more obvious economic formula, negotiating a loosening of the formal restraints in exchange for the maintenance of a loosened relationship. Each time the parties accomplished their goals (at least for the short run, which is all that can be accomplished anyway) without making concessions they believed they could not make, and in so doing created integrative outcomes consistent with economic equilibria.

Notes

[1] For an excellent discussion of the entire issue involved here, see Millman (1995). For analysis of the EMS and its purposes, see Giavazzi *et al.* (1988), Guerrieri and Padoan (1989), and Fratianni and von Hagen (1992).

[2] When confidence is restored at the end of a successful operation, moneys spent to shore up the weak currencies are recovered on the market. If the currency devalues, however, such expenditures become a loss to the countries involved.

Section 4

Trade Issues

Chapter 8

The Uruguay Round Negotiations on Services: Economic Basis, Political Outcome

Anders Ahnlid

8.1   Introduction

The General Agreement on Trade in Services (GATS) is to trade in services what the General Agreement on Tariffs and Trade (GATT) is to trade in goods. GATS was negotiated as part of the Uruguay Round of trade negotiations, launched under the auspices of GATT in 1986 and formally concluded in April 1994.

The Uruguay Round was the most comprehensive trade negotiation ever embarked upon, in terms of both participation – 117 nations took part – and scope of the agenda. The negotiations covered several traditional trade issues as well as several "new areas," of which services was one.

Within the round, the services negotiation formed a large negotiation in its own right. It comprised a number of subnegotiations, involving different participants and negotiating styles and techniques. However, they all aimed at the establishment of either trade rules or detailed commitments specifying the conditions for trade by nation and sector.

This paper does not attempt to provide a comprehensive account of the negotiating process in its entirety. Neither does it systematically analyze to what extent the outcome was affected by the fact that the subject matter was fairly new to the participants. Instead, it focuses on the extent to which two sets of theories – classical and neoclassical trade theory on the one hand and negotiation theory on the other hand – explain the outcome of the negotiations.[1]

In doing so, emphasis will be put on two aspects of the negotiating process: first, the formulation of central GATS rules, and second, the negotiations on commitments, or "concessions," in key service sectors. In this context, the analysis will focus on the crucial concept of nondiscrimination as embodied in the rule on most-favored-nation (MFN) treatment. Furthermore, the paper concentrates on the strategies of the United States, which was instrumental in launching the negotiations and had a large impact on the outcome. The paper also addresses the effects of changing economic power, i.e., the results of the changed status of the United States, which went from being sole economic leader when GATT was formed to becoming part of a leading troika during the negotiations on GATS. It will be argued that structural changes of this kind have to be taken into account in any explanation of the result.

8.2   Explanatory Power of Trade Theory

Is classical and neoclassical trade theory, whose original aim was to explain trade in goods, applicable to trade in services as well? The answer is not self evident, in particular since the definition of "trade in services" used in GATS differs substantially from what is normally viewed as trade in goods.

Uruguay Round participants spent four years discussing the definition of trade in services. According to the final agreement, such trade is defined as the supply of a service through any of four "modes of delivery": first, cross-border delivery of service, which corresponds to "normal" trade in goods; second, consumption abroad; third, the establishment of a juridical person producing services in another country, i.e., direct investments; and, fourth, movement of a natural person from one country to another with the aim of supplying a service. It is evident that trade in services thus defined is very different from trade in goods, in particular as it involves the movement of capital and labor (Drake and Nicolaides, 1992; Bergquist, 1993).

Comparative advantage is a key element of neoclassical trade theory. This notion assumes that production factors do *not* move across borders, which raises questions as to the applicability of the theory to trade in services. However, for the purpose of this chapter, suffice it to say that economists as well as national governments tend to agree that trade theory is applicable to trade in services (Feketekuty, 1988). Consequently, it is generally held that such trade, in accordance with the principle of comparative advantage, results in economic gains in the same way as trade in goods, and that barriers to trade in services are costly to society just as restrictions to trade in goods.

However, if classical and neoclassical trade theory were to be used to predict the outcome of the negotiations on GATS, one would expect a result involving far-reaching, if not complete, liberalization of trade on the basis of MFN treatment, meaning that no country receives treatment that is less favorable than the treatment given to the most favored trading country. Given the way international trade agreements are normally constructed, such an outcome would, first, include general and strong *rules*, of the kind found in GATT. These rules would apply to all countries and all services, and would prohibit discrimination both among countries (MFN) and between national and foreign service suppliers ("national treatment"). Second, the ideal result would contain binding *commitments* on liberalization by all countries in all service sectors to guarantee predictability for future service trade.

Not surprisingly, a result of this kind did not occur in the Uruguay Round, neither with regard to the rules of GATS, nor in relation to the country-specific commitments under the agreement. The ground rules included in the framework agreement are neither general nor particularly strong when compared to GATT. In fact, no substantive GATS article is general in the sense referred to above. The basic GATS rule on MFN is not unconditional in the same way as the corresponding provision in GATT. GATS allows for MFN exemptions, under which discrimination among trading partners may continue, at the time the agreement enters into force. From the point of view of economic theory it does not make sense to discriminate among trading partners by raising higher barriers against trade from one particular country than from others.

Two other general rules of key importance in GATT – on national treatment and prohibition of quantitative restrictions – have been transformed into negotiated specific commitments on national treatment and "market access" in GATS. Even in sectors where the rules apply, the construction of the agreement makes it possible for countries to make reservations that allow trade barriers and continued discrimination. These elements of GATS are not in accordance with policy advice drawn from trade theory.

In the negotiations on specific commitments on market access and national treatment, countries failed to agree on permanent and meaningful inclusion of key service sectors. While all major participants made commitments on financial services, the application of the commitments was initially not guaranteed beyond the first six months of GATS' existence. Thereafter, the interim period was prolonged until 1997 (however, without full participation by the United States). Several participants agreed to commitments on maritime services and some covered aspects of basic telecommunication services. However, neither the United States nor the EC made commitments in these sectors, which were, therefore, not meaningfully covered by GATS. Furthermore, participants did not agree on commitments on audiovisual services, and the quest by developing countries for commitments concerning movement of persons, i.e., individual service suppliers, was also rendered futile.

Thus, at its entry into force, GATS mainly covered less controversial sectors such as tourism, business, professional, and distribution services (GATT Document GNS/W/120). Furthermore, most commitments reflected existing regulatory regimes rather than liberalization; or "stand-still" rather than "rollback" in terms of the negotiating jargon. By not accepting liberalizing commitments across the board, participants failed to follow the general prescription given by economic theory, i.e., to give up costly trade barriers to gain long-term welfare benefits.

Against this background, the main functions of GATS originally were first, to contribute to increased predictability in services markets and second, to provide a basis for future liberalization. This is similar to the role played by GATT for trade in goods during the first phase of its existence; the bulk of the liberalization under GATT came later. Having the parallel to GATT in mind, GATS was an economically valuable result of the Uruguay Round, even if it was far from the ideal outcome as measured by the standard of trade theory.

8.2.1   Rationale for negotiations

It is evident that trade theory alone does not provide an adequate explanation of the form and content of GATS. However, this should come as no surprise. Trade theory is not constructed to explain outcomes in multilateral trade negotiations. Rather, it seeks to explain why trade occurs.

The main question regarding the role of trade theory in trade negotiations then is to what extent governments seek to achieve results that are commensurate with the theory. There are indeed signs that trade theory did matter in the services negotiations. Just as considerations based on trade theory have been instrumental in the creation and maintenance of the regime for trade in goods during the post-war period (Goldstein, 1986), trade theory provided "a broad justification" for why the United States took the lead in the process that led toward inclusion of services in Uruguay Round (Drake and Nicolaides, 1992).

US Trade Representative William Brock, who played a key role in the events leading to the launching of the round, made it clear that US gains from liberalization of trade in services would come through an increase of both exports and imports. "Trade in services provides the same mutual economic gains [that are] made possible by trade in goods," he wrote. "It permits international specialization on the basis of comparative advantage. It increases the efficiency of domestic industries through increased competition. And it enriches consumer choice by widening the range of available services ... ." Against this background, barriers to trade in services "... should be of major concern to policy makers interested in seeing the creation of new jobs and in improving economic efficiency, for they are costly in terms of lost economic opportunities" (Brock, 1992).

According to Brock, pressures for protection of service industries, at home or abroad, put the potential gains from trade at risk. Hence, the need arose for an international agreement that would restrain such pressures and remove existing barriers to trade in services. Several other high-level US officials used similar economic arguments for the creation of GATS (Feketekuty, 1988).

From a trade theory point of view, a nation would be expected to seek abolishment of trade barriers in other countries, particularly in sectors where it has a comparative advantage, as well as to revoke its own trade barriers. Thereby, it would maximize the gains from trade in accordance with the theory. Policymakers in Washington generally assumed that the United States had a comparative advantage in most service sectors. The fact that services accounted for approximately 70% of US gross national product substantiated the assumption in the view of many (Reyna, 1993). Domestic policies based on economic theory also played a role. In the mid-1980s, deregulation already under way at the national level in sectors such as aviation and banking contributed to the quest for international liberalization, which, thus, "... conformed to the general philosophy of deregulation in the United States" (Balassa, 1990:129). Experiences from internal deregulation were also important in determining why the EC turned into a strong supporter of the services negotiations after some initial hesitation (Messerlin, 1990).

Most developing countries were initially skeptical of the US campaign for negotiations on services. Infant-industry related arguments were used to voice the opposition. However, the theory of comparative advantages helped to identify the interest of these countries in the negotiations. Given that labor is the abundant factor of production in most developing countries, the theory suggests that these countries should specialize in delivery of services that are relatively labor intensive. Hence, several developing countries, with India at the forefront, followed the advice given by economists and started to request commitments concerning labor-intensive services, including movement of persons from developed countries.

8.2.2   Political limitations

According to classical and neoclassical trade theory, economic gains can be obtained unilaterally, i.e., by opening up one's own market regardless of what other nations do. As pointed out by Kremenyuk *et al.* (1994), unilateral liberalization is, however, often not feasible politically, due to resistance from groups that would be negatively affected by domestic adjustment costs if barriers to trade were dismantled.

In accordance with traditional public choice theory, small groups of producers that lose a great deal from liberalization are likely to be more vocal and influential on the political scene than the larger number of consumers that benefit, but just a little, from the reform. Politicians who seek re-election are likely to listen to the opposition and forgo unilateral liberalization, particularly if other countries maintain barriers similar to those that are candidates for liberalization at home. Thus, unilateral liberalization of trade in services, just as of trade in goods, pays economically, but is often not feasible for political reasons (Messerlin, 1990).

The interest of governments in international trade negotiations based on the principle of reciprocity can be explained in this context. Feketekuty (1988:17) has noted that such negotiations facilitate liberalization because they enable:

> ... each government to provide a convincing rationale for reductions in barriers that adversely affect specific economic interest groups. The government can thus say: We cannot expect other countries to take painful steps that will help us, unless we are prepared to take some painful steps ourselves.

The political constraints on one's own liberalization explain why governments mostly refer to export interests when they publicly defend participation in international negotiations. The prospects of export increases are generally more positively received by the public than promises of increased imports, which are likely to lead to adjustment costs, for instance through the closure of uncompetitive firms.

Against this background, the fact that the US administration wanted to obtain economic gains – from both exports and imports – by liberalizing trade in services did not provide sufficient ground for the campaign of US Trade Representative Brock for multilateral negotiations on trade in services. The administration needed, and found, allies in domestic interest groups that wanted to expand service exports. US societal impetus for liberalization originated within sectors such as insurance, financial services, travel and tourism, and information-based services. Intensive lobbying by these groups was an important element in the process that led Congress to include services in the mandate that was given to the administration as the platform for US participation in the Uruguay Round. The interest of these lobbying groups was mercantilist in nature, i.e., it was focused on removal of trade restrictions in other countries, which would benefit US sales, without recognizing the need to liberalize at home.

However, to achieve this mercantilist goal, the United States would have to reciprocate by reducing its own trade barriers. Therefore, the US quest for liberalization abroad implied acceptance of market openings at home as well. Consequently, the foundation was laid for results in accordance with trade theory, intentionally so from the viewpoint of the administration, but unintentionally so from the perspective of mercantilist interest groups. In this way, reciprocity "hitch[ed] the mercantilist tractor to the welfare-maximizer's plough" (Winters, 1987:46), and thus served to guarantee economically efficient results despite political constraints.

8.2.3 Traces of trade theory

GATT contains numerous references to the norm of liberalization and indications of the guiding role of economic and trade theory. A correspondence to trade theory can also be found in the negotiating process leading to the establishment of GATS, as well as in the final result of the Uruguay Round. The so-called Punta del Este declaration, which constituted the agreed mandate for the Uruguay Round, was explicitly inspired by trade theory. Thus, the aim for the negotiations on services should be to:

> ... establish a multilateral framework of principles and rules for trade in services ... with a view to expansion of such trade under conditions of transparency and progressive liberalization and as a means of promoting economic growth of all trading partners and the development of developing countries. [Punta del Este Declaration, GATT/1396:11]

The growth stimulus referred to would result from increases in exports as well as in imports. The aim of the negotiations was later turned into an objective of the resulting agreement, and the above language was incorporated in the preamble of GATS.

Another example of trade theory influence is found in Part IV of GATS, labeled Progressive Liberalization. Article XIX on Negotiation of Specific Commitments states:

> In pursuance of the objectives of this Agreement, Members shall enter into successive rounds of negotiations, beginning not later than five years from the entry into force of the Agreement ... and periodically thereafter, with a view to achieving a progressively higher level of liberalization. Such negotiations shall be directed to the reduction or elimination of the adverse effects on trade in services of measures as a means of providing effective market access. This process shall take place with a view to promoting the interests of all participants on a mutually advantageous basis and to securing an overall balance of rights and obligations. [GATS, Art. XIX]

While this provision defines the economic basis for GATS, it also highlights the importance of the reciprocity norm, which is political in nature and crucial for an explanation of the outcome of the negotiations.

8.3   Explanatory Power of Negotiation Theory

The analytical tools and concepts found under the label negotiation theory, as defined by Kremenyuk *et al.* (1994), contribute to an explanation of the outcome in the services negotiations. However, narrowly defined, negotiation theory has to be complemented by an analysis of national and international political factors. Such factors largely explain why the negotiated result deviates from the outcome predicted by economic theory.

8.3.1   Changing notion of reciprocity

It has already been noted that reciprocity plays a special role in international trade negotiations by linking economic ends to political means. In international relations reciprocity refers to "exchanges of roughly equivalent values in which the actions of each party are contingent on the prior actions of the others in such a way that good is returned for good, and bad for bad" (Keohane, 1986). Under the auspices of GATT, exchanges are made within the negotiations on commitments, while the regime itself seeks to prevent cheating. As pointed out by Kremenyuk, Sjöstedt, and Zartman in the Introduction to this volume, the concept of reciprocity is both ambiguous and flexible. Still, it is the key to success in negotiations of the kind found in the Uruguay Round, which are to a large extent "concessionary" in nature.

Results from multilateral trade negotiations have to be perceived as balanced, or reciprocal, by all participants involved. It is often not possible to determine the attainment of such a balance in quantitative or objective terms. Instead, a judgment has to be made on political and qualitative grounds. Thus, in trade negotiations the concept of reciprocity involves a substantial level of subjectivity. This feature is even more pronounced in negotiations on services than in negotiations on goods. The fact that services was a new and therefore not very familiar subject matter for trade negotiators added to the difficulties involved in assessing the value of a given negotiated result. However, in the final analysis, and concerning goods as well as services, what counts is the ability of governments to defend a deal as reciprocal in the domestic arena, not whether the result is reciprocal in an objective sense.

Under the broad and admittedly imprecise definition referred to above, several forms of reciprocity can be detected. Keohane, for instance, usefully distinguishes between diffuse and specific reciprocity. Under the former, countries seek rough equivalence of concessions within a group, while under the latter, they strive for precise equivalence in relation to specific participants (Keohane, 1986).

Negotiation theory provides little guidance with regard to which type of reciprocity will characterize a particular negotiation. A comparison between the negotiations on GATT in 1947 and GATS in 1986–1994 suggests that the international power structure must be taken into account in order to establish which form of reciprocity will prevail. This, in turn, will have considerable impact on the outcome.

At the end of World War II the United States was the dominant economic power in the international system. As such, it had a strong interest in preventing a repetition of the mistakes of the 1930s, when trade frictions contributed to economic depression which, in turn, in the view of many, considerably contributed to the outbreak of war. Therefore, the United States was willing, and able, to "pay" relatively more than other countries for the establishment of a liberal international trade regime that would contribute to peace and stability. Consequently, the United States accepted diffuse reciprocity as the basis for GATT, despite the free rider problem that followed. America was, for example, willing to "... reduce its tariffs more than proportionately" and to "pay" third countries to secure Japan's accession to GATT in the 1950s (Lipson, 1983). The United States largely acted as predicted by so-called hegemonic stability theory, i.e., it was willing to provide free trade in a form that resembled a public good.

Between the creation of GATT and GATS, respectively, economic power was profoundly redistributed in the international system. In the 1980s the trading system was governed "... under the multilateral auspices of the United States, the European Community (EC), and to a lesser extent Japan" (Lipson, 1983). No single champion of free trade was at hand, willing to pay disproportionately for free trade by accepting diffuse reciprocity.

While worldwide prosperity and peace were important aims when the United States pushed for GATT, its quest for GATS was more based on national economic considerations that were largely determined by a seemingly ever-mounting trade deficit. The US strategy was based on such perceptions of reality as the one summarized by Lloyd Bentsen, the chairman of the Senate Finance Committee:

> For years, we have given many countries a "free ride" in the trading system. In past GATT Rounds, the big players ... would negotiate steep tariff cuts. But there was no incentive for many others to play along because the most favored-nation principle guaranteed that everyone would get the benefit of tariff reductions. The result: At the beginning of the Uruguay Round, the United States' average tariff was less than 5%. India's was 118% ... . [The Uruguay] Round offers us an opportunity to correct that imbalance. The world has changed dramatically since the last round of multilateral trade talks ... . Countries that were not major players in world trade then are assuming increased importance today ... . [B]ut they will be even more important 10 years from now. That's why we have to lock in the benefits today. And that means no more free riders. [Bentsen, 1992]

The administration acted accordingly. In 1993 US Trade Representative Brock aimed at the creation of a "global trading system that fits the 1990s, that recognizes the world as it is rather than as it once was. We want shared responsibility [and] no free riders" (*Financial Times*, 5 March 1993).

Thus, in the Uruguay Round in general, and in the negotiations on services in particular, the United States insisted on specific reciprocity in order to avoid free riders. This had a fundamental impact on the outcome regarding services, both in relation to the rules of GATS and with regard to the country-specific commitments thereunder.

8.3.2   GATS versus GATT

In legal terms GATS is weaker than GATT. While GATT relies on a number of key rules of a general nature, GATS does not. This is partly explained by the difference between trade in goods and services. From a political point of view, it is more difficult to grant full national treatment and to abstain from quantitative restrictions when the movement of capital and labor is involved, as is the case in trade in services, than when goods are moved across borders. However, the difficulties caused by the specific nature of trade in services could very well have been accommodated under a more liberal set of rules than the one contained in GATS. For instance, in the initial phase of the negotiations on GATS the United States supported a wider and more ambitious concept of national treatment than the one found in the final result. The United States argued that national treatment ought to apply generally, unless otherwise specified. Under this "negative approach" countries would have been able to tackle problems related to the specific characteristics of trade in services by reservations to national treatment. However, the negative approach was not accepted by some other participants, for example the EC, India, and Brazil. This group advocated a "positive approach" under which commitments on national treatment would be "positively" recorded. If no recording was made, national treatment should not apply.

The final solution built on the latter approach. However, it also provided for the possibility of making reservations that preserved the right to discriminate in sectors where commitments were made. The solution originally proposed by the United States would probably have resulted in a more liberal outcome, since it would have comprised a standstill in sectors where no reservations were taken.

The debate on national treatment in the Uruguay Round may be compared to a similar discussion during the 1947 negotiations on GATT, in which the United States, arguing for a general rule on national treatment, was able to force its will through despite opposition from others (Jackson, 1969). The comparison suggests that the lack of a strong free trade champion in the negotiations on GATS rendered that agreement weaker with respect to national treatment than was necessary due to the differences between trade in goods and services. This, in turn, indicates that the new structure of power influenced the form of GATS.

The influence of the power structure is even more evident with regard to the rule on MFN treatment. The difference between trade in goods and services can hardly explain why all foreign services or service providers should not in general terms be given the same treatment by a signatory to GATS. Thus, a political explanation is needed for why MFN is weaker in GATS than in GATT. The lack of a hegemon willing to take on a disproportionate share of the "cost" for international openness, and thereby provide for diffuse reciprocity, forms an important part of that explanation.

Of all subnegotiations on specific GATS rules (the agreement consists of 29 articles), the negotiation leading to article II on MFN was the most sensitive and difficult. It also highlights the different circumstances under which GATT and GATS were created.

In the negotiations on GATT, the United States insisted that unconditional MFN should be a general cornerstone of the agreement. During the negotiations on GATS the former hegemon was the most vigorous proponent of a more conditional form of MFN for two main reasons. First, the United States wanted to prevent free riding. It was not willing to extend liberalizing commitments to countries that were not open to US suppliers. Second, the United States wanted to retain its right to discriminate among other countries in sectors where it was not willing to make commitments of its own for protectionist reasons. In both cases, the United States wanted to retain its ability to act unilaterally against countries that upheld barriers to trade that US authorities perceived as unacceptable. Sanctions of this kind would be prohibited under unconditional MFN.

Consequently, the United States, most often in splendid isolation, argued against the inclusion of unconditional MFN in GATS (GATT, 1990a:5). At one stage the American delegate suggested that MFN be made a negotiated commitment, equivalent to commitments on market access and national treatment, under the agreement. This position was unanimously rejected by other parties. The EC, for instance, held that elimination of general MFN would remove "all substance" from GATS (GATT, 1990a:7).

Against this background, the United States changed its position slightly and declared its willingness to apply MFN in all service sectors except maritime and aviation services, provided that sufficient market access and national treatment commitments, as defined by the United States, were given by others. US Trade Representative Hills explained the US position:

> Absent market access commitments an MFN requirement means that countries with open markets must stay open to everyone, while

countries with closed markets stay closed to everyone, and have no incentive to open to anyone. [GATT, 1990b]

However, other participants, including the EC, Japan, and leading developing countries rejected the link between MFN and commitments on market access and strongly supported the inclusion of an unconditional MFN clause in GATS. However, many developing countries either wanted to include important sectors under the agreement or requested substantial reservations within sectors for which commitments were made.

Against this background, negotiators could not agree on an MFN provision that was generally acceptable. Even if the United States was isolated, it was strong enough to persist in its resistance against unconditional MFN. Consequently, in 1991, when the MFN issue was to be settled in the Draft Final Act, which included a draft Agreement on Trade in Services meant to form the basis for the final negotiations, the chairman of the negotiations had to "arbitrate" the text of the article on MFN. In doing so, the American position had to be covered. The United States had made it quite clear that it was not willing to sign an agreement on the basis of unconditional MFN, and that it preferred the status quo to such an outcome. Furthermore, the chairman knew that an agreement without the United States was not a viable outcome. As the Uruguay Round constituted "a single undertaking," failure concerning services would have led to the collapse of the entire round, which in turn would have jeopardized the multilateral trading system as a whole. Thus, in order to accommodate the US position, the chairman put forward an article that included the possibility of making exemptions from MFN at the time of entry into force of the agreement. Thereafter, unconditional MFN should apply (GATT, 1990a:4).

Given the US isolation in the negotiations, others strongly criticized the arbitrated result, which they felt gave too much to the United States. However, tacitly it was recognized that the suggested text accurately reflected political realities, and everybody was therefore prepared to live with it.

Once the negotiation on the text of the MFN provision was over (the possibility of revising the text was formally held open but no real attempt was made to reopen the negotiations on the article) the battle over MFN treatment continued in the negotiations on country-specific commitments in key sectors, which included the issue of whether MFN exemptions in accordance with article II should be made or not. These negotiations were held 1992–1993. The United States made the most far-reaching use of the possibility to request MFN exemptions. For instance, it requested open and sector-wide exemptions concerning financial and telecommunication services that would be lifted if others made sufficient commitments concerning market access and national treatment. Consequently, the granting of MFN became a bargaining chip in a way unknown under GATT. In addition, the United States requested a sector-wide exemption for trade in maritime services.

The US ambassador to GATT elaborated on this link between MFN and market access/national treatment in early 1992:

> [A]n agreement would only be satisfactory if there was an adequate balance between those partners with open markets who maintained that openness through the MFN principle, and others who made substantial national treatment and market access commitments. The United States was prepared to withdraw its intended MFN exemptions if the overall level of liberalization of markets was acceptable ... . The intention was to achieve an overall result in the negotiations that would commit the major markets of the world, both developed and developing, to a more open regime of international services trade. While accepting that some delegations saw this approach as an inappropriate use of leverage, a final result which committed the United States to maintaining an open regime while not securing openness from other participants would be unbalanced and would create a significant free-rider problem. [GATT, 1992]

The US stand on MFN remained a major issue in the services negotiations until the very end. The most far-reaching US requests for MFN exemptions were rejected by other participants. For instance, the EC responded to the US intervention cited above by warning that "... if the present scope of commitments and MFN exemptions were maintained, there would be little likelihood of an outcome that the European Community could accept" (GATT, 1992:4). New Zealand claimed that "... [t]he use of MFN as a bargaining chip was an inappropriate and dangerous misuse of the provision [that] would send a retrogressive signal to the negotiations" (GATT, 1992:4). Others threatened to withdraw their offers if the US exemptions were maintained.

8.3.3   In search for the "critical mass"

The United States was not willing to lift its MFN exemptions unless a sufficient number of parties, often referred to as "the critical mass," made satisfactory commitments. Thus, what the United States sought was not specific reciprocity exactly as defined by Keohane (1986), but rather a specific form of plurilateral reciprocity. This indicates that it would not be necessary to go all the way to conditional MFN, which Keohane has suggested as the recipe for preventing free riding when large numbers of actors are involved, in order to achieve cooperation after hegemony. As long as reciprocity is established among the most important trading nations within a particular sector, regime leaders tolerate that countries of less importance are given free rides.

The search for sufficient commitments from a critical mass of parties can usefully be analyzed in terms of Snidal's model for collective action by intermediate groups, which builds on an n-person Prisoners' Dilemma (Snidal, 1985). Snidal argues that the existence of a hegemon is not necessary for establishment of free trade as a public good. A group of leading states may also be willing and able to guarantee such a good, if the benefits from cooperation within the group outweigh the costs. Snidal labels privileged groups of this kind "k-groups." A k-group consists of the countries that have an incentive to cooperate with the aim of providing the public good and, therefore, forgo the option of noncooperation or free riding. Without suggesting a specific number, Snidal assumes that k-groups are "small," and that they consist of relatively large nations.

The negotiations on GATS suggest that the formation of a k-group, involving a few rather large nations, is not sufficient for establishment of free trade commitments. In the Uruguay Round four major participants – the EC, the United States, Japan, and Canada – cooperated closely within the so-called "quad-group," the most influential of the many informal groupings within the negotiating process. The four belonged to the biggest suppliers in almost all service sectors, and the quad-group bore the characteristics of a k-group. However, in no sector was a liberalizing deal within "the quad" sufficient to produce a successful outcome. The quad- or k-group was not willing to give outsiders a free ride. Free trade would only be established if outsiders with no a priori incentive to cooperate could be coerced to forgo their free rider option. Thus, a model involving elements of strategic bargaining and coercion seems to be needed to analyze the GATS negotiations on specific commitments.

As pointed out by Snidal, in such a model "states in the k-group, in addition to contributing to the public good, must coordinate their coercive capacities to enforce contributions from other states" (Snidal, 1985). Quad members sought to coordinate their efforts against the target countries in the critical mass. However, the outcome suggests that they were not very successful in their endeavor.

The critical mass was defined by the k-group. It comprised countries whose commitments were perceived, by the k-group, as a necessary condition to produce commitments from the k-group itself. In the Uruguay Round services negotiations, the composition of the critical mass varied among sectors. Typically, it consisted of the Organisation for Economic Co-operation and Development (OECD) countries plus some advanced developing countries, between 15 and 20 countries in all (counting the EC as one). However, the exact composition of the critical mass, as well as the judgment of what constituted "sufficient" commitments, were highly subjective in nature, confirming that reciprocity is "... determined by the perceptions of the actors involved" (Rhodes, 1989). Thus, it was perceived reciprocity rather than objective equivalence that was important to k-group members.

The quest for plurilateral reciprocity of this kind was underpinned by domestic US interests. As the meaning of liberalization or commitments in the area of services became clear during the negotiating process, domestic opposition grew in a number of sectors, including in some that had initially favored negotiations (Drake and Nicolaides, 1992; Ryan, 1990). In response to pressures of this kind the US administration required a very high level of commitments from others in order to lift its MFN exemptions. The security points of the United States and the EC were at such a high level that it worsened the prospect for a successful conclusion of the negotiations (Kremenyuk *et al.*, 1994). In this context it is worth noting that the security point of the United States is always likely to be at a substantially higher level than the security points of small countries, given that the United States has a larger potential for pursuing its interests uni- or bilaterally. Therefore, the United States is better suited to do well under conditions of status quo than small countries are.

In the final phase of the negotiations in 1993 it was evident that critical masses would not be obtained concerning financial, maritime, and basic telecommunication services. Alternatively put, it became clear that k-group members had failed to coerce other critical mass countries to make sufficient concessions. As a result, the three sectors were initially excluded from effective and permanent coverage under GATS.

8.3.4   Financial services

The financial services sector in the United States belonged to the initial proponents of the service negotiations, but became more cautious the longer the process continued. In response to the positions taken by the financial services lobby, the administration set a very high security point in the negotiations on commitments in this sector. The United States was only willing to extend access to what US negotiators described as the "already very open" American market on an MFN basis if other countries, representing significant financial markets, committed to making their markets equally open (Ryan, 1990). If such commitments were not achieved, the United States would be better off retaining the right to unilaterally punish countries that were closed to US financial institutions. Thus, status quo was seen as the BATNA pending a sufficient level of commitments from others (Kremenyuk *et al.*, 1994).

In particular it was argued that offers by "... a core of roughly a dozen important emerging market countries and Japan... " had to be improved (Summers, 1993). The group referred to included countries such as Korea, Hong Kong, Singapore, Malaysia, Thailand, India, and Brazil. Several of the target countries argued that they had not reached an internal level of development that made it possible for them to meet the US requests.

Still, the US strategy, which to a considerable extent was supported by the EC and Canada, met with some success in the final phase of the Uruguay Round. Some countries improved their offers in response to the pressure from the k-group. However, a number of countries considered to belong to the critical mass – e.g., Brazil, Indonesia, and Malaysia – did not move. In view of their relatively weak domestic financial services industries, these countries did not perceive punishment, in the form of closure of the US market to their exports of financial services, as a real threat. They were not interested in exports. Some of them would probably not have had anything against the complete exclusion of the sector from GATS. Thus, to a certain extent, these countries and the k-group members did not play the same negotiating game. The "target countries" feared neither status quo nor potential American sanctions.

In light of these developments, the United States reconsidered its sector-wide MFN exemption toward the end of the negotiations. The United States was now willing to extend its existing financial services regime to all participants on an MFN basis. However, only countries with a high level of commitments were to be granted the benefits of future US liberalization in the sector. The US delegation submitted a revised request for an MFN exemption that would allow for such a "two-tier approach," and presented it as a major improvement. Others, including the EC, were not willing to accept any form of conditional MFN in a key sector such as financial services.

In mid-November 1993, the director general of GATT, in an unusual move, warned that:

> "... certain positions taken recently on financial services might prove to be counterproductive. Indeed, there was evidence that unless there was an urgent review of these positions, not only would past and current efforts to improve existing offers falter, but the important progress already achieved might begin to unravel. [The Director General] called upon the United States, in particular, to find workable solutions." [GATT, 1993]

However, the United States did not bend. The commitments of many target countries were still deemed to be insufficient, and a two-tier outcome was seen as the only possible negotiated result. A compromise was worked out in the final days before the deadline set for the negotiation, 15 December 1993. To save the situation countries were given more time – six months after the entry into force of GATS (1 January 1995) – for negotiations aimed at reaching a level of commitments that would permit a solution based on unconditional MFN. Meanwhile offers were transformed into commitments which, together with the need for MFN exemptions, could be revised after the six-month period. As a quid pro quo for accepting this formula, developing countries, led by India, required, and got, prolonged negotiations on movement of "natural persons" as well.

The six months for extended negotiations did not suffice to solve the problem in line with US interests. The negotiations were the subject of a hearing of the Senate Banking, Housing and Urban Affairs Committee three weeks before the new deadline, 30 June 1995. A US Senator sent a very clear message to the top US negotiators:

> ... I have no doubt that the World Trade Organization officials, and your counterparts in other nations, are probably calling to urge you to sign a deal – any deal. Our message today is – and I think it's clear – don't let them play us for a sucker. If it's a bad deal, don't sign it. It's as simple as that. [Bond, 1995]

The US Treasury and the US Trade Representative found it to be a bad deal. Shortly before the deadline US negotiators declared that progress was not sufficient for the United States to grant full MFN treatment in the financial sector. Thus the United States stuck to the offer under which MFN treatment was granted for operations under the existing national regime only, while any improvements in US regulations would be implemented without an MFN obligation included in GATS.

Against this background the EC, in an unusual move, took the lead at the end of the six-month period and managed to prevent the unraveling of the package of commitments that would have occurred if others had followed the United States by limiting commitments and taking MFN exemptions. Strong EC lobbying resulted in the binding of "best offers" on an MFN basis by almost 30 countries, including the EC itself, Japan, and a number of countries that had been the "targets" of the US strategy, during yet another interim period lasting until the end of 1997. This made the United States a "free rider" under the MFN offers by 30 other countries. This showed that the EC, and others that followed the EC lead, had security points that were substantially lower than the largely politically determined security point of the United States.

The deal that resulted from the EC initiative, which showed that trade theory-related considerations weighed heavily within the EC with regard to trade in financial services, was labeled "a very good second best" by the Secretary General of the WTO, the institution that succeeded GATT on 1 January 1995 as a result of the Uruguay Round. Before the end of the interim period, 31 December 1997, new negotiations are likely to take place on financial services. The EC and the other participants in the interim solution no doubt hope that the time gained will help to lower the US security point to a more realistic level so that a permanent solution can be achieved on a full MFN basis (Kremenyuk *et al.*, 1994).

8.3.5   Maritime services

In maritime services the EC, Japan, and the Nordic countries were the main demandeurs, forming the k-group. The United States belonged to the main targets,
as did a number of advanced developing countries. Initially the US administration,
responding to the strongly protectionist interest of the domestic industry, refused to
discuss any commitments on market access and national treatment in the sector. Simultaneously, the United States requested a sector-wide MFN exemption covering
all relevant measures. Status quo was clearly the preferred option for the United
States.

First, the Nordic countries and then the EC led a group of countries that worked
toward securing sufficient commitments concerning market access and national
treatment from a critical mass of participants by developing a set of model commitments. However, here, as well, security points were at high levels. The sector
was by and large already characterized by a substantial degree of liberalization.
In particular large shipping nations, such as Greece and Denmark within the EC
and Norway, were not willing to settle for anything less than a codification of the
rule of the "open seas." An outcome at an intermediate level, which would lead
to recognition of unilateral restrictions that had so far never been recognized under
international law, was regarded as unacceptable. These countries also found the
status quo, meaning a lack of formalized restrictions, preferable to an agreement
that contained questionable reservations, and therefore a sort of legitimation, for
various barriers and discriminatory practices.

In the final phase of the negotiations, mainly as a quid pro quo for the EC's
readiness to discuss commitments concerning audiovisual services, the United
States showed willingness to take on maritime commitments concerning international shipping, the disputed subsector, and join the search for a critical mass.
However, the EC found the US offer far from satisfactory, and just before the
deadline, when it was clear that no deal would emerge for audiovisual services,
the United States and the EC agreed that the critical mass had not made sufficient
commitments concerning maritime services. Again, lack of export interests was an
important explanation for weak or abstract commitments from a number of target
countries. When it became clear that the basis for an agreement did not exist, both
the United States and the EC withdrew their maritime offers, and the negotiations
were prolonged in this sector as well, until June 1996. Given that the United States,
as well as leading shipping nations within the EC, saw status quo as an acceptable, or even preferable outcome, albeit for different reasons, this outcome was not
surprising.

8.3.6   Telecommunication services

The situation concerning basic telecommunication services was somewhat different compared to financial and maritime services because real negotiations on commitments never started within the framework of the Uruguay Round. Initially, participants thought that it would not be possible to agree on commitments in this sector, which was characterized by monopolies in many countries, i.e., within most EC member states. However, during the course of the round rapid technological evolution made it clear that attempts to protect national monopolies would soon be overtaken by events. The United States deregulated its market in the 1980s and the EC launched an ambitious plan for internal deregulation.

In late 1991 the United States requested a wide MFN exemption for basic telecommunications in order to safeguard its ability unilaterally to sanction countries that were closed to US telecommunication companies. However, at the same time the United States declared its willingness to remove the exemption if specified countries – all the OECD countries plus Mexico, Korea, Hong Kong, and Singapore – were willing to make commitments reciprocal to those offered by the United States in the area of long-distance telephony.

However, it was clear, in particular because internal EC deregulation would not be achieved until 1998, that the commitments the United States needed for a reciprocal outcome could not be reached within the time frame of the Uruguay Round. Recognizing this, negotiators decided to settle for a mandate for continued negotiations concerning basic telecommunications as the result of the Uruguay Round. Thereafter, time and effort were spent on working out the text of the mandate, and on securing participation in these negotiations from a critical mass of countries. Finally, participants agreed to prolong the negotiations until April 1996. In fact, this agreement served as the model for the outcome on maritime services referred to above.

8.4   Concluding Remarks

In this chapter, trade negotiations have been viewed as processes through which governments seek to achieve economically desirable results within the limits of national and international political constraints. The presentation has shown, first, how negotiators in the Uruguay Round services negotiations managed to agree on common rules for trade in services. Key rules such as MFN, were, however, weaker than the corresponding rules in GATT. Second, the chapter has elaborated on how negotiators failed to reach agreement on permanent and meaningful commitments in important service sectors. How can this outcome be explained in terms of trade theory and negotiation theory, respectively?

Not surprisingly, neither trade theory nor negotiation theory fully explains the result. At the same time, both are relevant for such an explanation, but at different stages of the negotiating process. When testing the applicability of the theories the findings of the paper suggest that two questions should be separated: namely, why do countries enter into trade negotiations, and why does a particular outcome occur?

8.4.1   Trade theory

The negotiations on GATS indicate that trade theory contributes to an answer to the first question. The gains from international trade and the resulting economic growth, as predicted by classical and neoclassical trade theory, explain why governments are eager to engage in trade negotiations. But trade theory cannot explain why negotiations succeed or fail, or, if they succeed, the outcome.

As pointed out above, if participants in the Uruguay Round had followed the prescriptions of classical and neoclassical trade theory, the shape and content of GATS would have been very different from the final outcome. The ideal regime would have provided for unrestricted trade in services among the 117 participants on the basis of comparative advantages. Such a regime would have promoted exports of labor-intensive services from developing to developed countries and exports of capital-intensive services – such as financial and telecommunication services – in the opposite direction, to the benefit of all. However, this type of result did not occur in the Uruguay Round. Furthermore, participants failed to agree on commitments regarding national treatment and market access within key sectors.

Thus, trade theory explains neither why the rules of GATS are weaker than the rules of GATT, nor why participants were not able to agree on commitments in key service sectors. This should come as no surprise, since trade theory is not constructed to explain outcomes in international negotiations. For instance, trade theory does not take into account political constraints on the ability of governments to act. From a trade negotiation perspective, trade theory instead performs as an ideal roadmap for participants that seek economically beneficial results despite political constraints. The EU leadership, resulting in the interim solution on financial services, shows that the ability of an actor to follow the map varies.

Finally, it should be noted that new trade theories, which often advocate "strategic trade policy" involving various forms of protection, have not been examined in this chapter. Such theories might explain outcomes in trade negotiations better than classical and neoclassical trade theory. However, these theories have a weak spot when it comes to empirical testing. The results of most new trade theories can be neutralized through retaliation, i.e., by strategic action. Since retaliation is likely to occur in the trading system, the potential gains implied by the theory would probably seldom be obtained. Furthermore, GATS, as well as GATT, can be seen as regimes whose purpose is to institutionalize retaliation of this kind, and thereby render opportunistic first moves on the basis of new trade theories futile (Richardson, 1990; Ekholm and Torstensson, 1989).

8.4.2 Negotiation theory

Negotiation theory is a necessary, but not sufficient, tool for an explanation of the shape and content of the final Uruguay Round outcome on services. In particular, the admittedly imprecise concept of reciprocity, which performs an important function in the border zone between areas covered by economic and political theory, is crucial to such an explanation.

However, the analytical tools that fall under the label of negotiation theory have to be complemented by consideration of structural factors, notably the distribution of power both in the international system and domestically. Stronger international structural constraints made a number of GATS rules weaker than the corresponding rules under GATT. The transition from a hegemonic structure of international economic power to one involving a need for collective leadership explains why the negotiations on GATS were characterized by searches for specific, rather than diffuse, forms of reciprocity. It also shows why major actors, with the United States in the lead, backed by domestic business interests, formed k-groups and concentrated on achieving a sufficient level of commitment from a critical mass of countries. However, the security points of k-group members were set at high levels, which led to demands at equally high levels that were too high for the rest of the target countries. Many of them declined to meet requests, referring to infant industry-related arguments, and lack of export interests rendered threats of closure of other markets ineffective. The k-group members failed to realize that the potential free riders did not value the free rider option highly.

When only part of the "critical mass" made satisfactory contributions, the liberalizing effort in financial, maritime, and telecommunication services failed to produce liberalizing results. The United States in particular was not willing to agree to solutions that would give free rides to countries that had been defined as belonging to the critical mass. Demands largely formulated by domestic service providers could not be lowered. Thus, large participants, such as the United States and, to a lesser extent, the EC, found themselves caught in the Negotiator's Dilemma, referred to by Kremenyuk, Sjöstedt, and Zartman in the introductory chapter. Inflated demands led to no rewards. In this situation links to other parts of the agenda of the Uruguay Round served as a safety net. A complete failure in any of the three main sectors would have put the whole services negotiation, and thereby the entire Uruguay Round, at risk. In order to save the situation, participants had to agree to continue negotiations. In the financial services sector these negotiations ended in yet another interim solution, which could be achieved once the EC escaped the dilemma of the mercantilist negotiator. The United States, however, is still held fast by mercantilist fetters.

The meager initial results in key sectors do not imply that agreements on liberalization cannot be found in these areas, but they do suggest that the attainment of such agreements under the present structure of power is more time consuming, and technically more difficult, than in a hegemonic system. In this regard, it is important that reciprocity is ultimately a subjective concept. When more time is given for negotiations, participants have an opportunity to lower their security points, which the EC has already done in the financial services sector, and to find compromise solutions without losing face.

The Uruguay Round experience of negotiations on trade in services shows that the lack of a hegemon willing to accept diffuse reciprocity puts a larger part of the responsibility for a liberal outcome on potential free riders, i.e., on often small and medium-sized countries to which the major participants' requests are directed, and whose commitments are necessary to build the critical mass. Part of the failure to include important sectors under the provisions of GATS can be blamed on mercantilist sentiments in the United States and disagreement between the United States and the EC. However, the failure of newly industrialized countries and some developing countries in Latin America and Asia to deliver sufficient commitments in response to requests from the leaders also contributed. These countries will have to come up with better commitments in the prolonged negotiations that are still under way, and in future negotiations. If not, it might not be possible to establish a comprehensive and liberal regime for trade in services. Likewise, the United States and, to a lesser extent, the EC will probably have to lower their demands somewhat in order to reach an equilibrium point. If the participants in the prolonged negotiations were able to follow the road map provided by trade theory, they would not hesitate to make their contributions.

Note

[1] This chapter was completed in September 1995 and does not take into account events that have taken place thereafter, including important WTO agreements concerning trade in telecommunication and financial services.

Chapter 9

Negotiations on Setting Up a Common Trade Regime in the Commonwealth of Independent States

Maria G. Vlasova

9.1 Introduction

This chapter examines the explanatory power of both economic and negotiation theories in regard to economic talks among the Commonwealth of Independent States (CIS) nations within four years after the breakup of the Soviet Union. Intrinsic features of the economic agenda in the CIS are determined by traditional cooperation, historical economic ties, and interdependence of the entities that used to comprise a single economy organized on the principles of centralized planning, government fiat, and heavy social programming. Since the USSR collapsed, ex-Soviet republics have become sovereign actors that recognize no superior authority and are not subject to any supranational ruling body. Under such circumstances the only peaceful way left for them to settle various issues pertaining to economic distribution and coordination is to conduct negotiations. Issues under debate that require participation of all member nations embrace various economic matters, including division of economic assets and liabilities of the former USSR, in particular, external debt and property abroad, and valuable entities such as the Black Sea Fleet and Baikonur Space Center, as well as preservation of economic ties and coordination of trade, monetary, and financial policies.

Negotiation in the CIS is a complex, ongoing process characterized by typical properties of international negotiations: "multiple-actor, multiple-issue, multiple-stage events" (Dupont and Faure, 1991). Various activities, decisions, and declarations of the CIS members, both regional and individual, affect the negotiating context and every round of talks, thereby shaping the negotiators' perceptions of the interests, positions, intentions, and capabilities of their own constituency and of other parties. Only through examining this negotiation background is it possible to grasp the cause/effect links between negotiators' interests and negotiation results.

Before examining the properties of economic negotiations in the CIS it seems appropriate to identify several methodological restrictions. In this case attention should mainly be addressed to the analysis of the pretext, issues, forms, and outcomes of negotiations rather than individual and group interests and influences involved in the bargaining, although their importance is recognized. We shall not consider cultural and ethnic differences among the CIS negotiators, as the impact of this variable has been limited in economic negotiations between the new states, which inherited a common cultural background that had existed more than 70 years.

Since its foundation the CIS faces a multitude of problems in the social, political, and economic areas. Unstable social and economic development, a high degree of uncertainty in the evolution of a common market, and the maintenance of joint military and strategic security space give grounds for the contradictory evaluations, comparisons, and prognoses of experts, politicians, and public opinion polls that from time to time appear in the Russian and foreign press. "The question arises whether the CIS exists to date. Maybe, yes, but only to little extent. Since the agreement in Belovezhskaya Puscha was made, over 400 agreements have been signed but hardly any agreement has been backed by any concrete deed" (Rogov, 1994).

What forces lead to the present ambiguous relationships between the countries in the CIS, which, in turn, from time to time prompt them to negotiate for better terms of economic partnership, or ignore certain meetings and withdraw from joint agreements on economic alliances? What factors determine actor strategies and the outcomes of economic negotiations between the CIS nations?

In answering these questions we first need to highlight the properties of economic negotiations in the CIS to establish whether they differ from other types of bargaining and distinguish their specific characteristics. Second, we must determine variables that share an impact on negotiation dynamics and economic strategies of the CIS members. Third, we need to address attempts by the Newly

Independent States (NIS) to identify and pursue their own sovereign interests in the economic sphere and see how these moves can build a common trade regime.

9.2   Reasons to Negotiate Trade

The development of the CIS reveals the increasing role of negotiations in the transitional period confronting the CIS members engaged in nation building. Why did nations of the CIS choose to negotiate for common trade regulation after they became independent? When they were parts of the Soviet economy, there was scarcely any need for economic negotiations. Government orders pertaining to goods, materials, services, distribution channels of supply, and sales were established by the centrally regulated structures on a command and control basis. Money resources were allocated by the decisions of the supreme authorities of the Communist Party. Leaders of the Soviet republics came to Moscow to request allocations for their domain's development and to report on their achievements. Economic considerations were limited to the need to maintain social order and to obtain required external financing through exports of oil, gas, raw materials, and military equipment. Foreign trade was controlled by state quotas and centrally distributed licenses.

The breakup of the centralized economy of the USSR gave rise to new economic actors within the CIS and the need to establish ties on the level of both governments and enterprises. Fundamental change in the CIS economies has entailed a shift from a centrally planned economy to many new economic entities building up market relationships. This brought about the need to respond to demand and to evaluate results in terms of economic efficiency, which in turn had an impact on the development of a negotiation process between the CIS members.

What are the challenges confronting the CIS negotiators and how can one explain negotiating dynamics? In highlighting major topics of economic negotiations in the CIS one needs to take into consideration systemic traits comprising political transformation and market development in the post-Soviet republics. They affect the positions and attitudes toward economic alliance in the CIS countries. Since the collapse of the USSR two major trends prevailed in the CIS. First, members sought to ensure economic sovereignty by isolationist and protectionist measures in an attempt to reduce the disadvantages of strategic dependence on the Moscow center and the ensuing unequal economic exchange. Second, they wished to restore manufacturing and technological ties based on differences in available resources, the advantages of a single network of transportation and communication, and a high integration of scientific and technological conditions and standards.

These two trends have had both economic and symbolic meaning. Protectionism was rooted in the long-held view of the Soviet center as the main evil to republics. It was later associated with Russia and the questions "Who feeds whom?"

and "Whose economy suffers?" i.e., whether Russia provided cheap resources to other NIS, or whether the NIS provided invaluable economic gains for Russia. This distributive calculation of gains and losses created discontent with existing economic ties and doubts about the benefits of a common market, and resulted in divergence in the aims of the NIS. Differences between the former Soviet republics have been strengthened by different rates of transition to market and economic reform, including price liberalization and privatization of industry.

Preservation of "a common economic space" (later altered to "the reviving of economic ties") was mandated by the results of the referendum on "the union of a new type" (March 1991) and public opinion favoring moves toward integration, as well as by traditional division of labor, interindustry and intraindustry specialization, and cooperation that produced a high degree of interdependence among the CIS economies. In an interdependent system, the viability of the CIS economies depends on the economic channels within the CIS, prompting them to negotiate for better terms of economic cooperation in the transitional period. Hence, the major challenge of economic negotiations in the CIS comprises a contradiction between long-term aims (sustainability of each national economy) and short-term means (viability of economic exchange on privileged terms within the CIS). In the remainder of this analysis, we intend to highlight the following features:

- Economic negotiations in the CIS are handled mainly by governments.
- Economic negotiations comprise three levels of decision making.
- The CIS negotiating style is affected by the heritage of the Soviet negotiating style.
- Economic issues are linked to political matters.

9.3   Economic Regulation by Governments

While the free play of market forces is now gaining recognition in the CIS, government regulation of internal and external economic relations is the dominant feature of the CIS economies. Government penetration into the economic sphere is not limited to emerging transitional economies; instead it is a common vehicle used by sovereign states to achieve their political and economic goals. As Gilpin (1987) concedes, "... whereas economists think in terms of aggregate solutions and global equilibrium, governments and special interests think in terms of specific sectors and are therefore primarily concerned about who produces what products." However, the role of the state in the CIS economies has had some peculiarities. In general, governments have performed three economic functions: as owners of valuable assets, enterprises, and resources; as legislators designing the legal framework for economic activities; and as administrators supervising and regulating the mechanics of cooperation and distribution.

Governments have been the main actors in the negotiations, including summits of the heads of state and heads of government, meetings of ministers (defense, internal affairs, security, transport, oil and gas, etc.), discussions with the heads of foreign economic ministries, and sessions of the CIS Customs Council and of the Economic Coordination and Consultation Committee. Actors other than governments, including the Inter-Republic Parliamentary Assembly, national central banks, and Russian monopolist producers (Russian Gas Corporation; Russian Contract Corporation; Russian Agricultural Corporation), have participated in the negotiation process, but their role has been reduced to facilitation and support. Overall, economic negotiations have been subject to governmental regulation, which generally leads to bureaucratic delays in decision making. One objective of such regulation has been to accommodate interest groups.

There are two main reasons for the paramount role of the governments as economic negotiators. First, the NIS have not yet finished restructuring their economies through privatization, liberalization, and deregulation to provide room for economic initiative by firms and individuals. In the transitional period NIS governments have retained regulatory leverage in both domestic and foreign economic activities by establishing restrictions and rewards, providing economic aid and credits, issuing licenses, imposing trade barriers, determining currency and terms of payments, etc. Second, economic exchange within the CIS involves strategic resources and is conducted mainly in the form of barter, "interstate order supplies," and credit-linked deliveries. Therefore, the governments have a major say and a viable "visible hand" in securing vital commodities through imports and in obtaining financial reserves by exporting merchandise through intergovernmental arrangements.

9.4 The Structure of the Agenda in the CIS Economic Talks

The current economic situation affects the prioritization of goals for CIS negotiation. Recession creates incentives to defect from collective agreements in order to reduce vulnerability and dependence. Hence, depression strengthens calls for immediate solutions and some gains that might seem immediately available. "Cooperation becomes riskier in the short run and less valued over the long haul" (Lipson, 1984).

Due to the economic decline in all CIS countries, the value placed on short-term economic benefits has exceeded perceived gains from future prospects of economic cooperation for the majority of member states. This situation stimulated their pre-occupation with immediate issues of annual deliveries and credits. However, because of economic interdependence and structural imbalance, CIS members were also concerned with obtaining stability in their trade relations through common patterns and standards. Some member states sought broader integrative arrangements and benefits from closer coordination. This was rooted in the intrinsic characteristics of economic issues, which tend to be "characterized by elaborate networks of rules, norms, and institutions, grounded in reasonably stable convergent expectations" (Lipson, 1984). These stable expectations may be developed and maintained with the help of regimes that are primarily designed to "establish stable mutual expectations about patterns of behavior and to develop working relations" (Keohane, 1984), as they reduce transaction costs, produce repeated behavior, and in general, reinforce and institutionalize reciprocity (Axelrod, 1984). The differing interests of the CIS nations have generated diverse types of multilateral talks and different outcomes in the form of multilateral agreements.

The first level includes talks focusing on concrete issues of maintaining existing trade ties and negotiating such factors as price and amount of exports/imports, type of currency, and the system of clearance and settlement between the CIS countries. These talks have resulted in various agreements: on multilateral, interstate specialization of production and delivery of high-quality and hybrid seeds of agricultural crops; on interaction in the fields of land surveying, cartography, registering, and scanning; on joint actions to provide the economy and the public with electricity and heat in the autumn–winter period; and on cooperation in such sectors as construction or chemical production.

The second level deals with another type of negotiations, aimed at trade relations, at establishing a propitious trade and customs regime, and at coordinating monetary and credit policies in the CIS that alleviate barriers to trade and minimize the political impact on economic affairs. This type of negotiation indicates a larger degree of coordination between the CIS members. The outcomes include agreements on the mutual recognition of property rights and on regulation of property relations, on the concept of the payment union, and on the customs union, etc., as well as a draft standard bilateral agreement to set the exchange of national currencies between the CIS states and a draft agreement on a free trade zone.

The third level reveals broader attempts to conduct negotiations that entail economic integration of the CIS countries through creation of common economic structures and oversee their implementation in areas defined as spheres of common economic regulation of the CIS members. It comprises agreements on common institutions designed to expand mutual economic coordination, including an economic court, an interstate bank, an interstate economic committee under the auspices of the CIS heads of state, etc.

How can one predict the general inclinations of the CIS negotiators with regard to the depth of economic integration and the type of talks they are ready to participate in? As Snyder and Robinson (1960) have indicated, the process of negotiation involves mutual attempts to influence the choices of the parties and movement of parties to a "commonly acceptable point of agreement." Similarly, Raiffa (1982) argued that a final contract lies in the "zone of agreement" confined by "reservation prices" of the parties. BATNA represents the security point or the "estimate of costs and benefits without agreement" (Zartman and Berman, 1982). The reservation prices or security points serve as limits of parties' flexibility in terms of their policy choices, room for concessions, and vulnerability to pressure. A zone of agreement may be enhanced by the integrative potential of a negotiation, meaning "the possibility of finding new options that are better for both parties than those that are obvious at first" (Pruitt, 1991).

Economic negotiations in the CIS were characterized by a common security point – that of maintaining political sovereignty and an independent status in regulating the internal economy. Given that background, CIS negotiators were unable successfully to tackle economic issues in a direct way. However, they did achieve the integrative potential through package agreements that satisfied their need to be perceived as "important" and equal trade partners and that were above their security points. Different degrees of flexibility in the security points of the CIS members affected the varying economic arrangements agreed upon by negotiators in the trade area, ranging from a mild form of a free trade zone to a strict form of common economic space.

9.5 Negotiation Process

What are the implications of the negotiation architecture for the negotiation dynamics? Negotiations are usually characterized by two general phases: a formula phase and a detail phase. While the first phase seems to imply a sufficient amount of cooperation and coordination, the second calls for competitive bargaining (Zartman and Berman, 1982; Dupont and Faure, 1991). Under CIS constraints, this led to success in the first phase, where negotiators agreed on broad declarations of intentions, and to disagreement over specific articles requiring economic contributions or political sacrifices.

For instance, on 13 March 1992, leaders of Russia and four Asian republics signed an agreement on the principles of a common customs policy and established the regulations of the customs council. Numerous meetings of customs experts preceded the event. The customs union was expected to be recognized as the subject of international law and was designed to introduce a unified system of customs duties and internal taxation of goods moving within the customs territories. All CIS members displayed interest in a single customs policy for trade with third countries. However, at the CIS summit only five heads of government were ready to sign the agreement on the creation of a customs union, meaning "a common customs territory, common rules and an absence of internal customs barriers." This was despite Russia's attempt to coordinate the efforts to construct the customs union. Armenia, Belarus, and Moldova signed only some articles; representatives of Ukraine did not have authority to sign the agreement; Azerbaijan did not sign it either. Hence, while the CIS negotiators displayed consensus and a desire to cooperate at the stage of formula discussion, which did not require specific commitments, at the detail stage they withdrew from agreement because they remained within the security point of independence and status quo and were reluctant to make concessions.

Economic negotiations have been affected by the heritage of the Soviet negotiating style, particularly the desire to be treated as equals by the economic Great Powers. This style includes a tendency to seek generally worded accords, a view of compromise as weakness, the use of negotiations to maximize power, and the priority of relations over agreements as the essential output of negotiations: "The Soviets may not always seek an agreement from negotiations; to the contrary, they may only wish that some sort of dialogue be maintained" (Sloss and Davis, 1987). A continuation of the Soviet negotiating style is natural, because NIS negotiators have been influenced by Soviet organizational culture, have retained common perceptions, and have not yet developed individual styles in economic negotiations. Differences in their strategies and tactics (full membership/associate/observer, attendance/avoidance of summits, signing/reservations/withdrawal from signing of agreements, compliance/not, etc.) hinge on various power resources available and on the negotiators' diverse perceptions of status, gains, and losses.

9.6   Prioritization of Issues

The fourth feature of economic negotiations in the CIS is the difficulty in negotiating purely economic issues because of the need to subordinate the economic agenda to political considerations. General issues that have been raised in talks on economic alliance in the CIS include maintaining a common economic space, a ruble zone, and a common currency; providing credits; creating a clearing and payments mechanism; settling mutual debts; determining ownership and supply of resources; and coordinating economic structures and economic policies. Trade issues included primarily transit policies, customs policies, means of payment, agreement about mutual supplies, and border control. However, economic issues in the CIS are closely linked to political circumstances and are often overridden by them. Domestic politics, social and military conflicts, and migration comprise the negotiating context in the CIS and have a great impact on the outcomes of economic negotiations. Considering these circumstances, two questions arise: What was the impact of the economic agenda on the negotiation output, and how did political concerns affect the resolution of economic issues?

On the one hand, in contrast to security issues, economic issues are more likely to be transparent for the monitoring needed to verify compliance, thus providing guarantees for enforcement and reciprocity. It has also been contended that economic issues are more likely to be characterized by two organizational conditions for cooperation: "(1) the future is not highly discounted and (2) the penalty for unreciprocated cooperation is not devastating" (Lipson, 1984).

Properties of economic issues in the CIS influenced negotiating performance and the attitudes of the NIS considerably. In particular, demand for the distribution of assets of the former USSR brought about a distributive approach and a calculation of who would get how much and under what conditions. The need to supply national economies with strategic resources, including fuel and energy, and to provide industries with sufficient orders made negotiators quite rational in evaluating terms of agreements on shipments and delivery. The propensity of the NIS to establish common economic arrangements was strengthened by the possibility of measuring the benefits for each party (e.g., annual agreements on free trade), by weak penalties or lack of measures against violators of trade agreements, and by the prospects of long-term mutual interdependence (e.g., customs union).

On the other hand, settlement of economic issues was complicated by the regard for equality and status maintenance. Status-versus-welfare calculations have been typical for international negotiations, where they bring about different expectations and interactive patterns (Lipson, 1984). When the aim of the interaction is to maximize the difference between one's own score and that of opponents, a "status game" is involved (Shubik, 1971). It transforms a variable-sum game into a competitive struggle with little possibility for joint gains, in which status considerations prevail over welfare calculations (Lipson, 1984). The zero-sum approach and prevalence of the basic concern for status have been impediments to cooperative conventions in both security and economic talks. Both types of negotiation include a mixture of status and welfare calculations "but in economic negotiations, status goals are seldom a significant end in themselves," while talks on security issues are perceived as "strictly competitive struggles," which make economic issues more likely to bring about a cooperative outcome (Lipson, 1984). However, in the transitional period the NIS tended to link economic issues to status considerations and to choose options that were not optimal for their welfare, but that seemed best to meet the perception of independent status (e.g., the decision to issue weak national currencies to be used in trade settlements between the NIS).

Another dimension of the problem refers to different perceptions regarding the equality of negotiators in bilateral and multilateral negotiations. "Parties are both equal and unequal in their roles and status in multilateral negotiation, whereas they are assumed to be equal in status (even if not in power) in bilateral negotiation" (Zartman, 1991:74). The CIS members are unequal in terms of power, which exposes them to frustration and attempts to display their actual or perceived weight.

Russia is the strongest economy of the CIS, and is essential for the stability and security in the region (Kremenyuk, 1992). Based on its absolute and relative power, Russia tends to play the dominant role in the CIS, but other CIS nations are strong enough to oppose its dominance by trying to use mutual interdependence and alignment with more powerful neighbors. To improve their own relative standing and the distribution of payoffs, parties in the CIS tend to convert multilateral talks into bilateral bargaining. This provides a stronger basis for their perceptions of equal status regarding the customs union, ruble zone, etc. (Sagorskij, 1993). Given the economic interdependence of Russia and other CIS countries, Russia cannot effectively threaten to use military tools to achieve its economic goals, despite its military dominance. Instead, Russia must try tit-for-tat and conditional bargaining over economic issues with other CIS states less equipped with military means but possessing values in other areas.

Thus, the economic agenda affected the performance of the CIS negotiators in different ways. It colored the distributive character of the process. It prompted a fairly rational approach to determining choices deriving from the ability to measure options and results. The influence of political considerations reflected the priority placed on maintaining status and sustaining the equality of negotiating parties. Economic efforts that required multilateral integration usually were not successfully resolved in the CIS due to the lack of mechanisms for compliance and enforcement and a preference for quick fixes over long-term gains.

9.7   Options for Negotiating the Common Trade Policy

9.7.1   Static dimension

Negotiating outcomes in the CIS included legitimation, institutionalization, and enforcement of an emerging trade regime. To work out a common regime, the NIS have tried several institutional arrangements to maintain, or procure, benefits of trade cooperation and reduce potential losses. They include:

- A free trade zone based on the regulation of trade policies within the regional bloc (1991–1995).
- A customs union, originally planned on the basis of a common CIS customs territory (1992) and finally established by a trilateral agreement (1995).

- A monetary union, originally with the ruble as the common currency (1992–1993) and then discussed as a second stage of strengthening monetary integration (1994–1995).
- A "common economic space" (as a "market" was only emerging slowly), originally based on transparent borders for the movement of labor, capital, goods and with the ruble as a common monetary unit (1992–1993) and then viewed as a prospect for the economic reintegration of core states (1994–1995).

What are the national interests behind the choice among possible types of trade regime in the CIS? The priorities of the NIS depend on a variety of factors. Negotiating demands in the CIS are determined by the economic and political transition, which comprises a shift from the unified Soviet state to independent nations, from the planned economic system to a mixed economy, from the socialist ideology to the ideology of nationalism, and from an authoritarian regime to a political system based on democratic elections, and also reflects an "overall shift from vertical social relations to horizontal social relations" (Ury, 1992). Yet this shift is not uniform. Varying trends in the NIS became evident at certain phases of their independent development.

The choice of degree of involvement in the economic alliance in the CIS was determined by structural factors (relative power and interdependence), as well as by the dynamic characteristics of actors (perception of gains and losses). The components of power available to the CIS negotiators included international prestige, political viability, involvement in military conflicts, and the degree of economic significance and dependence.

The international prestige of the NIS pertains to international recognition, participation in international organizations, summit meetings with foreign leaders, the coverage of the country by the international press, etc. The largest countries of the CIS – Russia, Ukraine, and to a lesser extent Belarus – are recognized internationally because of their size and traditional membership in the UN. Georgia and Kazakhstan have to a large extent been visible and important due to the proactive role of their leaders. Other states may lean on relations with stronger neighbors to strengthen their negotiating positions. While those with high prestige have used the tactics of political pressure to pursue their objectives, the smaller countries have requested special treatment and economic aid.

Internal political struggle in some of the NIS has also conditioned national interests in economic negotiations and policy choices. The more intense the political strife, the smaller is the likelihood of agreements on economic coordination and the more do national interests reflect noneconomic matters. The opposition in NIS has usually been critical of integrative moves and has tended to interpret them as detrimental to their independent status. Ruling elites have used bilateral agreements to obtain required resources and to attain economic stabilization. Another important factor is political independence as perceived by newly sovereign countries. The more independence is considered vital, the more unlikely is the success of economic integration, due to the lack of internal political incentives for coordination and cooperation. A concern for independence will also make it more difficult for more developed countries to take advantage of this economic dependence for pressure and unilateral gains.

Involvement in military conflicts also has implications for economic negotiations. Six of the 12 member states have been engaged in military conflicts, sometimes with the involvement of neighboring states and the Russian army. At the initial phase of conflict, there was no need for negotiations, as states preferred military means to achieve their goals. The longer the conflict lasted, the greater was the deprivation of resources and economic plight and, thus, the dependence on Russia, the most powerful member of the bloc. The use of negotiation to obtain economic and military aid increased as the conflicts unfolded.

Economic disparities and overall economic decline have affected the relative power of the NIS. As a result of the breakup of the USSR, the gaps among CIS members with regard to their economic performance have increased. The CIS Committee on Statistics indicated that GDP per capita by the end of 1993 was 10% less in Ukraine than in Russia, 30–34% less in Kazakhstan, and 80% less in Uzbekistan (*Vnezhnyaya Torgovlya*, #12, 1993). Despite the decline in industrial output, as illustrated in *Table 9.1*, and the decrease in volume of CIS trade, CIS trade relations are rather intensive. According to the CIS Statistics Committee, 40% of the aggregate external trade took place within the CIS in 1994. As a result, all NIS have become dependent on trade agreements negotiated among themselves.

The level of external dependence has been a major determinant of the opportunities offered by the CIS. Statistical findings prove that the smaller the territory, population, and economic potential of the country, the more a nation depends on cross-regional ties (Granberg, 1994). The significance of dependence should be considered in both absolute and relative terms. The assessment should also distinguish between the dependence on other countries and the impact made on them. The degree of impact within a regional bloc could be estimated on the basis of the monetary, industrial, agricultural, or mineral resources of a country that are demanded by other members of the bloc. Economic impact in the CIS essentially depends on fuel and energy resources, agricultural resources, the volume of industrial output, the size of currency reserves, and control of other valuable property. The degree of dependence is a function of the degree to which required resources must be imported from other countries, taking the cost factor into consideration.

Table 9.1. Indexes of GDP in the CIS states.[a]

	In % to previous year increase, reduction (−)				In % to 1990, reduction (−)		
	1991	1992	1993	1994	1992	1993	1994
Azerbaijan	−0.7	−22.6	−23.1	−22.0	−23.1	−40.9	−53.8
Armenia	−8.8	−52.3	−14.8	−5.5	−56.5	−62.9	−60.9
Belarus	−1.2	−9.6	−10.6	−20.0	−10.7	−20.2	−36.3
Georgia	−20.1	−40.3	−39.4	−30.0	−52.3	−71.1	−79.8
Kazakhstan	−11.8	−13.0	−12.9	−25.0	−23.3	−33.2	−50.1
Kyrgystan	−4.2	−16.4	−16.4	−25.0	−19.9	−33.0	−50.0
Moldova	−18.7	−28.3	−4.8	−30.0	−41.7	−44.5	−61.2
Russia	−12.8	−19.0	−12.0	−15.0	−29.4	−37.8	−47.2
Tajikistan	−	−	−17.3	−12.0[b]	−	−	−
Uzbekistan	−0.5	−11.1	−2.4	−4.0	−11.5	−13.7	−16.7
Ukraine	−11.6	−13.7	−14.2	−19.0[b]	−23.7	−34.5	−47.0[b]

[a]No data on Turkmenistan.
[b]Estimate.
Source: Interfax, Statistichesky Vestnik, 26 May 1995, #21 (140).

The distribution of economic power and the degree of external dependence determine the divergence of individual strategies of the CIS members in the search for greater gains. In particular, Russia and Ukraine tend to diversify their economic relations to reduce direct dependence on other CIS economies, while at the same time maintaining a considerable impact on CIS processes. Belarus, Kazakhstan, and Uzbekistan, which are less competitive at the world market than the first two and more dependent on Russia, have tried to derive benefits from the economic relations within the CIS. Armenia, Georgia, Kyrgystan, and Tajikistan seek arrangements to subsidize their economies by means of external aid. Azerbaijan, Moldova, and Turkmenistan have used available resources and/or cooperation with their neighbors to reduce dependence on the CIS economic bloc.

In the interdependent CIS, all economies have something to offer, either exclusive products or competitive prices. Belarus exports products of its machine-building industry and agricultural products. Ukraine exports steel, vegetable oil, mineral fertilizers, and metals. Azerbaijan may use its oil deposits as an export product. Moldova exports wines, vegetables, and fruits. Turkmenistan exports gas. Uzbekistan exports cotton, energy, and natural gas as well as vegetables and fruits. Kazakhstan exports grain, coal, and nonferrous metals.

Russia is the main supplier of energy, oil, and gas in the CIS. It also represents an enormous market with its own ruble currency and hard currency reserves. Russia has the lion's share of the extractive industries: it accounts for over 90% of oil, over 75% of gas, 57% of coal, 46% of ferrous ore, and about 64% of bauxite. Likewise, Russia has the largest processing industries: over 55% of steel and ferrous metals production; 60% of steel pipes; about 90–100% of the production of aluminium, nickel, and tin; over 60% of mineral fertilizers and cement; and 80% of asbestos (according to 1990 data). However, Russia needs some important resources from external sources, which it used to get from the former Soviet republics. Russia has only 5% of known reserves of manganese, and less than 3% of chromium, while it consumed 55% of the manganese and about 40% of the chromium of the totals produced in the entire USSR. As for uranium, Russia produces 25% of the total uranium output in the CIS and meets only 65% of its demand, covering the rest with the help of the reserve created by previous supplies from Kazakhstan and Ukraine (Mirlin and Pelymsky, 1995).

Differences in production expenses and location of extraction and processing industries determine the pattern of interdependence of the NIS. Russia has a trade surplus with all NIS, which is of vital importance for ensuring market outlets for its commodities. Scarce resources available to the majority of the CIS nations have made them dependent on Russian supply of fuel and energy. Trade imbalances created by diminishing export opportunities and stable import demand have affected their asymmetrical financial stances. Loans from international financial organizations and credits from Russia's Central Bank only increase their overall debt. Attempts to restrict economic ties with other CIS members and protect the domestic market from the negative impact of the neighboring countries were not effective because of the extremely weak national currencies, high internal debt to enterprises, and weak monetary policies. Hence, mutual dependence serves as the main stimulus and condition for economic negotiations in the CIS.

Outcomes of trade negotiations are subject to economic and political considerations determined by both "comparative advantage, product complementarity, economic distance" and "such factors as geographic proximity, ethnic, cultural, linguistic similarity, traditional affinities and formal international political linkages and commitments" (Alker and Puchala, 1968). Integrational factors relevant in the case of CIS include geographical closeness, interdependence, traditional economic ties between enterprises and ministries, common language, and common technological standards. CIS members inherited a shared organizational culture, mentality, and language for communication. This heritage facilitates economic negotiations that are otherwise complex and difficult to conduct. A large number of participants (12 states) with differently structured economies have had difficulties in finding a common ground. No country has been able, or willing, to perform as a leader in the integration process. Short-term economic interests of the CIS members, such as obtaining credits and mineral resources or settling debts, have come into contradiction with their long-term strategies for modernization and advanced economic development. This dilemma has resulted in inconsistent economic strategies.

9.7.2 Dynamic dimension

Participation in a negotiation means an attempt to meet one's own interests and to promote outcomes that will bring gains and minimize losses. The expected payoff will have an impact on the positions of other negotiating parties and their perception of relative gains and losses from the negotiated outcome. This process has been depicted in terms of give-or-take dilemmas pertaining to the creation of "public goods": the key questions are how much of a shared resource to take and how much to give in order to sustain a collective resource (Aquino *et al.*, 1992). The resolution of these dilemmas is found in relative terms because actors assess gains and losses by comparing them to gains and losses attained by others. Two explanations of noncooperative behavior have been offered: the free rider hypothesis, i.e., a party has an opportunity to accrue benefits without making any sacrifices; and the "sucker effect," i.e., a party defects to avoid paying for the benefits accrued by other parties (Aquino *et al.*, 1992:667).

The relative power of individual CIS members and available alternatives to economic cooperation among the CIS countries have become one of the dominant factors of their negotiating performance. The relatively more powerful states tend to use negotiations to make others comply with their conditions (the sucker effect). The relatively less powerful countries tend to negotiate for generally better terms while avoiding specific binding clauses (the free rider effect). For example, some of the smaller CIS countries participated in negotiations and signed general declarations pertaining to the establishment of a customs union, although their main purpose was to obtain privileges from Russia. Russia, in turn, was eager to coordinate its trade policies with the relatively more powerful CIS members to avoid having its donor role heavily criticized by the domestic political opposition.

The perception of benefits and losses from common trade policies in the CIS underwent several changes over time. The initial general perception in the former Soviet republics was that it would be possible to advance an independent economic policy. Their independence was, however, soon seriously undermined by deteriorating economic conditions. Most Central Asian republics have been especially active supporters of closer economic integration due to their dependence on economic cooperation with Russia (see, for example, Schuenemann, 1995; Halbach and Tiller, 1994). However, Azerbaijan, Moldova, Turkmenistan, and Ukraine have preferred to abstain from any coordination and obligations that might impede their independent development.

The strategies of self-reliance underwent certain changes, associated with political overhaul and parliamentary and presidential elections in Azerbaijan, Belarus, Georgia, Moldova, and Ukraine. These elections brought politicians to the forefront who have stressed the benefits of economic cooperation in the CIS, particularly when Russia expressed intentions of obtaining economic aid from stronger partners in the West. It is difficult, however, to make a fair assessment of the commitment to cooperation in the CIS. While the NIS have been unanimous in broad economic declarations, it has been more difficult to find consensus on specific issues. Economic goals remain subordinated to domestic political considerations. National leaders have focused their attention on urgent political and security issues, including the settlement of military conflicts in Armenia, Azerbaijan, Chechenya, Georgia, Moldova, and Tajikistan that have taken most of their time and negotiating efforts. Nonetheless, due to their economic plight the NIS have not managed to find viable alternatives to economic interdependence within the CIS. As they need cooperation with other CIS member states, they have opted to drift with the tide by supplying the most essential commodities with the help of bilateral agreements.

9.8   Trade Policies of the CIS Countries

The trade policy choices of CIS governments have been rooted in different combinations of benefits and costs of participation in a regional economic bloc. Since the breakup of the Soviet economic system, the NIS have had several trade options:

- Import-oriented policies to satisfy market demand, or import restrictions to protect domestic producers.
- Export-oriented policies to support foreign sales, or export restrictions to retain goods on the domestic market.
- Policies of self-reliance aimed at the reduction of trade ties and the development of domestic industries for domestic consumption.

Exports were at first perceived as damaging for the emerging market economies, as they created a scarcity of goods on domestic markets. This brought about strong protectionist measures aimed at minimizing the outflow of commodities by means of administrative measures, e.g., checkpoints on borders, lists of strategic resources, or licensing of exporters. This type of trade policy was called "protectionism inside out," i.e., export restrictions outstripped import restriction (Shishkov, 1994).

Later, as an effect of the introduction of weak national currencies by CIS states, exports were perceived as a source of monetary profit. Consequently, the NIS undertook measures to liberalize foreign trade, reduce lists of strategic commodities, cancel quotas, etc. It became more important to export outside the CIS to obtain hard currency reserves. At the same time, this resulted in reduced imports among the CIS and increased imports from countries outside the CIS. The imports proved competitive in the home market of CIS countries and hurt the interests of domestic producers, a development that has, in turn, stimulated intraregional trade in the CIS.

9.9 Negotiations on the Customs Union in the CIS

Customs regulations have been an integral part of the common trade regime in the CIS and have been negotiated by the NIS throughout the existence of the CIS. Independent customs versus customs unification were assumed to bring either losses or gains (Viner, 1950). Customs union means an association of two or more countries that not only eliminate tariffs between themselves but also erect common external tariffs against third countries. The combination of preferential policies among members and protectionist measures against outside countries poses the question of benefits of the customs union over national customs that may arise from changes in relative prices (separately explored by Meade, 1956; Gehrels, 1956–1957; Lipsey, 1957), and the difference between "inter-country substitution" (one country is substituted for another as a source of a commodity) and "inter-commodity substitution" (substitution of one commodity for another due to a relative price shift and an ensuing increase in the volume of imports; Lipsey, 1960:503–505). These studies have laid the foundation for a theory indicating that welfare may either rise or fall after customs unification (Bhagwati, 1983), which provides room for both advocates and opponents of customs unions to put forward their arguments.

In the CIS some functions of national customs policy were seen as sources of revenues and as barriers to a customs union. Customs duties play an important role in replenishing the budget with currency; for example, Russian customs channeled 14.2 billion rubles into the country in 1994. Customs border checkpoints have been used to prevent the exports of illegal commodities and to restrict the outflow of goods; in 1994, customs in Smolensk levied 2.5 billion rubles in fines and confiscated goods and materials worth double that sum. The removal of customs duties deprives the state of a substantial income. Moreover, identifying the country of origin at customs points helps to limit re-export of goods, particularly of strategic raw materials supplied in accordance with intergovernmental agreements.

Other effects of national customs laws were perceived as favorable to customs unification. Customs duties, excises, and taxes impose additional expenses for exporters and importers. The unification of customs regulation simplifies trade procedures, removes bureaucratic delays, and makes transactions less costly.

Negotiations on a customs union in the CIS have been guided by a number of common conceptions of the actors involved, and by the perception of a customs union as first and foremost a political construction. Member states recognize the potential damage of refusing to coordinate their policies with the Russian customs policy, as they would have the status of "foreign countries." Other factors favoring union include the utilization of the media to influence negotiating partners, a tactic used especially by Russia, the country most interested in common regulation to reduce transactional costs. The Baltic states have been held up as examples of "bad" behavior, such as the introduction of customs borders and checkpoints, and contrasted with the EC experience as a showcase of customs unification. Finally, advocates stress the openness of any undertaking aimed at customs unification for all the NIS.

9.9.1   Issue power: package agreements

Interdependence is a "function of political power and political choice" that explains both imperial and autarkic strivings in terms of dependence because "states seek to control what they depend upon or to lessen the extent of their dependence" (Waltz, 1979). It has also been asserted that military force usually dominates economic means. However, under "complex interdependence" militarily strong states find it more difficult to use their overall dominance to control outcomes (Keohane and Nye, 1977) because military force is more costly to use and less effective than economic power. Issue-specific power assets often prevail and issue linkages become useful tactics.

Due to economic interdependence and the importance of political autonomy in emerging nation-states, trade relations in the CIS have been characterized by bilateralism, the dominance of the relationship between Russia and other CIS states, the impact of Russian legislation and institutions on trade agreements, and the development of new common trade institutions. The trilateral union of Russia, Belarus, and Ukraine was seen by Russia as its best option. This preference was explained by economic factors and supported by arguments referring to cultural and historical unity. The benefits of a cross-regional economic bloc were examined by Russian academician A. Granberg, who devised a mathematical model of efficient coalitions using the Pareto optimum as a basis of evaluation and employed it to study the economic ties between Soviet regions based on 1987 statistics. He found that the most efficient option would be a trilateral economic coalition of Russia, Ukraine, and Belarus; the second best group would consist of Russia, Ukraine, Belarus, and Kazakhstan; the third best Russia, Ukraine, and Kazakhstan; and the fourth Russia, Belarus, and Kazakhstan (Granberg, 1994:155).

An enduring aim of Russia's economic policies has been to integrate Ukraine into the economic union. However, Ukraine found a way to expand its trade relations outside the CIS (the greatest increase in exports to non-CIS states during 10 months of 1994 was an estimated 42% rise recorded by Ukraine) and to maintain required supplies, mainly of energy and fuel, from Russia based on bilateral agreements on trade and economic cooperation. Ukraine could escape any binding accords by threatening to stop the transit of Russian gas to Eastern Europe through its territory.

Belarus was in a different situation. It was closely tied to Russia, since it had to use its trade surplus with the NIS in its trade with Russia and desperately needed imported fuel and energy for its heavy industries. Russia consumed 86% of its exports, and accounted for 84% of its imports. Russia has also been the main trade partner of Kazakhstan: Russia receives 48.7% of Kazakh exports (coal, oil products, grain, wool) and delivers 61% of Kazakh imports (mainly timber, oil products, trucks, and buses). According to Kazakh prime minister at that time, Akezhan Kazhegeldin, the main priority has been the "restoration of the former single economic space (represented by the Soviet Union) outside which we simply cannot survive" (*Moscow News*, 24 February 1995).

Given the different situations of the NIS, the development of the customs regime in the CIS has been a balanced policy of maintaining the previous common economic space and the common external customs tariffs and avoiding new tariffs between CIS members with the help of free trade agreements and the coordination of customs policies. CIS governments tried first to maintain common external customs taxes and to avoid additional internal taxes. Then they wanted to restrict exports and ensure an income for the state with the help of internal taxes. Eventually some states sought to eliminate those taxes to adjust to the Russian external customs regime and to obtain preferential trade conditions.

The NIS developed the customs union in several stages. First came the preservation of the unified customs territory, 1991–1992. The disintegration of the common customs regulation, accompanied by attempts to establish a common economic space and a ruble zone, occurred at the end of 1992–1993. Next came bilateral agreements on free trade and the establishment of a customs union based on Russian legislation and regulation, which took place in 1994–1995. Finally, a trilateral customs union was created in 1995. Frequent topics of talks on a customs union in the CIS were relative transparency, the use of unilateral administrative and economic regulations to pressure other parties, the linkage of political and economic issues, the institutionalization of a customs regulation, and the discrepancy between the formula and detail phases of the negotiation process.

Establishing a customs policy in the CIS was a rather transparent process. Statistical data and legal regulations had been published. Customs services conducted regular press conferences and meetings of customs officers to learn from the EC experience.

As a response to lack of compliance by NIS, some countries – notably Russia – took unilateral protectionist measures. Such economic penalties made other NIS join the common customs declarations. However, the preoccupation of the NIS with their own good brought about the disintegration of the common customs territory through erection of internal customs taxes and borders. For example, in October 1992 the Russian government introduced rigid customs controls on its borders to prevent illegal export of strategic raw materials (nonferrous metals, precious gems, oil, and gas) and doubled the number of customs posts to 600 on the borders with Azerbaijan, Georgia, Ukraine, and the Baltic states. In November 1992, Russia established customs points with the eight remaining NIS members to protect itself from re-export. The common customs territory disintegrated.

By contrast to multilateral arrangements and unilateral undertakings, which have rarely proved to be fruitful so far, the CIS has successfully linked issues both within the same area (called "log rolling") and among different areas (side payments; Lindberg and Scheingold, 1970). Hence, log rolling package deals were used in the talks between Russia and Kazakhstan linking customs regulation, the settlement of debts, and the delivery of strategic goods. On 12 September 1993, the premiers of the two countries agreed to abolish customs controls on the common border as of 20 September 1993, to shorten the list of commodities subject to customs duties, and to set up 67 points to curb smuggling of arms, drugs, and jewelry across the border. An arrangement was made to ensure the supply of 300,000 tons of petrol, 540,000 tons of diesel fuel, 64,000 tons of condensed gas, and other fuel to Kazakhstan; as well as 2.7 million tons of grain to Russia. Grain and oil products were to be traded on the basis of clearing the Kazakh debts for products received from Russia during the first eight months of 1993, amounting to over US$160 million. Side payments, or packaging security and welfare issues, also proved fruitful. On 28 March 1994, Russia and Kazakhstan signed agreements to set up a transnational oil corporation, the lease of Baikonur, and a customs regime on a joint basis. Linkage was successful because it added value to the agreements for all parties involved. This, in turn, reduced the risk that Russia might be perceived as a "sucker" by domestic politicians.

Belarus used linkage of economic and strategic issues in a series of agreements with Russia to establish a single customs zone in the two republics. Minsk was given access to cheap Russian raw materials and energy, and in turn accepted that Russia would maintain two military bases in Belarus for the next 25 years. Officials in Belarus estimated it would save $400 million a year once the duties on oil were lifted because Russia would sell energy and raw materials at its own lower internal prices.

The discrepancy between the formula and detail phases has been a permanent feature of the customs talks. The political interests of the NIS made them abstain from a multilateral agreement on a customs union; the general accords adopted in the first half of 1992 have never been ratified. The customs regime was instead regulated by bilateral agreements that represented a mixture of free and managed trade.

The revival of the multilateral talks on a customs union dated back to July 1994 when the council of the heads of CIS customs services approved a draft framework for customs legislation and signed agreements to simplify customs procedures. There followed an agreement reached at the October 1994 CIS summit on the concept of a customs and payments union. However, when the council had to take concrete steps to adopt the draft agreement on a customs union in November 1994, Tajikistan, Turkmenistan, and Ukraine abstained from approving it. In fact, after the NIS agreed on the general formula, only Russia and Belarus were ready to enter the customs union. One explanation was the reluctance of sovereign states to accept Russian customs legislation and procedures.

9.9.2 Negotiating a trilateral customs union

The trilateral customs union among Russia, Belarus, and Kazakhstan was based on the Russian import-export tariff regime and was signed by Prime Ministers Chernomyrdin, Chigir, and Kazhegeldin. They agreed to introduce standard methods to levy customs duties, to produce statistics, and to run the customs services. They also agreed to lift customs duties on goods traded among them, to establish common duties, and to remove customs controls at their joint borders. The prerequisites for the trilateral customs union were established by bilateral agreements on economic and trade cooperation in the period 1993–1995.

The negotiations on the trilateral customs union revealed several contradictory features of the CIS trade talks. First, Russia tried to promote both its economic and political interests, while the other NIS were mostly concerned with the management of the current economic recession. Second, experts and politicians assessed the benefits of a customs unification differently. For example, Belarus Prime Minister Chigir estimated that Belarus would get $26 per ton of oil without customs duty, which meant a benefit of about $400 million a year once duties on oil were lifted. In contrast, the opposition leader in the Belarus parliament, Sergei Naumchik, stated that customs agreements would lead to liquidation of Belarus as an independent economic entity. The chairman of the shadow cabinet of the Belarus Popular Front, V. Zablotski, suggested that a bilateral treaty on a customs union would inflict a US$2 billion annual damage on the republic. Experts calculated difficulties connected with changing excise rates in accordance with Russian customs rates because the level of revenues was built into the budget. Russia had customs duties on the import of spare parts for motor vehicles while Belarus did not, and their introduction would hurt Belarussian makers of motor vehicles.

A third feature was a discrepancy between executive and legislative powers with regard to customs unification. While the executive powers put forward and implemented this idea, legislators criticized and opposed it, pointing out the damage to political independence and sovereign prestige. Because of the opposition in the Belarus parliament to a customs union, the Belarus government adopted secret resolutions to secure implementation of the signed package of documents. Later the Belarus president held a referendum to attain public support for his intention to "remain in the sphere of Russian political influence." In Kazakhstan the president dissolved the parliament in order to avoid a political battle with the opposition.

Time pressure has been identified as an impediment to smooth customs unification. Vladimir Pokrovsky, Russian deputy minister for cooperation with the CIS, stated that the customs agreement was first of all a political decision for which the participants turned out to be technically unprepared. He said, "In the West they usually calculate first and then sign an agreement. We can't act in this way as we lack time" (*Kommersant*, #10, 1995:69). Perceived time pressure caused difficulties in timely implementation of the agreement. Definite deadlines to enforce integration were set. According to Russian sources, Belarus failed to fulfill the first agreements as of April 1994. Dismantling of the customs points on the border of Russia with Kazakhstan caused confusion in March 1995. Learning from earlier failures to implement decisions adopted at the highest political levels, several steps were undertaken to avoid this default: setting deadlines, holding follow-up meetings, and signing delivery acceptance protocols.

As for the legislative basis of the customs union, Russian representative V. Mescheryakov, deputy chairman of the State Customs Committee, stated that Russian customs regulations were to be used as a basis. However, according to Kazakh officials the parties arrived at a compromise with an orientation toward international legal norms. As for Belarus, because of the many differences in customs taxes some failures to stick to agreements have been registered. According to a report by customs offices, 4,000 VAZ cars were exported without taxes within three months of 1995. In general, new taxes stemming from unification of customs excises were applied to only a third of those goods on the list, while cars, precious metals, petroleum, and other commodities were exported without taxes.

Although the customs union was meant to be open for membership by other CIS states, aides to the Belarus president frequently stated that the expansion of the customs union to incorporate Kazakhstan was not expected or desired by Belarus. Other CIS entities wanted to join as well: the Crimean Supreme Council wanted Ukraine to join the CIS customs union to restore links with Russia; Uzbek and Tajik leaders visited Kazakhstan to discuss entering into the customs union; Tajikistan and Kyrgystan submitted an application to the CIS Interstate Economic Committee requesting admission to the customs union. A. Tugaev, the Kyrgys vice-prime minister, revealed a plan to join the customs union. Conditions for joining the customs union included coordination of economic reform; unification of foreign trade; legislation governing customs, currency, finances, pricing and taxation; a common policy toward third countries; common rules for currency markets; common defense of external borders; and joint utilization of defense facilities (*Kommersant-daily*, 21 April 1995, p. 2). They reflected an approach of linking security and economic issues. This, in turn, implied an instant reluctance to expand membership, since it might lead to difficulties in reaching agreements and monitoring compliance.

9.10   Structural Aspects of Trade Negotiations in the CIS

We can clearly identify the following features of the trade negotiations in the CIS: trade talks on three political levels of complexity; contradictory economic and political factors; and a loose framework despite emerging legitimation and institutionalization.

The trade regime achieved through negotiations in the CIS comprises three levels, each of which reflects the degree of readiness of different CIS states to integrate their economies. The first level pertains to negotiations on specific deliveries, supplies, or credits of a routine character. The second level represents the establishment of a propitious regime in trade and customs and is characterized by prevailing Russian legislation and regulation. The third level includes broader undertakings to deepen integration, create joint institutions, and unify legislation to regulate the economic sphere jointly. The multilevel structure of negotiations in the CIS displays shifts in the dispositions of the various republics on the issue of economic alliance. The output of the current economic negotiations was determined by financial and economic policies of the sovereign republics, their economic interdependence, and geographical closeness.

The economic agenda has been suppressed by the political context, which encompasses establishing and building up independence by CIS countries, acquiring features of nation-states, and achieving world recognition. Internal political fights to gain and retain power, and parliamentary elections also play a role. Thus, despite "complementary interdependence" (Granberg, 1994), benefits of cooperation, and existing long-term ties between the CIS economies, political preferences often overwhelm economic necessity, leading to attempts at currency self-reliance and restrictions on the exchange of goods, services, and capital.

The experience of negotiating trade alliances in the CIS may be compared to that of the EC, Benelux countries, and NAFTA. Economic negotiations in the CIS are distinguished from similar rounds of talks on other economic alliances by the goals and the outcome of actions taken by the participants. Whereas European nations went from the independence of nation-states toward integration and unification, members of the CIS intended first to gain full independence after being part of the Soviet Union for so long. Later they became willing to maintain economic ties with former partners, but only to a certain extent. They have struggled for diversification of economic contacts and alliances.

A primitive system of exchange and bilateral deals has prevailed in the CIS trade, resembling economic relations in the former East European Council for Mutual Economic Assistance (CMEA), where market regulation was replaced by a political settlement system, the transfer of clearing accounts, and a clearing ruble as instruments of payment. Political and economic reform in Eastern Europe caused dissolution of the CMEA economic bloc and changed the economic orientations of its former members. Similarly, when the NIS moved to restructure their economies, inequalities among them were strengthened. Deficits of goods and industrial decline brought about the need to increase imports and reduce the outflow of resources to neighboring countries. Currency deficits entailed the dissolution of a common ruble zone and put weak but independent currencies into circulation. Political considerations have undermined the possible gains from economic cooperation. Market notions and terms are new to the ideologies and political economies of the NIS. Supply and demand, free trade, and consumer needs have only begun to gain recognition. This makes the neoliberal approach relatively irrelevant for the explanation of the economic transition in the CIS (McFaul, 1995). Economic assessments have typically been based on a mixture of values reflecting both the former planning system and the new economic realities.

Along with allocation of resources, a number of noneconomic considerations have influenced the CIS negotiations on a customs union: ethnic and cultural unity, involvement in military conflicts, political stability, and foreign assistance. The more resources it has, the more options a country has. Resources are unequally distributed among NIS, fostering a mutual dependence of their economies and an interest in economic exchange through negotiations. Ethnic and cultural unity supports integration, but this unity is not typical for the NIS, which have heterogeneous populations embracing various nationalities, religions, cultures, and languages, and lack a shared ideology or common enemy. Countries involved in military conflicts either on their own territory or on the territory of their neighbors are likely to allocate considerable resources to the war effort, which diminishes export possibilities and import opportunities due to lack of funds and investment and unstable currency. Six CIS republics have been directly involved in military conflicts. Internal political struggles have led to frequent changes in economic policies and a failure to implement the decisions adopted. Internal political strife in the NIS has also led to political instability and economic crises, weakening the nations affected. Finally, foreign assistance fosters the opening of economies, deregulation, and the devaluation of economic cooperation between the CIS countries. It creates competition among NIS for a share of the economic assistance.

A major hindrance to negotiations is the lack of reliable sources of information and established communications flows between the negotiators. This partially explains why it is difficult for them to track the implementation of agreements, even when they wish to do so. Evolving institutionalization designed to standardize communication patterns, information flows, and behavior was impeded by the reluctance to create any supranational structure. (For example, although Kazakhstan was one of the advocates of CIS integration it objected to the supranational functions and rights to legislative initiative of the customs council; *Kommersant-daily*,

21 April 1995, p. 2). The CIS framework is rather vague and weak. The negotiation process has been more important than its results, as the negotiations have been perceived as tools to maintain relations between negotiators and countries.

9.11 Conclusion

This chapter has addressed the role of negotiations in establishing and developing a common trade regime in CIS. The case study reveals certain specific properties of the negotiating process in the CIS.

Most important is that the main participants engaged in trade negotiations are governments, which continue to pursue economic regulation. Government penetration of the economic sphere remains the dominant feature of the context of economic negotiations. There have been various regional attempts to speed up integration, such as the economic agreement of 16 regions of Russia, Ukraine, and Belarus and the Central Asian accords on cooperation, and to increase the involvement of commercial actors (mainly banks) in securing economic links. However, governments have retained much impact on the market through intergovernmental trade agreements, internal banking regulation and taxation, the provision of subsidies and loans, and the restrictive regulation of export and import.

The economies of the CIS countries continue to depend heavily on each other. There is a clear discrepancy among the economic goals and economic performance of the CIS members. Although all ex-Soviet republics have moved to build up their economies and to maximize economic gains, they are prone to employ diverse economic means that range from protectionist policies and self-reliance to cooperative development. Russia remains the dominant power; it is the main creditor, supplier of oil and gas to the CIS market, and producer of over 70% of the CIS GDP (in 1993), while accounting for only half of its population. The other CIS members lack a stable currency and the resources to be equal trade partners with Russia.

The inequality of participating economies leads to asymmetrical negotiations and tends to turn multilateral rounds of talks into bilateral meetings and agreements. The latter provide more room for reciprocal bargaining and equivalent economic exchange, while the former require unanimous decisions, which are hard to achieve given the variety of economic objectives and opportunities available to the CIS countries. Moreover, bilateral bargaining provides conditions that may help CIS members to feel more equal than they do in multilateral negotiation.

The lack of real alternatives to optimize the economic payoffs of the CIS members is the main impetus for the republics to remain in the CIS orbit. Their search for other options, including support from the EU, international financial organizations, and such foreign countries as Germany or Turkey is not adequate to meet their current needs.

All CIS economies face the complications of shifting from a command-and-control-based economy to one responding to market demand and economic efficiency. Thus, the free play of market forces contributes little to explaining the motives of the main negotiators, although an understanding of the necessity to react in accordance with supply and demand is widespread among the new actors of the economic talks. They include, for instance, financial and industrial groups and commercial banks participating actively (but prudently) in CIS economic affairs.

The failure to gain from free market play makes joint decision making at the intergovernmental level more complicated. The lack of a ruling authority recognized by all members determines the hectic development of various rounds of talks, and gives all participants the opportunity not to sign the agreements or even to break them. No alternative mechanisms for enforcing common decisions have developed due to each nation's fear of giving up "sovereign control" over its national economy.

The CIS perceive negotiations mainly in terms of a zero-sum game, or concessions versus victory, and view compromises as a sign of weakness. A frequent strategy is to lock the negotiations or avoid implementation of the agreements, pending better resolution in the future.

Linkage of economic and political issues and package agreements are the pervading features of the economic bargaining between the CIS nations. The republics are tempted to use diverse power instruments available to them, including economic leverage, military force, strategic pressure, or long-term promises, to compensate for the lack of other tools, to avoid giving away their security points, and to promote their economic positions.

Negotiations over trade issues in the CIS can be viewed through the prisms of both economic and negotiation theories. The economic approach makes it possible to grasp the causes and contents of issues raised at the negotiating table, and to evaluate the quantitative benefits of outcomes, the alternatives and incentives of participants based on their economic interests, the degree of involvement in cooperation and division of labor, and the dependence on trade relations and financial ties. Negotiation theory provides solid ground for analysis of the strategies and tactics of negotiating parties that endeavor to achieve objectives determined by their perception of their interests at stake. Both theoretical frameworks possess value in explaining the process of economic negotiations in the CIS. They embrace the complexity of economic issues and the divergence of resources of the negotiators, given the combination of conflicting and cooperative strategies of the CIS nations, the willingness of participants to get as much as possible from cooperation and division of labor, their unwillingness to share the burden of economic disorder, and the recurrent need to balance political preferences and economic considerations.

Chapter 10

Silicon for the Masses: How AT&T Licensed its Intellectual Property in the 1970s to Facilitate the Development of a Worldwide Semiconductor Industry

Robert E. Kerwin and Richard A. DeFelice

10.1 Introduction

This case study reviews the structure and process of negotiations in which AT&T Corporation engaged with semiconductor manufacturers during the 1970s. These were the early years of the burgeoning growth of the semiconductor industry in the United States and the world. Analysis of the specific results of each negotiation is precluded due to the proprietary nature of the negotiated settlements and the nature of intellectual property agreements in general; however, it is possible to derive a generic model of the negotiations for purposes of analysis, which will serve as the means for developing this study.

Intellectual property license agreements have proven to be a key element in the international economic growth of technologically sophisticated industries such as electronics. They have been necessary for stimulating the growth and spread of products and markets for high technology while protecting and rewarding the key innovators. The crafting of these agreements is particularly demanding of negotiation skills because of the often indeterminate nature of the value of intellectual property rights in rapidly advancing fields.

Intellectual property rights, such as patents and copyrights, are legal means authorized by governments to stimulate industrial development and economic growth while allowing individuals and companies to protect their investments in innovation. Patent laws provide the patent holder with monopoly rights (albeit temporary) to exclude others from making, selling, or using certain items of commerce. These exclusionary rights may be waived and licenses granted to others through licensing agreements negotiated to obtain varying combinations of rights to the others' intellectual property, enhancements to market position, and collection of revenue through royalties. Major international electronics firms use the exchange – or nonexchange – of intellectual property rights as part of their competitive strategies.

Certainly, the evaluation of the outcomes of these negotiations is subjective and depends upon the objectives of the engaged parties and the perspective of the individual attempting the evaluation. It is possible, however, to understand the results in the context of the explosive growth of the semiconductor industry that took place during and following the time period selected for analysis. Today, the semiconductor industry exceeds US$100 billion in sales per year with over 200 companies worldwide that have significant operations involving the design and production of semiconductor products – not including those associated companies that produce raw materials, processing equipment, and computer-aided design software.

This case study focuses upon AT&T's negotiations of patent license contracts covering semiconductor technology – contracts that have helped sustain the most rapidly changing technology of the last three decades. It begins with a description of the negotiation process utilized by AT&T during the 1970s, an overview of the structure of the negotiating teams, and a discussion of the impact of governmental influence and of typical issues that required resolution. The applicability of negotiation theory and economic theory will be explored as means for accurate prediction of the possible outcomes of intellectual property negotiations.

10.2 Background

10.2.1 AT&T

AT&T, originally American Telephone & Telegraph, was the world's largest telephone company during the 1970s. In 1976, it became the first company in history to earn over US$1 billion in a single quarter (Auw, 1983:18). As an instrument to facilitate its primary business of supplying telephone equipment and services to the

United States, AT&T operated a large semiconductor manufacturing and research business in its Western Electric subsidiary and Bell Laboratories.

AT&T was founded in the 1870s by Alexander Graham Bell following his invention and patenting of the telephone. Since that time, AT&T has always been a leader in advancing technology. During its history, the company has been the subject of antitrust investigations by the US Department of Justice, the results of which have, to a certain extent, shaped AT&T's business and direction. Although focused upon US telephone service, AT&T has at various times owned holdings in international ventures. AT&T's Western Electric subsidiary operated telephone manufacturing businesses in places such as Antwerp, Barcelona, and Budapest; it sold these businesses to ITT during the 1920s partly because of the threat of antitrust action (Brooks, 1975:170).

Since the Nobel Prize-winning invention of the transistor by J. Bardeen, W.H. Brattain, and W.B. Shockley at AT&T's Bell Laboratories in 1948, the company has played a major role in the development of semiconductor devices and integrated circuits. Dozens of seminal developments in this field have resulted in key patents assigned to AT&T through the 1950s, 1960s, and 1970s. These patents include the fundamental polysilicon self-aligned gate process (still used in all semiconductor memory and microprocessor devices today; Kerwin *et al.*, 1969), the Metal Oxide Semiconductor Field Effect Transistor (Kahng, 1970), and the process of oxide diffusion masking (Derrick and Frosch, 1957).

10.2.2 Why negotiate?

AT&T used its intellectual property rights aggressively for the several decades after the invention of the telephone in 1875 (Fagen, 1975) to establish and control its markets. Later, when it was subject to antitrust settlements and regulatory considerations, AT&T traded intellectual property rights with other major players in electronics through licensing agreements to acquire the rights to combine its own technology with the technology of others (referred to as design freedom) to provide new, more efficient products and services and thus lower the costs of communications within the United States.

Under the 1956 Consent Decree that settled an antitrust investigation begun by the US Department of Justice in 1949 (Auw, 1983), AT&T was ordered to license all of its US patents and some of its technology to all who requested licenses at "reasonable and non-discriminatory rates." Beyond this compulsion to license, however, there were other reasons to enter into licensing agreements.

AT&T, like most creative, technologically sophisticated companies, may well call itself an intellectual property company. It publicly protects its inventions, software, and company product names by obtaining legal rights through patents, copyrights, and trademarks. AT&T privately protects its technical and business information as trade secrets. By these actions, AT&T generates a substantial business asset known as intellectual property. This asset consists of the legal right to exclude others from the use of these inventions, software, and trademarks, and it may be managed to produce substantial business advantage. To achieve this business advantage, the patent, copyright, and trademark assets may be licensed broadly, licensed selectively, or not licensed at all to generate revenue or manage the competitive environment and marketing strategies for products and services. Royalty revenue would be generated by enforcing rights against those who infringe, either via lawsuits or by negotiating the exchange of rights for value with other companies. Another important value would be exchanging the rights to use each other's intellectual property (referred to as cross-licensing).

Cross-licensing in the semiconductor industry became prevalent in part because the manufacture of semiconductor devices requires the use of multiple technologies. Through the 1960s and 1970s, the key materials and process patents were held by a handful of the major US electronics corporations. If a company wished to enter the industry, it was necessary to have a license to these patents. At present, many strong competitors hold patents and have inventive potential in this field. For the past decade, nearly half of the top 20 recipients of US patents each year have been major companies competing in microelectronics (see *Figure 10.1*). Thus, the semiconductor industry and its suppliers of sophisticated processing equipment have become interdependent, while at the same time sustaining the most rapid development pace in the history of engineering. In the United States, merchant sales of semiconductors grew from essentially US$0 in 1958 to over US$8 billion in 1980 to over US$100 billion today. The industry has developed on the basis of a strategy of cross-licensing process technologies broadly while being very selective in the licensing of product designs. This can be attributed in part to the fact that intellectual property protection was well established for processes, but until 1986, no country – including the United States – had laws providing intellectual property protection for semiconductor designs (Howell *et al.*, 1988:207).

Meanwhile, European semiconductor and computer companies found it necessary to obtain licenses for semiconductor technology in order to remain competitive due to their lagging technological level (Howell *et al.*, 1988:165). Still, the investment in research and development (R&D) and capital equipment by US electronics firms continued to increase dramatically through this period, as illustrated in *Table 10.1*.

Through its Western Electric subsidiary and Bell Laboratories, AT&T sustained an extensive R&D program in the semiconductor field during the decades following its invention of the transistor. The patents resulting from that investment made up a portfolio of material and process patents that was the strongest in the industry (Sah, 1988).

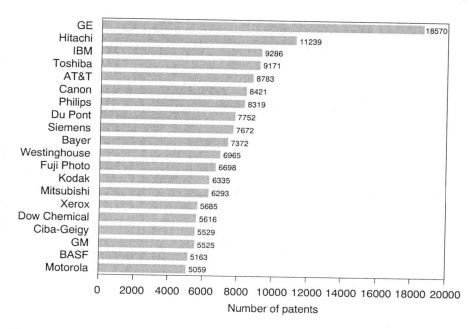

Figure 10.1. Top recipients of US utility patents, 1976–1992. Source: US Patent and Trademark Office.

Table 10.1. US semiconductor R&D and capital spending (US$ million).

	1976	1977	1978	1979	1980	1981	1982	1983
R&D	228	300	384	470	625	776	875	944
Capital	306	413	650	887	1,300	1,424	1,188	1,323

Source: SIA.

10.3   The Negotiations

10.3.1   Parties

Despite its many innovations, AT&T did not invent patent licensing. This practice had been used extensively for decades in many industries such as oil, pharmaceuticals, radio and automobiles. Certainly though, AT&T did lead the way in the establishment of licensing practices in the semiconductor industry.

In addition to the patent attorneys who were responsible for writing the applications filed at the US and world patent offices, AT&T employed lawyers who specialized in intellectual property matters to ensure that the corporation complied with the guidelines of the 1956 Consent Decree. However, it was not these lawyers who negotiated AT&T's licensing agreements.

AT&T chose to approach patent licensing from a business rather than a legal perspective. Attorneys were intimately involved in structuring and reviewing policies and contracts, but for its negotiating activities, AT&T established a department of business managers. These executive managers typically came from strong technical backgrounds and were charged with the responsibility of negotiating patent and technology licenses on behalf of the corporation. The legal departments cooperated in this endeavor to assert and defend patent claims, to craft the contract language, and to ensure compliance with the 1956 Consent Decree.

AT&T licensing managers would negotiate directly with the CEOs, managing directors, or general attorneys of many potential licensees. Other companies with more intellectual property experience would delegate this responsibility to their internal organizations that specialized in this field. It is not surprising that many licensees began emulating AT&T's management of intellectual property by establishing patent licensing organizations as their own portfolios grew. A culture developed wherein licensing managers established networks and communicated professionally with one another to maintain their relationships. These relationships served to facilitate the negotiation process when the time came to renew licenses.

10.3.2 Getting to the table

Sometimes getting a potential licensee to come to the table for meaningful discussions was difficult. Few potential licensees were much happier to see an AT&T licensing manager than to see a landlord or tax collector. Many small startup ventures hoped to avoid paying royalties. Some even cried foul and accused AT&T of anticompetitive practices. Still others ignored requests – hoping to fall through the cracks. AT&T's comprehensive and systematic approach to the semiconductor industry however, meant that few – if any – companies were lost in the activity of that period. Some were more difficult than others to bring to the table, but in the end, most came to negotiate a license. In only a few cases was legal action required.

To overcome this general reluctance on the part of the potential licensees to begin discussions, AT&T developed an approach that it employed with consistent success. The corporation would write a letter introducing AT&T and its patent licensing department and requesting a meeting to provide an overview of AT&T and explain its licensing policy.

In the 1970s, AT&T was a household name in the United States, but was generally known abroad only as the US telephone company. The corporation developed roadshows to present at initial meetings that were tailored to appeal to the business, technical, and/or legal community based upon the participants confirmed for the meetings. The presentations showcased the advanced developments and innovations from Bell Laboratories in the semiconductor field, provided a high-level perspective on the investment in research and development (R&D) committed by

AT&T to further advancements, and described the immense patent portfolio that AT&T had built, covering many of the basic materials and processes required for the manufacture of semiconductor devices. These introductory meetings tended to be cordial, with each party seeking to identify the other's decision makers and understand their underlying interests.

10.3.3 The parties' interests

Since the US government required AT&T to license its patents, AT&T's interests were fairly straightforward. The corporation was precluded from using its patents to exclude competitors from the marketplace; furthermore, AT&T had agreed to limit the royalty it would collect in return for granting licenses ("reasonable and non-discriminatory rates" – although these terms were not explicitly defined). Beyond this, AT&T was permitted to negotiate terms so long as it respected the limits mentioned above.

The continued development of the semiconductor industry required vast infusions of both investment and talent. Although much of the early work had been carried out by a few institutions, it quickly became impossible for any one development organization to provide the research needed to satisfy the growing industry. AT&T found that it could benefit greatly by "licensing in" technologies patented by other researchers entering the rapidly developing field. Since the corporation's prime directive was to deliver the best telephone service possible, AT&T sought the freedom to allow its developers to incorporate all new innovations into its telephone systems without limits.

Despite this quest for design freedom, AT&T did not lose sight of the fact that it also wanted to recoup a fair return on the millions of dollars of investment put into its R&D program. This world-renowned program has delivered an average of one patent per working day since AT&T Bell Laboratories was founded in 1925. Therefore, while it was necessary to ensure that the royalty rates used in its patent license agreements met the guidelines imposed as part of the 1956 Consent Decree, AT&T was keenly interested in ensuring that it received commensurate value for its intellectual property. The specific order of priority for these two aspects of reciprocal value – rights versus royalties – during the time period of this study is still a matter of debate among the historians of the corporation.

AT&T also understood the value of maintaining good relationships with its licensees. Many US licensees were also valued customers and suppliers of AT&T. Semiconductor technology was advancing so rapidly that it was accepted practice for the parties to reevaluate the relative strengths of each other's patent portfolios and negotiate new license terms every five years.

The other parties to these negotiations were companies, universities, and individuals from around the world, each with their own interests and priorities.

However, it can be argued that their interests were principally technology driven. By this time, Bell Laboratories had established itself as one of the prime movers at the leading edge of the semiconductor industry. Licensees sought rights to the vast store of technological developments that were produced daily at Bell Laboratories. More specifically, Bell Laboratories could be viewed as essentially a "one stop shop" where a licensee could select from many of the technologies it would need to set up and operate its business. Since semiconductor research at Bell Laboratories ran the gamut from process development to fabrication of equipment to physical chemistry and basic research, AT&T's semiconductor patent portfolio was the most comprehensive in the world. Taking a license with AT&T would allow rights to enough technology to participate in the industry without a significant risk that another patent holder could shut down the operation. While AT&T never promoted itself as an umbrella of protection for its licensees, it was recognized that licensees saw value in this capability.

Prestige also played a role that is not altogether separable from the technical interests. The name Bell Laboratories is recognized and respected worldwide. Licensees saw value in being able to report that they had entered a cross-licensing agreement with AT&T that allowed them to enjoy the benefits of the excellent research performed by Bell Laboratories.

Finally, there was a financial advantage to executing a patent cross-licensing agreement with AT&T: the rates were reasonable by definition. Furthermore, licensees could be assured that they were receiving comparable rates to those enjoyed by the rest of the industry and were thus playing on a level field. Competitors' prices would reflect differences in the manufacturing, design, marketing, and management of their businesses, and not any preferential treatment from the technology developers.

This does not suggest that AT&T was the world's department store of technology where companies could stroll in to select prepriced items from the shelves and pay the cashier at the door. The requirements of the 1956 Consent Decree were complex, and, as previously noted, AT&T employed a division of lawyers and business managers to ensure its compliance and meet the needs of its business interests.

10.3.4   The impact of government

As mentioned earlier, AT&T's licensing negotiation practices were strongly influenced by US government policy. Flexibility in developing licensing strategies is a key tool that allows major competitive corporations with extensive patent portfolios to compete in the marketplace; for example, companies need the flexibility to license standard technologies broadly while not licensing key technologies underlying new products and services. During the early development and growth phase of the semiconductor/integrated circuit industry, AT&T was precluded from such a flexible strategy; the Consent Decree with the US government in 1956 set specific guidelines regarding AT&T's licensing of its patents.

These requirements were eventually lifted in 1984 in the Modified Final Judgment (MFJ) concluded with the US Department of Justice. Under the MFJ, AT&T divested itself of the regional Bell operating companies and the associated local telephone business, while keeping the long distance telephone service business, Western Electric manufacturing, and Bell Laboratories. Perhaps more importantly, AT&T was finally permitted to chart its own destiny as suggested four years before the settlement in the following excerpt from its 1980 annual report:

> No longer do we perceive that our business will be limited to telephony or, for that matter, to telecommunications. Ours is the business of information-handling, the knowledge business. And the market we seek to serve is global.

However, during the 1970s, the requirement for AT&T to license its patents to all who asked at "reasonable and non-discriminatory rates" obviously steered AT&T's licensing strategy and negotiation processes. The resulting "open door" licensing program became focused upon the exchange of rights to patents impacting the new advancing technology. This had the effect of creating a culture of open exchange, which catalyzed the entrance of numerous small entrepreneurial companies into the semiconductor industry. The large influx of new talent and ideas is largely responsible for the explosive growth that has characterized the semiconductor industry.

10.3.5 Reaching an agreement

The first phase of nearly all negotiations in the time period of this study began with the identification of potential licensees and concluded with a successful introductory meeting. The second phase was typically completed back at headquarters. AT&T's licensing department would identify the other parties' interests, perform the necessary homework, and develop a negotiating strategy that anticipated the issues and concerns that might be raised during the course of the upcoming discussions. The homework included development of company profiles using information found in the public and private sectors, and possibly even included the acquisition of products for subsequent analytical study.

During the third phase, face-to-face meetings with a potential licensee would resume. The primary purposes of this phase were to present a compelling argument justifying the need for an agreement and to reach a "handshake" on high-level terms for that agreement. This phase sometimes took more than a year to complete. While this may appear to be an extended time to reach an understanding, it is important to realize that intellectual property goes right to the core of a company's business. Discussions of patent claims are extremely complex and require expert understanding of technology and law. Business managers are not quick to concede that the products they have developed infringe upon the patents of others. They are even less inclined to add the cost of patent royalties to their cost of doing business.

The question of value was perhaps the most intensely discussed issue in the negotiations between the parties. The negotiations moved into this phase following the initial introductory meetings at which the lead negotiators outlined the boundary conditions and expectations of their companies. A contract zone would be established early in the negotiation process. Then the parties would address the value issue, which could be broken into two steps: patent assertion and balance of values.

One of the key elements of the preparation for patent negotiations was the development of a comprehensive analysis of the impact of AT&T patents upon the products of the other party. AT&T used the resources of its manufacturing subsidiaries and Bell Laboratories to assist in identifying competing products that might infringe AT&T's patents. Because AT&T owned fundamental and broadly impacting patents in the materials and processes of semiconductor technology during the 1970s, the mere fact that integrated circuits were manufactured by the other party was sufficient information to suggest patent infringement in that time period.

Detailed analytical studies called "reverse engineering" were performed on representative products to identify and document the patented processes used by the other party in their manufacturing processes. Sufficient detail was required to provide demonstrable evidence that AT&T's patents were in fact infringed. In addition, a thorough market study was performed to identify the types of products manufactured and sold, as well as the estimated revenue resulting from sales. Information for the study of past and future sales was gathered from annual reports, and from statistics provided by companies such as Integrated Circuit Engineering Corporation and Morgan Stanley and Company.

AT&T also evaluated its interest in the patents held by the other negotiating party. AT&T would compile production estimates from its Western Electric subsidiary and combine them with the information collected on the other party's products to create the basis for royalty rate calculations.

The assertion of patent infringement identified through reverse engineering was presented over the course of several meetings to give both sides the opportunity to question, study, refute, and provide new information. Establishment of patent impact is a crucial step toward resolving the value issue, and considerable emphasis was placed upon this aspect of the negotiation. Rarely did the other party openly admit to infringement – regardless of the information presented. Typically, it was only conceded that there was interest in developing a business solution to resolve the entire matter.

Once this concession had been made, the resolution of the value issue moved on to the second step: balancing the value. The valuation of the impact of infringement is not an exact science. The company must consider the cost of alternatives, such as design-around or even litigation. During the period after the 1956 Consent Decree, AT&T used a 2.5% royalty rate for semiconductor technology (the rate was 5% prior to that time). At times, the discussion would return to the patent impact phase when one or the other party believed that it was not receiving appropriate value for its patents. During the course of this lengthy exchange, both parties would often share information regarding their possible future directions in products, technology, and research efforts so as to resolve the value issue as favorably as possible. Toward the end of the 1970s, when significantly more companies began asserting their growing patent portfolios, these discussions became more complex and protracted because the cumulative effect of multiple royalty payments to many patent owners became substantial for patent users.

The negotiation of the value issue included considerable time spent discussing at a high level the scope and terms of the license. It was these discussions that gave both parties the best opportunity to verify their assumptions about the underlying interests of the other.

As mentioned earlier, one of AT&T's primary interests in licensing was to obtain rights to use advanced technology developed by others. Likewise, one of the interests of semiconductor companies was to obtain rights to use AT&T's basic patents. Thus, the desire for "patent peace" – the ability to use each others' patents without concern of litigation – was a common interest of the parties and helped establish the initial definition of a contract zone during negotiations.

A typical method used to address this mutual concern was to discuss provisions for a "lifetime rights" exchange of patents. This provided rights to each party to use the other's patents until the patents expired. However, limiting this exchange to only existing patents presented a new, but related, problem. Should one company (AT&T or the other party) develop a significant invention the day after an agreement was executed, and should that invention result in an issued patent, that patent would be unlicensed to the other company. The unlicensed party would have nothing left with which to bargain for rights to the patent because it would already have granted licenses to all of its patents. To solve this dilemma, the negotiators introduced the concept of licensing "futures" – the patents issued to a company during a specific future period. This arrangement ensured that both parties could enjoy patent peace for a mutually agreed upon period.

Achieving a level of understanding sufficient to obtain a handshake on a settlement did not end the negotiations. The lead negotiators were obligated to return to their management for review and approval of the terms. Following this, the lawyers began the complex task of crafting the contract language. Several drafts would be exchanged with suggestions for modifying definitions or scope or with requests for clarification of language before final executable documents were prepared. This began the fourth phase of the negotiations.

The language of intellectual property contracts is typically complex and the terms are often considered proprietary by the parties involved. AT&T's contract language was further complicated from 1956 to 1984 by its obligations to the US government. Significant effort was put into crafting provisions that protected AT&T's intellectual property and business operations while ensuring that AT&T complied with the "reasonable and non-discriminatory" requirements for licensing.

The contract serves as the governing legal document for the exchange of intellectual property rights between the two parties. It defines the scope and duration of the licenses granted, the royalties to be paid, and conditions and remedies for breach. In addition, it includes sections to specify miscellaneous provisions such as handling of taxes, communication, etc. In negotiations with new entrants to the semiconductor industry, the standard contract draft sometimes even served as a useful framework for the discussions during the second and third phases.

10.3.6   Closure and the postagreement agreement

While licensing managers were empowered to make decisions on behalf of the corporation at the negotiation table, they were obligated to obtain consensus approval from an internal management advisory committee consisting of senior licensing managers and attorneys. Sometimes the AT&T negotiator would be required to return to the table to clarify a point or renegotiate some of the terms and conditions previously settled. At other times companies found the accounting requirements contained in the standard contract for reporting and paying royalties on products that used patents too complex or burdensome. To resolve this issue, AT&T would often agree to use a commuted rate calculation or lump sum arrangement. These alternative payment provisions were offered only upon request and for the convenience of the other parties.

When a commuted rate was requested by a potential licensee, complex patent usage, royalty rate, and patent impact calculations were replaced with a single rate that was applied to publicly available gross revenue figures (e.g., annual reports) to calculate the royalty owed. With the lump sum provision, the parties negotiated mutually acceptable estimates of future sales affected and determined the royalty owed based upon the estimates. This royalty could then be paid in a single lump sum payment or in several payments spread over the period of the agreement.

The locations of the negotiation sessions frequently alternated between places selected by each party. While it was advantageous to use a "home" location such as Bell Laboratories while asserting AT&T's portfolio of patents, it was sometimes

advantageous to travel to the other party's desired location to reinforce the relationship being developed or to facilitate meeting schedules. These intellectual property
negotiations sometimes resulted in melodramatic resolutions that rivaled the lore of
secret service novels. On one occasion following a somewhat contentious round of
negotiations, the negotiators agreed to meet one last time at a neutral site. Several
private discussions took place between the negotiators and their support staff in an
attempt to iron out a settlement. In the end, the lead negotiators met in a symbolic
gesture halfway across a small bridge that spanned a pool at the hotel to shake
hands on a deal.

By the end of the 1970s, AT&T had executed approximately 200 licenses with
semiconductor technology companies. During this entire period, AT&T always
obtained royalty-free licenses.

The final execution of the patent license agreement marked the ending of the
fourth phase and the beginning of the fifth. It was the end of the negotiations,
but it was also the beginning of a relationship. This relationship involved more
than mere contract management (royalty payments and record keeping) because at
some point beyond the future period of patent peace, either or both parties would
find it advantageous to negotiate a renewal of the patent license agreement.

10.4   Analysis

10.4.1   Neoclassical economic theory

Neoclassical economic theory has limited use as a predictor of the outcomes of
intellectual property negotiations. The negotiations in which AT&T engaged with
international companies during the 1970s provided many opportunities to attempt
to apply neoclassical theory. For one, the negotiations took place in a setting where
it was possible for both parties to have access to information regarding products
manufactured and sales revenue generated. Access to this information was crucial
to constructing a mutually satisfactory model that balanced the value of each party's
patent portfolio. Additionally, the intellectual property at issue in these negotiations
was patents – public documents that may be obtained by any party by request to the
respective country's patent office. Therefore it was possible for both sides to review
and understand the relative intellectual property strengths of each prior to entering
negotiations. AT&T's dominant patent position in the semiconductor industry was
well known and could be easily verified by a search through public information.

A second element required for the application of economic theory is identification and prioritization of interests. This was facilitated for three reasons. First,
the legal premise of a patent is that the holder is granted monopoly rights to exclude or allow the use of the invention claimed in the patent. If a patentee owns
the rights to several key processes in a new and growing field, as AT&T did during

that time period, users of those processes must obtain rights to the key patents in order to practice their trade legally. AT&T was aware of its portfolio strength and therefore could logically determine that those with whom it negotiated required a license. Second, one of AT&T's significant interests was imposed upon it by the US government as a result of the Consent Decree of 1956. The conditions of the 1956 Consent Decree were widely known, so parties wishing to negotiate a patent license with AT&T knew that the company was obligated not merely to provide licenses, but to provide them at "reasonable" rates. Finally, patent license agreements typically had five-year lifetimes and were renewed through subsequent negotiations. This provided a reason for both parties to carry their knowledge of interests obtained in previous negotiations forward to the preparations for the next discussions.

Given the information and knowledge regarding each party's interests that was available prior to initiating patent license agreement negotiations, one might suggest that prioritization of the interests would be straightforward. However, this was not the case. While some of AT&T's interests may have been well known, the issues that concerned the company had a deeper and broader reach than merely complying with the requirements of the US government – however compelling that interest might be. As noted earlier, AT&T was also interested in maintaining its "design freedom" – namely, the ability of its designers to combine any new technology with their own to support the development and improvement of the US telephone system. This interest aligned well with the 1956 Consent Decree requirements but was contrary to the interest of obtaining a fair return on the research investment. If AT&T had only been interested in design freedom, then royalty-free cross-licenses would have been sufficient to satisfy that aspect. Prioritization of these primary and other secondary interests was difficult and perhaps never completely resolved.

The international companies negotiating with AT&T likewise had conflicting interests. On the one hand, they required licenses to the key semiconductor patents held by AT&T; but market forces compelled them to minimize the amount of royalty paid to maintain their competitiveness. While this was perhaps mitigated by the 1956 Consent Decree requirements, it was exacerbated by the complexity of the semiconductor manufacturing process and the numerous patent holders. One could not pay significant royalties to everyone and operate a competitive business.

The fact that the semiconductor industry of the 1970s time period did not fit the classical parameters of a perfect competition model is another reason for the inadequacy of neoclassical economic theory as a predictor of the outcomes of international intellectual property negotiations. As noted by Kenneth Flamm, classical competitive markets assume a mature, widely diffused technology used to produce a standard commodity (Flamm, 1987). A technology-intensive product such as integrated circuits follows a competitive model that includes substantial investment in continuous technological development, well differentiated products with patent-assured monopoly rights, and significant royalty returns on those monopoly rights. In addition, there is the added complexity that this industry benefited strongly from the economies of scale provided by access to international markets while simultaneously requiring technological innovations. The cost and market share arguments favor larger firms, while the rate of innovation may be better provided by a large number of small startup firms.

With respect to competition, it should be noted that during this period AT&T did not compete in the commercial semiconductor market place with any of its licensees. All semiconductor products manufactured by AT&T were consumed by AT&T; i.e., it was a captive supplier. Further, classical supply/demand considerations did not apply to AT&T's patent licensing during the 1970s because of the 1956 Consent Decree requirements to license all comers at reasonable terms and conditions.

Finally, in the case of negotiating for rights to a single critical patent, the patent holder with monopoly rights holds all the cards. Only when each party has significant patent holdings may a more classical market for intellectual property rights be established.

10.4.2   Negotiation theory

Negotiation theory and economic theory share certain elements. Both require that the parties involved have sufficient information available to understand and prioritize their interests. It is of paramount importance for each party to recognize fully and define for itself specifically what it desires as the outcome of a negotiation. Negotiation theory goes further and suggests that it is also beneficial to invest time to try to understand the needs and interests of the other party before initiating discussions, and to spend as much time as possible during the negotiations listening to understand the competing interests of both. As stated in the previous analysis, intellectual property negotiations do provide the opportunity to obtain sufficient information prior to and during discussions to satisfy this element.

The preparation phase was particularly important. AT&T invested significant time, effort, and money in understanding the value of its patent portfolio and the impact of its patents on the products of the companies with which it negotiated cross-licenses. This valuation process facilitated the prioritization of interests for the negotiators and provided key insights into the interests of the other party.

Another element of negotiation theory concerns the role of power in negotiations. AT&T's power was strengthened and at the same time encumbered by government policy. Without the monopoly rights provided by patents, neither AT&T nor any other company would have the power to protect and license its intellectual property. AT&T's power was enhanced because it owned many of the key patents necessary for the manufacture of advanced semiconductor devices during the 1970s. Companies required a license to these patents to use the processes involved legally. At the same time, the terms of the 1956 Consent Decree limited AT&T's use of the monopoly power granted under patent law.

Power can be real and perceived. AT&T was effective at establishing its reputation as a leading innovator that protected its intellectual property rights in the rapidly developing semiconductor industry. This reputation was developed through the excellent research performed at its Bell Laboratories, its strong intellectual property licensing program, and the prudent use of litigation.

Alternatives to a negotiated settlement were also considered. The theory of negotiation predicts that an agreement will result when the BATNA of the parties is less attractive than the terms that can be obtained through negotiation.

Companies that infringed AT&T's semiconductor technology patents had two alternatives to a negotiated agreement: cease to use the infringing material/process and revert to alternative technologies, or risk a lawsuit. These were unattractive alternatives, since they put their competitive advantage in the marketplace at risk. The economies of scale are significant in the semiconductor industry, and patented improvements in processes represented significant cost advantages for the user. Furthermore, future improvements would build from the latest technological base and companies that did not keep pace in this rapidly developing field would quickly be overtaken by competitors.

Another alternative was to design around the infringing material or process by inventing and developing a new method. In this period, few of the entrepreneurial semiconductor manufacturers had the technical and financial resources to be continuously developing new, noninfringing technologies.

A patent user could also choose to continue its infringement without seeking a license. However, it then faced the likelihood of litigation. This was perhaps an even less attractive alternative because of the high costs associated with patent infringement lawsuits. In addition to the cost of the preparation and actual defense of the litigation (estimated to run between US$500,000 and US$1 million), analysis has shown that infringement lawsuits have a net negative effect on the stock prices of publicly held companies, both through the filing of the litigation and by the verdict (Umesh, 1994).

None of these alternatives was significantly better than entering a licensing agreement with AT&T at a 2.5% royalty rate. The net effect of widespread cross-licensing in the semiconductor industry was a significant factor in the most rapid technological development rate in the history of engineering. Through this period, shared process and material inventions led to the doubling of complexity and capability of integrated circuits each year. This in turn has led directly to the enormous impact of computers and communications in all aspects of life today.

Chapter 11

The NAFTA Negotiation: Economic and Negotiation Perspectives

Gilbert R. Winham and Annie M. Finn

11.1   Introduction

This case study analyzes the negotiation among the governments of Canada, Mexico and the United States that resulted in the 1994 NAFTA. The 1985–1988 negotiation for the Canada–United States Free Trade Agreement (FTA) is intimately tied into this analysis, as the FTA can be identified as the substantive basis underlying the NAFTA negotiation. In this sense, the FTA model has greatly influenced the NAFTA model. In assessing the outcome of the negotiations, we will review elements of the negotiation process as well as the major substantive provisions of the NAFTA.

The NAFTA negotiation exhibits all the elements of a modern high-level international economic negotiation. It involves the participation of three governments – two large industrialized countries with market economies and the third, namely Mexico, having undergone substantial economic reform and deregulation prior to the initiation of the NAFTA negotiation. A distinguishing feature of the NAFTA negotiation is that it was essentially conducted on an even footing between developed and developing countries.

This case study provides an analysis of the NAFTA negotiation through reference to negotiation theory and a more broadly based economic theory. While it does not provide a detailed account of the process of the negotiation, it does present a Canadian perspective on the structure and process of the negotiation. As will become clear in this case study, each country had differing reasons and objectives for becoming involved in the negotiations. An analysis of the outcomes shows that while negotiation theory may explain some elements of the NAFTA negotiation, the outcomes may be better understood through an understanding of the economic conditions that underlay the negotiation.

11.2   Objectives

In terms of foreign economic policy, both Canada and Mexico focus on the United States, which for both countries accounts for about three-fourths of their international trade. This trade dependence has, in the past decade, led both the smaller nations to propose a free trade agreement with the United States. In 1985, Ottawa proposed to negotiate bilateral free trade with Washington, following a lengthy internal review of Canada's economic prospects. This review was conducted in the Liberal and Conservative governments of Prime Ministers Pierre Trudeau and Brian Mulroney, respectively, as well as by the independent Royal Commission on the Economic Union and Development Prospects for Canada (the Macdonald Commission). It was prompted in large measure by the recession of 1981/1982, which shook Canadian confidence because it appeared to have a deeper and more lasting impact on Canada than on the United States. The recommendation to negotiate free trade with the Americans that followed this review effectively reversed the national policy of 1879 which, *inter alia*, provided a margin of protectionism against US products.

In June 1990, Mexico, led by President Carlos Salinas de Gortari, initiated a bilateral free trade agreement with the United States based on similar reasoning, namely, the large Mexican–US trade flow. Prior to this initiative, Mexico had undergone extensive economic reforms characterized by liberalization and stabilization. In the early 1980s, several factors prompted the Mexican government to re-evaluate its economic policies: the Mexican debt crisis in 1982, combined with a weak international oil market and little external funding. As a result, Mexico made advances toward greater trade and investment liberalization, and toward less government intervention in the economy, i.e., toward a more market-oriented economy. Since 1985, Mexico had steered away from its protectionist import-substitution-industrialization (ISI) policy, recognizing the inefficiencies in productivity such a policy instills. In 1986, Mexico joined the GATT, and in compliance reduced its tariffs through a phaseout plan from 100% to 20% between 1985 and

1990. By shifting from ISI policies and placing heavier emphasis on manufacturing goods, Mexico became more reliant on US markets for its exported products. Mexico's vulnerability to the application of American laws to remedy unfair trade (i.e., antidumping and countervailing duties) became increasingly apparent, encouraging Mexico's interest in gaining a freer trading regime between the two countries.

Mexico had several objectives in participating in a free trade agreement with the United States. The primary goal was to gain and ensure more open and secure access to the US market. Attracting and increasing foreign investment and capital inflows from the United States was a second objective for Mexico. Mexico was also concerned with possible trade diversion to the EC, as well as with Canada's preferred access to the US market resulting from the FTA. Mexico's internal domestic reforms would be solidly enhanced and entrenched through the establishment of free trade with the United States. Moreover, while Canada was not a major trading partner with Mexico, Canada's involvement with the NAFTA meant a broadened export market for Mexico and represented a potential source of future investment. The NAFTA would also enhance foreign direct investment (FDI) in sectors of the economy where Mexico exhibited a comparative advantage, which would invariably help to create employment within Mexico. FDI would also assist Mexico in servicing its foreign debt. Finally, the NAFTA, it was hoped, would force greater economic efficiency through the introduction of international competition. Each of these goals would promote the restructuring and growth of the Mexican economy.

The United States had both political and economic interests in pursuing the NAFTA and thereby expanding its trade with Mexico. The agreement was seen by the United States as an opportunity for widening its export markets as well as promoting the efficient use of labor and natural resources within the free trade region, while also improving international competitiveness and productivity of American firms.

It has been argued that a major objective of the United States in negotiating NAFTA was to promote greater political and economic stability within Mexican borders (Hufbauer and Schott, 1992). For example, the establishment of the NAFTA would help to reinforce Mexican attempts at liberalization of foreign investment restrictions and protection of intellectual property, which would obviously benefit US multinationals. A final, often-cited objective of the United States in negotiating the NAFTA was the hope that growth and an increase in jobs in the Mexican economy would stem the tide of illegal immigration into the United States.

Canada's objectives in negotiating the NAFTA were different from its objectives in initiating the FTA. In the latter, Canada – like Mexico in the NAFTA – was a smaller nation initiating a free trade negotiation with a much larger principal trading partner. In the NAFTA, however, Canada was in the position of responding to an initiative launched by a third party, and particularly one with which trade flows were not economically significant.

Initially, Canada's interests in joining the NAFTA may have been defensive. The primary objective was to ensure that gains it had made under the FTA with the United States were not diluted in any way through a bilateral deal between the United States and Mexico. Also of importance was Canada's desire to ensure that it received the same access provisions to the Mexican market as the Americans. Most importantly, however, Canada was concerned with the emergence of a bilateral trade agreement between Mexico and the United States existing alongside its own bilateral trade agreement with the United States. Another important objective for Canada, and possibly the United States as well, was that the NAFTA provided an opportunity for both parties to improve the FTA. Finally, Canada also hoped to gain access to the Mexican market, since Canada had come to recognize the large export market and increased investment opportunities in Mexico, and the potential for enhanced competitiveness of Canadian firms. While initially motivated by defensive concerns, Canada did have significant interests in the benefits the NAFTA would provide.

In sum, while all of the negotiating parties may have had their own separate objectives for entering into the negotiations, they each perceived NAFTA would effectively improve the efficiency of their respective industries and labor force. This, in turn, would enhance the international competitiveness of each party.

11.3   Structure and Process of the Negotiation: Canada

Canada structured its NAFTA negotiations differently than the FTA negotiations. The FTA negotiation structure can be described as more political, while the NAFTA structure was more intimately tied to the Canadian bureaucracy. Perhaps the reason for the structural differences between the FTA and the NAFTA was that the FTA represented a bigger change in policy direction for Canada, and hence was more problematic for the government.

The FTA negotiations were conducted by the Trade Negotiation Office (TNO), a newly established body set up by the Canadian government. The TNO, by its very structure, was separated from the Canadian bureaucracy. Some would argue that the stakes were too great to leave negotiations of this magnitude and importance to state bureaucrats. The government appointed Simon Reisman, a former government official, to lead the Canadian negotiations. He in turn selected a staff of 100 individuals to manage the TNO bureaucracy. Though largely independent, the TNO operated under the cabinet through the trade minister, at the time Patricia Carney. As the FTA negotiations progressed, the TNO reported more directly to Prime Minister Brian Mulroney, and his chief of staff Derek Burney. Burney's role in the negotiations intensified as he became involved in the final stages of the negotiations. While the provinces had large stakes in the FTA negotiations, their participation was limited to a few First Ministers' Conferences and an integrated role in meetings with TNO officials through a body called the Continuing Committee on Trade Negotiations.

By contrast, the Canadian structure of the NAFTA negotiations was more fully integrated into the Canadian federal bureaucracy. The Office of Trilateral Trade Negotiations (OTTN), located in External Affairs and International Trade Canada, comprised the Canadian negotiating team, which was headed by chief negotiator John Weekes, a career official. Negotiations were conducted by specialists from various federal departments, while the OTTN coordinated the process and provided for managerial accountability.

The political structure of the NAFTA negotiation commenced from a cabinet committee chaired by then Minister of International Trade Michael Wilson. The cabinet committee directed the negotiation, and received briefings from Deputy Minister of International Trade Don Campbell, the chief negotiator, and others. Operating below the cabinet committee, with responsibility for policy coordination and direction and representing all interested departments, was the Assistant Deputy Ministers (ADM) Committee. A "Core ADM" Committee representing the ADMs of Finance, Investment, Agriculture, the Privy Council Office, and Industry, Science and Technology met weekly and led the ADM in providing operational direction for the negotiation. Involvement with the provincial governments was considerably less intense than in the FTA negotiations. There was formal federal–provincial interaction, taking the form of briefings from specialists in the federal line departments who received input from provincial counterparts on technical matters. Political issues, however, were aired at the ministerial level.

The NAFTA negotiations were conducted over 14 months in six marathon negotiating sessions. In the intervals between these sessions, smaller ad hoc sessions took place as necessary. Specific subjects would be negotiated simultaneously during the marathon sessions, while the chief negotiators would be in almost permanent session in a separate meeting. Only if problems arose in the specific meetings would the chief negotiators become involved in working through or resolving specific problems; otherwise the issues would be passed on to ministers. Therefore, the negotiators in the specific sessions were expected to agree on as much substance as possible. In this respect, considerable decision-making power was delegated down the chain of command of the negotiation.

Together the United States and Canada pressed Mexico to adopt significant trade policy changes. Grayson (1993) states that the US chief negotiator, Jules Katz, along with his Mexican and Canadian counterparts, Herminio Blanco and John Weekes, respectively, made an important advance in the negotiation at the

17–21 February 1992 plenary session in Dallas, Texas. Katz made it clear that Mexican "tit-for-tat" concessions to the United States and Canada were unacceptable. Mexico acquiesced when Katz emphasized that Mexico, the most protectionist of the parties, would have to reduce its barriers by more than its partners if economic integration were to be achieved. Apparently, news of this understanding passed quickly to the 19 working groups that had convened in the so-called jamboree negotiating session. Notable progress was made within six weeks on investment, intellectual property, textiles, standards, sanitary practices, customs administration, financial services, banking, and surface transportation.

In an earlier session, one Mexican official reported a breakthrough for the Mexican negotiators after the 9–10 February meeting of trade ministers in Chantilly, Virginia. The official had announced that his country finally understood that the NAFTA was not based on "horse-trading" between the parties, but rather on a set of underlying principles that the United States and Canada had understood from the beginning of the negotiations. All three parties were expected to remove tariffs over time. The four key tenets of a principle-based accord were: complete elimination of all barriers to trade, equal treatment in each country for all goods and services produced in North America, a commitment not to erect additional commercial obstacles between and among the signatories once the pact was signed, and extending the MFN treatment accorded a third country to North American partners (Grayson, 1993).

In the NAFTA negotiation, the Canadian and American governments took the opportunity to refine areas that were unsatisfactory in the FTA. Additionally, Canada and the United States had other, more pressing concerns. As noted earlier, Canada's main operational concern in negotiating the NAFTA was to protect the gains it had achieved through tough negotiations in the FTA. Similarly, the United States closely monitored the NAFTA with a view to protecting the carefully negotiated compromises of the FTA. Together, Canada and the United States pressed Mexico to accept the enhanced NAFTA provisions modeled after the FTA. Because of the nature of the FTA provisions, both of the original participants preserved the gains made, and resisted any reconsideration of original non-negotiable areas. For example, the United States refused to reconsider any diminution in the energy package negotiated in the FTA. Likewise, Canada's general exception on culture in the FTA was a "non-issue" for the NAFTA, even though Mexico was willing to negotiate in this area. In addition, Canada flatly refused Mexico's proposal to eliminate all agricultural restrictions.

Canada also resisted change in the NAFTA on the Chapter 19 dispute settlement mechanism for antidumping and countervailing duties. As will be demonstrated, this mechanism was the subject of considerable debate in the FTA, and its creation as an alternative to Canada's major demand in the FTA in fact saved the entire negotiation from collapse. Given this delicate compromise struck in the FTA, Canada's reservations were warranted.

Interestingly, Mexico sought through the NAFTA to gain exceptions to the application of US laws to remedy unfair trade, just as Canada had done in the FTA. When the United States refused to move on this issue, Mexico sought access to the Chapter 19 dispute settlement, more specifically, to the binational panel mechanism to review parties' application of domestic antidumping and countervailing duties. However, both Canada and the United States had problems with this Mexican request. The binational review mechanism was carefully constructed and was based on the assumption that both Canada and the United States had similar administrative laws and procedures necessary to ensure the proper "due process" functioning of the panels. Hence, initially, it was believed that Mexico's civil law tradition would pose an obstacle to extending the panel review mechanism. Most problematic for Canada and the United States was their doubt that Mexican administrative law and procedures would guarantee the same level of due process for Canadian and American exporters to the Mexican market as Mexican exporters would receive in the American or Canadian market (Winham and Grant, 1994).

How this dilemma was resolved is interesting for negotiation theory analysis and demonstrates what may happen when considering plurilateral as opposed to bilateral bargaining. Assuming that the major issues were primarily between the United States and Mexico, Canada took a back seat role in this part of the negotiation, that is, until the last stages. The United States proposed a two-tiered approach to the problem. The tier 1 proposal essentially involved using US procedures for antidumping and countervailing duties as a model for Mexico to incorporate into its domestic system. Tier 2 was more ambitious, proposing to establish NAFTA standards for due process against which each party would be held accountable. Canada, and initially Mexico, resisted such a suggestion, interpreting it as too intrusive. However, the Mexicans abruptly appeared to settle on US proposals that followed mainly the tier 2 proposals and some changes to the FTA. The Canadians still would not accept this proposal, precipitating an anxious 36-hour period of bargaining near the final round of the NAFTA negotiations. In the end, the parties settled on the tier 1 proposals. A "safeguarding" provision was added in Article 1905 to ensure against any party acting to inhibit the proper functioning of the panels.

11.4 Substantive Provisions of the NAFTA

The NAFTA is a comprehensive trade agreement that ensures a more stable climate for trade and investment. The agreement creates mutual obligations among the three parties and achieves substantial liberalization of access to their markets. In many respects, it builds upon the substance of the FTA, yet expands beyond it in scope. In certain areas, the NAFTA acknowledges differences in each party's willingness to negotiate in certain areas.

Early discussions among the NAFTA parties resolved that the format of the agreement would conform to the FTA model. However, while following the model, the NAFTA elaborated and improved on some areas of the FTA, for example, investment and telecommunications, and reorganized other areas, namely national treatment and border measures. Intellectual property and a rudimentary chapter on competition policy were the only areas added to the agreement that were lacking in the FTA.

The NAFTA format set up core disciplines in the main articles of each chapter. While the core disciplines of the agreement remained fixed, the negotiations involved modifications and reservations to be accorded to the parties. Chapter annexes were used to modify those disciplines for specific nations. This is why the NAFTA contains a lengthy series of annexes at the end of the document to incorporate national reservations and exceptions in the new areas of investment, services and financial services.

The NAFTA comprises eight principal areas: objectives and scope of the agreement, trade in goods, technical barriers to trade, government procurement, investment and services, intellectual property, institutional provisions such as dispute settlement, and finally general provisions governing entry into force and accession. Supplemental agreements on the issues of labor and environment were reached in August 1993.

The following section will outline the general substantive areas of the NAFTA, as well as the side agreements. An analysis of the outcomes of the negotiation and whether it is best described or predicted by economic theory or negotiation theory will conclude the case study.

11.4.1   Tariff and nontariff barriers to trade

The cornerstone of any free trade agreement is the removal of tariff and nontariff barriers to trade. The reduction of inefficient protectionist policies to deregulate the market is a central tenet of neoclassical economic theory. The NAFTA provides for the elimination of all tariffs on goods traded between the parties in conformity with the GATT obligations of each of the parties. GATT Article XXIV requires the elimination of barriers to trade on substantially all goods traded between parties in order for the parties to comply with the exception to the principles of MFN and national treatment under the GATT.

The NAFTA provides for a gradual elimination of virtually all tariff barriers over an agreed timetable. Tariffs were either to be eliminated immediately, or phased out over periods of 5, 10, or 15 years. The scheduled phaseout of these barriers essentially provides temporary protection to sensitive industries and allows the parties to restructure and adapt to the new trading conditions. Canada, for example, succeeded in protecting footwear and clothing, traditionally sensitive industries, through a lengthy phaseout period. Similarly, Mexico was able to negotiate the protection of certain vegetables, powdered milk, and pharmaceutical products.

Mexico's position in negotiating this area was unique in that it had already substantially reduced its tariffs and gone a long way in eliminating other barriers to trade, such as import licensing requirements, during its years of reform leading up to the NAFTA negotiations. This area was therefore less contentious, since Mexico had already dealt with these barriers, which had posed serious obstacles to foreign producers in the past.

In recognition of the disparity between Mexico and the United States and Canada, the tariff schedule provides Mexico with faster access to the Canadian and US markets than vice versa. The agreement provides for safeguard measures to protect sensitive domestic industries injured by import surges resulting from the NAFTA.

Automobiles

The automobile sector accounts for the largest share of continental trade flows between the negotiating parties. Gaining access to Mexico's highly protected automotive market was a key objective for both American and Canadian negotiators. Canada further aimed to protect provisions in the 1965 United States–Canada Auto Pact, which was the basis for FTA negotiations in this area, from any dilution by a possible bilateral agreement between Mexico and the United States (Johnson, 1993). Each party succeeded in these objectives. The auto provisions aim for almost full integration of the North American market within 10 years. The NAFTA incorporates the duty remission schedule of the FTA. As a result, Mexico's previously insulated market will open up to Canadian and American exports of automobiles and auto parts over a phase-in period.

The rules of origin have also changed in the NAFTA, increasing the percentage of domestic content from 50% to 62.5% on cars, light trucks, and major parts, and 60% on other vehicles and parts. The NAFTA includes a tracing requirement to measure foreign components of autos so parties meet their own North American content requirements (minimum 60%).

Interestingly, powerful constituencies with competing interests played roles in influencing negotiations in this area. These included the US Big Three automakers (General Motors, Ford, and Chrysler), auto workers, and auto parts firms (Hufbauer and Schott, 1993). A key negotiating objective for the Big Three, in which they were successful, was to ensure that the terms for the gradual elimination of most of Mexico's nontariff barriers would not grant benefits to newly established manufacturers in Mexico.

Textiles and Apparel

The textile and apparel sector was heavily protected by Canada and the United States, because such special treatment was afforded to this sector in the FTA. The NAFTA succeeded in setting a 10-year phaseout of all tariffs on the textile and apparel trade among the parties. The rules of origin negotiated in the NAFTA are stricter than those in the FTA: essentially, their purpose is to eliminate non-NAFTA fabrics and yarns in the production of textiles and apparel. Preferential duties are applied to yarns, fabrics, and apparel originating in North America. Expanding upon similar exceptions in the FTA, NAFTA incorporated exceptions permitting certain specified quotas of products not meeting the NAFTA rules of origin.

Agriculture

The agriculture provisions in the NAFTA are unique, since two separate bilateral arrangements were negotiated between Canada and Mexico and the United States and Mexico (Hufbauer and Schott, 1993). The FTA provisions between Canada and the United States remain in effect. The NAFTA focuses on phasing out tariffs and other restrictive measures, such as import quotas and import licenses on agricultural products, over a specified period of time. Eggs, poultry, and dairy products were some of the agricultural products that Canada and Mexico were able to exclude from the agreement, allowing Canada to continue to impose import quotas on these products. The bilateral arrangements allow each party to impose health and safety standards on imports, provided there is a scientific basis justifying the imposition of such restrictions.

Energy

The NAFTA energy chapter extends the FTA provisions while expanding trade and investment opportunities trilaterally. The provisions mutually oblige the parties to eliminate or reduce trade and investment restrictions in the energy sector. However, Mexico's constitution prohibits foreign ownership and exploitation of its resources. Therefore, investment in and the provision of services in its oil and gas industries are just some of the exclusions from the application of the energy provisions. Conversely, Mexico does not receive benefit from liberalized access to US or Canadian markets in the excluded areas.

Services

Trade in commercial services is expanded from the FTA. NAFTA parties must mutually extend national treatment to many commercial services. Basic telecommunications are excluded from both the FTA and the NAFTA, yet some areas of enhanced services are within NAFTA's scope. New expanded areas in the NAFTA include land transportation and specialty air services. Furthermore, compared to the FTA the NAFTA provides greater transparency to the procedures governing the flow of business and professional personnel across respective borders.

Financial Services

Where a non-NAFTA party is granted a concession beyond the privileges extended to NAFTA parties, the financial services chapter establishes and incorporates the principles of national treatment, greater transparency in the regulation of financial sectors, and MFN. American and Canadian financial institutions will only achieve full access to Mexico's financial markets in the year 2000, after what appears to be a lengthy transition period for Mexico. In this regard, the rules of origin issue (i.e., the "true nationality" of the interested financial institution) was of concern to the parties. Furthermore, the NAFTA establishes dispute settlement provisions in this area where the FTA did not.

Government Procurement

The NAFTA opens up access to parties seeking government procurement contracts in goods, services, and construction. The NAFTA improved on the provisions in the FTA that set out the procedures governing tendering bids, challenging bids, and settling disputes.

Investment

The NAFTA investment provisions liberalize restrictions on investment flows between the parties; they essentially extend national and MFN treatment to investors from the NAFTA parties. The investment provisions explicitly prohibit trade distorting performance requirements for the export of goods and services, domestic content, domestic sourcing, the transfer of technology, and obligations to supply exclusively a certain regional or world market. Dispute resolution provisions are also established in the form of international arbitration on a state-to-state basis and at the investor-state level.

Intellectual Property

With some notable exceptions, NAFTA parties extend "national treatment in [their] intellectual property laws to corporations and citizens of the other NAFTA countries" (Hufbauer and Schott, 1993). The intellectual property provisions in the NAFTA essentially establish standards for the trade and transfer of intellectual property between the parties. The chapter further provides for their protection and enforcement. The Uruguay Round draft code helpfully lays the basis for the substance of these provisions. Also of use was the Agreement on Trade-Related Aspects of Intellectual Property Rights. Both of these agreements help to set standards designed to protect such property and remedial provisions to deal with infringements of these rights.

Dispute Settlement

Building on the FTA, two chapters (aside from the sector-specific provisions) in the NAFTA deal explicitly with dispute settlement among the parties. Chapter 20, incorporating Chapter 18 of the FTA, provides for basic institutional arrangements and dispute settlement procedures to resolve disputes over the interpretation and implementation of the NAFTA.

Chapter 19 of the FTA established a dispute settlement mechanism that deals specifically with disputes over countervailing and antidumping duties. The NAFTA adopted this mechanism, which provides for the establishment of binational panels to review the use of unfair trade remedy laws by member parties. As such, the panels replace domestic courts in reviewing final antidumping and countervailing duty findings by the respective domestic agencies. Negotiating this mechanism caused some concern to the original signatories of the FTA. Because the Mexican legal system was significantly different from that of the United States and Canada (the Mexican legal system is based on the civil law tradition, while Canada and the United States maintain a common law legal tradition) it was feared that application of administrative law of judicial review would not accord the same treatment to all the parties. Mexico agreed to change its domestic administrative laws to place them more in conformity with US and Canadian concerns for transparency. The NAFTA adds a new provision that essentially safeguards the panel process and the finality of panel decisions from the interference of domestic laws. If the benefits of this mechanism are denied to one party, this provisions allows recourse to be taken against the denying party.

11.4.2   The NAFTA side agreements on labor and the environment

The side agreements attempt to address concerns over the disparity in environmental and labor issues among the three parties. Where a party persistently fails to enforce laws on labor standards and environmental protection, the agreements essentially set up the machinery to address these issues through cooperation and dispute settlement. The mechanism is a commission consisting of a ministerial council, an independent secretariat, and a public advisory committee. The commission may undertake consultations with a party charged with nonenforcement of its relevant laws. A panel may be established to investigate a charge of nonenforcement of such legislation, which may lead to sanctions against the nonenforcing party or even to the withdrawal of equivalent NAFTA benefits to the offending party. However, while the NAFTA may be a landmark agreement for incorporating environmental issues in a trade agreement, it lacks progressive provisions to upgrade the enforcement of existing standards or to enhance existing standards.

11.5   Analysis of the NAFTA Negotiation

One important aspect of this analysis is to examine the extent to which international negotiations such as the FTA and NAFTA are best explained by resorting to economic or negotiation theory. Given the objectives for Canada to negotiate the FTA and Mexico to negotiate the NAFTA, and after reviewing the outcome of these negotiations, it appears the motivations of the parties – if not the actual bargaining behavior at the table – may better be explained through reference to the underlying economic variables rather than to negotiation variables. The following section will explore these two different theoretical perspectives. A key question in this analysis will be: why did Canada and Mexico negotiate the NAFTA?

11.5.1   Negotiation theory

Negotiation theory places emphasis on the capacity of the parties to define interests, to analyze alternatives, and to settle on some outcome(s) on the basis of quid pro quo. Reciprocity is important, and parties tend to avoid those outcomes where they believe they will receive a smaller share of the benefits compared to other parties. Are the outcomes of the NAFTA negotiation explained by negotiation theory? Certainly the NAFTA parties defined their interests, reached a joint decision, and made some concessions following the negotiation theory model of quid pro quo. There is some identification of common ground between the parties. Each party clearly hoped to achieve greater access to the others' markets. Identification of common ground is also apparent in the negotiations for sector-specific gains shown above. However, with regard to the basic motivations for each party to negotiate, economic theory may better explain the outcomes of the negotiations.

One aspect to examine is the objectives of the parties. If one were to listen to government pronouncements, the reasons for Canada entering into free trade with the United States was to "instill a trade and investment climate which could contribute ... to the creation ... of more and better employment opportunities" (Canadian Trade Negotiations, 1985). Further listed objectives included: attaining security of access through the avoidance of US trade remedy law; improving market access; and initiating an ordered adjustment toward increasing competitiveness of the Canadian economy (Winham, 1994).

Mexico's objectives for initiating free trade with the United States were similar to Canada's in initiating the FTA. Gaining secure access to the US market was a major Mexican objective. Certainly Mexico's decision to enter into negotiations represented a continuation of the nation's internal economic reform and liberalization policies. Other objectives included promotion of domestic and foreign investment, incorporation into a regional trade grouping, and improvement of bilateral political and economic relations with the United States and Canada.

In looking at the objectives of the parties, it appears that some objectives are not defined in relational terms. It is probably easier to apply negotiation theories involving quid pro quo where the definition of a party's interests necessarily involves the other side. This is most easily seen in classical distributional bargaining, such as union–management negotiation over wage rates. However, in cases where objectives are not defined relationally, it may be that the parties can accept a wide range of outcomes, and that those outcomes may not depend on any fixed notion of reciprocity. For example, one of Mexico's objectives in the NAFTA was to promote domestic and foreign investment, and the fact is that much of what Mexico did in the NAFTA to promote investment was to liberalize its investment laws, which could have been done unilaterally without any reference to Canada or the United States.

A second aspect to consider about negotiation theory is the relative balance or imbalance found in the negotiation. If the relationship between the parties is not balanced, it is inherently more difficult to apply such negotiation concepts as reciprocity, equality, or quid pro quo. The FTA and NAFTA negotiations were unbalanced in terms of size of the parties; however, negotiation theory has been able to cope effectively in analyzing negotiations between weak and strong parties. The imbalance in the FTA and NAFTA negotiations was due more to the relative desire of the parties for an agreement, and the initial trade policies of the parties involved. It was clear that both Canada and Mexico were demandeurs in the negotiations with the United States, and that they valued an agreement per se more than their larger partner did. This source of imbalance is problematic for negotiation theory, because it tends to shift the explanation of negotiating behavior away from the tradeoffs offered at the table, and toward the underlying motivations of the parties. The question becomes not so much why one tradeoff is better than another, but what motivations would make many tradeoffs acceptable, as long as an agreement could be reached.

On the imbalance produced by trade policies, both Canada and Mexico had deeper trade protection against US products prior to the FTA and NAFTA negotiations than the United States had against Canadian or Mexican products. For example, it was estimated that average Canadian tariffs were more than twice as high as those of the United States in bilateral trade. This being the case, if countries are to move to a free trade (i.e., tariff-free) regime, it is apparent in terms of reciprocal exchange that one side will give up twice as much protection as the other. The conclusion would appear to be that traditional notions of mercantile tariff bargaining, based on reciprocity and quid pro quo, are not particularly useful in analyzing bold initiatives such as free trade negotiations.

A third aspect worth noting in the FTA and NAFTA negotiations was the "security of access" issue. This term was a code word for Canada's (and Mexico's) desire to gain blanket exception from the use of American laws to remedy unfair trade practices (i.e., the use of antidumping and countervailing duties). These trade remedies have the effect of restricting exports from the trading partners of the United States, and both Canada and Mexico have been impacted by US trade remedy actions in the past. This issue was critically important to Canada and Mexico because it went to the heart of the negotiation: clearly, there was no point in negotiating a free trade regime if the principal partner in that regime remained free to take actions restricting trade. The United States refused to make any concession on unfair trade remedies. Instead, the parties settled on the agreement-saving mechanism of binational panel dispute settlement established in Chapter 19 as an alternative to Canada's major demand in the negotiations. The fact that Canada settled for this less far-reaching dispute settlement mechanism on its principal demand led Doern and Tomlin (1991) to conclude that Canada had been "out-negotiated" in the FTA.

It is true that politicians, especially in Canada, cited "security of access" reasoning as a principal justification for negotiating the FTA. However, in terms of negotiation theory, there are several questions left unanswered if one accepts Doern and Tomlin's view, which presumably is based on negotiation theory. The issue really turns on how important security of access in fact was to Canada, as opposed to how forcefully it was articulated. First, if it were true that Canada and Mexico had negotiated the FTA/NAFTA as a defensive response to American protectionist trade remedy laws, this could be interpreted as a forced negotiation, or rather a situation of negotiating under threat. The differential in power between the negotiating parties must be recognized in this light, but normally even weaker parties resist being forced to the table. Power in negotiation theory can be defined as "the ability to bring about outcomes they desire," or "... the ability to get things done the way one wants them done" (Salancik and Pfeffer, 1977).

Second, as was outlined above, both Canada in the FTA and Mexico in the NAFTA failed to achieve this primary demand in the negotiations. Instead, both countries accepted the dispute settlement mechanisms in Chapter 19. For both Mexico and Canada the outcome of the agreement in this area proved largely illusory. There was relatively little quid pro quo on this important issue between the greater power of the United States and the Mexican and Canadian negotiation teams. Therefore, if one continues to accept security of access as being Canada's principal objective in the negotiation, one is obliged to accept that Canada (and possibly Mexico) was pressured into these agreements because of the continuing coercive protectionism practiced by the United States through continued use of unfair trade remedy laws. This hypothesis appears implausible, given that a significant economic power with choices, such as Canada or Mexico, would not likely negotiate such a comprehensive agreement on the basis of coercive protectionism applied by a principal trading partner. One is inclined to think there were other objectives and reasons why Canada and Mexico negotiated free trade.

The conclusion is that negotiation theory does not give a full explanation of some of the most important aspects of the FTA/NAFTA negotiations. Certainly reciprocity and quid pro quo did explain some issues, especially the capacity of parties to keep items off the agenda or to drop items from the table. For example, Canada was successful in negotiating an exception for cultural issues, and the United States and Mexico were successful in keeping maritime transportation services and petroleum products out of the negotiation. What this may show is that small powers perhaps have greater power to avoid unfavorable results than to achieve beneficial results, which would likely be consistent with negotiation theory. However, to understand the FTA/NAFTA negotiations fully, one is obliged to look beyond the tools that negotiation theory brings to the analysis.

11.5.2   Economic theory

Recent developments in the international economy, notably international economic interdependence, the opening up of markets, deregulation, and international flow of investment policies through FDI immeasurably affected the economies of all of the parties to these agreements. Both Canada and Mexico have an overwhelming export dependence on the United States. This dependence meant that if either Canada or Mexico sought to liberalize trade, it would necessarily involve the United States. Canada learned earlier on, in the GATT multilateral tariff negotiations, that while medium powers could receive nonreciprocated benefits from trade liberalization by larger countries, initiating concessions from larger powers was much more difficult. The reason is that nations normally reach agreements in tariff negotiations with the principal supplier of a given product, and middle or smaller countries are rarely the principal suppliers of products to large countries. As a result, Canada found it could not fully achieve its export access demands in multilateral negotiations (Winham, 1988).

External pressures coming from the international system for trade liberalization led to substantial internal pressures in Canada and Mexico, and perhaps the United States, for trade liberalization and economic deregulation. Countries such as Canada and Mexico recognized international market forces and accepted their dictates in order to achieve economic development. These factors help to explain Mexico and Canada's reasoning for engaging in the FTA/NAFTA negotiations.

To summarize up to this point, the international movement toward a global economy led to internal revolutions in the domestic economies of both Canada and Mexico. The fact that both countries traded disproportionately with the United States, a larger economy, and that they were able to engage the United States in a free trade agreement, made that internal revolution easier for Mexico and Canada. That they were also able to obtain some reciprocity for what was essentially necessary domestic economic reform made the negotiations all the more fortuitous, but these reciprocities were not the sole basis for the negotiations.

International competitiveness was highlighted in both Canada and Mexico as a key concern for economic survival. Before entering into negotiations, both Canada and Mexico recognized the need to keep pace with international economic interdependence and international competition. Competitiveness necessarily complements free trade and the deregulation of tariffs on imports and exports. Modern productive technology and the internationalization of markets require greater economies of scale than could be achieved in the Canadian market and in the hitherto ISI-led Mexican economy. Adopting such a posture was a recognition by both parties of the inefficiencies that protectionism fostered.

Elsewhere it was argued that selling the FTA to the business community was made easier by identifying security of access as the Canadian objective, as opposed to selling what amounted to a total restructuring of the Canadian market on the basis of enhanced competitiveness. Nonetheless, enhanced competitiveness continued to be the Canadian prime objective in the FTA negotiations and can better explain the reasons for Canada's continuing in those negotiations even after it became obvious that Canada would not achieve appreciable inroads toward reducing US contingent protectionism. Two influential government documents reflect this objective: *Competitiveness and Security: Directions for Canada's International Relations*; and the Macdonald Commission report on economic policy. Competitiveness was also encouraged by Prime Minister Brian Mulroney before and during the FTA negotiations and by Finance Minister Michael Wilson in 1990. Mexico had similar motivations: the prospect that free trade would promote Mexican competitiveness (Herzog, 1994) may better explain the country's continuation in the

NAFTA negotiations than would the identification of commonality of interests approach posited by negotiation theory.

A second key concern for Canada and Mexico in negotiating free trade was their desire for domestic economic reform. This objective was clear for Mexico, as the NAFTA may be viewed as a corollary to or continuation of economic reform initiatives that began in the mid-1980s. Policies of deregulation of the economy and initiatives for export-led industrialization led to a necessary redefinition of the role of the state in the Mexican economy.

In Canada, free trade also emerged as the preferred approach to the management of economic policy, even though the government never really articulated a direct relationship between free trade and government reform. Free trade was identified by the Macdonald Commission as the key to balancing a reliance on market forces and the role of the state in Canada. Significantly, the Macdonald Commission could not identify any better alternatives to free trade for Canada in its need to restructure its economy through deregulation and through enhancing competitiveness. Hence, Canada had few alternatives to initiating FTA negotiations with its largest trading partner. One identifiable alternative would have been to accomplish its goals through internal domestic reform policies, however, this would have been more difficult to sell politically.

It can be concluded then that Mexico explicitly and Canada implicitly pursued the free trade negotiations as a means to promote and enhance reform of the government's role in the economy (i.e., deregulation), and to improve the competitiveness of their respective economies. These basic economic objectives appear to have been more important to the parties than the specific concessions exchanged during the negotiation process. What the negotiation did above all was to give Canada and Mexico an excuse to initiate and continue the process of domestic economic reform, which would have been more difficult politically to accomplish on a unilateral basis.

A final point to consider was Canada's decision to enter the NAFTA negotiation, which was initiated on different assumptions than its decision to seek participation in the FTA. For Canada, the FTA negotiation signaled a reversal of a long-standing trade policy and was taken after extensive internal deliberations. The NAFTA, on the other hand, was negotiated in a defensive manner, arguably so that Canada would not lose any of the gains it had negotiated in the FTA. The NAFTA negotiation was not warmly received by the Canadian government, which was just recovering from the bruising "free trade" election of 1988.

Diversification from traditional reliance on the US market could be identified as a reason for Canada to enter the NAFTA. Canada's desire to gain access to the Mexican market also became more apparent during the negotiations. Canada became aware of the advantages of reducing nontariff restrictions on Mexican producers and of access to the hitherto restricted Mexican markets for automobiles.

The best explanation, however, for Canada's decision to enter the NAFTA negotiations was described by economists Ronald Wonnacott and Richard Lipsey as the "hub-and-spoke" model (Wonnacott, 1990). The model is explained as follows: were the United States to extend a series of trade agreements to other countries, it would secure itself in the position of the hub, while the signatories to such bilateral agreements would occupy the spoke positions. The hub, of course, would benefit from liberalized trade and reduction of tariffs from each spoke, while each spoke would lack the benefits of the others' liberalization.

This hub and spoke model had immediate application for Canada when it was faced with the possibility of an emerging bilateral agreement between Mexico and the United States. Canada understood that Mexico would gain through a bilateral agreement with the United States the same reduction in tariffs and access to US markets that Canada had achieved in the FTA. Canada believed that this would threaten its own enhanced access to the US market, and further threaten other gains achieved in the FTA negotiation. Conversely, the United States would gain access to the Mexican market equivalent to its access to the Canadian market, while neither Mexico nor Canada would achieve greater access to each other's markets. This would leave the United States with a direct trading advantage over its bilateral partners. In the investment area, this would also mean a disadvantage to Canada and Mexico, as investors would settle in a preferred market such as the United States and gain equal access to the two other parties. For the same reason, the United States would be more attractive to prospective manufacturers, especially in the important automotive sector.

The alternative to this hub-and-spoke model is, of course, what the NAFTA represented: namely, a multilateral obligation between all the parties. Canada in this sense was faced with little alternative but to negotiate the NAFTA, not only to preserve its gains in the FTA, but also to forge ahead with a new relationship with Mexico. Again, it appears that Canadian behavior in the NAFTA may be better explained by economic analysis than by the variables put forward in negotiation theory.

11.6 Conclusion

We argue that both Canada and Mexico pursued free trade for reasons that were actually extrinsic to the relative exchanges produced by the bargaining process. This is especially emphasized by the fact that both parties failed to achieve the major goal of gaining exceptions to US unfair competition laws. Rather, as explained, the objectives of these parties – namely, competitiveness and economic reform – could have been achieved without entering into negotiations at all; that is, they could have been achieved unilaterally through domestic reform. This factor allowed both governments to be relatively indifferent to the balance of concessions identified by negotiation theorists as key in negotiations. Gaining such sectoral concessions as were outlined above in the substantive portion of this case study was of some interest to the parties, but cannot explain the full dynamics of and reasons underlying the negotiations. Rather, the FTA and the NAFTA negotiation offered both Mexico and Canada an acceptable rationale for restructuring and continuing difficult policies of domestic economic reform that would have been more difficult to initiate otherwise.

Hence, the "relative exchange" arguments of negotiation theories only partially explain the behavior of Canada and Mexico and the outcomes of the FTA and the NAFTA negotiations. Both Canada and Mexico reversed long-standing trade policies by initiating these negotiations. A fuller explanation of the negotiation is achieved by looking at recent developments in the international economic system that impacted heavily on Canada and Mexico, and encouraged these nations to initiate negotiations that would reform their economic policies, rather than by looking at the tradeoffs on specific issues reached during the process of negotiation. Hence, economic analysis appears to be more useful than negotiation analysis in explaining the important features of the FTA and NAFTA.

Chapter 12

Market Conditions and International Economic Negotiation: Japan and the United States in 1971

John S. Odell

12.1 Introduction

The most distinctive dimension of international economic negotiations – in contrast to those over diplomatic recognition, war termination, and arms control, for instance – is that economic bargaining is sensitive to market conditions. The main purposes of this chapter are to elucidate this broad point by laying out some specific market propositions and suggesting their empirical validity. Particular market conditions – such as international price levels, balance of payments positions, and industrial structures – bias initial negotiation strategy choices in predictable directions on average, and later changes in those conditions also shift negotiator behavior and outcomes in understandable ways. A typology of negotiation strategies is introduced to represent variance at the crucial initial stage in the negotiation process. For illustrations this chapter draws especially on overlapping negotiations between Japan and the United States over the textiles trade and exchange rates between 1969 and 1972, as well as other recent episodes.

12.2   Problems with Present Knowledge

We need much better understanding of economic conflict, negotiation, and cooperation among states, for theoretical as well as practical reasons. While much has been written on these subjects, our knowledge remains fragmented, incomplete, and possibly wrong in some respects. Several informal approaches developed in psychology and sociology have been suggested for international relations and many of these are interesting, but only a few causal propositions have been specified and tested even weakly on historical evidence from this field (Zartman, 1978, 1994). Impressive mathematical models of bargaining may be valid for interstate economic negotiations, but we do not know in the cases of the many conjectures that again have not passed even weak tests against empirical data from international history. One possible way forward is to "unpack" such models into basic components so that at least some dimensions might be tested. This chapter is one attempt in that direction.

Many empirically sophisticated case studies have illuminated particular events and some express theoretical payoffs (Wriggins, 1976; Winham, 1986; Haas, 1992; Martin, 1992, Part II; Friedheim, 1993). Despite their achievements, these studies, including some of my own, have failed collectively to accumulate into a consistent body of knowledge, or even into several sub-bodies each internally coherent, because they begin from a diversity of conceptual foundations. Some studies of international negotiations propose typologies – of components, stages, and influences upon the process – and show that their concepts can help describe multiple cases in the same language, but this work too stops short of identifying general links between causes and specific effects and conditions under which these relationships hold.

Political science studies of international economic cooperation conducted during the last decade have generated a new school of analysis and have also achieved much (Haggard and Simmons, 1987; Milner, 1992), but this literature too suffers from at least three significant limitations that are relevant here. It has effectively restricted "cooperation" to regime studies. This research has effectively drawn attention away from many international economic negotiations, and possibly the most consequential ones: those that take place bilaterally between states or between states and firms. In fact bilateral bargaining is actually a prerequisite for, or a dominant component of, many multilateral agreements. Possibly the most consequential international economic regime agreement of the twentieth century, reached at Bretton Woods in 1944, was actually negotiated bilaterally by the United Kingdom and the United States to a large extent before they invited other parties to join the process (Gardner, 1956). One veteran US negotiator has explained in a related sense that "what becomes apparent at the [multilateral] negotiation session is often less a product of that meeting than a result of the painstaking groundwork that has occurred, on a bilateral basis, in the weeks or months preceding" (Benedick, 1993).

Second, most of this literature has assumed, rather than demonstrated, that these international institutions cause the behavior of states and other actors to differ from what would have happened in the absence of the institution. Thus, for instance, while one might suppose that the mixed history of trade liberalization since 1947 was due to the GATT, we have little careful empirical research designed to inquire whether, in the absence of this regime, the major states would have accomplished through bilateral and plurilateral bargaining roughly the same pattern of barrier reductions and increases that has been observed. We even lack much disciplined counterfactual speculation to support this inference. Very recent research has begun to direct some empirical attention to regime effects and early results give the first sound evidence for such effects; with more time this picture might change (see Martin, 1992; Finnemore, 1993; Haas, Keohane and Levy, 1993; Strang and Chang, 1993; as well as related discussion in Young, 1991; Underdal, 1992; Chayes and Chayes, 1993; Müller, 1993. One of the most convincing is Mitchell, 1994).

Third, this school has generally attempted to explain regime formation and change by concentrating on the international power structure, hegemonic and otherwise, and the institutional framework thought to govern this interstate bargaining. A given power structure is, however, only the bare beginning of analysis; many different outcomes are consistent with a given structure. International institutions probably have only a small influence on bargaining outcomes, relative to other influences; at any rate, little empirical research has demonstrated otherwise. This school, with a few exceptions (e.g., Rhodes, 1989; Evans *et al.*, 1993), seems to assume that the international economic bargaining process – the parties' actual strategy choices and the interaction between them – has no significant effects on negotiation outcomes. One of the theoretical ideas most popular recently – that high transaction costs of operating otherwise are what drive states to cooperate via regimes – has yet to be substantiated with much close empirical research.

As an example consider one of the most seminal contributions, Robert Keohane's pioneering *After Hegemony*. Keohane selects the multilateral negotiation of the International Energy Agency (IEA) in the 1970s as the primary illustration of his theory, which effectively limits cooperation to international institution building. This book itself underlines repeatedly how marginal this agency's practical effects were (Keohane, 1984:224–240). By contrast, the book does not study the bilateral bargaining during roughly the same period between Algeria and France, which led eventually to agreement on a higher price and movement of billions of cubic meters of gas as well as improved political relations between the two states. Nor does the book help us understand why the parallel bilateral gas negotiations during the same period between Mexico and the United States ended in an agreement so small as to deviate only trivially from no agreement at all (Zartman and Bassani, 1987; Fagen and Nau, 1979; Bailey and Vega, 1989). Most important, the book does not report a close enough empirical investigation of the IEA negotiation process to show whether the main explanatory variable proposed – the desire to reduce high transaction costs of future bargaining – actually influenced any government's behavior. A full and fair evaluation will, however, need to take account of subsequent studies and critiques that this book and others have stimulated, which are still unfolding.

For now, presumably no one would deny that economic negotiations have something to do with markets. More specifically, though, just which market conditions cause official negotiators to respond, and in which directions? Are any general behavioral relationships indicated by a surplus of confirming evidence over anomalies? How are these market effects achieved? Under what conditions do government negotiators defy apparent market incentives? That is, how strong are specified market influences relative to other influences? As elemental as the general theme may seem to be, especially for economists, much of the available empirical theory on interstate economic negotiations is truncated and weakened by the failure to reach beyond political and psychological ideas to encompass market properties explicitly as well. At the same time, market hypotheses alone are not sufficient and are sometimes quite misleading. States do not always behave as reasonable market-based propositions would have led us to expect, even though they do so to a greater extent than is sometimes recognized.

12.3   Decision to Negotiate and Choice of Initial Strategy

The approach in this chapter builds especially on influential works by Walton and McKersie (1965), Raiffa (1982), and Lax and Sebenius (1986), among others. It uses "bargaining" and "negotiation" as synonyms, defined as the process whereby two or more parties, having at least some objectives in conflict, direct demands and offers at each other for the ostensible purpose of reaching agreement. The usage here is broad, encompassing actions such as threats and use of economic sanctions that, for instance, reduce the other party's no-agreement alternative. Sometimes such measures are instead classified as coercion and excluded from "negotiation." However, virtually no negotiation worthy of sustained study is purely free of the exercise of power. On reflection, defining "bargaining" so narrowly would leave us with little to study. Thus, the argument in this chapter does not assume that any negotiated agreement will make each party better off than it perceived itself to be before the bargaining. Parties sometimes accept agreements that represent losses relative to the status quo ante because the best alternative to the agreement available at that (subsequent) time is regarded as worse.

Let us begin with simple negotiation theory and impose some further temporary restrictions in order to think more deeply about this market angle of vision. Imagine a simplified world of two unitary states with a mix of overlapping and diverging objectives. Hypotheses framed in terms of two states are the logical starting place when building an analysis of a multilateral negotiation as well. Initially assume also that no internal divisions or national institutions affect their negotiating behavior. Later, when empirical anomalies demonstrate a need to do so, this assumption will be relaxed.

For clarity of exposition, this chapter concentrates on conditions that the practical negotiator must generally accept as given in the short run. Here market conditions are temporarily assumed to be exogenous for negotiators, even though in a more complex, realistic theory causal arrows would often run in the opposite direction as well, at least in the long run. Most these propositions are intended to apply to all economic issues. A few are specific to sectoral trade issues.

This chapter generally assumes rational decision making. This does not mean that negotiators care only about economic objectives or the short run. Rationality is equally consistent with other objectives such as power, security, and status. This chapter also generally assumes that negotiators will perceive conditions without biases due to culture, education, or the nature of cognition. In fact, such an approach will probably not prove sufficient. Elsewhere we have developed at length a case for adding propositions concerning variations in leaders' policy beliefs (Odell, 1982b). Only limits of space rule out greater attention to such hypotheses in this study.

Market forces are certainly not the only important influences on economic negotiations. Each of these hypotheses is thus meant as partial and ceteris paribus, or valid when all other causal variables are constant.

What, then, will lead states to decide to negotiate, and what will determine their resistance (security) points and strategies in bargaining over international trade, investment, and money? For analytical clarity, the distinction between the party's decision to negotiate and its initial strategy choice, and then the subsequent bargaining process and its outcome, will be helpful. Each of these phases in the process can vary over a significant range of possibilities, and they are not correlated perfectly. Understanding the first step is crucial, especially for states dealing with the most powerful players, such as the EU in trade matters and the United States on most economic issues. These major powers often make such initial decisions without consulting outsiders, and yet this initial choice is likely to limit firmly the set of possible agreements that can be reached. In these and most other cases, choosing to travel down one path is likely to stimulate one particular set of reactions from the other side more often than another set, and hence to block paths that would be open otherwise. Each possible strategy raises its distinctive set of risks or possible barriers to greater gain for the deciding party. After considering these initial decisions, this chapter will turn more briefly to market influences on the subsequent process and outcomes.

One of the most basic premises of all rational negotiation theory is that the decision maker will compare the likely gains and losses from a proposed agreement with the value of the BATNA available at the time. The basic insight that resistance points are determined by the party's BATNA appeared explicitly at least as early as Frederik Zeuthen's *Problems of Monopoly and Economic Warfare*, first published in 1930, and was reiterated in Iklé and Leites (1962). If the deal's net value is expected to be less than the party's reservation value, it will decide not to negotiate. In economic affairs, "leaving it to the market" often stands as at least a potential alternative to any official agreement. When the market alternative is expected to be superior or equivalent to a negotiated deal on balance, the leader will avoid official bargaining, and otherwise will negotiate. The more the market alternative improves in value, the smaller the odds that the state will enter official negotiations and the higher the negotiator's resistance point for agreement. A deteriorating market alternative increases the possible gain from a given agreement (by definition, if gain is understood as surplus relative to the best alternative available), and implies a behavior shift in the opposite direction.

Sometimes, a change in relevant market conditions is the proximate trigger for a negotiation. One simple application is found in trade issues. For states that concentrate on the export of a particular commodity, the greater the decline in the commodity's international price, the greater the odds of a decision to negotiate or renegotiate intergovernmental agreements to support or raise the price, and the lower the negotiator's resistance point for a given deal, ceteris paribus. For example, compare the international prices of coffee in each year after 1950 (*Figure 12.1*). The hypothesis and these data would suggest that we look for negotiations perhaps after 1950–1953 and at least after the steep decline from 1954 to 1961. Periodically through the twentieth century Brazil's government attempted to support world prices by unilateral management, and then by producer-only agreements. After one such arrangement was signed in 1957, the international price rose briefly, but then fell again as world production and exports exceeded demand despite the agreement. The worse the market alternative became, the greater the effort to negotiate official price support arrangements, at least for this commodity in this period. In 1958 Brazil and others decided to widen the agreements to encompass 15 Latin American states, but prices continued to fall in Latin America and also in newer African exporting states. In 1959 a larger group of exporting states, including French Africa and Portuguese Angola, decided to negotiate a grand producer-only agreement. Eventually the exporters decided they would not be able to hold prices unless importing states, especially the United States, agreed to join an agreement to enforce

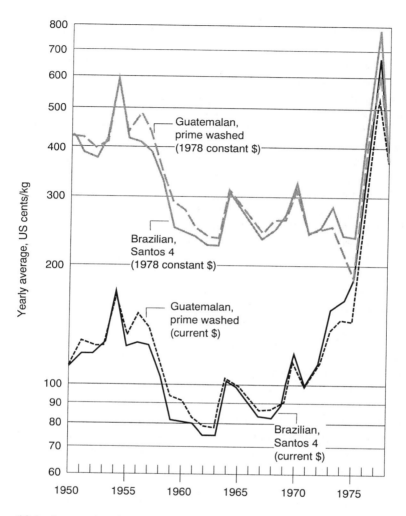

Figure 12.1. International coffee prices, 1950–1978. Source: World Bank, *Commodity Trade and Price Trends*, August 1979, p. 39.

it by refusing to buy from exporters who overshipped their quotas. The result was the 1962 United Nations Conference on Coffee, which created the International Coffee Agreement, headquartered in London (Fisher, 1972; Krasner, 1973).

A second application comes at the aggregate level on macroeconomic issues. A state with a policy goal of maintaining a stable exchange rate will be sensitive to its balance of payments and level of monetary reserves. The larger its payments deficit and the lower its reserves, other things being equal, the greater the odds it will decide to negotiate foreign loans, a currency depreciation, or some combination of the two. As the reserve stock dwindles, the market (which, in a more complex recursive model, would reflect previous actions by governments as well as private firms) takes away the government's alternative of waiting for the payments picture to right itself, and thereby reduces the negotiator's resistance point for a given international deal. Recent illustrations have been seen in the payments balances of the United States in 1969–1971, the EMS member states in 1990–1993, and Mexico in 1994–1995.

To be sure, governments under pressure can act unilaterally, as demonstrated by London's collapse in September 1931 and the US decisions of April 1933 and August 1971. By stepping back, though, we can also recognize such actions as moves in bargaining processes, whether or not the actors so intended them at the time. Each of these actions influenced the expectations and behavior of other players and markets, whose own moves in the short run determined the value of the outcome for the country that moved first. The 1971 episode will be discussed in more detail below.

The good's price, for trade issues, and the currency's price and the country's balance of payments, for international monetary issues, are all proximate variables that actually stand for a complex mix of other, causally prior, influences. In the coffee trade, for example, periodic freezes destroy production capacity while new investment increases supply. Changes in consumer taste or declining prices of substitute goods can reduce demand. At the aggregate level, payments balances register and combine such influences as changing levels of income and saving at home and abroad, as well as those that determine capital flows, such as competition from alternative recipients of foreign investment and changing interest rate differentials. One implication for negotiation analysts is that a better "early warning system" for anticipating policy changes, conflicts, and negotiations on economic issues entails monitoring some of these prior, as well as the proximate, influences on negotiator behavior. Again, a fuller political-economic theory would recognize some market changes as partly endogenous (Stein, 1992, also analyzes decisions to negotiate).

12.4   Strategies

Suppose, then, that a state has decided to attempt to negotiate an international economic agreement. What strategy will it adopt? In order to improve negotiation and cooperation theory empirically, we need a typology that is more discriminating than the popular dichotomy between "defect" and "cooperate." This tool simply discards too much of the information we observe. In addition to not bargaining, then, suppose the government has three broad strategy options: value claiming, value creating, and between the two, the combined strategy.

12.4.1 Value-claiming strategy

The first, the value-claiming or distributive strategy, is defined as a set of activities that promote the attainment of one party's goals when they are in conflict with those of the other party (Walton and McKersie, 1965, chapter II; Lax and Sebenius, 1986, chapter 2). It is a rational response to a situation in which no settlement acceptable to both could make both better off than they are at the outset. State A, as a value-claiming or distributive negotiator, proposes or insists on an agreement under which state B will lose value and A will gain value from them, relative to the status quo ante. (If gain and loss are defined instead relative to the party's best alternative at the moment, then presumably neither party would sign an agreement that would cause it to lose, unless it acts irrationally.) Applications vary as to the severity of the tactics used. Most generally, state A insists that it will make no concessions and resists doing so. Particular distinctive claiming tactics include a high opening position; concealing information about one's own true objectives and priorities; and criticizing the other's unfavorable positions. As a value claimer, A concedes at a slow rate; delays; attempts to manipulate B's beliefs about its own alternatives and A's; and may attempt actually to worsen B's alternatives and to improve A's. In some cases the value-claimer attempts to establish a commitment to a particular demand in order to lower the other's resistance point and rule out certain points in the bargaining range, for instance by making an explicit threat. Various ancillary tactics are used to increase credibility. Many sources develop lists of tactics, including such modern classics as Schelling (1960), Schelling (1966), and Walton and McKersie (1965).

Actually making concessions – agreeing to give up something A values that partially offsets the value A will receive – can be consistent with a distributive strategy if concessions are held back until several rounds have passed. Simply lowering demands for unrequited concessions is not by itself a transfer of value from A to B and hence should not be confused with "making concessions." Of course not all these tactics need be found in a given episode. If the situation presents a conflict of objectives, we can expect to see some of these tactics from each side.

The dominant risk of the strict claiming strategy is that it will stimulate manipulation and claiming from other parties and that even if an agreement is reached, the process will fail to uncover potential joint value that might have been created through negotiation, if the parties' objectives turn out to overlap to some extent. Many actual interstate negotiations, conducted with bounded rationality and imperfect information, are probably inefficient in this sense, even though each state might have been better off if the outcome had been more efficient. Some gains for state A cannot be achieved without the cooperation and benefit of state B, in which case a more efficient outcome is not only consistent with, but also necessary for, maximization of A's interests.

The United States and the EU have employed claiming many times to force another country to reduce its exports of textiles or apparel below levels that would prevail otherwise. The importing side declares that it seeks an agreement in which an exporting state will make a concession but the importing side will make no concessions of its own, such as increasing its imports of other products from the restraining state. For example, the US government began a famous case of claiming from Japan over the textiles trade in October 1969. Washington's aide-mémoire described its objectives concerning "the textile problem" purely in terms of American concerns: apprehension on the part of American management and labor over the rapid rise in imports of textiles and the adverse effect this can have on investment decisions and on employment, and the importance that the government of the United States attaches to the creation and preservation of employment opportunities for minority groups in the United States.

The message called on Japan's government to accept a comprehensive five-year bilateral agreement establishing a quantitative limit on every wool and synthetic fiber textile and apparel product produced in Japan to be exported to the United States. This document, issued before negotiations started, already explicitly pointed to "strong sentiment in the United States Congress for a legislated solution should the attempt to achieve a negotiated solution fail (United States aide-mémoire of 2 October 1969; reprinted in Destler *et al.*, 1979:339–341). After two years of fruitless bargaining with Japan, President Nixon turned this thinly veiled threat into an unambiguous public threat to impose such limits unilaterally under the US Trading with the Enemy Act. At that point Japan settled for such an agreement, as did Hong Kong and South Korea.

The US side decided to start negotiations because of a domestic political deal made during the 1968 presidential campaign. Richard Nixon, as he was bidding for the Republican Party's nomination against Ronald Reagan, secured the support of Senator Strom Thurmond of South Carolina by promising to support protection for the US textile industry. With this deal in hand, Thurmond worked vigorously at the Republican convention that summer to bring Southern delegates into the Nixon column. Nixon launched negotiations that conflicted with his general foreign and trade policies because, like political leaders in many countries, he felt he could not afford to renege on this domestic political commitment (Destler *et al.*, 1979:66–72). In the first meetings, the Japanese side adamantly and uniformly refused to consider any agreement on synthetic textiles at all, somewhat to the Americans' surprise. Late in 1969, however, Tokyo's position softened and serious negotiations began.

Distributive strategy is also seen in monetary bargaining. Another, more famous example is Washington's August 1971 unilateral suspension of the dollar's convertibility into gold and the US demand that Japan, West Germany, and other financial powers revalue their currencies against it. The Nixon Administration also imposed a 10% tariff surcharge on all dutiable imports, which Nixon said was a temporary measure that would be ended when foreign "unfair exchange rates" were ended. This too was a case in which the parties' immediate objectives conflicted sharply. Japan opposed any yen appreciation by any means. The major European states also opposed appreciation by more than a very small margin (Odell, 1982a, chapter 4; Gowa, 1983).

12.4.2 Value-creating strategy

The second broad strategy option, value-creating or integrative bargaining, is also an ideal type and a dramatically different one. This approach consists of activities that promote the attainment of goals that are not in fundamental conflict with those of the other party. As an integrative negotiator, state A proposes that state B negotiate toward an agreement designed to yield gain for both simultaneously. This strategy does not necessarily refer to altruistic behavior. It may be a rational response to a different payoff structure, a situation in which the parties' true objectives are unrelated, complementary, or mutually dependent.

In a world of unbounded rationality and perfect information, each government would know its own and the others' goals and priorities, and thus would know whenever a Pareto-improving deal was possible. They would adopt the appropriate strategies and reach the best agreement permitted by their utility functions. In the actual world of highly imperfect information, however, each government is typically uncertain, prior to bargaining, about the other's true priorities – and sometimes about its own – and hence negotiators are uncertain about whether such potential to create value exists. An integrative negotiator's tactical goals, therefore, are to clear away the haze, discover or even create the two parties' preferences, and search for any convergences or profitable exchanges of concessions. By the way, initial uncertainty also implies that two negotiators faithfully using this strategy need not reach a value-creating agreement. Their true but imperfectly known objectives could turn out to be largely opposed, or the parties' reservation values on the issues of concern could rule out a positive zone of agreement.

A very different set of tactics is instrumental for this process. In Walton and McKersie's formulation (1965, chapters IV and V), the ideal-type integrative process moves through three phases. At first the parties explore, discover, and reveal the nature of the problem and their own objectives and priorities. Here and throughout, frankness and openness about information are at a premium. Positions are stated so as to facilitate identification of underlying concerns rather than to conceal them. Parties listen carefully and probe for underlying reasoning, rather than responding immediately with a counterargument criticizing the other. Efforts to manipulate and conceal information would risk stimulating mirror-image behavior and blocking the discovery of opportunities. Negotiators operate less like institutional role-players with a fixed brief to read, and more like individuals assigned to take the initiative toward solving practical problems affecting both sides simultaneously.

The second phase is a joint search for alternative potential solutions, which may not be standardized and obvious, and for their likely consequences over a range of objectives. Desired solutions are stated in specific terms rather than in sermons about abstract principles. Here too inventiveness and creativity are rewarded. In the final phase the problem solvers combine their utility functions in some way and test the alternative solutions devised against them. If not earlier, then at this stage the parties explore for concessions that might be valued differently and possible trades. All partial agreements are considered provisional until everything else is settled, to avoid excluding a possible later repackaging of the parts that would move the outcome closer to the Pareto frontier.

The dominant risk of the integrative strategy is that B's negotiator will use A's openness to B's distributional advantage, for example by discovering A's true resistance point and quickly offering to settle there and no higher. In fact, for this reason use of this ideal type of strategy alone may be rare in international relations.

12.4.3   Combined strategy

Probably more common is a third strategy type, ranking between claiming and creating. Using a combined strategy, the state employs features of both integrative and distributive approaches more or less simultaneously and in roughly equal proportions. In announcing the decision to negotiate by this approach and not by pure claiming, state A's negotiators commit their government to search for an agreement that will benefit both parties. They do not rule out possible concessions by their side, but they also delay their own concessions and attempt to bias the distribution of gains in A's direction. They may propose a principle of fairness or a formula for agreement that will achieve joint gains but shift their distribution toward A's side (see Winham, 1977, for illustrations and Zartman and Berman, 1982, for the concept of the negotiation formula). A variant of combined bargaining is the sequenced strategy, wherein the negotiator alternates between integrating and claiming as the process unfolds. The tit for tat strategy is a special case of combined strategy.

A year after the Nixon shock regarding the dollar, the United States also illustrated the combined strategy in monetary negotiation. At the 1972 annual meeting of the IMF, the United States offered a new plan for creating a more flexible monetary system that still remained within the Bretton Woods framework. One key goal behind the proposed rules was to create effective new disciplines on surplus countries like Japan to make revaluations more timely. In contrast to 1971, however, the US position also explicitly addressed the shared interests of all members and implied that it would not rule out changes of US policy as part of a package deal. Clearly Washington had switched back to the type of strategy used in 1965 to reform international liquidity and in 1943 to create the IMF in the first place.

Two other clear examples of this strategy are the positions of Canada and the United States in 1985 and 1986 regarding trade between them. Canada proposed that they negotiate a free trade area, and the United States agreed to bargain toward that goal (see Chapter 11 in this book). By definition, offering to negotiate free trade means lowering one's own tariffs as part of a package agreement. Prime Minister Brian Mulroney and President Ronald Reagan each set a goal of "the broadest possible package of mutually beneficial reductions in barriers to trade in goods and services" (Mulroney statement, quoted in Hart *et al.*, 1994:104–105). At the same time, each side clearly attempted to claim value from the other on particular issues. The Canadians were keen to control US antidumping and countervailing duty investigations into Canadian business and government programs, which they viewed as a new form of protectionism. They wanted to exclude some American concerns, such as Canada's policies protecting its media on nationalist grounds, from the talks, and they wanted American concessions to be implemented immediately while Canada could phase in its changes slowly. The US side wanted improved protection for intellectual property rights, elimination of Canada's industrial and regional subsidy programs, and reduced regulation of corporate investment.

12.5 Common and Opposite Economic Effects and Strategy Choice

If negotiators in general have three strategy options, which path will they then choose? One set of hypotheses for any issue begins from common and opposite interests or effects. States that will gain or suffer from the same change are thought especially likely to succeed in reaching a mutually beneficial agreement between them, and hence to use a combined or value-creating strategy, while those experiencing opposite effects are more likely to attempt to claim from each other. For economic issues, two variants of this hypothesis will be suggested.

First, if a decline in an international price harms state A while it benefits state B, A is more likely to use a distributive strategy in negotiating on this issue with B. If a price decline benefits or harms both, A is more likely to choose a mixed or integrative strategy toward B. In the coffee trade, for instance, research should find that in the 1950s Brazil and Colombia, both coffee exporters that stood to gain from a price increase, used the combined or integrative strategy rather than strict claiming toward each other in negotiations concerning international coffee prices. If Brazil had attempted strict claiming, refusing to consider any concessions toward Colombia, it would probably have undermined possibilities for discovering alternative deals that would have been better for both. At the same time, a scheme to fix export quotas would also establish a fixed pie that would have to be divided eventually, creating incentives for claiming from Colombia as well. Coffee importing states, on the other side, stood to lose unambiguously from any price support scheme – that is, considering only their narrow objectives as coffee importers. They faced a win–lose situation in the prospect of such an international coffee agreement, and so this hypothesis would expect them to display strict claiming behavior toward the exporters or to decide not to negotiate at all.

Bart S. Fisher's study of the 1962 London negotiations to create the International Coffee Agreement (Fisher, 1972, chapters 4 and 8) provides some comparative evidence illustrating this basic hypothesis, while also revealing how actual episodes become more complex than any single hypothesis can reveal. A change in the coffee price affected all exporters in the same direction, and likewise for the importer countries. For exporters, at the same time, any scheme to support prices by restraining exports would require distributing the available quantities, where an increase for one supplier meant a decrease for another. The supply side of this market varied significantly both as to the size distribution of the exporting countries and as to coffee quality, measured by consumer taste. *Table 12.1* shows the market shares of exporting and importing countries in 1962. As to quality, the "milds" or highest quality beans came from Colombia and Central America. Brazil exported Arabicas, ranking in the middle, and during the preceding decade several African countries had begun to export Robustas, placed by buyers at the low end of the quality and price spectrum.

The main variance in negotiation behavior seems to have tracked what would be expected from the respective positions in the coffee market. In 1962 all the exporting states (with the possible exception of the Africans) clearly advocated and supported an international agreement to stabilize and raise coffee prices. The largest shippers, Brazil and Colombia, also attempted to claim the largest possible share value from other exporters with respect to the allocation of shares. The expanding African market share had come basically at Brazil's expense; meanwhile Colombia was competing most directly with small Central American states. Thus Brazil and Colombia attempted to preserve the status quo by proposing an export quota arrangement with the largest quotas for themselves and small quotas to limit the rising competitors. These smaller but expanding players, in turn, pushed hard for one-state–one-vote governance and for quotas as large as possible, and opposed an enforcement mechanism that would pose an effective barrier to their overshipping their quotas. There is some evidence that African exporters agreed to a limiting arrangement because they feared that otherwise Brazil would use its substantial production capacity to flood the market and break them, and because the negotiations succeeded in keeping the enforcement mechanism porous. (The source does

Table 12.1. World exports and imports of coffee by country, 1962.

Exporters	%	Importers	%
Brazil	35.4	USA	52.1
Colombia	14.2	Canada	2.6
Guatemala	3.4	Other Americas	1.2
El Salvador	3.2	West Germany	8.3
Mexico	3.2	France	7.4
Costa Rica	1.9	Italy	4.0
Ecuador	1.2	Netherlands	2.3
Dominican Republic	1.1	Belgium-Luxembourg	2.0
Other Central America, Caribbean	2.4	(total EEC	24.0)
Other Western hemisphere	2.9	Sweden	3.0
(Total Western hemisphere	68.9)	UK	2.4
Kenya, Uganda, and Tanganyika	7.0	Other Western Europe	8.0
Ivory Coast	5.8	USSR, Eastern Europe	2.5
Angola	5.7	Africa	2.3
Ethiopia	2.2	Asia, Oceania	1.9
Malagasy Republic	2.0		
Cameroun	1.4		
Congo-Kinshasa	1.3		
Other Africa	2.5		
(Total Africa	27.9)		
Indonesia	2.1		
Other Asia, Oceania	1.0		
(Total world	100.0)	(Total world	100.0)

Source: Fisher, 1972, Tables 4 and 5, based on data from the Pan American Coffee Bureau.

not report on bargaining strategies of particular exporters vis-à-vis other suppliers beyond the exceptions noted here.)

The largest anomaly for a simple market hypothesis in this episode is that in 1962 the dominant coffee importing party by far, the United States, did negotiate and ratify an international regime designed to place a floor under prices and lacking any mechanism for enforcing a price ceiling. Washington's decision and strategy choice reflected weight given to salient political-military goals in the Cold War and Latin America (Krasner, 1971:243–244). US leaders inferred from the 1959 Cuban revolution and Castro's later declaration that he was a communist that the odds of further pro-communist revolutions in Latin America were higher than before. They also believed that putting a floor under coffee prices could help preserve political stability in parts of Latin America and thus deny the Soviet Union or "world communism" a significant political encroachment. Latin American development should also help indirectly to promote US exports. Some elements of the US coffee producing industry also favored an official agreement that would stabilize prices and supplies. Thus, Washington evidently used a combined strategy rather than pure claiming.

The most important price of all is the rate of exchange between currencies, which affects most current and capital transactions. A well-known example of opposite economic effects is that when a country's currency depreciates, home-made products become more competitive and producers elsewhere are beggared, at least in the short run. Neighbors can thus be expected to claim vigorously if short-run commercial objectives dominate their decisions. In 1971, while Japan and the United States were fighting over textile market shares, each used strict claiming on the economically more significant exchange rate issue as well.

One variant of this hypothesis highlights a more subtle divergence of interest regarding exchange rate oscillation itself, regardless of direction, between countries whose economies are more deeply penetrated by international transactions and those that are more self sufficient. Germany, the Netherlands, and most small, less-developed states typify the first group, in contrast to China and the United States. In more open economies, large-scale oscillations raise the costs of adjustment and readjustment. In this sense, highly trade-penetrated states will tend to benefit more from exchange rate stabilization, regardless of their internal politics or culture. Thus, research should find that in negotiations on exchange rate issues, a state uses the partially integrative strategy to form coalitions with others with similarly penetrated economies, and uses the claiming strategy more often with other states.

While these simple, rational choice market hypotheses are a logical starting place, they will almost certainly prove insufficient as predictors of some government behavior. For example, today one might be tempted to wonder why in 1971 Japan's leaders clung so tenaciously to the undervalued yen, given Japan's large and growing payments surplus and given the yen's subsequent large realignment. Their stout claiming strategy brought much disruption to Japan's international commercial networks and created serious resentment, especially in Washington, which held the keys to Japan's long-term security – all for a lost cause. Why did they resist market and political signals so strenuously?

This question, though it leads to a tangent from this chapter, hints that a better theory will also need hypotheses arising from the subjective or cognitive level. The picture that may appear clear with hindsight often appears murky and clouded to the actual decision maker. Any forecast of a strategy's effects depends on how markets and other players will behave. For instance, in Japan in early 1971, a case could have been made for a scenario in which the dollar–yen parity remains unchanged, the United States and other countries clamp down as they should on domestic inflation and hence on import spending; Japan meanwhile reduces barriers to imports and stimulates home demand, drawing in more foreign products;

and both shifts move the currency market back toward balance. If US leaders had spoken strongly and acted in favor of such an adjustment scenario, currency traders might not have swamped Japan with as many dollars. As discussed below, Japan's monetary leaders believed in 1971 that their exchange controls would, if necessary, prevent financial inflows from forcing the yen upward. Nothing in their experience to that time had indicated otherwise. In uncertainty, all leaders are likely to rely on their most fundamental and firmly held policy beliefs and expectations. If experience has never dramatically contradicted these beliefs, they will tend to determine initial strategy choice, even if immediate market signals conflict with those beliefs. Exact conditions under which market signals will always prevail over prior beliefs, or vice versa, have not been identified.

12.6 Complementary Conditions and Strategy Choice

The first set of strategy propositions flows from situations of common or opposite effects or interests. A second, equally basic, family arises from situations of different but complementary conditions. When each of two countries will gain from an exchange of particular concessions between the two, the government of one is more likely to use value creation toward the other than in other conditions or toward other states. The basic idea here stems directly from the theory of comparative advantage. On economic issues, market conditions produce differences across countries that can be complementary, and hence concessions that can be traded, as well as common interests.

Such conditions can lead to official trading, in which government agencies negotiate purchases and sales on behalf of the country. More common are the gains that can arise from trading concessions on existing import barriers. If B values A's concession more than maintaining its own restrictions against A's goods, then an exchange of these concessions will create value on balance for B, and similarly for A. The presence of high tariff barriers after the Great Depression and the recognition of such potentials for expanding the pie drew the major trading states together repeatedly in successive rounds of reciprocal trade liberalizing negotiations after World War II.

History also throws up clear anomalies for this hypothesis, cases in which countries that could benefit from such exchanges instead used claiming strategies, including the harsher variety, against each other. The hypothesized link between potential joint gains of this type and value-creating or combined strategies is sometimes short circuited. For example, from the 1950s through the 1970s Japan produced a surplus of apparel and the United States did not produce enough to satisfy demand (see *Figure 12.2*). This was a well-known instance of the large potential

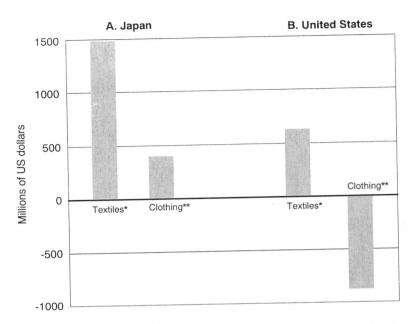

Figure 12.2. Japanese and US net exports of textiles and clothing, 1969. Source: United Nations, *Yearbook of International Trade Statistics 1970–1971*.
*SITC Code 65 "textile yarn, fabric, etc." **SITC Code 84 "clothing."

for nations to gain from exchange. This measure of revealed comparative advantage was distorted by import restrictions in both countries and hence is only a rough approximation. The textile mill sector's greater reliance on capital and energy to produce yarn and fabric would suggest, however, that the United States was probably less weak relative to the rest of the world in those products than in apparel manufacturing. Nevertheless, in 1955 Washington began to demand new Japanese limitations on exports of both apparel and textiles, using the distributive strategy. Japan initially responded in kind but later decided to comply.

During the same period and through the mid-1980s, according to trade theory many less-developed states could also have gained by trading their import restrictions for those of other developing and developed countries. Yet many of their negotiators participated in GATT negotiations by approximating the strict value-claiming strategy that demanded nonreciprocal concessions from the richer countries. Some of our simplifying assumptions must be relaxed before these anomalies can be understood.

12.7 Internal Politics, Sectoral Market Conditions, and Trade Negotiations

A highly simplified theory, then, suggests certain propositions about strategy choices that might prove valid across states with different cultures, historical experiences, and national political institutions. Yet negotiators do appear to defy such market incentives under certain conditions, some as yet unspecified, at least when the market propositions are this simple. Relaxing the assumption of monolithic states will now permit us to develop other market hypotheses that move us further along. Adding these hypotheses is analogous to introducing additional variables to a multivariate model, either additively or in interaction with others.

Specifically on trade and other regulatory issues, such as those between Japan and the United States, suppose the state's political institutions permit national producers to exercise disproportionate influence over the definition of national objectives in negotiations covering its economic sector. The internal mechanism could vary from relatively visible, ad hoc lobbying to more established and less visible corporatist relational linkages, to particularistic back-channels to the ruler in a dictatorship. In a world of states of this type, where special producer interests can bias the setting of negotiation objectives over their sector in proportion to the relative size of their domestic political resources, differences in the same state's negotiation behavior across different sectoral issues become understandable to a theory that identifies the market characteristics most relevant for this behavior. Consider three types of market difference across sectors (and changes through time) that will lead to predictable variation in trade negotiation behavior.

First, increasing import penetration should increase the chance of international conflict and claiming strategies in general. When a producer group has sufficient domestic political resources, even slight penetration by imports may be sufficient. In the United States, imports of synthetic textiles and garments had cornered less than 10% of the aggregate market when Washington demanded export restraints from Asian states. This producer complex was a giant, however, in political size. With 2 million worker-voters, it was several times the size of even the automobile or steel sectors, for example. Only its congressional caucus had demonstrated the capacity to hold national legislation hostage in Congress until it received concessions regarding imports. By contrast, footwear imports expanded their share to more than half the US market during the late 1960s and 1970s. This much smaller and dwindling industry demanded import restrictions with no less intensity than its counterparts in clothing, yet Washington repeatedly turned it away. Presidents Ford and Carter both rejected recommendations to impose global quotas. Carter negotiated export restraint agreements with two exporting countries and left the others alone, and in 1981 President Reagan allowed these restraints to expire.

Second, in a world with significant domestic producer influence the degree of an industry's concentration and other industry economic properties will bias government strategy choice in trade negotiations. When the producers of an upstream industrial input are relatively concentrated, the odds are greatest that a cartel will form to hold domestic prices above competitive levels. Furthermore, when the downstream user industry is also concentrated, when the upstream goods are standardized, and when they constitute a smaller percentage of downstream producers' costs, the chances are greater for an informal arrangement between the two industries to help enforce those high prices for upstream goods, and to create informal barriers against competing imports to keep those prices above the world price level. Under these circumstances the home government is especially likely to employ a claiming strategy, avoiding concessions completely if possible, when bargaining about these sectors. In return for helping the sellers, domestic buyers will get assurances of supply, perhaps buttressed by an implicit threat that it would be cut off if they fail to cooperate.

In Japan, at least, producers of cement maintain such a cartel with the help of their customers, the construction industry (Tilton, 1994). Each is a relatively concentrated industry and their markets correspond to this hypothesis. Representatives from the respective industry associations actually meet face-to-face to set prices, and imports have been remarkably stable and low. Campaign contributions to Diet members helped, at least until very recently, to ensure that the government kept the large government procurement market for construction closed to cement from abroad. In contrast, more dispersed Japanese industries, such as textiles and machine tools, have been unable to form cartels because of the free riding problem. If upstream products are differentiated, coordinating on prices is more difficult. Furthermore, if the product accounts for a larger share of downstream costs, as do aluminium ingots for aluminium refiners, the downstream sector would have more difficulty absorbing the premium and would be more likely to seek imported alternatives, as aluminium refiners have reportedly done. US institutions make such collusion much less likely in America, but US competition law is much stronger than that in many countries.

Here too, however, political resources will condition the industry concentration effect. An industry that is small in terms of employment or campaign funding contributions is less likely than a huge industry to enjoy this sort of bargaining support. In the case of Japan, on the other hand, the Ministry of International Trade and Industry has also reportedly identified certain (but not all) concentrated industries as critical to national development. Distributive bargaining is most likely in those strategically chosen sectors, regardless of their domestic political resources.

A third sectoral market hypothesis for states sensitive to producer pressure turns on economies of scale in production and steep learning curves (this hypothesis is inspired by Milner and Yoffie, 1989). When economies of scale are large and learning curves steep, and when another government expands its support to competitors abroad, the home firm exporting these goods is likely to change its expressed policy preference from free trade at home with mixed bargaining to contingent distributive bargaining, and its government will tend to act in that direction. In this case, the negotiator threatens economic sanctions against countries benefiting from these industrial policies, but promises not to implement the threat if their governments end these practices. Support includes import protection and financial and other rewards linked to production and exports. This distributive bargaining is expected to promote exports that this industry, unlike one with small-scale economies, needs for profitability. Ordinary unconditional import protection would be counterproductive, since it would provoke retaliation against those exports. Conversely, when the market changes in the opposite direction, bargaining strategy should shift from distributive to combined. This hypothesis is likely to apply only in states with relatively large home markets, for obvious reasons.

Milner and Yoffie (1989) report contrasts between selected industries where economic properties, foreign government support, political pressure exerted by US firms, and US official negotiation strategies varied in keeping with this idea during the 1970s and 1980s. Because of technological changes, the US semiconductor, commercial aircraft, and telecommunications equipment industries all experienced sharp increases in economies of scale as well as steep learning curves during this time. Machine tools witnessed lesser increases in the same direction. The larger scale requirements indicate that even firms based in the largest home markets need exports for profitability. Meanwhile Japan and the EC also increased support for their own producers, so that US firms complained of both increased competition in America and official biases against them in Japan and Europe. Until then, each sector had long expressed a preference for US free trade.

Of the four, semiconductors lost the most in profits and market share, and they moved the most quickly and aggressively, filing legal petitions to force US government retaliation against Japanese firms. They maintained that the Japanese were vigorously claiming value from the United States and that a response in kind was needed. Washington responded after 1985 by demanding, on pain of sanctions, what became the 1986 Japan–United States semiconductor agreement (which did not include any concessions in US policy). Then, alleging noncompliance in 1987, the Reagan Administration carried out its threat and imposed economic sanctions against Japanese goods (*Biztrend (Japan)*, 18 June 1986; *Business Week*, 1 July 1985; *Economist*, 12 July 1986; *Far Eastern Economic Review*, 4 July 1985, 17 July 1986, 9 April 1987; *New York Times*, 4, 5, and 26 July 1986, 2 August 1986; *Seikai shuho (Japan)*, 29 July 1986; *Washington Post*, 24 December 1985, 21 February 1986). Washington has also concentrated some negotiating effort on the commercial aircraft and telecommunications equipment sectors and has generally used a claiming strategy that demands concessions, sometimes by means of explicit threats, while ruling out serious compromises of its own policies in return.

The US machine tool industry, in contrast, did not press for strategic trade bargaining. The changes in scale economies were not as great, this industry was much less concentrated, and its firms employed more diverse corporate strategies. Larger firms tended to adjust commercially, avoiding Japanese competition by moving into high-technology market segments. Many smaller firms went out of business. Other industries such as steel, garments, and footwear have not experienced significant increases in scale economies during the same period, and have not made demands on the US government for conditional export claiming. Thus, opening the state into its components allows sectoral market hypotheses to make more sense of trade negotiating strategies that seem anomalous with the simplest theory.

12.8   Market Conditions, Relative Vulnerability, and Outcomes in 1971

Initial strategy choices, the main subject of this chapter, are of course only the beginning of the negotiation process. More generally, no theory, no matter how complete, will be sufficient to interpret any single event. Thus, let us fill out the remainder of two stories of the overlapping 1971 conflicts between Japan and the United States concerning the textile trade and exchange rates. In this way a fuller sense of the process's actual endogeneity will also come through.

These accounts will also suggest two more general points about the process. The monetary case reinforces the lesson that, as with initial decisions, in economic negotiations the more a market's supply exceeds its demand – i.e., as the market alternatives for the exporter worsen – the greater the odds of concessions by a government seeking a higher price, and vice versa. Here Japan sought a higher price for the dollar, but the dollar supply in the Tokyo foreign exchange market became enormous. As a qualification, the monetary case reminds us, too, that governments (here the United States) can trigger or enhance short-run market shifts as tactical moves during a negotiation. Second, both events illustrate the more general point that if a less vulnerable party issues a credible threat of unilateral sanctions (or actual contingent sanctions), it will worsen a more dependent party's alternative to agreement and thus lower its perceived resistance point. In other words, despite strongly held prior beliefs and the resentment such rough tactics undoubtedly engender, the Japanese government still decided to change and reach agreement.

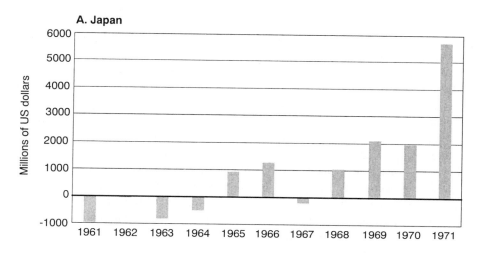

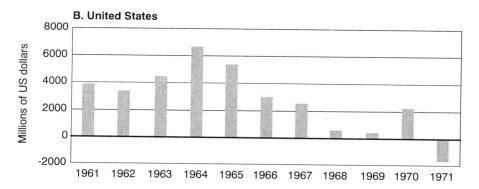

Figure 12.3. Japanese and US global current account balances, 1961–1971. Source: IMF, *International Financial Statistics Yearbook*, 1985.

In each negotiation, again, each government began with a strict claiming strategy. On the textile trade, the United States in 1969 had asked for unrequited concessions and Japan had planted its feet firmly and refused for more than two years. On exchange rates, Washington did not ask Japan specifically for yen revaluation before 15 August 1971. In the IMF, however, the United States had tentatively suggested study of new rules allowing for greater but limited exchange rate flexibility, and Japan's delegates had opposed these moves, which did not lead to any reforms.

Japan's current account with the rest of the world moved into surplus in 1968. The surplus doubled in 1969 and hardly declined at all in 1970, even while the

home economy accelerated (see *Figure 12.3*). Every month in early 1971 produced further sharp accumulation of foreign exchange reserves, as market participants probably began to protect themselves against, or speculate on, the chance
of a yen appreciation. Each month's report touched off public discussion in Japan
about how to satisfy foreign complaints about the surplus. By March and April
the nation's most prominent business leaders began to indicate publicly that they
no longer had confidence that the Ministry of Finance's "stand fast" policy on yen
revaluation would solve the problem. In May West Germany responded to similar surplus pressures by allowing the deutsche mark to float upward. In Tokyo the
Finance Ministry responded to these pressures by reaffirming denials that the yen
could be revalued and by quickly organizing an "Eight-Point Program to Avoid
Yen Revaluation." The alternatives offered were greater liberalization of imports,
international investment, foreign aid, and reconsideration of export promotion programs. Almost no observers outside the Japanese government, at home or abroad,
viewed this response as close to proportional to the size of the surplus problem.
The ministry's international monetary specialists did not draw up any contingency
plans for responding to unilateral US action (Angel, 1991:88).

One possible explanation for the Japanese government's refusal to change its
yen policy was an honest belief that in fact the Japanese balance of payments was
still not permanently in surplus. A deficit had driven reserves quite low as recently
as four years earlier, and, "We therefore still believed ourselves to be very vulnerable," according to Toyoo Gyohten, then a junior Finance Ministry official who held
its highest appointive post in international monetary policy during the 1980s. He
added:

> We thought [the large surpluses of 1970 and 1971 were] the result of
> the cyclical domestic slowdown during those years. Corporate prof-
> its were deteriorating, stock prices were falling, and production was
> very stagnant. We thought the appropriate counter-measure was not
> to revalue the yen, because that only would have aggravated our do-
> mestic slowdown. We preferred to boost the domestic economy by ex-
> pansionary fiscal and monetary policy and to liberalize imports further.
> [Volcker and Gyohten, 1992:91–92]

Gyohten immediately casts doubt, however, on this interpretation, saying, "I
frankly suspect this argument did not reflect a genuine belief on the part of the
Japanese and was to some extent a bargaining tactic against outside pressure to
revalue the yen." Indeed, Robert Angel finds that regular confidential forecasts by
the ministry's own economists in 1970 agreed with those of the IMF, the OECD,
and the GATT, which all found Japan to have shifted permanently to surplus status
(Angel, 1991:61–62).

Even so, the widespread fear in Japan that yen revaluation would harm the economy might still have been genuine, if confused. The rate of 360 to the dollar, fixed since the occupation, was associated psychologically with the whole of Japan's economic progress since the war. For senior monetary policy makers, two other tactical assumptions were probably highly salient. One was that if the bankers tried to sell too many dollars to the Bank of Japan, exchange controls would again work as they had before. The ministry had long experience controlling the Japanese banking sector with formal and informal guidance, and that experience generally indicated that the ministry had the tools it would need to keep its economy insulated from international financial market pressure.

The other assumption was a broader one about international relations: namely, that the responsibility for managing the global economic system lay somewhere other than Japan, and that the government's highest duty in the realm of international economic affairs was to promote and safeguard Japan's economic competitiveness relative to the rest of the world. When other countries complained and criticized, experience showed that these pressures could often be diffused substantially by means of "the prolonged yes," a technique also perfected during the occupation. This approach entailed expressions of sympathy with foreign problems, repeated requests for clarification and revision, and large-scale public relations campaigns to explain foreign "misunderstandings" of special Japanese conditions (Angel, 1991, chapter 2). Thus the day of reckoning could at least be postponed.

Figure 12.3 shows that the US current account with the entire world, not only with Japan, deteriorated after the mid-1960s. Inflation had picked up, relative to the rest of the industrial world, as the government injected Vietnam War spending into the economy for three years without a tax increase. The growing increase in the supply of dollars relative to demand in the foreign exchange market made a dollar depreciation by some means increasingly likely.

Two prior beliefs in particular led the United States to the means chosen to seek this depreciation. John Connally took office as secretary of the treasury in early 1971. He believed that in economic affairs Japan and also Europe were taking advantage of America and harming it. Connally told a congressional committee: "Much of the condition that we find ourselves in today is the result not of our actions but the actions of other nations who have strengthened their own position, and during the last decade both Germany and Japan have immeasurably strengthened their position" (US Senate Finance Committee, 1971:80). At one cabinet-level meeting with the President, according to an official who was present, he delivered "an unbelievable diatribe" against the EC and Japan, implying they were America's real enemies.

The second belief, reached during the summer of 1971, was that defense of the dollar at its present rate of exchange was bound to fail, short of a domestic recession that would be worse than the disease. Paul Volcker, Treasury under secretary for monetary affairs, whose career had specialized in international monetary and banking matters, tells us that already by early that year he had become concerned enough about the dollar's prospects to raise a warning about the possibility of devaluation in his first substantive briefing for the new secretary (Volcker and Gyohten, 1992:72). Soon a Treasury economist secretly estimated that the magnitude of devaluation needed to restore equilibrium in the foreign exchange market would fall between 10% and 15%. During the following summer, the IMF staff also estimated that a dollar depreciation of 10% was needed (de Vries, 1976, Vol. 1, pp. 537–538).

As a lifelong defender of the Bretton Woods system, Volcker preferred to defend the dollar, but also drew up a contingency plan under which, if the time for decision came, Washington could take the initiative and keep it, rather than seeming to collapse in defeat. He says he was certain that any attempt to negotiate a global exchange rate realignment with the gold window open would inevitably leak to the press and provoke massive, disruptive money movements. This situation would create an irresistible incentive for some governments to convert their soon-to-be devalued dollars while they could; otherwise they would fail in their duty to their own citizens. Very soon other central banks would line up and force the United States to suspend convertibility anyhow, in a disorderly manner (Volcker and Gyohten, 1992:73, 78; extensive interview research in the United States in 1975 confirmed some of these belief statements from other sources, and no evidence contradicting them was discovered.) He says his plan included means of restoring some degree of US convertibility after the negotiations. In early August a new run on the dollar and a British request for cover of some of its dollar holdings convinced Volcker that the time for maintaining the initiative might soon slip away forever.

To review, the initial US strategy was claiming along three issue dimensions. After years of vowing to make dollars as good as gold at $35 an ounce on demand, Washington now said it would not convert them after all and that it wanted the dollar to depreciate in market value. The United States soon stoutly refused to raise the dollar–gold price as a means to that end. It made no concrete proposals for settling the immediate crisis or for designing a restored monetary system for the longer term. Nor had the Nixon Administration ever secretly asked Japan to revalue the yen before 15 August (Angel, 1991:111).

This claiming exemplified the harsh variant. Reversing field suddenly without any advance notice, going beyond a high opener, and bypassing threats of sanctions, Washington also imposed a conditional 10% tariff surcharge in its first move. This blow alone, to be lifted when currency concessions were on the table, immediately worsened the no-agreement alternative for the others' exports. Beyond the main monetary issue, the United States also sought reductions in other governments' barriers to US exports and investments as well as increases in other states' contributions to mutual defense. President Nixon's speech bluntly blamed the crisis on "international speculators" and "unfair exchange rates" and certainly not on Americans. To say the least, the Americans did not in this case propose negotiations designed to benefit others as well as themselves.

On the morning after President Nixon's bombshell speech, few close observers were confident what the outcome would be. Would agreement be reached or would hostile countermeasures eventually unravel the entire postwar trade and monetary systems? To what degree would domestic constituencies constrain their governments? Would Tokyo and other capitals accept all the political pain of adjustment if Washington made no concessions on US policy, as it insisted? If they could reach agreement, would they put a consistent monetary system back together or only patch over the now-gaping hole? Even among the cognoscenti, a significant degree of uncertainty reigned. With hindsight and from the market standpoint another puzzle arises: if markets were pointing toward general yen appreciation and dollar depreciation, why did it take four months to negotiate the realignment? In fact, considering that a year after the Smithsonian conference, the dollar and the yen each moved even further after another disruptive conflict, why did the negotiated realignment not simply go further in the first place?

Clearly this shocking US demarche did nothing to encourage other governments to place heavy weight on creating joint value for the long run. In fairness, it must also be acknowledged that Tokyo had given evidence that it would have been equally tenacious, if not more so, in resisting yen appreciation if Washington had used a more balanced strategy. In any case, this negotiation process was thereafter marked almost exclusively by claiming tactics and hardly at all by value-creating measures. Each government concentrated on haggling over bilateral currency rates as shifters of sales and jobs in the short run, meaning that going down was good and moving up was a concession. With each party thus dug in and publicly committed, the bargaining took four months to complete.

Meanwhile, currency markets, though manipulated or disrupted during certain periods by official intervention and statements, also provided a tangible indication of the equilibrium rate, and hence of the sustainability of any given negotiating position on the currency issue. Japan's large and growing aggregate surplus led currency traders worldwide to continue to bet on yen revaluation, so that regular business plus speculation kept the money flowing to Tokyo. After two weeks, the government allowed the yen to float upward, but Japanese politicians pressed the Finance Ministry desperately to hold the rise down as much as possible. Still, a large market imbalance forced the ministry reluctantly but repeatedly to raise Japan's implicit reservation value from the 360 level during the fall. *Figure 12.4* depicts the huge intake of dollars during August and the rising market rate thereafter. That the Bank of Japan continued to add to its reserves during the fall implies that in a free float, the yen would have risen more than it did. Later Japan's monetary regulators inferred a vivid lesson – that their most draconian controls were in fact no longer adequate to insulate the national economy from the world market (Volcker and Gyohten, 1992:91).

In September Secretary Connally showed he was in no hurry to settle this crisis. He felt far less pressure from commercial constituents than did his counterparts in Japan and Europe, and did not rush to propose specific deals. Japan's finance minister Mikio Mizuta learned during sessions in Europe, Washington, and Ottawa that no one abroad accepted the ministry's dogged diagnosis that Japan could avoid a revaluation. Connally demanded a 24% yen increase vis-à-vis the dollar, as well as a substantial increase from West Germany and lesser movements from other major states according to their payments positions. These other governments offered nothing like what would be needed to depreciate the dollar globally by 10%, let alone 15%.

Meanwhile, the textile negotiations had dragged on since late 1969 without yielding an agreement. Nixon had not, however, forgotten the domestic political "pledge that the president apparently felt more strongly about than gold," as Volcker later dubbed it (Volcker and Gyohten, 1992:79). On 20 September the American textile negotiator in Tokyo delivered a strong and simple ultimatum: agree to the last US demand for export restrictions by 1 October, or the United States would impose quotas unilaterally, effective 15 October (Destler *et al.*, 1979:299–312). In the end, Japan's leaders believed the American threat and accepted an agreement on American terms rather than accept unilateral action.

In November the United States took a significant step forward on exchange rates, when at a multilateral ministerial session in Rome Volcker responded to abstract demands for a US contribution by asking, "... how would you respond if we increased the price by 10% to 15%?" President Nixon and his national security assistant Henry Kissinger had scheduled their historic trips to Moscow and Peking (Beijing) for early 1972, and they wanted to solidify the anticommunist alliance in preparation. By now Nixon clearly wanted to be done with this monetary problem (Volcker and Gyohten, 1992:88), and was willing to settle for somewhat less if necessary. Nixon played the dollar devaluation card in a bilateral meeting with French Prime Minister Georges Pompidou, agreeing to raise the dollar–gold price to $38 and leaving Connally the surcharge removal as his last lever.

By 18 December, the day before the Smithsonian settlement, the yen had risen to 320 to the dollar, about 13%, in Tokyo. Finance Minister Mizuta later claimed that Prime Minister Sato had authorized him to agree to a settlement as high as 300 yen per dollar, or a 20% revaluation, just before that conference. In fact Mizuta managed to stop Connally at 308 yen, or 16.9%. Overall, after tough distributive bargaining America's partners had conceded an effective dollar depreciation of only

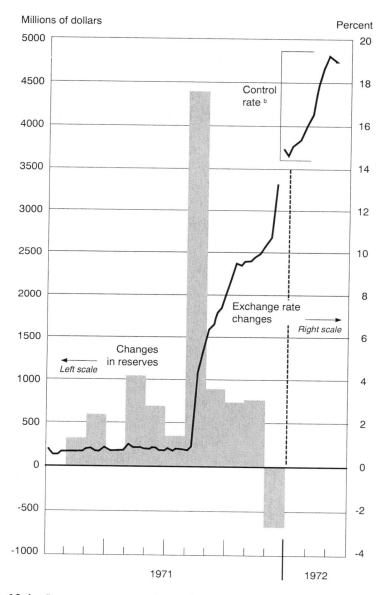

Millions of dollars

Percent

Figure 12.4. Japan: movements in exchange rate and official reserves, 1971.[a]
Source: US Federal Reserve Bank of New York *Monthly Report*, March 1972, chart ix. [a]Exchange rate movements are measured as percentage deviations of weekly averages of New York noon offered rates from the official parity at the beginning of 1971. Changes in reserves are computed from figures shown in the IMF's *International Financial Statistics*.
[b]Upper and lower intervention limits established in December 1971.

about 8%, less than the US Treasury had calculated would be needed to produce a stable balance of payments (Volcker testimony, US House Banking Committee, 1973:74). Citing this shortfall, the United States declined to pledge to defend the new exchange rates and did not resume convertibility. Nor did other states make any significant concessions on trade or military burdens during this negotiation. Thus, although the governments officially renewed their loyalty to Bretton Woods rules regarding pegged official exchange rates, negotiators never discussed long-term arrangements that would ensure future adjustment under these new conditions.

Stepping back from these 1960s and 1970s stories, broader endogenous relations between markets and official negotiators also come into view. For instance, the swelling force of currency market pressure felt by monetary regulators was partly the result of the formation and growth of the Eurocurrency banks and markets during the 1960s, which in turn were made possible by 1950s government decisions to lift currency controls and by differences in national banking regulations. Banks in London began to accept deposits denominated in US dollars, outside the Americans' regulatory reach. When multinational banks and corporate treasurers had large regular dollar accounts in several countries, they magnified the amounts that could quickly flood into currency markets and the speed with which they could do so. The size of the daily flow of dollars into foreign exchange markets could swell sharply even if many multinationals simply made ordinary payments today that were scheduled to occur next week.

In turn, the tumultuous official monetary conflict and bargaining of 1971 through 1973 also generated or accelerated subsequent changes in the world currency market. As firms learned to their dismay that contracts spanning different currencies might entail much greater risk than they had realized, with a magnitude often great enough to wipe out the transaction's business profit, they demanded new ways to lay off this risk. Multinational banks greatly expanded their foreign exchange trading departments, and forward currency markets expanded. By adding forward contracts, the largest firms could reduce currency risk at a price. As a result, international trade and capital movements did not suffer as much from exchange rate flexibility as some had projected from analogies of the interwar period. Presumably, where these market innovations were available, they reduced political pressure on governments to return to exchange rate fixity from what they would have felt otherwise.

Despite some initial uncertainty, there was no doubt about the relative alternatives ultimately available to Japan and the United States. Judging from the share of its GNP exported to the other country, Japan was roughly six times as dependent on the huge American economy as the United States was on Japan (data from IMF, *Direction of Trade*, various years, and *World Bank Atlas*, 1972; see Odell, 1982b, Table 6, chapter 4). Japan held much of its international money in US dollars.

Moreover, with the Soviet Union, China, and North Korea nearby and only a small military force of its own, Japan had no alternative to relying on America for its military security. Japan was much more vulnerable to US power, should it be exercised, than vice versa. Lack of perfect information about how Americans would act was sufficient to permit a conflict to begin, but, as we would expect, the party to yield the most during the process was the more vulnerable party, despite its strong state and strongly held contrary prior beliefs about the prospects for standing fast. In fact, considering Japan's vulnerability, its negotiators' tenacity and patience were remarkable and more than some of President Nixon's advisers had expected.

12.9 Summary and Implications

Government negotiations over economic issues stand apart from other negotiations because of their sensitivity to market conditions. Our present knowledge is lacking partly because of a shortage of explicit causal hypotheses about the negotiation process. Thus this chapter introduces a new typology for the empirical study of international negotiations, as well as several concrete conjectures regarding initial strategy choice and subsequent negotiation behavior. *Figure 12.5* reviews these propositions graphically. This summary is formulated in terms of decisions and strategies by a state A toward a state B, and each proposition is stated in terms of a change in the causal variable in only one direction, leaving the converse implicit for simplicity.

Again, this theoretical angle of vision is only one of several. Even incorporating internal politics, it will be insufficient particularly as long as we abstract from the endogenous give and take between parties after negotiation begins, and from the negotiators' own perceptions of market conditions and their noneconomic objectives.

From this study flow two modest implications each for negotiators and scholars. Of course we need much better knowledge of what leads to what before we can make confident recommendations to practitioners. In the interim, nevertheless, these propositions at least suggest useful preliminary guidelines for preparation and applied analysis. Even points that seem fairly obvious when made explicit are still not always observed in practice.

First, sound preparation for economic negotiations implies making explicit assumptions about the main economic and other influences affecting the market to be discussed, absent official negotiations. A baseline forecast of future prices, quantities, payments balances, and their consequences will aid in ascertaining parties' alternatives to agreement and their "relative bargaining power." In fact, some projection is essential to a rational decision about whether to negotiate at all. Proposals to negotiate should be viewed with caution, at least until the most likely negotiated

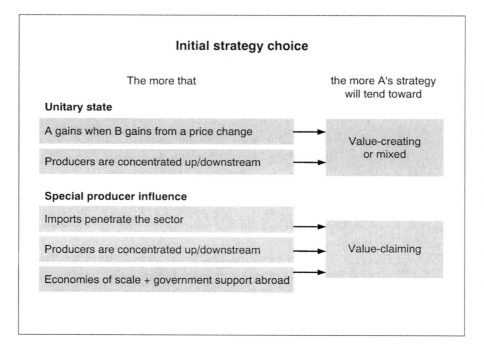

Figure 12.5. Markets, strategy choice, and subsequent behavior.

outcome is estimated as significantly superior to the situation that would probably evolve without official bargaining. Market analysis also holds potential for creating early warning indicators of future economic conflicts and negotiations.

This study, like others, also implies systematically analyzing and taking the temperature of internal politics in each country – such as expressed preferences of the economic groups affected and possible divisions within the groups – as an aid to estimating likely negotiation objectives, moves, and responses, and thus judging whether a zone of agreement exists or could be created. In 1969 Washington underestimated the internal difficulties that would face any Japanese prime minister seeking to carry out promises to restrict Japanese textile exports to the United States and hence the price that would have to be paid to achieve Nixon's goal (Destler *et al.*, 1979). Japan's planners underestimated the weight President Nixon attached to such concessions. On the other hand, more recent US negotiators have sometimes overestimated their own constituents' support for harsh claiming, with embarrassing consequences (Odell, 1993). A prospective strict distributive strategy should, for example, take into account the chance that the other party will respond in kind with measures that are not significant on the national scale but that target some key constituents. There is also the risk that the other government will yield so little, because it lacks domestic room for maneuver, that in the end the political costs of bargaining will exceed the economic gain. A preliminary decision to attempt a strict integrative strategy should likewise be tested against the risk that revealing information at the bargaining table fairly freely will result in an agreement that benefits one's side on balance but fails to generate sufficient gain for special groups that can block ratification.

Second, during negotiations the team should monitor market conditions for possible changes and estimate how they will affect the negotiators. Such subsequent aggregate or sectoral market developments might open new opportunities for creating joint gain or for shifting the distribution of the gain in favor of one's own side or of another party. Similarly, subsequent changes in internal politics will also reduce the inevitable uncertainty prevailing at the time of initial strategy choice. A team member should be assigned to evaluate the consequences of that choice on a regular basis, and to recommend adjustments that seem necessary.

For scholars of negotiation and cooperation, the most obvious implication is that these hypotheses need further conceptual and empirical study. Actual tests would require specifying more precise rules for classifying actual strategies and other variables. We should attempt to falsify these ideas and to the extent that they survive, to improve and integrate them into wider negotiation and cooperation analysis.

More generally, analysts should design more empirical research on the international negotiation process using comparisons structured according to explicit causal hypotheses. Separate single-case studies can also make valuable contributions to our accumulating knowledge, especially when they are designed specifically to go beyond available knowledge. Indeed, it is difficult to imagine how the essential facts about the negotiation process could even be gathered without detailed study of particular cases. But the single-case method, even at its best, reaches diminishing returns before long. Research that involves two or more contrasting observations along a causal variable and a supposed effect variable will certainly permit stronger inferences and make a greater contribution toward a negotiation theory that is both more general and more valid empirically. These multiple observations can, but need not, reflect different countries. Often we can often find more than one observation in a single "case" study, as this term is often used. (For other examples see King *et al.*, 1994.) For instance, regarding a hypothesis that a worsening market price will speed an exporting state's concession rate, variation can be obtained by comparing the same government's negotiation on this product on two occasions, when the price was relatively high and relatively low, respectively.

A few published studies demonstrate that research designed to employ purposeful comparison can permit stronger inferences about negotiation. Some employ qualitative methods (George *et al.*, 1971; Zartman, 1987b; Putnam and Bayne, 1987; Odell, 1988; several chapters in Evans *et al.*, 1993; Schoppa, 1993), while others use quantitative techniques (Hopmann, 1974; Odell, 1985; Martin, 1992; Bayard and Elliott, 1994). We will progress further in the future if scholars of co-operation devote more attention to the negotiation process, and if studies of this process move beyond untested models and ad hoc single-case studies to greater use of comparative empirical research to evaluate explicit causal hypotheses, and most of all if they work from a common conceptual foundation.

Acknowledgments

This chapter was written in 1995 while the author was visiting scholar at the Institute for International Studies, Stanford University. He is grateful for the Institute's support, as well as to the Ford Foundation, the Social Science Research Council, the Pew Charitable Trusts, and the University of Southern California Center for International Studies for earlier support of research on this subject. His book *Negotiating the World Economy* (Cornell University Press, 2000) gives a fuller statement of his more recent ideas.

Part III

Analysis

The following three chapters analyze the case studies from the viewpoint of the approach that the editors suggested: economic theory and negotiation analysis. It was the task of the authors of the case studies to look at their respective cases through the lenses of the two disciplines in order to give sufficient evidence for the analytical part to conceptualize from them. That is why the analytical part, structurally as well as substantively, consists of three main topics: what lessons and conclusions can be drawn from the cases for the economic theory approach (Robert Neugeboren), for the negotiation analysis approach (I. William Zartman), and how both can be interrelated in analyzing international economic negotiation (Gunnar Sjöstedt).

The analysis itself is worth attention. First of all, it provides a tool for all those – practitioners or academics – who want to understand better what is happening in world market transactions. In this sense, it also helps the reader to gain insight from the analytical component of the case studies. Second, it substantiates the ideas and concepts suggested in the first, introductory part of this study. Third, it actually develops and provides detail on the whole concept of the book.

Neugeboren approaches the central issue of the study with the understanding that, once political barriers treated by the Cold War were removed, market forces became dominant in shaping the landscape of international economic negotiation. It should also be added that the current situation in these talks permits us to see the extent to which economic forces supported the Cold War relationship or worked against it. In any case, the economic dimension of major world economic deals has gained considerable ground and deserves attention in studying the current state of affairs.

Zartman does not question this postulate. But his view permits us to identify what role negotiation skills and negotiation analysis may play in the context of current realities in the world market, and to understand better that the outcome of economic deals in international relations is not simply a result of blind market forces, but very often depends on whether the people entrusted with the task are prepared to carry it out effectively. In other words, even the most powerful economic entities may be poor negotiators and, by contrast, even the economically weakest parties may perform well as negotiators.

Sjöstedt tries to synthesize the two views and to avoid a comparative approach. On the contrary, his idea is that the two may tightly interrelate and together attain maximum effectiveness as analytic tools. Even more important, he sees in negotiations a certain redistributive function that helps to spread the economic benefits achieved by the most successful parties without making such sharing a burden and turning it into an impediment to economic development. His point is that international economic negotiation is a major tool in helping the most advanced entities to function as engines of development, while giving the less advanced the possibility to enjoy the fruits of economic achievements abroad.

All in all, the analytical section is a promising endeavor that may help both to advance our knowledge on the subject and to teach states and organizations how to use negotiation skills to optimize economic development.

Chapter 13

The Economic Approach to International Negotiation

Robert Neugeboren

Now that the ideological barriers to economic integration have fallen, market forces are playing a much larger role in international affairs. Foreign policy is increasingly concerned with matters of trade and finance; national security is seen as tied to international competitiveness. Yet it is not at all clear that countries compete in the same way individual firms do, and economists are divided, some advocating continued liberalization, others calling for strategic trade policies to spur exports and growth. The world today is a testing ground for an array of economic strategies vying for a place in the international trading system, with governments and private business interests seeking investments and myriad, untapped consumers in newly emerging markets worldwide. The rules of the new game are still unclear, however, and as the shadow of the Cold War recedes, there is a need to negotiate new international agreements to secure the ground for sustained economic growth and development.

Recent shifts in the international balance of power have greatly transformed the stakes and the players in the game. The rise of multinational corporations over the past few decades has fundamentally altered the relationship between states and firms, while continued technological and organizational innovation has greatly reduced the costs of doing business internationally. Lower transportation and communication costs, in turn, have led to a period of heightened economic interdependence, increased capital mobility, and globalized market competition. The Cold War has ended, and a new era has begun in which "there now is greatly intensified competition among states for world market share. That competition is forcing states to bargain with foreign firms to locate their operations within the territory of the state, and with national firms not to leave" (Strange, 1992:5).

Today, states and firms use negotiations for a wide range of purposes, including to secure market access, coordinate financial arrangements, exploit economies of large-scale production, and establish strategic alliances across national borders. As the editors of this volume put it in the introductory chapter, "Since the criteria of economic performance today include, together with the technological and financial base, currency exchange rate, investment in research and development, and a sound economic foreign policy, both governments and private exporters have to pay great attention to negotiation over these issues as a tool to promote their interests and power in the world."

The case studies in this volume cover negotiations on trade in goods and services, financial and monetary relations, joint ventures, intellectual property rights and other areas of economic activity. They include bi- and multilateral, business/business, business/government, and government/government negotiations. Some were successful, others were not. Some involve parties that, only a few years ago, would not have gathered around the same table to negotiate economic issues, because during the Cold War trade was organized under the imperatives of a bipolar security system. But the collapse of the Soviet Union has changed all that. Long-established patterns of dependency are receding, and a more diversified and interdependent world order is on the rise.

The globalization of economic relations in the post-Cold War era promises increasing prosperity to East and West, North and South. Yet in even the rosiest scenario, reasonable people may disagree on the rules of the new economic game and how to divide the ensuing gains from trade. The purpose of this chapter is to explore to what extent, and under what conditions, economic theory may be helpful in understanding and resolving these disputes. Section 13.1 reviews classical trade theory and the development of strategic trade theory. Section 13.2 describes the economic approach to international negotiations as built up from the assumption of rational behavior. Section 13.3 offers a brief review of the case studies, organized with the help of three models of international economic negotiation.

13.1   Trade Theory and Practice

In the time of Smith and Ricardo, when nations went to war to bring home gold and other treasures, the notion of free trade had yet to be established. Why trade for what could be taken by force? In answering this question, the classical economists addressed themselves to the political leaders of their day, offering trade policies and tariff schemes as alternatives to war and plunder.

Considerable refinement has been added to the argument over the years, but the basic explanation for why countries should trade is to be found in the classical notion of comparative advantage. Because countries differ in natural and technological endowments, efficiency-improving exchanges are possible, where each exports the good whose production is intensive in the factors with which it is better endowed. To borrow a contemporary example from Paul Krugman: "Canada exports wheat to Japan because Canada has so much more arable land per capita, and as a result in the absence of trade wheat would be much cheaper in Canada" (Krugman, 1994:2). Trade allows countries to exploit their natural differences, expanding the range of products available to consumers and broadening the market for producers.

When this picture of free trade is combined with the standard assumption of perfect competition, tariffs, subsidies, quotas, and other protectionist measures can be shown to yield only short-lived advantages, since any rents would eventually be competed away by the workings of the market. It follows that such barriers create a drag on the economy, and that social welfare is optimized when producers and consumers have the greatest possible access to each other and to the material and technological resources needed for production. In a world of free trade, production naturally tends toward its most efficient site (i.e., lowest relative factor costs), and everyone gains as a result.

According to this classical case for free trade, therefore, a country that wants to improve its national welfare should remove whatever impediments exist to the flow of trade across its borders. This is true no matter what other countries choose to do. Yet this classical view is confounded by reality. Indeed, were it true, "there would be no need for trade treaties: global free trade would emerge spontaneously from the unrestricted pursuit of national interest" (Krugman, 1997:113). That countries, on the one hand, pursue protectionist trade policies and, on the other hand, invest time, money, and national prestige in international trade agreements to reduce these barriers suggest something is wrong with this classical picture. At least some work needs to be done to overcome the distance between theory and reality.

The classical case for free trade is rendered in wholly static terms. It assumes that resources, technology, capital stock, and so on are given and that countries trade to take advantage of differences in these fixed endowments. Yet, as has been well known at least since Ricardo, and emphasized by modern theorists from Ohlin on, where economies of scale exist, the benefits from specialization give countries a reason to trade in the absence of any differences in factor endowments. This is because access to international markets lets firms expand production, move down their average cost curves, and earn enough over time to recover the costs of R&D (Krugman, 1994). It follows that measures such as tariffs, subsidies, quotas, and the like can be used to create a comparative advantage by shifting world specialization so as to favor the home nation (Krugman, 1994:3). In a dynamic environment, a small initial disparity in competitiveness can lead to growing inequality over time. Until recently, however, trade theorists paid surprisingly little attention to scale economies, learning-by-doing, and other dynamic phenomena. This is because there has not been a satisfactory way to deal with their implications in terms of a mathematically tractable formalism (Krugman, 1994:11).[1] Today's "rethinking of international trade" moves away from the static formalizations of perfect competition and constant returns, and what emerges is a world where comparative advantage can be created and strategic concerns come to the fore.

In a static environment, each actor can take the behavior of others as fixed, reduced to parameters of a relatively simple maximization problem. In a dynamic environment, on the other hand, each actor must consider that outcomes will depend on not only on his or her own decisions but also on the decisions of others, and that they know this, and so on. This strategic interdependence means that what is best for each will depend on the behavior of all, and coordinated decision making may be preferred to decision making in isolation. A coordinated reduction of trade barriers is a case in point. But where there is bargaining power to be exploited, attempts to claim a larger share of the pie may have the effect of reducing its size (Sebenius, 1991:211). In the international arena, where no supervening authority exists to enforce agreements, mutually advantageous agreements may be very difficult to secure.

By taking seriously increasing returns and imperfect competition, the new, strategic trade theories show that even if one accepts the proposition that perfectly free trade would be best for all, one cannot rule out the possibility that an individual country may have an incentive to protect a domestic industry. Likewise, it may make sense to demand that foreign trading partners lower their barriers in a reciprocal fashion. In general, what is optimal for one country will depend on what other countries choose to do, and it may indeed be rational to invest in mechanisms to coordinate trade policies and avoid harmful conflicts. It is here that we may wish to solicit advice from the artful negotiator "on how to make agreements when trust and good faith are lacking and there is no legal recourse for breach of contract" (Schelling, 1960:18–20). Indeed, such expertise is crucial today, if the gains from trade are to be realized rather than left on the blackboard.

13.2   The Economic Approach to International Economic Negotiation

Formal economic analyses of international negotiations are built on a simple methodological proposition: that the parties are rational. That they are assumed to be rational means they prefer more of what they want to less – a modest and, at the same time, extremely powerful proposition. It is modest because it seems a minimal requirement to render human behavior intelligible, and powerful because it offers a rigorous theoretical framework within which to study negotiation processes and outcomes. A wide range of theoretical models have been erected on this basis, all unified by the belief that human behavior can best be explained by assuming agents are rational (Camerer and Thaler, 1995). Indeed, what distinguishes economics from other social sciences is not the nature of the objects under its investigation (e.g., money or the market sector) but the "persistent, rigorous application of the assumption of rational behavior" (Becker, 1976).

The economic approach to international negotiations envisions players who try to maximize their utilities, or payoffs, in a game of strategy, subject to the condition that others are behaving likewise. Each chooses a strategy (which is a complete plan of action for the entire game) calculated to yield the best chance to "win," i.e., to receive the highest expected payoff.[2] Each player must reckon: what course of action should I follow, given that the outcome will depend not only on my strategy but also on theirs, which in turn will depend upon their expectations of my strategy, and so on? This kind of problem (i.e., recursive reasoning) seems to involve an infinite regress, defying logical analysis, but game theory has shown it may be possible to reach a solution via the notion of a strategic equilibrium (Elster, 1979:19).

Consider a simple bargaining problem. Two players are to agree on the price of a loaf of bread. Buyer is willing to pay up to US$1 for the loaf, the price she could pay for an equivalent loaf elsewhere (Buyer's reservation price, which equals the BATNA). Seller is willing to sell for anything over US$0.50, which is his best available offer (Seller's reservation price). The game is played in a finite number, n, of alternating offers. Buyer makes the first offer; Seller can either accept or counteroffer, and so on. The game continues until an offer is accepted, or n is reached. If a bargain is struck, each player gets the difference between his or her reservation price and the accepted offer; if no offer is accepted, the players both get zero. How should the game be played?

It turns out that if n is known, the game has a unique equilibrium, arrived at by backward induction. For example if n is 5, then on the fifth round of the game Buyer will make the smallest possible offer, say US$0.51, and Seller will accept, because it is better for Seller than no agreement. Knowing this, Buyer can make the same offer on the first round and Seller will accept; this pair of strategies is the equilibrium. Furthermore, this outcome supports an agreement made before the game, because once it is achieved neither player has an incentive to deviate or cheat, i.e., the outcome is self enforcing. More generally, a strategic equilibrium is defined as a set of strategies (one for each player) that maximizes each player's expected payoff, given the choice of the other player(s). It is a set of "best response" strategies identifying a terminal state of the game (Rapoport, 1966), a stable resting point, or a balance of power, enforced only by the self-interest of the players. In 1951, John Nash proved that every finite game has at least one equilibrium.

It also turns out, however, that if n is unknown, there are multiple equilibria, i.e., the game could have more than one terminal state.[3] Moreover, it appears that multiple equilibria are the rule rather than the exception. Furthermore, in many cases the set of equilibria can be Pareto ranked, i.e., inefficient equilibria are possible. Thus, an equilibrium is a very general solution concept that allows us to rule out certain (sets of) strategies as inconsistent, but it cannot specify (predict/prescribe) the finer-grain processes through which the terminal state is achieved. And hence, while the existence of an equilibrium tells us we shall not be attempting the impossible in searching for a game's solution, it does not tell us how to go about finding it (Rapoport, 1966:78). We know, for example, that chess is among the class of games with a well-defined solution, and yet the existence of a solution does not indicate how to win the game.

Rather than a scientific theory offering unique prescriptions for rational behavior, therefore, the economic approach to international negotiation should be seen in more modest terms. Starting from the assumption that the parties are rational, the approach allows us to rule out from consideration strategies that are not mutually compatible. Indeed, a successful negotiation must produce an agreement that allows agents to form stable expectations over the longer run, and economic theory will no doubt be helpful in identifying terms of exchange with this equilibrium property. How such a solution is to be achieved, on the other hand, requires tact, reasonableness, and creativity to find new possibilities for agreement.

Before going on, therefore, it will help to put the relationship between economic theory and negotiation practice as succinctly as possible: where equilibria are unique (e.g., monopoly or perfect competition), economic theory fully determines rational behavior and there is no room for negotiation[4]; where multiple equilibria exist (e.g., oligopoly or imperfect competition), behavior is, strictly speaking, underdetermined. This is the realm of bargaining and negotiation expertise. In the international trade arena, where no supervening authority exists to enforce agreements and imperfect market conditions are likely to prevail, the scope for negotiation is especially significant. In this context, as Howard Raiffa wrote, "international negotiations are essential mechanisms for the peaceful resolution of disputes and for maintaining stability and a degree of predictability in international relations. The balance between war and peace may not be a matter of the nature of the differences that divide us but of the process we use to resolve those differences" (Raiffa, 1991:9).

13.3 Three Models of International Economic Negotiations

Over the past 50 years, international economic negotiations have become a vital part of statecraft. In the 1940s, the need to reconstruct Europe and organize the postwar economy gave rise to Bretton Woods. Eventually, the World Bank and the IMF were established to stabilize currency exchanges and provide for an orderly system of balance of payments financing. In the 1950s, the GATT codified the rules for a vast expansion of international trade, which is generally seen as having contributed to an extraordinary period of economic growth.[5] Increasing the flow of international trade was the driving force behind these negotiations. By the 1960s, "the aims of multilateral trade negotiations were easily discernible and had a clear unifying orientation: liberalization by means of the elimination of trade barriers at the border" (Sjöstedt, 1991:330). Today, the nature and locus of international economic negotiations have been fundamentally altered by the rise of MNCs and by recent changes in the global balance of power. This section describes three models (in loose chronological order) that can be helpful in understanding these developments.

13.3.1 Multilateral trade negotiation

The multilateral trade negotiation (MTN) model focuses on the problem of securing large-scale international agreements to reduce trade barriers against the temptation for countries to cheat. The model depicts securing such agreements as a kind of collective action problem that arises in the provision of a public good (Olson, 1965). In particular, while reducing trade barriers may be good for all, there may also be incentives for individual countries to pursue gains for themselves. Where more than two countries are involved, some will have the opportunity to free-ride on the liberal trade policies of others, and this is more likely where the number of countries involved is large or their behavior is hard to monitor. Indeed, without some mechanism to ensure or coerce behavior, the economic approach predicts that compliance with international trade agreements will be suboptimal (Chayes and Chayes, 1993). The goal of the MTN, therefore, is the creation of a credible commitment mechanism by means of which agreements to reduce trade barriers can be enforced.

Consider, for example, the problem of reducing a protective tariff on widgets. Assume that all would prefer reducing the tariff to the status quo, for the traditional free trade reasons. But each would most prefer that the others reduce *their* tariffs while it would leave its own in place, because the expanded export market would allow domestic widget producers to gain advantages of scale over their foreign competitors. This is what we would expect where economies of scale exist, as argued in Section 13.1. Conversely, none wants to remove its protective tariff if others do not. What should the countries do?

It turns out that leaving the tariff in place is a strictly dominant strategy (i.e., best no matter what the others choose), even though all countries would be better off were each to remove the tariff. The difficulty in this PDG is that the cooperative outcome is not self enforcing, because each country gains still further by cheating when the others cooperate. Rational players will always defect in a one-shot game; however, if the game is repeated, it may be rational to cooperate. It has been argued that the repeated Prisoners' Dilemma is a better model for the analysis of multilateral economic relations, since many issue areas are prone to such "retaliatory linkage" (Keohane, 1984:104). These interdependencies have the effect of multiplying the interactions among states, so that the fear of retaliation tomorrow may keep potential defectors in line today.[6]

Thus, while the MTN model highlights the economic dimension of the problem of making international trade agreements, it also makes clear the need for a negotiated solution. In particular, as analysis of the repeated Prisoners' Dilemma demonstrates, cooperation requires a stable relationship such that the punishment of defectors can be ensured. During the Cold War, for instance, regular meetings among Western allies set the stage for the repeated interactions needed to reduce trade barriers. The stability and predictability of these ongoing relationships provided the credible commitment mechanism needed to rationalize and implement cooperative trade policies. The result was a sustained period of economic growth, under the umbrella of US security guarantees.

Odell's study of negotiations between the United States and Japan in the 1970s (Chapter 12) nicely demonstrates this interdependence of economic and political-security dimensions during the Cold War. Prior to a scheduled trip by Nixon and Kissinger to Moscow and Peking (Beijing) in 1972, the United States offered Japan concessions on textile and exchange rate policies in order to keep the anticommunist bloc unified. In the calculus of national wealth and power, the United States gave longer-term security interests priority over shorter-term economic ones. In Odell's words: "Washington's decisions and strategy choice reflected weight given to salient political-military goals in the Cold War."

The case of the EMS (Chapter 7) provides another example of the salience of political and security arrangements on an ongoing MTN. In Europe, monetary union is seen as part of a process toward a more general unification. It began in the 1980s with a series of exchange rate mechanisms, moving toward a single European currency. Because exchange rate volatility is seen as a barrier to trade, the benefit of monetary union is expected to be an expansion of commerce in the region. The cost, however, is a loss of sovereignty as domestic politicians give up control over key macroeconomic variables. Domestic calls for economic stimulus, for example, create a demand for monetary looseness, tempting member states to defect from agreed-upon exchange rate guidelines, as has happened in a number of European countries. Where the benefits seemed to outweigh the costs before 1989, the impetus toward unification since has waned and parochial interests have come to the fore.

Mesjasz's analysis of Poland's negotiations with Western banks in the period 1980–1994 (Chapter 6) likewise reflects an interdependence of political-security and economic forces as well as the shifting realities of Cold War dynamics. In the early stages of these negotiations, Western banks coordinated their lending strategies and generally dictated the terms to the Polish regime. By 1989, with the impending Soviet collapse, however, Poland enjoyed heightened bargaining power as Western governments sought leverage to further weaken the Eastern bloc. In both this and the previous case, the ending of the Cold War marked a fundamental change in the outcome of an ostensibly economic international negotiation.

In the aftermath of the Cold War, along with the shift in the international balance of power has come the rise of trading blocs. In an apparently defensive posture, more and more countries have sought new partners for fear of being left out of the regional trade game. Negotiating the NAFTA (Chapter 11) seems to have been motivated by just such concerns. In the former Soviet states, attempts to establish a free trade zone under the CIS have met with mixed results, as important security arrangements remain unsettled (Chapter 9). In the West, the focus of these multilateral negotiations has shifted from simple tariff issues to often subtle non-tariff barriers, and from goods to the more ambiguous category of "services," as described in Chapter 8. As a result, MTNs are giving way to other types of international economic negotiations, better suited to today's changing political and economic realities.

13.3.2 International business negotiation

The MTN model focuses on the competition among states over national wealth and power. In the last few decades, however, the growing size and influence of MNCs have greatly altered the nature of international economic negotiations. No longer can the firm be seen as merely the agent of the state's economic foreign policy. And while multilateral regimes (such as the new WTO) are still the loci of important economic negotiations, increasingly the focus is on the behavior of private business interests as they seek out new ventures in both established and emerging markets worldwide.

Dupont (1991) offers a model of international business negotiation (IBN), in which the MNC has replaced the state as the primary actor. Competition among firms over market share and profits extends beyond domestic borders, driven by the need to achieve ever larger economies of scale (see Chapter 11). In this strategic environment, firms must do more than ruthlessly outmaneuver their competitors; they must also seek out cooperative relationships that take advantage of complementary activities among firms of different nationalities. The goal of the IBN, therefore, is to secure the advantages of large-scale production and distribution through the establishment of joint ventures and other forms of vertically and horizontally integrated multinational enterprises.

The IBN is akin to the domestic variety of business negotiation, involving the acquisition of specialized production technologies, organizational structures, and management techniques. Because it can be difficult to measure the value for such hard-to-price assets, firms often use negotiations to establish a "fair" price in the absence of a market mechanism (Caves, 1982). Yet firms looking for foreign partners confront a number of special problems. First, cultural factors may greatly complicate the process of reaching an agreement, as a number of the cases in this volume demonstrate. For instance, Faure's study of a European company's attempt to establish a joint venture in China (Chapter 3) provides an excellent example of the difficulties inherent in such cross-cultural negotiations. The experience of the Disney Company in France confirms that cultural factors can affect the outcome of the negotiation process. In this case, Disney's prior experience in Japan seemed to bias its expectations of success in France (see Chapter 2). Second, and perhaps more important, domestic business negotiations take place in the shadow of the coercive power of the law, whereas IBNs are characterized by the absence of such a centralized legal authority. As a result, innovative organizational forms are needed to cope with the relatively higher risks of making agreements internationally.

The case study of AT&T (Chapter 10) provides a powerful example of a major multinational that used negotiations to establish international markets in the semiconductor industry. It also demonstrates the role of scale economies in international business strategy. First, "a technology-intensive product such as integrated circuits follows a competitive model that includes substantial investment in continuous technological development ... with patent-assured monopoly rights ... . In addition ... this industry benefited strongly from the economies of scale provided by access to international markets." A system of licensing fees was established to ensure that the parties "could enjoy 'patent peace' ... for a mutually agreed upon period." The keys to AT&T's success were both the acquisition of new semiconductor technologies as well as new contractual forms for collecting royalties on technologies shared internationally.

13.3.3   Negotiation between host countries and MNCs

In MTNs states are the players, whereas in IBNs the players are MNCs. The case studies suggest the outlines of a third model, however, that has been discussed by

Strange (1992). The emergence of a genuine world economy, made possible by technological as well as political changes, has produced "a fundamental change in the nature of diplomacy. Governments must now bargain not only with other governments, but also with firms or enterprises, while firms now bargain both with governments and with one another" (Strange, 1992:61).

In this third model, states bargain with firms to supply firm-specific assets, such as new technologies, managerial expertise, and jobs, to domestic constituencies. In return, states hold out the promise of a hospitable environment to firms seeking new business ventures abroad. By offering business-friendly regulations and other state-specific assets, they can lure firms to locate within their territories, and it may be cheaper to promote economic growth by inviting multinationals than by investing in the support of native industries. Indeed, many underdeveloped countries have taken this route, combining foreign capital, technology, and managerial expertise with relatively cheap domestic labor to create a comparative advantage in a variety of export markets.

Okogu's study of Nigeria (Chapter 5) offers one example of an oil exporting country's experience with negotiation as a development strategy. Weakness in the world oil market in the 1980s forced Nigeria, which was dependent on oil exports, into a structural adjustment program under the auspices of the IMF and the World Bank. Negotiations took place between the government and the international lenders and also between the government and key domestic actors, whose support was essential to implement the agreed-upon economic reforms. The result was that Nigeria's highly centralized military government was forced "to continually seek accommodation with opposing groups, and [was] prone to compromising its policies."

According to theorists of the dependency school, such arrangements only reinforce the underdevelopment of the host (Tarzi, 1991). This takes place through an extraction of wealth in the form of the natural resources of developing countries where, historically, property rights are ill defined. From this point of view, the role of MNCs in oil exporting during the 1960s is often cited as an example of post-colonial domination. Negotiation, in this context, is largely a matter of assertion and capitulation. By focusing on the strategic dimension, however, the new model allows for the analysis of a wider range of outcomes. In particular, we can expect that what happens will depend on the relative bargaining capabilities of the host and the multinational, including the negotiation skills of the parties among other factors.

Sawyerr's study of the VALCO Agreement between Ghana and a consortium of international aluminium companies (Chapter 4) offers a contrasting example of a developing country's negotiations with powerful foreign interests. In this case, as economic conditions changed to the consortium's advantage, the agreement was renegotiated, resulting in concessions by the consortium "to make the agreement more balanced in altered circumstances." Against the power of the consortium to extract still larger gains from the arrangement, Ghana's negotiators appealed to the "fairness" of a more balanced outcome and saw to it that the consortium paid for a key domestic service "at the rate paid on average by similar companies worldwide." Good negotiators, with an eye to the long-run mutual gains available, made the difference, and thus the author concludes, "... a party's economic and technical weakness need not always translate into a negative outcome."

13.4 Conclusions

Classical trade theory makes the case for unilateral reductions of trade barriers. After all, as Frederic Bastiat has said, should we block up our own ports just because other countries have rocky coasts? From this perspective there is little room for negotiation. Yet we know there are situations in which a country may choose to protect its markets at home or to demand access to markets abroad, and these trade practices make sense as soon as we admit economies of scale and imperfect competition into our viewpoint. Indeed, as a number of the case studies have shown, firms seeking the advantages that go with larger scales of production have a real incentive to expand abroad, and negotiations are needed to reach agreement on fair terms where market mechanisms do not (yet) exist. In the international arena, because no reliable authority exists to enforce agreements across national borders, any settlement must include a plan for its own enforcement (i.e., it must be self enforcing). This means that international economic agreements are often a game over the rules of the game rather than a game within a well-defined set of rules.

The case studies span the period 1970–1990 and demonstrate a marked shift in the nature of international economic negotiations around the end of the Cold War. Where once trade was conducted under reliable Cold War arrangements, today the rules of the game are themselves up for negotiation. The large-scale multilateral trade negotiation (of which GATT is the prime example) continues to have relevance, but increasingly other types of negotiations are becoming important. In some cases, firms negotiate with firms to secure the advantages of larger scale by finding international partners with access to markets abroad. In other cases, firms negotiate with states seeking to advance their technical capabilities and to increase employment; the states offer such incentives as low-cost labor and raw materials, and/or favorable tax treatment.

The end of the Cold War has created new opportunities as well as new risks. Negotiation has become increasingly important to both states and firms as a means to reduce uncertainty and coordinate exchanges of money, goods, and services across national borders. The zero-sum and bipolar worldview of the Cold War has gradually given way to a nonzero-sum and multipolar one (Rosenau, 1990). For the class of zero-sum games, John von Neumann's minimax theorem offered a unique solution that guaranteed a minimum payoff. Yet bargaining and negotiation can only take place where there is the possibility of mutual gain or the risk of mutual loss. For the class of nonzero-sum games, however, it seems that multiple (nonequivalent[7]) equilibria are the rule. Both the simple bargaining problem in Section 13.2 and the repeated Prisoners' Dilemma in Section 13.3 give rise to multiple equilibria. In such cases, many outcomes are consistent with the predictions of the theory. Where multiple equilibria exist, in other words, a coordination problem arises: How, from among a set of possible equilibria, do players come to arrive at the same one? "And here," as Schelling argues, "it becomes emphatically clear that the intellectual process of choosing a strategy in pure conflict and choosing a strategy of coordination are of wholly different sorts" (Schelling, 1960:96).

The minimax theorem assumes only that the players are following preferences and decision rules each has determined for himself, i.e., monologically. To put things another way, opponents in pure conflict necessarily try "to avoid any meeting of the minds, even an inadvertent one" (Schelling, 1960:96). Solving a coordination problem, on the other hand, requires the players to reach a solution in which (in some minimal sense) they must agree. To put things another way, pure conflict can only be played by opponents; whereas coordination requires that players adopt the attitude of partners in a dialogue (Habermas, 1984). From this point of view, we can say that trust is the problem to be solved. It is no simple matter to provide reasons for another's trust – why one should be believed to mean what is said and intend what is proposed – but to succeed those involved must regard the terms of their agreement as mutually binding, and this may be subverted by strategic attempts to manipulate the process.

Instead of bargaining from the relative strength of their interest positions and achieving a compromise circumscribed by their given positions, international economic agreements require that negotiators first try to understand each other. In so doing they may come to understand their own positions in a new light. In this way, negotiators may discover a realm for possible agreement where there had been none before. As many of the case studies demonstrate, successful negotiations often begin with just such an exchange. In international economic negotiations, the problem, of course, is to balance the rational desire for more of what we want with the need for trust in achieving solutions to what are becoming truly global problems.

Notes

[1] In perfectly competitive markets, firms set prices equal to marginal costs. But if production is subject to increasing returns, then marginal costs are always decreasing, so that all firms are making losses in equilibrium! (See Krugman, 1994.)

[2] Here "winning ... does not have a strictly competitive meaning; it is not winning relative to one's adversary. It means gaining an advantage relative to one's own value system; and this may be done by bargaining, by mutual accommodation, and by the avoidance of mutually disastrous behavior" (Schelling, 1960:4–5).

[3] In a "shrinking-pie" version of the game (i.e., with discounting), there is a unique (subgame perfect) equilibrium (Rubinstein, 1982). Camerer *et al.* (1993) offer some interesting experimental results.

[4] Under full information conditions. If information is incomplete, then negotiation can been seen as part of the process through which information is exchanged, which itself may be subject to strategic manipulations.

[5] For a less sanguine interpretation of the history of GATT, see Irwin (1995).

[6] Linkage is also possible between concurrent issue areas through the use of side payments. Hence: "Much as iterated Prisoners' Dilemma [sic] lead to very different results from the single-play version of the game, so does an analysis of a given regime in the context of others produce a different structure of incentives than considering each regime in isolation" (Keohane, 1984:100).

[7] Multiple equilibria can also arise in the zero-sum context, but only in a technical sense. Operationally, the equilibria are equivalent, and a player can choose any strategy that supports any equilibrium and expect a unique payoff, i.e., the game's value. In nonzero-sum games, different equilibria have different payoffs, i.e., there is no unique value. In these cases, what strategy to choose remains underdetermined, hence a coordination problem exists.

Chapter 14

Negotiation Analysis Perspective in International Economic Negotiation

I. William Zartman

In the preceding cases, which can be taken as representative of economic negotiations, economic theory was generally not enough to explain the negotiated outcomes. While it often indicated what parties should do (if they were to attain specific ends), it did not explain how or why they did what they actually did. On occasion, it also explained limits on their behavior, although at other times the parties contravened those limits (with consequences often predictable by economic theory). It takes negotiation analysis – since theory is probably too big a word to be applicable – to explain the reality of human interaction, even on economic matters. It is therefore instructive to summarize the results, so as to learn more about negotiation analysis and behavior. The following summary will focus on the means by which outcomes were achieved, the value and validity of process assumptions, and the effects and determinants of tactical, outcome, and methodological choices made by the parties.

14.1   Power and Manipulable Values

It has been noted that the essence of the negotiation process is to change the parties' conflicting values in order to enable them to coincide in an agreement. Initially, these values are neither precise nor fixed nor compatible. Parties start out with some general notions, perhaps a few positions, and some underlying interests. Out of this uncertainty, the negotiation process is designed to develop precise and compatible positions. The parties do this by pushing on each other, by resisting each other's pressure, and by revising their own positions, not merely by registering the coincidence or convergence of those positions. The instrument is power, an action taken to move the other party's position in an intended direction (Tawney, 1931; Simon, 1953; Dahl, 1957; Thibaut and Kelley, 1959; Habeeb, 1988; Rubin and Zartman, 1995). What is the source or basis of that action?

The cases show overwhelmingly that the primary source of power is the security point of the two parties, establishing a predominance of opportunity power over demand power. An attractive alternative to a negotiated outcome allows parties to hold firm and an unattractive alternative makes the offered outcome look better. Parties try to buttress their own alternatives and undermine those of the other party, at the same time as they try to make their offer for a negotiated outcome more attractive. However, as the cases show, more negotiation action and effort is spent on maintaining or worsening alternatives than on improving offers; the offers are made to look relatively, not absolutely, better.

Making offers and alternatives more or less attractive means adding perceived value – positive or negative. Negotiating power is therefore an action that purports to add value to a course of activity. Further categorization can divide these positive and negative exercises – gratification and deprivation – into two types: those involving voluntary additions and those involving simply the consequences of involuntary additions. The first are termed promises and threats, the second predictions and warnings, respectively. Warnings are frequently preferable because they involve no effort, merely an indication of likely negative consequences of an indicated action, but they cannot be turned off and on, as can be threats. Predictions are inherent in the positive-sum outcome; promises are additional voluntary sweeteners.

In these cases, parties most frequently made use of warnings to move the other party toward agreement by devaluing the security point of the other party, sometimes backing up those warnings with some coercive threats, and resisting the efforts of the other similarly to devalue their own alternative courses of action. Usually they also offered predictions of benefits, sometimes backed by additional promises, to make the negotiated outcome attractive. The combination of contingent gratifications with deprivations makes for positive-sum or integrative bargaining, to be discussed below, whereas contingent deprivations alone mark zero-sum or distributive bargaining.

In the European cases, France was successful in bargaining for German support in 1992 and then for a loosened but maintained EMS by evoking the worst case scenario of European collapse as the sole – and unacceptable – alternative. The predicted benefits of holding onto the EMS were agreed on at Maastricht; neither France nor Germany made any additional promises to improve the outcome, either in 1992 or 1993. The Polish debt negotiations with the IMF were a play and counterplay of warnings: the IMF's warnings of consequences (for Poland) if Poland defaulted were accepted until political reform began, then countered with Poland's warnings of consequences (for the West) if the liberalizing system were allowed to collapse. From time to time, the banks or the IMF would improve the terms of agreement to reward Poland for compliance, or to make that compliance possible, but these were embellishments on the basic power of alternatives. Similarly, in the very different world of Mickey Mouse, Disney kept its security point in Spain higher in appearance than in reality, whereas France committed itself early and publicly to a Disney deal; predictably, Disney made the deal favorable for itself. Any additional promises were the consequence, not the component, of the basic power relation. In US–Japanese negotiations, it was noted that "often a threat of even worse unilateral action is credible and hence lowers the exporting states' resistance [security] points and results in agreement that transfers value."

This asymmetry in relative demand was formalized into a real structural imbalance in two cases, which can be neatly expressed in game theoretical terms. One party preferred giving in to having a deadlock, whereas the other's preferences were the reverse; in other words, the first party saw a CDG whereas the second saw a PDG, or again, one party said that evoking a worst case scenario did not impress it, contrary to the cases above, since it did not agree that the scenario was the worst case. In the GATS section of the Uruguay Round, "the US had made it quite clear that it was not willing to sign an agreement on the basis of unconditional MFN and that it preferred status quo to such an outcome ... . [O]thers preferred an agreement which included the objectionable provision [for exemptions from MFN], and the US, to no agreement at all or status quo." This distribution of security point values both supported and framed the negotiations: it put the United States, with a higher security point, in a stronger position in determining the terms of trade, but the United States would lose that power if ever it would opt definitively for status quo. The result, predictably, was continuing but inconclusive negotiations.

In negotiating the terms for continued exploitation of the Volta River aluminium concession, Ghana was in the same PDG position, whereas VALCO was the Chicken; Ghana preferred no plant operation to operation on the old terms, whereas VALCO viewed termination of operations as unacceptable (at least under any of the terms under consideration). Ghana brought the point home by turning off the electricity, on the (real) pretext of low water, thus practicing coercive diplomacy (George *et al.*, 1971). It also made and made good on promises to provide additional benefits through a lowered exchange rate, not specific to VALCO, and tax adjustments; these down payments did not bring immediate concessions from VALCO. It is no wonder that VALCO ended up paying a higher rate for electricity than the unmanipulated contract zones would have indicated.

In the intellectual property rights negotiations between AT&T and semiconductor companies, the security point was shared and operated for mutual benefit. The high cost of the alternatives for both sides kept all the parties on track toward a mutually satisfactory solution – licensed cooperation rather than separation or litigation. At the same time, both sides had a protected retreat, "the monopoly rights provided by patents, ... [which gave them] the power to protect and license intellectual property" and also gave them something to bargain with, as promises and predictions of benefits. Little warning and few threats were necessary, since they worked more or less equally on both sides.

The reverse – and perverse – situation obtained in the negotiations for a customs union in the former Soviet Union. All the parties were tied together by trade, although some more closely than others, and Ukraine created a more favorable security point that permitted it to opt out of the deal by cultivating relations with Europe. No party had any ability to threaten sanctions or to promise additional benefits for any other. Russia tried, by threatening less favorable bilateral treatment (not by promising any additional benefits), but to no avail; it could not change their Prisoners' Dilemma into a Chicken Dilemma view of the game. Many of the parties refused to recognize their interdependence because of their political pride in their newfound independence, and therefore entered into a distributive status game. As a result, all ended up in a negative-sum outcome, the three final partners by forming the most unfavorable union, the others by not joining and thus neither making the union more favorable nor improving their own situation. Indeed, had the parties had greater latitude in manipulating their security points, they might have been able to bring each other to a universally more favorable agreement. The cases show that alternatives give power, and bargaining power is necessary to overcome the initial conflict in values and demands. But the effectiveness of that power depends on the subjective willingness of the parties to be moved and their skill in persuasiveness at moving each other.

If the opportunity power provided by the perceived alternatives is the dynamic by which the parties within the negotiations arrive at a common position, the assumptions provide the limits to their manipulations. If negotiations do not meet the parties' expectations of positive sum, equivalence, and reciprocity, the parties will suspend or leave the process. This effect has already been seen in the discussion of the positive-sum nature of negotiations as a basis of power. Parties that did not see benefits in agreement greater than their security points either held back from agreement, like the United States in GATS, China in joint venture negotiations, and initially, Ghana in regard to VALCO, or left the negotiations entirely, like most of the ex-Soviet states. Suspension and delay were tactically effective in eliciting better terms for the dissatisfied party, illustrating the first effect. By contrast, leaving the negotiations was decisive, not just a threat, in the CIS case, and produced no changes in positions.

Whereas in the Positive-Sum Assumption the reference is the party's own security point, in the Equivalence and Reciprocity Assumptions it is the action of the other party, in outcome and in process. Parties believed that their benefits must be equivalent to those received and their concessions reciprocated by those given by the other party. This was the basis of the intellectual property rights negotiations, where the parties gave up exclusiveness in exchange for fair and reasonable returns; "due value," "commensurate value exchange," and "continuing equal value" were the guidelines for both sides of an acceptable outcome. Indeed, if a party "believed that it was not receiving due value for its patents," negotiation returned to the diagnosis phase on patent impact, since the basic formula was fixed. Reciprocity even carried over into venue and drafting: parties alternated locations for negotiations, and exchanged drafts in the final editing process. Similarly, in the GATS negotiations, as in GATT itself, the parties negotiated MFN status based on the very principle of reciprocity and the process of reciprocated concessions. Even in arguing for conditional MFN the United States used the reciprocity argument: "maintaining an open regime while not securing openness from other participants would be unbalanced." Significantly, the American principle of limited or plurilateral equivalence was a tinkering with the concept, not a replacement of it. But against the American notion of fairness were set the different views of the Europeans, Japanese, and others, and sectors of services were left out of GATS or covered in such a way that it was the United States that became the free rider.

In the EMS negotiations, the limits of fairness were breached for some countries, such as Britain and Italy, which would have had to make disproportionate sacrifices to stay in the snake, and so left, blaming Germany for not being willing to share the burden equitably. Most of the former Soviet republics acted in a similar way when they left the CIS customs union. The perceived limits of fairness also troubled the Chinese negotiating joint ventures, as they feared that the foreign company was getting hidden and unequal benefits; otherwise it would not be seeking to enter the Chinese market. As a result, China dragged its feet and often aborted negotiations. Ghana too felt that the previous agreement with VALCO was unjust and that it deserved more equitable benefits, built on equivalence with other rates around the world. These notions of fairness and justice are based on perceptions of equivalent benefits to those enjoyed by the other party, not on the meeting point of incremental concessions or of bargaining on the basis of security points (Zartman *et al.*, 1996; Zartman, 1997). As such, they form the limits to the arena within which the bargaining takes place.

14.2   Process and Patterns

On the tactical dimension of process, it is the Negotiator's Dilemma that demands an answer from each party. That answer depends in part on the answer of the other party, raising problems of infinite regress that lock in the dilemma. The question is not only, "When should I be tough and when soft?" but, "When should I be tough or soft in response to the other party's toughness or softness?"

A number of patterns are visible. To begin with, some negotiations began as relatively soft, as Shopkeepers should. Disney and the French, AT&T and its competitors, GATS negotiators – all typical businessmen – opened reasonably. The common feature was the perception that failure would be costly and undesirable for all. Most of these also closed reasonably (too reasonably, some would say, in regard to the French who got Mickey-Moused). The set that did not continue soft to the end was the GATS negotiations, where general softness ran into American toughness and created responsive toughness and stalemate in return, in a Bazaar variation on the Shopkeeper. There are as many explanations for the differences in the two sets of endgames as there are analytical variables, from culture to relative demand (Faure and Rubin, 1993; Bartos, 1974, 1978). In the terms of the initial analysis, the cost and catastrophe associated with failure diminished in participants' – and particularly Americans' – eyes as the GATS negotiations continued.

The rest of the cases opened tough, as the parties tried to impose their positions on each other. This might well be considered a normal opener, since in the diagnosis or prenegotiation phase parties can be expected to try to impress on each other the importance of their demands. The questions of cost of concession versus cost of nonagreement that underlies the Toughness Dilemma is not yet posed. The important distinctions therefore come afterward. In some cases, toughness led to softness, that is, one party caved in and the two came to an agreement closer to one side than to the other. The EMS cases, the Chinese joint venture, the Polish debt negotiations, and, after a while, the Ghanaian bauxite negotiations all produced lopsided outcomes that nonetheless satisfied all sides to the point of winning agreement. In the CIS, GATS, and early Ghanaian negotiations, toughness led to toughness and stalemate. Again, the difference seems to result not from any pre-established predilection of the parties – Shopkeepers versus Warriors – but from the elements of opportunity and relative demand – security points and justice levels – in comparative evaluations. Members of the CIS, Chinese, non-American GATS, and

Ghanaian teams felt that they were not getting enough in terms of relative justice, and so hung tough, even to the point of refusal. Once the sense of justice is satisfied, the parties can usually reach an agreement. At that point, they begin working on each other's security points, using opportunity demand against opportunity power, to define an acceptable outcome.

The second dimension of process concerns first the decision to work for positive-sum or zero-sum negotiations, and then the ways in which that decision can itself be influenced. Many of the cases presented here began with a recognition by both sides that a positive-sum outcome was the key to success in the negotiations. Each side felt that in order to obtain its goals, it had to allow the other side to obtain its goals as well and that joint attainment guaranteed implementation. That is what the intellectual property rights negotiations were all about, as they sought shared value for profit, patent peace, and an exchange of rights to commensurate value. That too was the aim of the entire GATS agenda, based on the notion of comparative advantage and gains from trade expansion; the whole EMS was based on joint gains from convertibility and stability; and NAFTA was to benefit all three members through comparative advantage, free movement of the factors of production, and elimination of customs barriers. The detailed negotiations on these subjects hung on the best way to achieve these goals, not on objections to the positive-sum principle. The CIS customs union negotiations began on the same Positive-Sum Assumptions. Even the Euro Disney negotiations were very much among Shopkeepers looking for a deal: Disney would make France benefit, France would make Disney benefit.

Other cases were stuck in a zero-sum approach, and suffered from it. Notably, once started, the CIS customs union negotiations became plagued by zero-sum thinking, as parties charged that joining would only come at the expense of their economic and sovereign well-being. That argument carried the day among many of the intended partners. One party's distributive approach reinforced the others' and obscured the potentiality for joint gains; Russia played a sucker strategy toward the NIS and they responded in reverse with a free rider strategy. Similar criticisms were launched in the NAFTA debates, but they did not prevent the negotiations from reaching agreement. In the GATS negotiation, the United States and particularly some of the domestic pressure groups were criticized for "mercantilism," seeking liberalizing concessions only from others without making any themselves, although the official delegation tried to allay this approach. In China, zero-sum fears and attitudes by the government became self-proving hypotheses, as would-be joint venture partners were worn down and scared away by the negotiating process. Yet in all these cases, the outcome sought was characterized conceptually as a mutually beneficial regime; none of these cases concern inherently and solely distributive negotiations. (It is hard to categorize the Polish debt negotiators one way or the other in this regard).

What accounts for such attitudes, so divergent from the theoretical nature of the subject under negotiation? To begin with, it was – again paradoxically – the integrative nature of the outcome that made distributive attitudes possible. Zero-sum parties assumed that the result would not be a larger pie, and instead focused their attention on getting as large a piece of it for themselves as possible. This in turn suggests that at least not all parties are zero sum by nature, but rather adopt that approach when the circumstances lend themselves.

Thereafter, determination is more difficult to specify. The original hypothesis, that parties turned to zero-sum perceptions when the basic assumptions were not fulfilled, that is, when a party did not believe that the other subscribed to the initial norms, is only loosely supported. The strongest evidence comes from US–Japanese exchange rate negotiations, where Secretary Connally came to office with the notion that the United States was not receiving equitable treatment from Japan and so launched into distributive bargaining. A similar vicious circle of mistrust and distributive bargaining occurred in the Chinese joint venture negotiations, where the Chinese attitude was colored by historic references and allusions to the West's interest only in exploitation and the Westerners were alerted by warnings about Chinese attitudes.

A second set of hypotheses, from the US–Japanese cases, suggest that the negotiated outcome strategy depends on the external "market" conditions and is self perpetuating. Positive-sum behavior occurs when both parties already share or exchange benefits and zero-sum behavior is perpetuated when the parties are already locked in direct and active competition. Not all cases provide clear examples, but NAFTA and EU negotiations illustrate the positive effect and CIS negotiations illustrate the negative one (Lebedeva, 1996; Vlasova, 1996). A simpler correlation suggests that more powerful parties have a greater tendency to distributive thinking than less powerful parties, but this proposition would have to be refined to overcome serious problems in conceptualizing "more powerful" (Zartman and Rubin, 1999). A fourth observation is that distributive thinking is a product and heritage of the *kto-kogo* communist political attitudes (Leites, 1950). While these are promising suggestions, more work must be done on the subject, for the cases do show that distributive thinking keeps parties from seeing or reaching more individually and mutually beneficial positive-sum outcomes. In any case, in all four hypotheses, zero- and positive-sum thinking appear to be self-fulfilling, for different reasons, but that does not tell which is trumps.

Finally, in regard to the process sequencing, although economic analysis would suggest a process of quantitative convergence, the cases provided no clear examples of inductive negotiations. The AT&T, Chinese joint venture, Polish, and, to some extent, CIS negotiations concentrated on details under a preexisting formula, not the same thing as an inductive or constructive creation of a formula, even though there were often subtle attempts to change the formula.

In the event, the cases support the idea that negotiations are battles for or between general formulas or framework principles – a conflict over the best way to solve the conflict – before being able to progress to the settlement of details by deduction from the formula. The Polish debt negotiations, like all other debt negotiations, were a contest to select the applicable principles, with the actual figures trailing behind. The GATS negotiations never got to figures at all, but consisted of a struggle to determine the appropriate formula or formulas. The EMS negotiations in 1992 were over the defense of the current formula; in 1993, they were over the degree of change that the formula would allow without changing the formula! The Disney negotiations first concentrated on establishing a comprehensive framework in the Master Agreement, which provided a deductive standard for the subsequent negotiations on details. Finally, perceptively, Ghana held out for a deductive process against the efforts of VALCO, calling for a principle to determine electricity rates rather than just engaging in concession/convergence haggling over numbers.

This universal behavior in negotiation allows the analysis to be pushed a step further. If negotiation to define a joint position is not a matter of incremental concessions to a point of convergence, but a matter of finding a principle acceptable to the conflicting parties, what makes a winning case in the battle over formulas? Two different answers are available from some of the cases, answers that can be roughly categorized as substantive and procedural. The substantive answer addresses the question in its own terms, focusing on appropriate characteristics of the winning formula. The EMS and GATS cases show that the formula that prevailed was the original one, tinkered with in such a way as to preserve its integrity while overcoming the current objections, not a new and different formula, no matter how encompassing. Thus, in the European monetary committee meeting of 1–2 August 1993, of the many suggestions offered the one that won approval was a loosened ERM that maintained all the basic characteristics – universality, no currency control, limited float – of the original mechanism. Similarly, in the GATS negotiations, of the many proposals to bridge the European and American formulas, the one that gained agreement maintained the principle of unconditional MFN and incorporated the US position by allowing exceptions to be declared before the unconditional principle would be put into operation. Then, in the three excepted sectors, the formula was applied by a critical mass in financial services but no formula could be accepted in the maritime and telecommunications sectors, leaving the negotiations to be continued. In both cases, only tinkering preserved the integrity of the formula that enabled agreement.

These cases concerned the maintenance of an established formula under attack; in other cases, a formula that was salient because of its prominence in similar cases was adopted without much debate. There was no conflict on the formula for the joint venture; the dynamics of bargaining centered on the implementing details. Nor was there conflict on the free trade area formula of NAFTA, where negotiation centered on the subformulas and details of implementation. In the limiting case of CIS trade regime negotiations, on the other hand, the parties agreed easily on the customs union formula because they had no intention of agreeing on its implementing details.

The procedural answer concerns power. In some cases, a particular formula was adopted because of the decisive power of one or more of the parties, either through their ability to worsen the opposition's security points or through their ability to veto alternative proposals. In the EMS negotiations, the Paris–Bonn axis defending the European momentum was the basis of a winning coalition in the Community. In the GATS, the importance of the United States to a functioning agreement and to the other parties' preference scale balanced the others' critical mass, meaning that a formula would meet the concerns of both sides or would not be adopted. In the US–Japanese negotiations and the VALCO negotiations, it was simply the threatened or executed closedown of operations that caused one side's formula to prevail over the other's, not the characteristics of the formula itself. The fact that some cases can be singled out as examples of power as the deciding factor reinforces those other cases where characteristics of a winning formula can be identified.

14.3   Conclusions

This study has shown that economics enters into negotiations on economic issues before and after the negotiations. The issues and context are defined by economic considerations, and the agreement resulting from negotiations is then tested for durability by further economic conditions. If the negotiators would only leave the matters in between to be resolved by those same economic conditions and theories, administered and monitored by technicians, they might see a technically neater solution (if the technicians could agree), but one that would not take into account the political considerations of value and power – a little like deciding the outcome of a football game by weight and kinetic formulas rather than by actually playing the game. How then are these outcomes arrived at?

The process has been defined in terms of values, alternatives, and justice, inflected by power also defined in terms of values and alternatives. These items combine (in yet unidentifiable ways) to produce a price for an item in each party's mind and to move that price until it meets the other party's price, similarly determined. The price can be in terms either of items exchanged by the other side (promises) or of consequences produced as a result of the agreement (predictions). Most of the agreements studied here are examples of exchanged promises, except for the Polish debt and the EU monetary agreements, which were bought with predicted outcomes (which in the first EU case did not hold).

The assumptions under which this process operates have been shown to be not only normatively descriptive but also explanatory of particular approaches. While following the rules of the game tends to lead to positive-sum, integrative outcomes, not following them or suspecting that the other party will not do so leads to distributive or fixed-sum perceptions and behavior.

Combined with the fundamental possibility that a party may leave the negotiations when the process or the result does not meet its values and needs, these characteristics suggest the conclusions – not surprising but nonetheless worthy of reaffirmation – that negotiation is the best way to ensure satisfaction of both parties in creating a positive result in economic (and doubtless other) issues and conflicts. Impelled by a need for an agreement, a set of values, and ways of bringing the other party (similarly impelled) toward a mutually acceptable outcome, and pursuing a process governed by certain assumptions or rules of the game, parties tend to seek and often find mutually beneficial agreements that are usually durable and sometimes even efficient.

Chapter 15

How Does Economic Theory Interrelate with Negotiation Analysis for the Understanding of International Economic Negotiation?

Gunnar Sjöstedt

This chapter investigates the extent to which economic theory and negotiation analysis may help to explain the outcome of international economic negotiation. Simply raising this issue implies the hypothesis that economic issues may have certain special, intrinsic qualities that make negotiation theory insufficient to achieve full understanding of how international economic negotiations evolve and what outcome they produce. Is this supposition warranted? Are economic questions really significantly dissimilar to other topics when they are viewed as issues of international negotiation? Should negotiators approach economic issues differently than other topics like, say, border disputes, environmental hazards, or human rights?

15.1   Typical Features of Economic Issues

These pertinent questions are difficult to answer unequivocally. Economic issues apparently have distinctive attributes that, furthermore, are likely to facilitate negotiation concerning them. Hence, the stakes of economic negotiations are typically framed in monetary terms. For example, in a negotiation concerning market access the bone of contention may be expressed in percentages of market shares and ultimately in dollars, deutsche marks, yen, or any other selected currency. Consequently, as a rule economic issues are easily distributive and in this sense fairly uncomplicated to handle at the negotiation table. Quantification of issue values simplifies quick assessment of offers and requests made by negotiating parties. Distributiveness of issues facilitates compromises and tradeoffs. These kinds of issue characteristics are unquestionably important in a negotiation concerning economic questions, but to what extent are they special to this kind of international encounter?

Easily distributive issues can presumably be found in any issue area. For example, the stakes of a politically complicated zero-sum territorial conflict may sometimes be defined in terms of square kilometers or square meters. Environmental negotiations on air pollution typically have identified stakes – emissions of hazardous substances – that may be measured in tons and kilograms (Benedick, 1991; Susskind *et al.*, 1991). In any sector, negotiation strives to mold issues in such a way that they will become distributive. The incentives for two or more parties to initiate negotiation on a contentious question are likely to be greater if it is perceived as being distributive rather than nondistributive in nature. An important element of the art of negotiation is, furthermore, the ability to structure issues so they become manageable at the negotiating table (Zartman and Berman, 1982). Part of this task is to pave the way for a smooth distribution of issue stakes.[1]

It is difficult to make a general assessment of the extent to which observed characteristics of economic issues (such as distributiveness) are unique, or relatively special. There is no obvious criterion available for a straightforward and systematic comparison of economic and other topics as issues of international negotiation. No taxonomy exists offering a comprehensive set of critical, variable attributes that any issues on the agenda of international negotiation may possess.[2] In the absence of a satisfactory method of issue comparison, the question of what is special for economic issues has to be transformed into a less ambitious query: What are the typical features of economic issues on the agenda of international negotiation?

15.2 The Relative Significance of Negotiation Analysis and Economic Theory

One indication that economic issues have distinctive characteristics would be that in a negotiation they are processed differently from other issues. This project has not produced any hard evidence supporting that proposition. As demonstrated by Robert Neugeboren in Chapter 13, in theory situations exist where negotiation theory is completely irrelevant. Under conditions of full information the stipulations ordained by economic theory unequivocally determine rational behavior when game equilibria are unique, that is, when the game has only one terminal stage. These conditions are very rare and exist only in two exceptional situations: when there is either complete monopoly or perfect competition. In all other situations, where multiple equilibria exist, behavior is undetermined by the game situation as such. There is a need for joint solutions in all situations when parties perceive that they are becoming involved in strategic interaction; in other words, when the outcome of a decision depends partly on the choices made by some other party. In reality all international economic negotiations can be expected to incorporate elements of strategic interaction that make them suitable for negotiation analysis without necessarily making economic theory irrelevant.

William Zartman's analysis in Chapter 14 demonstrated that all the cases included in the investigation could easily be accommodated by negotiation theory. The questions addressed to the cases by negotiation analysis could be handled and answered as in any other issue area. None of the case analyses clearly deviates from a general pattern discernible in a typical international negotiation. For example, power is recurrently proven to be a critical determinant of the outcome. Fairness or justice requiring reciprocity between negotiating parties is likewise a recurrent feature when deals are struck in economic talks. Zartman notes that several of the cases could be described as "a play and a counterplay of warnings."

However, Zartman also recognizes that the cases of economic negotiation included in the project have indicated a possibly typical attribute of a process in which economic issues are negotiated. According to Zartman, one recurrent feature of all the cases was that negotiations were conducted on clearly defined Positive-Sum Assumptions.[3] Although some of the cases "were stuck in a zero-sum approach, and suffered from it" none of the them "concern inherently and solely distributive negotiations." A key question is, hence, why this is so?

The characteristics that economic issues seem to display at the negotiation table do not necessarily have to mirror objective, intrinsic attributes perfectly. Instead, the issue properties revealed may primarily reflect how parties think about the issues. Positive-Sum Assumptions are certainly somehow derived from the realities of the negotiation situation and from issue characteristics. However, they also depend on the perceptions of the parties concerned: on how they understand the situation, comprehend the agenda, and react to it. Perceptions and cognition influence how issues are framed (Rubin and Brown, 1975).

Issue complexity represents a case in point. In most of the cases analyzed in this book, parties seem to have had little difficulty in framing the issues in terms that were easily comprehensible not only to themselves but also to other parties to the talks. However, it is not equally evident that the topics dealt with in the economic negotiations lacked intrinsic complexity before they were framed as agenda items. For example, a large part of the earlier stages of the GATT negotiations on trade in services (the GATS case; see Chapter 8) was devoted to the clarification of the issues involved in order to make them negotiable (Feketekuty, 1988). The difficulties parties had in this regard represent one of the reasons why the GATT negotiations on trade in services constituted such a time-consuming and protracted process. Hence, economic issues in international talks sometimes lack complexity, are simple to calculate, and manifest themselves as easily distributive stakes because they have been constructed to have these attributes. This interpretation may be referred to as the regime-impact explanation. Its essence is that economic issues are fairly easy to cope with at the table because negotiation parties around the world employ more or less the same approaches and methods to evaluate them, all of which have been endorsed by international economic regimes.

According to a standard definition, an international regime is an issue-specific combination of formal rules, informal norms (soft law), consensual knowledge about the issues concerned (principles), as well as procedures for the internal management of the regime, around which actor expectations converge (Krasner, 1983). Most regime studies have focused on the hard backbone of the regime, the formal rules. Typically, the leading research question has been to what extent governments and other actors comply with the rules (Chayes and Handler-Chayes, 1995; Victor, 1996; Hutter, 1997). That analysis considered norms and consensual knowledge because they underpin the rules and hence contribute to making the regime more effective from a compliance perspective (Levy *et al.*, 1996). These softer regime elements may, however, also have an autonomous impact. One such effect relates to how, and to what extent, parties to international economic negotiations tend to perceive, understand, and cope with the issues in a consonant or even identical way (Sjöstedt, 1994).

In the sphere of international economic affairs comparatively strong regimes have developed since World War II. Looking at the rule element of these regimes, their relative strength varies considerably across economic subfields. Hence, the formal rules guiding the performance of governments are comparatively forceful and demanding in the trade area but much weaker with regard to monetary affairs or international investment (Hudec, 1990; James, 1996; Lucatelli, 1996; Preston and Windsor, 1997). Another regime element – consensual knowledge – is, however, more evenly distributed across economic subfields and seems to play a special and important role in all kinds of international interactions concerning economic issues. Economic consensual knowledge manifests itself in different ways. For example, it is institutionalized in the legal instruments of the world trade regime, in the conventions of WTO and its predecessor, GATT. The Preamble of GATT/WTO contains a reference to the guiding principles of neoclassical free trade theory, thus including them in the global trade regime. Similar references to neoclassical economic theory may be found in other conventions established at both the global and regional levels of world affairs (e.g., IMF, EU, or NAFTA; Bagwell and Staiger, 1997; Masson, 1995; Senti, 1996; Oliver, 1996).

The significance of the inclusion of widely accepted economic theory in international regimes may be construed in different ways. For example, an important feature of the consensual knowledge embedded in the global trade regime is that in today's world it need not be established in each particular negotiation by means of collective learning processes, as has often been the case in issue areas other than economic affairs. One illustration would be the grand effort in the Intergovernmental Panel on Climate Change (IPCC) to build up a common understanding of the climate problem, based on scientific knowledge, to convince national governments of the necessity to begin negotiations on climate warming (IPCC, 1995). In contrast, in the multilateral trade negotiations the existence of consensual knowledge was an important part of the structure in which recurrent negotiations – the GATT rounds – were initiated, structured, and conducted. The consensual knowledge of GATT/WTO and other economic regimes is shared by a multitude of decision makers in many countries. In the whole postwar period economic consensual knowledge has been communicated to key decision makers in private firms as well as in government institutions around the world by means of similar university education and training. This circle of like-minded officials and decision makers has gradually extended (see, for example, Fine *et al.*, 1994). The continuous process of collective learning pertains not merely to trade, but to all economic subfields. The consensual knowledge that is part of international economic regimes is not only spread worldwide among a very large number of individual decision makers in many countries, it has also become institutionalized in the organizational cultures of business firms, government agencies, and international institutions.

The case studies of this volume generally support the proposition that consensual knowledge does indeed have an impact on how economic negotiations are conducted and on the outcomes they produce. The strength of this influence varies across cases, but is typically diffuse and sometimes hard to define. However, a least common denominator in all the cases is that consensual knowledge seems generally to condition how economic issues are framed at the negotiation table. Except for this general impact of consensual knowledge its influence may be quite diverse, as it may affect actors, strategies, and structure of international economic negotiations in various ways at different analytical levels. As consensual knowledge is partly a method for elucidation and calculation applied to economic issues, it helps actors to understand their interests and to design appropriate strategies to pursue them. In a negotiation context the various parties sharing consensual knowledge are likely to use similar methods to analyze the problem situation and to design a policy to cope with it. Consequently, negotiation party A will have a fairly good understanding of how negotiation party B views the issues on the table. This acknowledgement of shared consensual knowledge may explain why, in the case of the Disney investment in France, the French government refrained from undertaking independent analysis of the profitability of the project. Once it was convinced that it had a common interest with Disney in undertaking the project, the French government apparently thought that it could rely on the assessments made by Disney, as they were based on the same kind of objective economic analysis that it would have undertaken itself if necessary.

The case of the GATS negotiation also demonstrates the significance of consensual knowledge, although in a different way. This case illustrates how different parties use consensual knowledge to frame a complex and fairly undefined set of issues in a compatible if not identical way in order to make it manageable at the table. A large part of this negotiation was devoted to setting up a conceptual framework for the identification of services as trade issues in terms of the language of the GATT regime and hence also in correspondence with prevailing economic consensual knowledge. Before the Uruguay Round, trade negotiations did not deal with such service issues as transport, banking, or insurance (Melvin, 1989). These topics were part of the agenda of various international institutions, but were not considered to pertain to the realm of international trade. Thus, before they could be installed in the agenda for the GATT talks they had to be transformed into trade issues, framed in terms of the current consensual knowledge.

Economic consensual knowledge not only helps negotiation parties generally to understand issues from a technical or substantive point of view; it is also so structured that it helps parties to identify common interests. Thus, the effect of economic consensual knowledge represents one likely explanation for the prevalence of Positive-Sum Assumptions that Zartman detected in all the cases included in the project. The case of GATS negotiation demonstrates how economic consensual knowledge may function to facilitate party interaction, and hence directly support the process – the overall pattern of party interaction unfolding during an entire negotiation. A similar facilitating impact on process can be detected in all the cases, although it is diffuse and hard to estimate.

The characteristics of economic consensual knowledge may also help explain the special role structure has played in many economic negotiations. Structure refers to the external and comparatively robust circumstances in the international system that may influence how an international negotiation unfolds and what results it eventually achieves (Zartman, 1991). Typical structural elements pertaining to most negotiations are, for instance, power relations between nations or international rules and other institutions (Frieden and Lake, 1995; Levy *et al.*, 1996). In the case of international negotiations on economic questions, relevant market conditions represent a significant element of the structural background conditions (Helpman and Krugman, 1985; Bourdet, 1988). The structural dimension of markets does not manifest itself in the content of particular market decisions on prices and volumes, but rather in the mechanisms by which such choices are made. In his chapter, John Odell points out that the most distinctive feature of economic negotiations is their dependence on the market. What parties do not settle in negotiation concerning the distribution of economic values will be determined by market forces. Hence, the market is a crucial, if not decisive, determinant of what parties perceive to be the BATNA. Market forces, therefore, influence when a particular government or other kind of actor decides to take part in a negotiation or move out of it. Odell also suggests that market conditions have a direct impact on how parties perform in the negotiation. For example, he asserts that a widening difference between supply and market demand will influence the initial choice of strategy.

Odell's assertion – that more research should be undertaken concerning the relationship between market conditions and economic negotiations – is well taken. It seems, however, that this contention should be somewhat widened. There is a need to study more extensively how structural background conditions generally affect negotiations on economic as well as other types of issues. If market conditions are envisaged as part of the general structure surrounding a negotiation they do not a priori stand out as such a special case as Odell seems to indicate. For example, in all cases where negotiation has the character of crisis management, the structural conditions representing determinants of the crisis are likely to have a strong and precise impact on the choices and strategies of actors as well as on process and outcome. It cannot be excluded that structural background conditions related to negotiations on issues other than economic questions may have an impact on actors and process that is basically rather similar to market influence on economic talks. In several environmental negotiations the problem area concerned has been described in a very precise way, including the quantification of key concepts whose interrelationships are described by means of a causal model. Ozone depletion is one case in point (Benedick, 1991). Such problem descriptions seem to have critical similarities to how market conditions may be determined and assessed by the parties to an economic negotiation.

Nevertheless, market conditions indisputably had an impact on negotiations in virtually all cases studied in this project, although the magnitude and significance of this influence varied considerably across negotiations. Case study authors generally report that at some point in the negotiation process individual parties had to consider market conditions. It is precisely the way parties consider (perceive and assess) the market that gives structural background conditions a special role, and possibly a special significance, in international economic negotiation. Again, this is due to the noteworthy effect of international regimes in the area of economic affairs. The consensual knowledge representing one of the pillars of economic regimes helps parties not only to "read the market," but also to do so in a similar way using essentially the same criteria and methods of calculation. Thus, consensual knowledge makes it much easier, and less risky, to take market conditions into consideration than to interpret and calculate the consequences of other significant elements of the negotiation structure such as, for example, pertinent power relationships between key actors.

The analysis of the case studies indicated that, at least in the perceptions and cognitions of a multitude of potential actors at the table, economic issues in international negotiations have certain typical features that may possibly be defined as special or even unique. This assessment recalls the project's second major query: to what extent economic theory or negotiation theory may help to explain the outcome of international economic negotiation. Recall that this problem definition does not imply the existence of two coherent master theories, one embodying cumulative knowledge about economics and the other pertaining to negotiation. Rather, the two sets of theories should be thought of as two heterogeneous families of approaches and analytical frameworks concerned with economic issues and negotiations respectively. The general characteristics of each of the two theoretical perspectives were described and discussed in Chapters 13 and 14, respectively.

Nevertheless, each of the two families of theories has certain idiosyncratic attributes with regard to both function and form. The function of economic theories is typically to explain, or prescribe, the appropriate avenue toward effective use of economic resources. By contrast, negotiation theory is instead concerned with the accommodation of conflicting interests in the search for a viable agreement supported, or at least accepted, by the two or more parties involved in a negotiation. Both economic and negotiation theory have a prescriptive purpose. One difference is that prescription in economic theory is usually more formalized and represents the logical consequence of the precise, causal relationships of the model. Sometimes, as in game theory, models for negotiation analysis may share the prescriptive ambition of economic theories and be structured in a similar way. However, negotiation analysis is usually satisfied to determine critical elements of a negotiation and to hypothesize about significant relationships between them.

One may ask if the observed differences between negotiation analysis and economic theory mean that one of the approaches offers a better guide to understanding
international economic negotiation than the other. Several of the case study authors
emphasize that this query is misguided. A comparison of economic theory and negotiation analysis cannot be framed as a contest of relevance or usefulness. Case
study authors claim that both economic theory and negotiation analysis are clearly
relevant in the assessment of economic negotiation. Thus, no categorical choice
can be made between economic theory and negotiation analysis. Instead, we need
to find ways to interrelate and combine the two approaches in a creative way.

However, the relative utility of economic theory or negotiation analysis for
the assessment of economic negotiations does warrant examination. The two approaches do not answer exactly the same questions. Hence, in a particular study
priority may have to be given to one of the theoretical perspectives, depending on
the objectives of the investigation and other particular circumstances at hand. Dissimilar research objectives are likely to require different research approaches. A
certain study may deliberately focus on questions pertaining particularly to either
negotiation analysis or economic theory. For example, a researcher interested in the
tactics and negotiation ploys employed by governments in economic talks cannot
expect to find a relevant frame of reference in economic theory.

It seems that different dimensions of economic negotiations may be more
closely associated with either economic theory or negotiation analysis. A negotiation is often a complex chain of events that may unfold along different patterns.
It includes quite different types of activity undertaken by the parties involved in
the process, depending on the circumstances at hand. For example, in positive-sum
games negotiators are usually concerned with value creation by means of cooperation before they share the "pie." In contrast, distributive bargaining tends to prevail
when the negotiation transforms into a zero-sum game. Positive-sum games and
zero-sum games will probably elicit different patterns of actor behavior. Actor
strategies in positive-sum negotiations are typically more flexible than the horse-
trading in a zero-sum context. The establishment of, or reference to, consensual
knowledge is probably more important in a positive-sum situation than when the
game becomes dominated by claiming strategies. Hence, economic theory is likely
to have a greater impact on positive-sum negotiations as compared to international
talks dominated by distributive bargaining. A further noteworthy observation is
that the general character of a negotiation, as determined by the mixture of cooperation and conflict resolution, influences the extent to which it is better interpreted
in terms of economic theory or negotiation analysis.

Different stages of the same negotiation may likewise exhibit quite dissimilar patterns of actor behavior, which in turn influence the direct applicability of
negotiation and economic theory. The early phases of a negotiation are typically

Table 15.1. Outcome across basic elements.

Actors:	Economic/negotiation theory
Strategy:	Economic/negotiation theory
Process:	*Negotiation theory*
Structure:	*Economic theory*
Outcome:	Economic/negotiation theory

dominated by search behavior; parties are engaged in setting the agenda, clarifying the questions introduced, determining initial positions on emerging issues, or even developing comprehensive strategies. The conditions for actor behavior represented by this process stage have some similarities to a positive-sum situation. Parties communicate extensively with one another and their exchange may be facilitated by the coordinating effects of consensual knowledge. Therefore, if search behavior in economic negotiation is conditioned by consensual knowledge strongly framed by economic theory, the analyst may also lean on the latter in trying to interpret what is happening in the process. In contrast, as it unfolds toward end game the choice process increasingly attains the features of distributive bargaining (Zartman and Berman, 1982). Determined strategic interaction characterized by claiming strategies begins to substitute for collective problem solving, decreasing the diffuse influence of the consensual knowledge common in the search stage of the process. This development evidently increases the relevance of negotiation theory, but possibly also of economic theories of negotiation focusing on rational choice. Accordingly, the relative applicability of negotiation and economic analysis can be expected to vary somewhat between the phases through which a negotiation unfolds, from prenegotiation to its final conclusion, the agreement.

A negotiation may be looked at from quite different points of departure. A common taxonomy of perspectives on negotiation makes a distinction between actors, strategies, process, structure, and outcome (Kremenyuk, 1991).[4] Looking at a negotiation on economic issues from these analytical perspectives, it seems that each pertains somewhat differently to economic and negotiation analysis. Indeed, a vague pattern is discernible, which is summarized in *Table 15.1*.

For three of the elements – actors, strategy, and outcome – economic and negotiation analysis essentially represent complementary perspectives. Both approaches are clearly applicable, and may be combined in various ways. However, the negotiation elements italicized in the table – process and structure – are different. In these two cases one of the two approaches is clearly more relevant than the other. Negotiation analysis relates strongly to process. Economic theory is especially relevant for the assessment of the structure of international economic negotiations.

Negotiation analysis certainly offers explanations why a certain actor, be it a government or a private firm, would choose to take part in a negotiation, regardless of the issues at stake. Zartman and Berman have formulated the basic motive to negotiate as follows: "Negotiation is appropriate when the parties see that a problem can only be resolved jointly and when they have the will to end an existing situation that they consider unacceptable, while admitting the other parties' claim to participate in that solution" (Zartman and Berman, 1982:66). Negotiation analysis points out the general circumstances that determine if a certain government or other type of organization will become a party to a negotiation. Therefore, negotiation analysis represents a logical point of departure in an assessment of what governments or other categories of organizations may become participants or indirect stakeholders in a negotiation.

However, economic theory may provide more concrete ideas regarding the actual motives for a particular actor to become a party to an economic negotiation. Negotiation theory offers an explanation of the conditions necessary for two or more actors to engage in a negotiation. Economic analysis helps to elucidate when these conditions are fulfilled. The investigation of the relevant economic circumstances may produce strong indications as to when two or more parties will have an incentive to start negotiation on, for example, FDI, a joint venture, or a project of regional trade liberalization.

Both economic and negotiation theory offer suggestions with regard to how parties choose and implement a strategy in an economic negotiation and how effective different strategies may be. A general conclusion from the case studies of this project is that the parties to the economic negotiations studied basically performed rationally as seen from an economic-theoretical point of view. Actor strategies were designed to secure as profitable a deal as possible for the party concerned. Several of the cases also demonstrated that parties were anxious to define a common economic interest shared by all parties, which could serve as a basis for an agreement. However, rationality was typically bounded. In several of the cases the parties did not undertake all the economic background studies that were evidently necessary for the design of a rational economic strategy. One stark case in point is the performance of the French government in its negotiation with the Disney Company. In some cases, for example the GATT negotiations on trade in services, the negotiation contained an element of joint analysis in search for an acceptable agreement. However, it is likewise clear that parties also resorted to standard negotiation tactics representing the exercise of power, such as the employment of threats and promises or the actual use of sanctions. This pattern of behavior is more consonant with negotiation analysis than economic theory.

The outcome of international economic negotiations can be defined and assessed in terms of either negotiation analysis or economic theory. However, a full understanding of why a particular outcome was produced requires combined insights from both economic and negotiation theory. Even if actor performance is consonant with the stipulations of negotiation theory, economic realities will constrain what is achievable.

Process is a concept belonging entirely to the family of negotiation theories (Dupont and Faure, 1991). Economic theory is entirely unsuitable for the analysis of process developments – how patterns of actor interaction unfold during a negotiation. However, the differentiation and understanding of process stages in terms of negotiation theory may clarify the conditions for the application of economic theory. The various process stages represent different combinations of conditions in this regard, e.g., with regard to the choice of party strategies.

The structural dimension of international economic negotiation represents an area where economic analysis may particularly enrich negotiation analysis. Several of the case study authors explicitly mention the significance of market conditions and other structural economic background factors. Case analyses identify at least two mechanisms by which structure may condition party performance and process development. The cases of negotiation on debt rescheduling and monetary crisis highlight the directly constraining impact of structure on outcome. In other cases the influence was more indirect and depended on how parties developed policies and strategy.

A particularly illuminating example is offered by the negotiations among Canada, Mexico, and the United States on the creation of NAFTA. This case study concludes that the agreement was the result of the common perception in the three countries that the structure of obstacles to free trade was very costly, as it prevented the effective exploitation of emerging continental markets in North America. The case study authors assert that many of the trade liberalization measures that Canada, Mexico, and the United States agreed upon in the NAFTA treaty could have been carried out unilaterally, without international negotiation. One important function of the negotiation was related to the domestic political scene: to make liberalization legitimate and necessary in the eyes of the public. Winham and Finn claim that to a large extent the creation of NAFTA should be seen as a set of autonomous national responses to structural conditions imposing themselves on governmental decision makers.

The NAFTA case, as well as the services negotiations in the Uruguay Round, illustrate the situation where two different types of structural elements influence actor performance in interaction with one another. One element is consensual knowledge founded in economic theory. The other is "real world" structural phenomena conditioning effective policies as prescribed by this consensual knowledge. Other cases demonstrate that parties sometimes "read" the signals for rational behavior coming from structural background conditions surprisingly badly. The negotiations between the French government and the Walt Disney Company represent the starkest illustration of this contingency. The Disney case was an encounter between two extremely resourceful parties. On one side of the table sat one of the biggest companies in the world, well known for its business competence. It confronted the government of one of the largest Middle Powers. Still, both of these formidable actors misinterpreted the market conditions for the amusement park that the Walt Disney Company wanted to set up outside Paris. Relying on its earlier successful experience in Japan, Disney overestimated the capacity of an amusement part located in northern France to attract people during the winter. The French government did not make any study of its own to elucidate the market situation and was satisfied to accept the calculations presented by Disney. As a result, neither party to the negotiation was sufficiently well informed about the economic background factors that had a potential to constrain the outcome of the negotiation. In other case studies, fully rational positions and strategies in an economic sense were prevented by the lack of sufficient information about the market and other background conditions. Thus, the way parties assess the economic background factors of a negotiation represents an important condition for how structure will influence a negotiation or its outcome. In this connection economic theory has an important role in explaining significant causal relationships.

15.3   A Final Word

A comparison of the cases investigated in the present project shows that the understanding of international economic negotiation may be improved by a more creative combination of negotiation and economic analysis. For such a theory-oriented research enterprise, negotiation analysis should serve as a basic frame of reference. Negotiation analysis offers the most comprehensive perspective and the most explicit conceptualization and explanation of negotiation. Integration of economic theory with negotiation analysis should usually not take place at a very high level of generalization. In order to attain useful synergy from such a combination of different theoretical perspectives and methodological approaches, researchers should avail themselves of the option to break down negotiation into useful subcategories such as dimensions (actors, strategies, process, structure, and outcome) or different types of party encounters such as win–win problem-solving games or zero-sum distribution games.

A major research task is to identify the nature of the relationship coupling elements of economic theory to negotiation analysis. In the present study a fairly crude distinction was made between the impact on a negotiation of, on the one hand, economic realities such as flows of transactions or market structure and, on the other hand, of economic, consensual knowledge. This, as well as other significant distinctions, must be further developed and assessed by means of continued research. The role of economic consensual knowledge, derived from economic theory or doctrine, represents a powerful instrument to facilitate international negotiations on economic questions. Several of the case studies demonstrated variations of this vital function of economic consensual knowledge.

An important question that must also be addressed in future research concerns the explanations of the special role and facilitating effect of consensual knowledge in international conflict resolution. Better understanding of these causes may make it possible to emulate successful methods of building economic knowledge in other issue areas, for instance in the sector of environmental problems. It is, however, also critical to sustain the now traditional role of economic consensual knowledge in future intergovernmental negotiations concerning trade, finance, multilateral firms, or monetary questions. Can economic, consensual knowledge be taken for granted? To what extent does it depend on strong economic regimes and bounded conflicts between major actors? There are signals visible that economic strife is mounting in the world after the end of the Cold War. Fair trade policies and regionalization will undermine global economic regimes if these processes go too far. Will these developments begin to weaken the consensual elements of economic knowledge embedded in global and regional economic regimes? These are urgent questions for theory and practice alike.

Notes

[1] The stake is the bone of contention regarding a certain issue on which a negotiation focuses. For example, if the issue is customs duties, the stake may be the range of possible tariff reductions with regard to a particular group of products (Mansbach and Vasquez, 1981).

[2] All empirical studies of international negotiations concern one or more issues. However, few studies exist that try to generalize about the role of issues in theory-oriented analyses. One exception is Mansbach and Vasquez (1981).

[3] For a discussion of the concrete meaning of Positive-Sum Assumptions see, for example, Landau and Rosenberg (1986) and Zartman (1986).

[4] "Actors" are those taking part in a negotiation. "Strategy" refers to the moves parties make in order to attain their objectives. "Process" represents the comprehensive pattern of party interaction. "Structure" pertains to stable and robust phenomena in the external environment influencing a negotiation. "Outcome" is the embodiment of the total results of a negotiation.

Conclusion

The goal of this study, as the opening chapter outlined, comprised several subgoals: first, to identify what is special about international economic negotiation compared to international negotiation on other topics; second, to determine how these specific features relate to the way international economic negotiations are conducted and concluded; and, third, to establish what type of advice, or lessons, may be extracted from this analysis for theory and practice. These tasks were rightfully called "ambitious," because hardly anyone engaged in the study of the world economic system or processes of international negotiation has attempted them.

The analysis of the first part of the study gave rise to some promising observations. Roughly speaking, international economic negotiations have two separate, though overlapping, aspects. First, these negotiations concentrate on economic matters and thus represent a typical case of the bargaining that accompanies all economic deals, regardless of whether they happen in the home or in the foreign market. Thus, they can be explained in the terms of economic theories. The other aspect identifies international economic negotiation as a specific type in the family of international talks that relate to the sphere of power relationships among nations. Therefore, international economic negotiations may and should be explained in the terms of negotiation analysis typical of the theories of international relations.

This overlap produces a highly specific type of integrative decision making where actors in the process seek two sets of different, though not always contradictory, goals: to maximize their direct profit from an economic deal and, in parallel, to coordinate it with national power interests that may either gain or lose from that profit. For a decision maker, this represents a complicated matrix of preferences that must first be clarified before a decision is taken and, second, negotiated with the other party.

The analysis of the second subgoal also yields some provocative thoughts. First of all, in every international economic negotiation there is an invisible but rather sensitive dichotomy in motivations and interests: the parties must seek an economic benefit in negotiating a deal, and at the same time they must, directly or

343

indirectly, correlate it with an established national interest. When the party is a government agency, this is done almost automatically and very often with the political aspect dominating; when the party is a private company or a TNC this is achieved through governmental control over both the process of negotiation and, especially, the outcome.

As a result, the real agenda of negotiation is split and has at least two separate blocks of issues that must be permanently coordinated and correlated. This makes the whole process of negotiation much more complicated, and demands that every party spend more time making final decisions because of the need to coordinate a desirable outcome with a wider than usual spectrum of concerned parties at home.

The other aspect of the same cluster of analysis is the need to coordinate an international economic negotiation with the other negotiations that proceed in parallel among the same parties but on other subjects – security, territory, environment, etc. There is definitely a strong feedback among all these talks. Political, security, and other interests strongly affect the economic negotiations, while expected gains in these latter negotiations strongly affect the former. As is evident even from Mesjasz's account of the interplay of economic and political considerations in Poland's negotiations with its creditors, there is no universal pattern as to how these different factors may correlate in international economic negotiations. But it is absolutely clear that international economic negotiations remain an important part of the whole global system of international negotiations. Moreover, they bear a significant part of the responsibility for the stability and predictability of that system, and have a significant imprint on it.

The essence of the analytical section of the book, which attempts to formulate lessons for theory and practice of international economic negotiation, may be summarized as follows. First, there are effective tools to evaluate these negotiations from the viewpoint of economic theories and negotiation analysis. Second, negotiators following these prescriptions can always try to identify (privately or publicly) their list of interests and preferences in negotiation, to build a certain model of priorities to be achieved – economic and noneconomic – and to work out a strategy that may help to build up appropriate negotiation tactics. Third, an effective negotiation strategy may help to avoid the pressure of a possible power asymmetry in negotiation that is related to unequal economic capabilities of negotiating parties. Fourth, in trying to achieve an optimal outcome, the parties must rely on both economic incentives and negotiating skills – a combination that is hard to construct but, once it is there, helps to achieve a mutually acceptable outcome.

There is every reason to conclude that almost all the tasks formulated at the beginning of the book were completed successfully. This leads us to hope that the current stage of analysis will be helpful to the interested audience, be it academic, or business, or government, or international bodies. But evidently the current practice of international economic negotiation has already acquired some new dimensions that demand new studies. Among these dimensions is the advent of global communication systems, which, besides being another area of economic activity, change the nature of communications between parties to economic negotiation. Another is the emergence of new types of goods and services due to breakthroughs in science and research (new sources of energy, environmental demands, population pressure, changing fertility of arable land, etc.), which will necessarily affect the current economic system and the associated negotiations. Many other new developments will either add to the existing agendas of international economic negotiations, produce dramatic results for the current hierarchy in the world market, or introduce the need for new international economic regimes and regulations. In any case, this monograph should not be regarded as the final work in the study of international economic negotiation, but instead as an opening for a new type of research.

References and Sources

Aggarwal, V.K., 1987, International debt threat: Bargaining among creditors and debtors in the 1980s, *Policy Papers in International Affairs*, No. 29, Institute of International Studies, University of California, Berkeley, CA, USA.

Aggarwal, V.K., and Allan, P., 1992, *Polish Debt Negotiation Games: 1981–Present*, Paper presented at the first Pan-European conference in international relations, ECPR Standing Group in International Relations, 16–20 September, Heidelberg, Germany.

Ajayi, I., 1986, The exchange rate issue, *First Bank Monthly Business and Economic Report*, July.

Alexander, S.S., 1952, The effects of devaluation on the trade balance, *IMF Staff Papers*, 2(April):263–278.

Alker, H., and Puchala, D., 1968, Trends in economic partnership: The North Atlantic area, 1928–1963, in J.D. Singer, ed., *Quantitative International Politics, Insights and Evidence*, The Free Press, New York, NY, USA, p. 291.

Angel, R.C., 1991, *Explaining Economic Policy Failure: Japan in the 1969–1971 International Monetary Crisis*, Columbia University Press, New York, NY, USA.

Antowska-Bartosiewicz, I., and Malecki, W., 1991, Poland's External Debt Problem, *Economic and Social Policy Paper 1*, Friedrich-Ebert Foundation, Warsaw, Poland.

Aquino, K., Steisel, V., and Kay, A., 1992, The effects of resource distribution: Voice and decision framing on the provision of public goods, *Journal of Conflict Resolution*, 36(4):665–687.

Arneberg, M., 1996, *Theory and Practice in the World Bank and IMF Economic Policy Models, Case Study Mozambique*, Statistisk sentralbyrå, Oslo, Norway.

Arora, V.B., 1993, Sovereign Debt: A Survey of Some Theoretical and Policy Issues, Working Paper WP/93/56, International Monetary Fund, Washington, DC, USA.

Arrow, K., ed., 1996, *The Rational Foundations of Economic Behaviour*, Macmillan, London, UK.

Atkeson, A., 1991, International lending with moral hazard and risk of repudiation, *Econometrica*, 59(4):1069–1089.

Auten, J.H., 1971, *The US International Competitive Position and the Potential Role of Exchange Rates in the Adjustment Process*, US Department of the Treasury, 28 May 1971, declassified 24 June 1974.

Auw, A., von, 1983, *Heritage and Destiny, Reflections on the Bell System in Transition*, Praeger Publishers, New York, NY, USA.

Axelrod, R., 1984, *The Evolution of Cooperation*, Basic Books, New York, NY, USA.

Aziz, C., 1992, Rich man, poor man at the gates of Disney, *Times*, 21 March.

Azocar, P., 1992, Euro Disney losses falling on the government, *Inter Press Service*, 6 August.

Bagwell, K., 1997, *An Economic Theory of GATT*, National Bureau of Economic Research, Cambridge, UK.

Bagwell, K., and Staiger, R., 1997, *An Economic Theory of GATT*, National Bureau of Economic Research, Cambridge, UK.

Bailey, J.J., and Vega Canovas, G., 1989, *The Mexico–U.S. Natural Gas Negotiations of 1977–1979*, Institute for the Study of Diplomacy, Georgetown University, Washington, DC, USA.

Balassa, B., 1990, The United States, in P. Messerlin and K. Sauvant, eds, *The Uruguay Round: Services in the World Economy*, World Bank and UN Centre on Transnational Corporations, Washington, DC, USA.

Barrat-Brown, M., 1993, *Fair Trade: Reform and Realities in the International Trading System*, Zed Books, London, UK.

Barro, R.J., 1977, Unanticipated money growth and unemployment in the United States, *American Economic Review*, **67**:101–115.

Barry, B., 1963, *Theories of Justice*, University of California Press, Berkeley, CA, USA.

Bartos, O.J., 1974, *Process and Outcome of Negotiation*, Columbia University Press, New York, NY, USA.

Bartos, O.J., 1978, Simple model of negotiation, in I.W. Zartman, ed., *The Negotiation Process: Theories and Applications*, Sage Publications, Beverly Hills, CA, USA.

Bartos, O.J., 1987, How predictable are negotiations, in I.W. Zartman, ed., *The 50% Solution: How to Bargain Successfully with Hijackers, Strikers, Bosses, Oil Magnates, Arabs, Russians, and Other Worthy Opponents in This Modern World*, Yale University Press, New Haven, CT, USA.

Bayard, T.O., and Elliott, K.A., 1994, *Reciprocity and Retaliation in US Trade Policy*, Institute for International Economics, Washington, DC, USA.

Becker, G., 1976, *The Economic Approach to Human Behavior*, Chicago University Press, Chicago, IL, USA.

Benedick, R.E., 1991, *Ozone Diplomacy: New Directions in Safeguarding the Planet*, Harvard University Press, Cambridge, MA, USA.

Benedick, R.E., 1993, Perspectives of a negotiation practitioner, in G. Sjöstedt, ed., *International Environmental Negotiation*, Sage Publications, Newbury Park, CA, USA, pp. 219–243.

Benjamin, N.C., Devarajan, S., and Weiner, R.J., 1986, Oil revenues and the "Dutch Disease" in a developing country: Cameroon, *OPEC Review*, **10**(2):143–162.

Bentsen, L., 1992, The Uruguay Round Table Negotiations, Statement before the US Senate, 6 February.

Bergquist, A., 1993, Sveriges internationella handel med tjänster, *Filosofie Licentiatavhandling*, Nationalekonomiska institutionen, Lund, Sweden.

Bhagwati, J., 1983, *Essays in International Economics*, MIT Press, Cambridge, MA, USA.

Bhagwati, J., 1988, *Protectionism*, MIT Press, Cambridge, MA, USA.

Bhagwati, J., and Hudec, R., eds, 1996, *Fair Trade and Harmonization: Prerequisites for Free Trade?* MIT Press, Cambridge, MA, USA.

Biersteker, T.J., ed., 1993, *Dealing with Debt: International Financial Negotiations and Adjustment Bargaining. Case Studies in International Affairs*, Westview Press, Boulder, CO, USA.

Blackman, C., 1997, *Negotiating China: Case Studies and Strategies*, Allen and Unwin, St. Leonards, Australia.

Bond, C., 1995, Statement before the Senate Committee on Banking, Housing and Urban Affairs, 8 June, Washington, DC, USA.

Bond, M., 1986, *The Psychology of the Chinese People, Hong Kong*, Oxford University Press, Oxford, UK.

Boon-Chye, L., 1993, *The Economics of International Debt Renegotiation: The Role of Bargaining and Information*, Westview Press, Boulder, CO, USA.

Bourdet, Y., 1988, *International Integration, Market Structure and Prices*, Routledge, London, UK.

Boyer, B., 1996, *Coalition Structures, Nonstate Actors, and Bargaining Orientation*, PhD Dissertation, University of Geneva, Switzerland.

Braithwaite, R., 1955, *Theory of Games as a Tool for the Moral Philosopher*, Cambridge University Press, New York, NY, USA.

Brams, S.J., 1985, *Rational Politics: Decisions, Games, and Strategy*, Congressional Quarterly Press, Washington, DC, USA.

Bret, C., 1992, Comment investir en Chine: Mode d'emploi, *Le Conseiller du Commerce Extérieur*, No. 415, Paris, France.

Brock, W., 1992, A simple plan for negotiating on trade in services, *The World Economy*, **5**(3):233.

Brooks, J., 1975, *Telephone: The First Hundred Years*, Harper & Row, New York, NY, USA.

Bulow, J., and Rogoff, K., 1988a, Multilateral negotiations for rescheduling developing country debt: A bargaining-theoretic framework, *IMF Staff Papers*, **35**(3):644–657.

Bulow, J., and Rogoff, K., 1988b, The buyback boondoggle, *Brookings Papers on Economic Activity*, **2**:675–698, The Brookings Institution, Washington, DC, USA.

Bulow, J., and Rogoff, K., 1989a, A constant recontracting model of sovereign debt, *Journal of Political Economy*, **97**(1):155–178.

Bulow, J., and Rogoff, K., 1989b, Sovereign debt: Is to forgive to forget? *American Economic Review*, **79**(1):43–50.

Bulow, J., and Rogoff, K., 1990, Cleaning up third world debt without getting taken to the cleaners, *Journal of Economic Perspectives*, **4**:31–42.

Bunn, G., 1992, *Arms Control by Committee*, Stanford University Press, Stanford, CA, USA.

Camerer, C., and Thaler, R., 1995, Ultimatums, dictators and manners, *Journal of Economic Perspectives*, **9**(2):209–219.

Camerer, C., Johnson, E., Rymon, T., and Sen, S., 1993, Cognition and framing in sequential bargaining for gains and losses, in K. Binmore, A. Kirman, and P. Tani, eds, *The Frontiers of Game Theory*, MIT Press, Cambridge, MA, USA.

Campbell, N., 1989, *A Strategic Guide to Equity Joint Ventures*, Pergamon Press, Oxford, UK.

Campbell, N., Plasschaerts, S., and Brown, D., eds, 1991, *Advances in Chinese Industrial Studies*, **2**.

Canada–United States trade negotiations: The elements involved, in *Canadian Trade Negotiations: Introduction, Selected Documents, Further Reading*, Department of External Affairs, Ottawa, Canada, 15 December 1985, p. 21.

Caves, R., 1982, *Multinational Enterprise and Economic Growth*, Cambridge University Press, Cambridge, MA, USA.

Chang, M., 1995, The electoral connection: Crisis and credibility in the European monetary system, Paper presented at the 1995 Annual Meeting of the American Political Science Association, 31 August–3 September, Chicago, IL, USA.

Chayes, A., and Chayes, A.H., 1993, On compliance, *International Organization*, **47**(2): 175–205.

Chayes, A., and Handler-Chayes, A., 1995, *The New Sovereignty: Compliance with International Regulatory Agreements*, Harvard University Press, Cambridge, MA, USA.

Chen, D., 1995, *Chinese Firms between Hierarchy and Market: The Contract Management Responsibility System in China*, Macmillan, London, UK.

Chen, D., and Faure, G.O., 1995, When Chinese companies negotiate with their government, *Organization Studies*, **16**:1, January.

Chermont, H., and Rayon, L., 1989, Euro Disneyland: Final Report, prepared by Chevreux de Virieu, Banque Indosuez Group, Paris, France, September.

Claessens, S., Diwan, I., Froot, K.A., and Krugman, P.R., 1991, Market-based debt reduction for developing countries, principles and prospects, *Policy and Research Series*, PRS 16, World Bank, Washington, DC, USA.

Claessens, S., Diwan, I., and Fernandez-Arias, E., 1992, Recent experience with commercial bank debt reduction, *Policy Research Working Papers*, WPS 995, World Bank, Washington, DC, USA.

Coase, R.H., 1960, The problem of social cost, *Journal of Law and Economics*, **3**:1–44.

Coats, A., ed., 1981, *Economists in Government: An International Comparative Study*, Duke University Press, Durham, NC, USA.

Cohen, B.J., 1986, In whose interest? *International Banking and American Foreign Policy*, Yale University Press, New Haven, CT, USA.

Cole, H., Dow, J., and English, W., 1989, Default, Settlement and Signaling: Lending Resumption in a Reputational Model of Sovereign Debt, CARESS Working Paper 89-26, December, University of Pennsylvania, Philadelphia, IL, USA.

Collins, T., and Dorley, T., 1992, *Les alliances stratégiques*, Interéditions, Paris, France.

Cooper, R., 1971, *Currency Devaluation in Developing Countries: Essays in International Finance*, Princeton University Press, Princeton, NJ, USA.

Corbin, J., 1994, *The Norway Channel*, Atlantic Monthly Press, New York, NY, USA.

Corden, W.M., 1981, Exchange rate policy and the resource boom, *Economic Record*, **58**(March).

Corden, W.M., and Neary, J.P., 1982, Booming sector and de-industrialisation in a small open economy, *Economic Journal*, **92**(December).

Cottrell, R., 1991, Disneyland, France: Overcoming a long-standing contempt for US culture, Paris is happy to import Mickey, Minnie and money, *Independent*, 26 May, p. 8.

Coughlin, P., ed., 1989, *Negotiations Management: Preparation, Strategy, and Tactics*, Commonwealth Secretariat, London, UK.

Cross, J.G., 1969, *The Economics of Bargaining*, Basic Books, New York, NY, USA.

Cyert, R., and March, J., 1992, *A Behavioral Theory of the Firm*, Second edition, Blackwell, Cambridge, UK.

Dahl, R., 1957, The concept of power, *Behavioral Science*, **2**(2):201–215.

De Keijzer, A.J., 1992, *China: Business Strategies for the '90s*, Pacific View Press, Berkeley, CA, USA.

Department of External Affairs, 1985, *Competitiveness and Security: Directions for Canada's International Relations*, Department of External Affairs, Ottawa, Canada.

Derrick, L., and Frosch, C.J., 1957, Manufacture of silicon devices, US Patent 2,804,405.

Deslandres, V., and Deschandol, J.M., 1986, *Droit et pratique des investissements français en Chine Populaire*, International Development, Paris, France.

Destler, I.M., Fukui, H., and Sato, H., 1979, *The Textile Wrangle: Conflict in Japanese–American Relations, 1969–1971*, Cornell University Press, Ithaca, NY, USA.

de Vries, M.G., 1976, *The International Monetary Fund 1966–1971: The System under Stress*, 2 volumes, International Monetary Fund, Washington, DC, USA.

Doern, G.B., and Tomlin, B.W., 1991, *The Free Trade Story: Faith and Fear*, Stoddart Publishing Co. Ltd., Toronto, Canada.

Dornbusch, R., 1989, Reducing transfers from debtor countries, in R. Dornbusch, J. Makin, and D. Zlowe, eds, *Alternative Solutions to Developing Country Debt Problems*, American Enterprise Institute, Washington, DC, USA, pp. 21–42.

Drake, W., and Nicolaides, K., 1992, Ideas, interests, and institutionalization: Trade in services and the Uruguay Round, *International Organization*, **46**(1):45.

Dupont, C., 1991, International business negotiations, in V. Kremenyuk, ed., *International Negotiation: Analysis, Approaches, Issues*, Jossey-Bass, San Francisco, CA, USA.

Dupont, C., 1994, *La négociation*, Dalloz, Paris, France.

Dupont, C., and Faure, G.O., 1991, The negotiation process, in V.A. Kremenyuk, ed., *International Negotiation: Analysis, Approaches, Issues*, Jossey-Bass, San Francisco, CA, USA, pp. 40–57.

Eaton, J., 1990, Debt relief and the international enforcement of loan contracts, *Journal of Economic Perspectives*, **4**:43–56.

Eaton, J., and Gersovitz, M., 1981, Debt with potential repudiation: Theoretical and empirical analysis, *Review of Economic Studies*, **48**:289–309.

Economist Intelligence Unit, 1984, *Quarterly Economic Review*, No. 3.

Edgeworth, F., 1961, *Mathematical Physics*, Kegan Paul, London, UK.

Eichengreen, B., and Lindert, P.H., eds, 1989, *The International Debt Crisis in Historical Perspective*, MIT Press, Cambridge, MA, USA.

Eichengreen, B., and Wyplosz, C., 1993, The unstable EMS, *Brookings Papers on Economic Activity*, **1**.

Eiteman, D.K., 1990, American executives' perceptions of negotiating joint ventures with the P.R.C.: Lessons learned, *Columbia Journal of World Business*, **25**:4.

Ekholm, K., and Torstensson, J., 1989, Svensk handelspolitik i ljuset av ny handelsteori, *Ekonomisk Debatt*, **6**.

Elster, J., 1979, *Ulysses and the Sirens: Studies in Rationality and Irrationality*, Cambridge University Press, Cambridge, UK.

Evans, P., Jacobson, H.K., and Putnam, R.D., eds, 1993, *Double-Edged Diplomacy: International Bargaining and Domestic Politics*, University of California Press, Berkeley, CA, USA.

External Debt, Definition, Statistical Coverage and Methodology, various issues, World Bank, IMF, BIS, OECD.

Faber, M., 1990, The Volta River project: For whom the smelter tolled, in J. Pickett and H. Singer, eds, *Towards Economic Recovery in Sub-Saharan Africa: Essays in Honour of Robert Gardiner*, Chapter 4, Routledge, London, UK.

Fagen, M.D., ed., 1975, *A History of Engineering and Science in the Bell System*, Bell Telephone Laboratories, Inc., New York, NY, USA.

Fagen, R.R., and Nau, H.R., 1979, Mexican gas: The northern connection, in R.R. Fagen, ed., *Capitalism and the State in U.S.–Latin American Relations*, Stanford University Press, Stanford, CA, USA, pp. 382–424.

Fang, T., 1999, *Chinese Business Negotiating Style*, Sage, Thousand Oaks, CA, USA.

Faure, G.O., 1995a, Conflict formulation: The cross cultural challenge, in B. Bunker and J.Z. Rubin, eds, *Conflict, Cooperation, and Justice*, Jossey-Bass, San Francisco, CA, USA.

Faure, G.O., 1995b, Nonverbal negotiation in China, *Negotiation Journal*, **11**(1).

Faure, G.O., 1998, Negotiations: The Chinese concept, *Negotiation Journal*, **14**(1).

Faure, G.O., 1999, The cultural dimension of negotiation: The Chinese case, *Group Decision and Negotiation*, **8**.

Faure, G.O., and Chen, D., 1997, Chinese negotiators: Profiles and behaviors, *Journal of Euro-Asian Management*, **3**(2).

Faure, G.O., and Rubin, J.Z., eds, 1993, *Culture and Negotiation*, Sage, Newbury Park, CA, USA.

Faure, G.O., *et al.*, 1998 *La Négociation: Situations et Problématiques*, Nathan, Paris, France.

Faure-Bouteiller, A., 1998, *La Chine: Clefs pour s'implanter sur le dernier grand marché*, JV & DS, Paris, France.

Feketekuty, G., 1988, *International Trade in Services: An Overview and Blueprint for Negotiations*, Ballinger Publishing Company, Cambridge, MA, USA.

Fine, J., Lyakurwa, W., and Drabek, A., eds, 1994, *PhD Education in Economics in Sub-Saharan Africa: Lessons and Prospects*, East African Educational Publishers, Nairobi, Kenya.

Finlayson, J., and Zacher, M., 1983, The GATT and the regulation of trade barriers: Regime dynamics and functions, in S. Krasner, ed., *International Regimes*, Cornell University Press, Ithaca, NY, USA, p. 282.

Finnemore, M., 1993, International organizations as teachers of norms: The United Nations Educational, Scientific, and Cultural Organization and science policy, *International Organization*, **47**:565–598.

Fischer, H.H., 1993, Joint venturing in China: A negotiating experience, *East Asia Executive Reports*, **15**:5.

Fisher, I., 1930, *The Theory of Interest*, Macmillan, New York, NY, USA.

Fisher, B.S., 1972, *The International Coffee Agreement: A Study in Coffee Diplomacy*, Praeger, New York, NY, USA.

Fisher, G., 1980, *International Negotiation: A Cross-Cultural Perspective*, Intercultural Press, Chicago, IL, USA.

Fisher, R., 1991, Negotiating inside out, in J.W. Breslin and J.Z. Rubin, eds, *Negotiation Theory and Practice*, Program on Negotiation Books, Cambridge, MA, USA, pp. 71–79.

Fisher, R., and Ury, W., 1981, *Getting to Yes: Negotiating Agreement Without Giving In*, Houghton Mifflin, Boston, MA, USA.

Fisher, R., and Ury, W., 1991, *Getting to Yes: Negotiating Agreement Without Giving In*, B. Patton, ed., Houghton Mifflin, Boston, MA, USA.

Flamm, K., 1987, *Targeting the Computer*, The Brookings Institution, Washington, DC, USA.

Fratianni, M., and von Hagen, J., 1992, *The European Monetary System and the European Monetary Union*, Westview Press, Boulder, CO, USA.

Freeman, C., 1997, *The Diplomats' Dictionary*, US Institute of Peace, Washington, DC, USA.

Frenkel, J.A., and Johnson, H.G., 1976, *The Monetary Approach to the Balance of Payments*, George Allen and Unwin, London, UK.

Frieden, A., and Lake, D., 1995, *International Political Economy: Perspectives on Global Power and Wealth*, Routledge, London, UK.

Friedheim, R.L., 1993, *Negotiating the New Ocean Regime*, University of South Carolina Press, Columbia, SC, USA.

Friedman, M., 1968, The role of monetary policy, *American Economic Review*, **58**:1–17.

Friman, H.R., 1993, Side-payments versus security cards: Domestic bargaining tactics in international economic negotiations, *International Organization*, **47**(3):387–410.

Fudenberg, D., and Maskin, E., 1986, The folk theorem in repeated games with discounting or with incomplete information, *Econometrica*, **54**:533–554.

Furubotn, E.G., and Pejovich, S., 1974, *The Economics of Property Rights*, Ballinger, Cambridge, MA, USA.

Gardner, R.N., 1956, *Sterling–Dollar Diplomacy: Anglo-American Collaboration in the Reconstruction of Multilateral Trade*, Clarendon Press, Oxford, UK.

GATT, 1990a, Uruguay Round document, MTN.GNS/40.

GATT, 1990b, Uruguay Round document, MTN.TNC/MIN(90)/ST/24.

GATT, 1992, Uruguay Round document, MTN.GNS/47.

GATT, 1993, Uruguay Round document, MTN.TNC/37.

Gehrels, F., 1956–1957, Customs Unions from a Single Country Viewpoint, *Review of Economic Studies*, **24**(1):63.

George, A.L., Hall, D.K., and Simons, W.E., 1971, *The Limits of Coercive Diplomacy: Laos, Cuba, Vietnam*, Little, Brown, Boston, MA, USA.

Giavazzi, F., Micossi, S., and Miller, M., eds, 1988, *The European Monetary System*, Cambridge University Press, Cambridge, UK.

Gilpin, R., 1987, *The Political Economy of International Relations,* Princeton University Press, Princeton, NJ, USA.

Goldenberg, S., 1988, *International Joint Ventures in Action*, Harvard Business School Press, Boston, MA, USA.

Goldstein, J., 1986, The political economy of trade: Institutions of protection, *American Political Science Review*, **80**(1):161.

Gomes, L., 1990, *Neoclassical International Economics: An Historical Survey*, Macmillan, London, UK.

Gowa, J., 1983, *Closing the Gold Window: Domestic Politics and the End of Bretton Woods*, Cornell University Press, Ithaca, NY, USA.

Graham, R.W., 1982, *The Aluminium Industry and the Third World: Multinational Corporations and Under-Development*, Zed Press, London, UK.

Granberg, A., 1994, Metodologicheskie Aspekty Analiza Ekonomicheskogo Vzaimodeistviya Respublik Byvshego SSSR, v Perekhodnyie Prozessy: Problemy SNG, Nauka, Moscow, Russia.

Gray, B., and Yan, A., 1992, A negotiation model of joint venture formation, structure and performance, *Advances in International Comparative Management*, **7**, JAI Press, Greenwich, CT, USA.

Gray, P., 1985, *Free Trade or Protection? A Pragmatic Analysis*, Macmillan, Basingstoke, UK.

Grayson, G.W., 1993, *The North American Free Trade Agreement – Canada, USA, Mexico*, Headline Series No. 299, Foreign Policy Association, Science Press, New York, NY, USA.

Greenhouse, S., 1991a, Disney's only fear with European park is being too successful, *Chicago Tribune*, 17 March, p. 9D.

Greenhouse, S., 1991b, Playing Disney in the Parisian fields, *New York Times*, 17 February, section 3, p. 1.

Grossman, H., and Van Huyck, J.B., 1988, Sovereign debt as a contingent claim: Excusable default, repudiation and reputation, *American Economic Review*, **78**(5):1088–1097.

Guerrieri, P., and Padoan, P.C., 1989, *The Political Economy of European Integration*, Barnes & Noble, Savage, NJ, USA.

Gulati, R., Khanna, T., and Nohria, N., 1994, Unilateral commitments and the importance of process in alliances, *Sloan Management Review*, Spring.

Haas, P.M., 1992, Special issue: Knowledge, power, and international policy coordination, *International Organization*, **46**.

Haas, P.M., Keohane, R.O., and Levy, M.A., eds, 1993, *Institutions for the Earth*, MIT Press, Cambridge, MA, USA.

Habeeb, W.M., 1988, *Power and Tactics in International Negotiation*, Johns Hopkins University Press, Baltimore, MD, USA.

Habermas, J., 1984, *The Theory of Communicative Action*, Heinemann, London, UK.

Haggard, S., and Simmons, B.A., 1987, Theories of international regimes, *International Organization*, **41**:491–517.

Hakam, A.N., and Chan, K.Y., 1990, Negotiations between Singaporeans and firms in China, *Advances in Chinese Industrial Studies*, **1**.

Halbach, U., and Tiller, H., 1994, Rußland und seine Südflanke, *Außenpolitik*, No. 2, pp. 156–165.

Harberger, A.C., 1950, Currency depreciation, income and the balance of trade, *Journal of Political Economy*, **5**.

Harrigan, K., 1988, Strategic alliances and partner asymmetries, in F.J. Contractor and P. Lorange, eds, *Cooperative Strategies in International Business*, Lexington Books, Lexington, MA, USA.

Hart, M., Dymond, B., and Robertson, C., 1994, *Decision at Midnight: Inside the Canada–US Free-Trade Negotiations*, UBC Press, Vancouver, Canada.

Helpman, E., and Krugman, P., 1985, *Market Structure and Foreign Trade: Increasing Returns, Imperfect Competition and the International Economy*, MIT Press, Cambridge, MA, USA.

Henley, J., and Mee-Kau, N., 1991, The system of management and performance of joint ventures in China, *Advances in Chinese Industrial Studies*, **2**.

Hennart, J.F., 1988, A transaction cost theory of equity joint ventures, *Strategic Management Journal*, **9**:4.

Herzog, J.S., 1994, Introduction, in V. Bulmer-Thomas, N. Craske, and M. Serrano, eds, *Mexico and the North American Free Trade Agreement: Who Will Benefit?* St. Martin's Press, New York, NY, USA.

Hicks, J.R., 1939, The foundations of welfare economics, *Economic Journal*, **49**:696–712.

Hopmann, P.T., 1974, Bargaining in arms control negotiations: The sea beds denuclearization treaty, *International Organization*, **28**:313–443.

Hopmann, P.T., 1996, *The Negotiation Process and the Resolution of International Conflicts*, University of South Carolina Press, Columbia, SC, USA.

Howell, T.R., *et al.*, eds, 1988, *The Microelectronics Race: The Impact of Government Policy on International Competition*, Westview Press, Boulder, CO, USA.

Howse, R., 1995, *Regulation of International Trade*, Routledge, London, UK.

Hudec, R., 1990, *The GATT Legal System and World Trade Diplomacy*, Butterworth Legal Publishers, Salem, MA, USA.

Hufbauer, G.C., and Schott, J.J., 1992, *North American Free Trade: Issues and Recommendations*, Institute for International Economics, Washington, DC, USA.

Hufbauer, G.C., and Schott, J.J., 1993, *NAFTA: An Assessment*, Institute for International Economics, Washington, DC, USA.

Hutter, B., 1997, *Compliance: Regulation and Environment*, Clarendon, Oxford, UK.

Ikenberry, G.J., 1988, Market solutions for state problems: The international and domestic politics of American oil decontrol, *International Organization*, **42**(1):151–177.

Iklé, F., and Leites, N., 1962, Political negotiation as a process of modifying utilities, *Journal of Conflict Resolution*, **VI**(1):19–28.

IMF, *International Financial Statistics Yearbook*, various issues, Washington, DC, USA.

IMF, Annual Report, various issues, Washington, DC, USA.

International Working Group on External Debt Statistics, 1988.

IPCC Second Assessment of Climate Change: A Report of the Intergovernmental Panel on Climate Change, 1995, United Nations, New York, NY, USA.

Irwin, D., 1995, The GATT in historical perspective, *American Economic Review Papers and Proceedings*, **85**(2):323–334.

Israelewicz, I., and Lazare, F., 1992a, La bataille du franc I, *Le Monde*, 29 December.

Israelewicz, I., and Lazare, F., 1992b, La bataille du franc II, *Le Monde*, 30 December.

Jackson, J., 1969, *World Trade and the Law of GATT*, The Bobbs-Merrill Company, Indianapolis, IN, USA.

James, H., 1996, *International Monetary Cooperation Since Bretton Woods*, Oxford University Press, New York, NY, USA.

Johnson, J., 1993, NAFTA and the trade in automotive goods, in S. Globerman and M. Walker, eds, *Assessing NAFTA: A Trinational Analysis*, The Fraser Institute, Vancouver, Canada, pp. 37–43.

Kahng, D., 1970, Field effect semiconductor apparatus with memory involving entrapment of charge carriers, US Patent 3,500,142.

Kaldor, N., 1939, Welfare propositions in economics and interpersonal comparisons of utility, *Economic Journal*, **49**:549–552.

Kaletsky, A., 1985, *The Costs of Default*, Priority Press, New York, NY, USA.

Kaneko, M., and Prokop, J., 1993, A game theoretical approach to the international debt overhang, *Journal of Economics* (Zeitschrift für Nationalökonomie), **58**(1):1–24.

Kearney, K.R., 1987, *Managing Joint Venture Success*, Lexington Books, Lexington, MA, USA.

Kenen, P., 1990, Organizing debt relief: The need for a new institution, *Journal of Economic Perspectives*, **4**:7–18.

Kennedy, P.K., 1987, *The Rise and Fall of the Great Powers*, Random House, New York, NY, USA.

Keohane, R.O., 1984, *After Hegemony: Cooperation and Discord in the World Political Economy*, Princeton University Press, Princeton, NJ, USA.

Keohane, R.O., 1986, Reciprocity in international relations, *International Organization*, **40**(Winter):4.

Keohane, R.O., and Nye, J.S., 1977, *Power and Interdependence: World Politics in Transition*, Little, Brown, Boston, MA, USA.

Keohane, R.O., and Nye, J.S., 1986, *Interdependence and International Politics*, Little, Brown, Boston, MA, USA.

Kerwin, R.E., Klein, D.L., and Sarace, J.C., 1969, Method for making MIS structures, US Patent 3,475,234.

Kindel, T.I., 1990, A cultural approach to negotiations, in N. Campbell, ed., *Advances in Chinese Industrial Studies*, **1B**, JAI Press, Greenwich, CT, USA.

King, G., Keohane, R.O., and Verba, S., 1994, *Designing Social Inquiry: Scientific Inference in Qualitative Research*, Princeton University Press, Princeton, NY, USA.

Kogut, B., 1988, A Study of the life cycle of joint ventures, in F.J. Contractor and P. Lorange, eds, *Cooperative Strategies in International Business*, Lexington Books, Lexington, MA, USA.

Krasner, S.D., 1971, The Politics of Primary Commodities: A Study of Coffee 1900–1970, Ph.D. dissertation, Harvard University, Cambridge, MA, USA.

Krasner, S.D., 1973, Business government relations: The case of the international coffee agreement, *International Organization*, **27**: 495–516.

Krasner, S.D., ed., 1983, *International Regimes*, Cornell University Press, Ithaca, NY, USA.

Kremenyuk, V.A., ed., 1991, *International Negotiation: Analysis, Approaches, Issues*, Jossey-Bass, San Francisco, CA, USA.

Kremenyuk, V.A., 1992, Smutnoye Vremya: Mezhdunarodnye Posledstviya v Mezhdunarodnaya Zhizn, No. 11, pp. 21–31.

Kremenyuk, V.A., Sjöstedt, G., and Zartman, I.W., 1994, International Economic Negotiations, Unpublished paper, International Institute for Applied Systems Analysis, Laxenburg, Austria.

Kritek, P.B., 1994, *Negotiating at an Uneven Table*, Jossey-Bass, San Francisco, CA, USA.

Krugman, P., 1994, *Rethinking International Trade*, MIT Press, Cambridge, MA, USA.

Krugman, P., 1997, What should trade negotiators negotiate about? *Journal of Economic Literature,* **25**(1):113–120.

Krugman, P., and Taylor, L., 1978, Contractionary effects of devaluation, *Journal of International Economics*, August.

Landau, R., and Rosenberg, N., eds, 1986, *The Positive Sum Strategy: Harnessing Technology for Economic Growth*, National Academy, Washington, DC, USA.

Lang, N.S., 1998, *Intercultural Management in China*, D.W.V., Wiesbaden, Germany.

Langguth, G., 1993, Interdependenz von wirtschaftlicher und politischer Integration, *Außenpolitik,* No. 2, pp. 173–180.

Larson, D.W., 1988, The psychology of reciprocity in international relations, *Negotiation Journal*, **4**(3):281–301.

Lax, D.A., and Sebenius, J.K., 1986, *The Manager as Negotiator: Bargaining for Cooperation and Competitive Gain*, Free Press, New York, NY, USA.

Lax, D.A., and Sebenius, J.K., 1991a, Interests: The measure of negotiation, in J.W. Breslin and J.Z. Rubin, eds, *Negotiation Theory and Practice*, Program on Negotiation Books, Cambridge, MA, USA, pp. 161–180.

Lax, D.A., and Sebenius, J.K., 1991b, The power of alternatives or the limits to negotiation, in J.W. Breslin and J.Z. Rubin, eds, *Negotiation Theory and Practice*, Program on Negotiation Books, Cambridge, MA, USA, pp. 97–113.

Leamer, E., 1984, *Sources of International Comparative Advantage: Theory and Evidence*, MIT Press, Cambridge, MA, USA.

Lebedeva, M., 1996, Why conflicts in the former Soviet Union are so difficult to moderate and negotiate, *International Negotiation*, **13**:409–421.

Leites, N., 1950, *The Study of Bolshevism*, Free Press, New York, NY, USA.

Lerner, A.P., 1944, *The Economics of Control*, Macmillan, New York, NY, USA.

Lever, R., 1992, Next, maybe Mickey will go to Lawyerland: It took 10 years, 25 firms and a 10-pound contract to create the foundation for Euro Disneyland, *Recorder*, 23 July.

Levy, M., Young, O., and Zürn, M., 1996, The Study of International Regimes, RR-96-007, International Institute for Applied Systems Analysis, Laxenburg, Austria.

Lewicki, R.J., Litterer, J.A., Minton, J.W., and Saunders, D.M., 1994, *Negotiation*, Second edition, Irwin, Burr Ridge, IL, USA.

Lewis, J., 1990, *Partnership for Profit: Structuring and Managing Strategic Alliances*, Free Press, New York, NY, USA.

Li, Z., 1994, *The Successful Experiences on the Development of International Joint Ventures in China*, Enterprises Management Publishing House, Beijing, China [in Chinese].

Li, X., 1999, *Chinese–Dutch Business Negotiations*, Rodopi, Amsterdam, Netherlands.

Lieberman, S., 1988, *The Economic and Political Roots of the New Protectionism*, Rowman & Littlefield Publishers Inc., London, UK.

Lindberg, L., and Maier, C., eds, 1985, *The Politics of Inflation and Economic Stagnation: Theoretical Approaches and International Case Studies*, Brookings Institution, Washington, DC, USA.

Lindberg, L., and Scheingold, S., 1970, *Europe's Would-Be Polity: Patterns of Change in the European Community*, Prentice Hall, Englewood Cliffs, NJ, USA.

Lindert, P.H., and Morton, P.J., 1989, How sovereign debt has worked, in J.D. Sachs, ed., *Developing Country Debt and the World Economy*, NBER Project Report Series, University of Chicago Press, Chicago, IL, USA, pp. 225–235.

Lipsey, R.G., 1957, The theory of customs unions: Trade diversion and welfare, *Economica*, **24**(93):February.

Lipsey, R.G., 1960, The theory of customs unions: A general survey, *Economic Journal*, **70**(3):496–519.

Lipson, C., 1983, The transformation of trade: The sources and effects of regime change, in S. Krasner, ed., *International Regimes*, Cornell University Press, Ithaca, NY, USA, pp. 256–257.

Lipson, C., 1984, International cooperation in economic and security affairs, *World Politics*, **37**(1)October:6–13.

Lipson, C., 1986, Bankers' dilemmas: Private cooperation in rescheduling sovereign debts, in K.A. Oye, ed., *Cooperation under Anarchy*, Princeton University Press, Princeton, NJ, USA, pp. 200–225.

Lorange, P., and Roos, J., 1987, *Cooperative Ventures: The Role of the Preventure Design*, RP/12, Institute of International Business, Stockholm School of Economics, Stockholm, Sweden.

Lucas, R.E., 1975, An equilibrium model of the business cycle, *Journal of Political Economy*, **83**:111–144.

Lucatelli, A., 1996, *Finance and World Order: Financial Fragility, Systemic Risk and Transnational Regimes*, Greenwood Press, Westport, CT, USA.

Małecki, W., 1994, Zarządzanie długiem zagranicznym Polski w okresie transformacji (Management of Poland's Debt in the Transformation Process), Paper presented at the Conference of the Institute of Finance, 14–16 June 1994, Wilga, Poland.

Mann, J., 1989, *Beijing Jeep*, Simon and Schuster, New York, NY, USA.

Mansbach, R., and Vasquez, J., 1981, *In Search of Theory: A New Paradigm for World Politics*, Columbia University Press, New York, NY, USA.

Markesun, J., 1995, The boundaries of multinational enterprises and the theory of international trade, *The Journal of Economic Perspectives*, **9**(2):169–189.

Marshall, A., 1924, *Money, Credit and Commerce*, Macmillan, New York, NY, USA.

Masson, P., 1995, The Role of the IMF: Financing and its Adjustment and Surveillance, International Monetary Fund, Washington, DC, USA.

Martin, L.L., 1992, *Coercive Cooperation: Explaining Multilateral Economic Sanctions*, Princeton University Press, Princeton, NJ, USA.

Mathur, I., and Chen, J., 1987, *Strategies for Joint Ventures in the People's Republic of China*, Praeger, New York, NY, USA.

Mayer, F.W., 1992, Managing domestic differences in international negotiations: The strategic use of internal side-payments, *International Organization*, **46**(4):793–818.

Mayer, C., Jing, L.H., and Hui, F.L., 1991, Joint venture performances: Six case studies from Tianjin, *Advances in Chinese Industrial Studies*, **2**.

McCord, N., ed., 1970, *Free Trade: Theory and Practices from Adam Smith to Keynes*, David & Charles Ltd., Newton Abbot, UK.

McFaul, M., 1995, Why Russia's politics matter, *Foreign Affairs*, **74**(1):87–98.

Meade, J.E., 1956, *The Theory of Customs Unions*, North Holland Publishing Company, Amsterdam, Netherlands.

Melvin, J., 1989, Trade in Services: A Theoretical Analysis, Institute for Research on Public Policy, Halifax, Canada.

Messerlin, P., 1990, The European Community, in P. Messerlin and K. Sauvant, eds, *The Uruguay Round: Services in the World Economy*, The World Bank and the UN Centre on Transnational Corporations, Washington, DC, USA.

Mikelbank, P., 1991, Slipping Paris a Mickey – Disneyland is coming to France: The French are not amused, *Washington Post*, 31 March, p. F1.

Millman, G., 1995, *The Vandal's Crown: How Rebel Currency Traders Overthrew the World's Central Banks*, Free Press, New York, NY, USA.

Milner, H., 1992, International theories of cooperation among nations: Strengths and weaknesses, *World Politics*, **44**:466–496.

Milner, H., and Yoffie, D.B., 1989, Between free trade and protectionism: Strategic trade policy and a theory of corporate trade demands, *International Organization*, **43**(2):239–272.

Mining Journal, 1984, **301**(7717):37–38.

Mirlin, G.A., and Pelymsky, G.A., 1995, Problemy otraslevoi, mezhotraslevoi i regionalnoi economiki v Vestnik Moskovskogo Universiteta, No. 6, Ekonomika, No. 3, pp. 31–40.

Mitchell, R.B., 1994, Regime design matters: Intentional oil pollution and treaty compliance, *International Organization*, **48**:425–458.

Mohr, E., 1991, *Economic Theory and Sovereign International Debt*, Harcourt Brace Jovanovich, Academic Press, London, UK.

Mostyn, C., 1992, Column one, *Vancouver Sun*, 13 April.

Müller, H., 1993, The internalization of principles, norms, and rules by governments: The case of security regimes, in V. Rittberger and P. Mayer, eds, *Regime Theory and International Relations*, Clarendon Press, Oxford, UK, pp. 361–390.

Nash, J.F., 1950, The bargaining problem, *Econometrica*, **18**:155–162.

Neary, J.P., and Van Wijnbergen, S., 1986, Natural resources and the macro-economy: A theoretical framework, in J.P. Neary and S. Van Wijnbergen, eds, *Natural Resources and the Macroeconomy*, MIT Press, Cambridge, MA, USA.

Neunuebel, E.R.J., 1995, Pre-contract considerations and negotiations, in D. Lewis, ed., *The Life and the Death of a Joint Venture in China*, Asia Law and Practice, Hong Kong, China.

Nicolson, H., 1939, *Peacemaking 1919*, Oxford University Press, New York, NY, USA.

Nicolson, H., 1963, *Diplomacy*, Oxford University Press, Oxford, UK.

Norman, P., 1992, The day Germany planted a currency time bomb, *Financial Times*, 12 December.

Norman, P., and Barber, L., 1992, The tragedy of errors, *Financial Times*, 11 December, p. 2.

North, D., 1990, *Institutions, Institutional Change and Economic Performance*, Cambridge University Press, Cambridge, UK.

Obstfeld, M., 1986, Rational and self-fulfilling balance-of-payments crises, *American Economic Review*, **76**(1):72–81.

Odell, J.S., 1982a, Bretton Woods and international political disintegration: Implications for monetary diplomacy, in R. Lombra and W. Witte, eds, *The Political Economy of Domestic and International Monetary Relations*, Iowa State University Press, Ames, IA, USA, pp. 39–58.

Odell, J.S., 1982b, *U.S. International Monetary Policy*, Princeton University Press, Princeton, NJ, USA.

Odell, J.S., 1985, The outcomes of international trade conflicts: The U.S. and South Korea, 1960–1981, *International Studies Quarterly*, **29**:263–286.

Odell, J.S., 1988, From London to Bretton Woods: Sources of change in bargaining strategies and outcomes, *Journal of Public Policy*, **8**:287–316.

Odell, J.S., 1993, International threats and internal politics: Brazil, the European Community, and the United States, 1985–1987, in P. Evans, H.K. Jacobson, and R.D. Putnam, eds, *Double-Edged Diplomacy: International Bargaining and Domestic Politics*, University of California Press, Berkeley, CA, USA.

Okogu, B.E., 1987, Structural adjustment in African countries: A theoretical assessment, *Zeitschrift für Afrikastudien*, **1**(1).

Okogu, B.E., 1992, *Africa and Economic Structural Adjustment: Case Studies of Ghana, Nigeria and Zambia*, The OPEC Fund for International Development, Pamphlet series No. 29, OPEC Fund, Vienna, Austria.

Okogu, B.E., 1995, Issues in Nigerian petroleum product pricing, *Journal of African Economies*, **4**(3).

Oliver, P., 1996, Free Movement of Goods in the European Community: Under Articles 30 through 36 of the Rome Treaty, Sweet and Maxwell, London, UK.

Olson, M., 1965, *The Logic of Collective Action*, Harvard University Press, Cambridge, MA, USA.

Osagie, E., 1986, Operating SFEM in the Nigerian setting, *Nigerian Journal of Economic and Social Studies*, **28**(1).

Oye, K.A., ed., 1986, *Cooperation under Anarchy*, Princeton University Press, Princeton, NJ, USA.

Özler, S., 1993, Have commercial banks ignored history? *American Economic Review*, **83**(3):608–620.

Özler, S., and Tabellini, G., 1991, External Debt and Political Instability, NBER Working Paper No. 3772, July.

Pechman, J., ed., 1989, *The Role of the Economist in Government: An International Perspective*, Harvester Wheatsheaf, New York, NY, USA.

Pen, J., 1952, A general theory of bargaining, *The American Economic Review*, **42**.

Porter, R.C., and Ranney, S.I., 1982, An eclectic model of recent LDC macroeconomic policy analysis, *World Development*, **10**(8).

Preston, L., and Windsor, D., 1997, *The Rules of the Game in the Global Economy: Policy Regimes for International Business*, Kluwer Academic Publishers, Boston, MA, USA.

Pruitt, D.G., 1991, Strategy in negotiation, in V.A. Kremenyuk, ed., *International Negotiation: Analysis, Approaches, Issues*, Jossey-Bass, San Francisco, CA, USA, pp. 78–89.

Putnam, D., 1988, Diplomacy and domestic politics: The logic of two-level games, *International Organization*, **42**(3):427–460.

Putnam, R., and Bayne, N., 1987, *Hanging Together: Cooperation and Conflict in the Seven-Power Summits*, Sage Publications, London, UK.

Pye, L., 1982, *Chinese Commercial Negotiating Style*, Oelschlager, New York, NY, USA.

Quarterly Economic Review of Poland, 1981, **3**:15.

Raiffa, H., 1982, *The Art and Science of Negotiation*, Harvard University Press, Cambridge, MA, USA.

Raiffa, H., 1991, Contributions of applied systems analysis to international negotiation, in V. Kremenyuk, ed., *International Negotiation: Analysis, Approaches, Issues*, Jossey-Bass, San Francisco, CA, USA, pp. 5–21.

Rapoport, A., 1966, *Two-Person Game Theory: The Essential Ideas*, University of Michigan Press, Ann Arbor, MI, USA.

Report of the Royal Commission on the Economic Union and Development Prospects for Canada, 1985, 3 volumes, Supply and Management Services, Ottawa, Canada.

Resener, M., 1992, *Business Wire*, Morgen-Walker Associates S.A., Paris, France.

Reyna, J., 1993, Services, in T. Stewart, ed., *The GATT Uruguay Round: A Negotiating History (1986–1992)*, Kluwer Law and Taxation Publishers, Deventer, Netherlands.

Rhodes, C., 1989, Reciprocity in trade: The utility of a bargaining strategy, *International Organization*, **43**(2):273–300.

Richardson, D., 1990, The political economy of strategic trade policy, *International Organization*, **44**(1).

Riché, P., and Wyplosz, C., 1993, *L'Union Monétaire de l'Europe*, Seuil-Point, Paris, France.

Rogov, S., 1994, Itog Pechalen, No Vykhod Iz Tupika Est, *NG Newspaper*, 31 December.

Rosenau, J., 1990, *Turbulence in World Politics: A Theory of Change and Continuity*, Princeton University Press, Princeton, NJ, USA.

Roth, R., 1992, Doors open one hour early for waiting crowd at EuroDisney, *United Press International*, 12 April.

Rubin, J.Z., ed., 1981, *Dynamics of Third Party Intervention: Kissinger in the Middle East*, Praeger, New York, NY, USA.

Rubin, J.Z, and Brown, B.R., 1975, *The Social Psychology of Bargaining and Negotiations*, Academic Press, New York, NY, USA.

Rubin, J.Z., and Zartman, I.W., 1995, Asymmetrical negotiations: Some survey results that may surprise, *Negotiation Journal*, **11**(4):349–364.

Rubinstein, A., 1982, Perfect equilibrium in a bargaining model, *Econometrica*, **50**(1):97–109.

Rubinstein, A., 1991, Comments on the interpretation of game theory, *Econometrica*, **59**(4):909–924.

Ryan, C., 1990, Trade liberalisation and financial services, *The World Economy*, **13**(3).

Sachs, J.D., 1984, Theoretical issues in international borrowing, *Princeton Studies in International Finance*, No. 54, Department of Economics, Princeton University, Princeton, NJ, USA.

Sachs, J.D., 1988, Comprehensive debt retirement: The Bolivian example, *Brookings Papers on Economic Activity*, **2**:705–713.

Sachs, J.D., ed., 1989, Developing country debt and the world economy, NBER Project Report Series, University of Chicago Press, Chicago, IL, USA.

Sachs, J.D., and Larraine, P., 1992, *Macroeconomics for the Global Economy*, Prentice Hall, New York, NY, USA.

Sagorskij, A., 1993, Entwicklungen in der GUS: Herausforderungen für Rußland, *Außenpolitik,* No. 2, pp. 144–152.

Sah, C.-T., 1988, Evolution of the MOS transistor: From conception to VLSI, *Proceedings of the IEEE*, **76**(10):1285–1290.

Salancik, G., and Pfeffer, J., 1977, Who gets power and how they hold on to it: A strategic-contingency model of power, *Organizational Dynamics*, **5**:3–21.

Sargent, T.J., 1998, Rational expectations, the real rate of interest and the natural rate of unemployment, *Brookings Papers on Economic Activity*, **2**:429–472.

Saunders, H., and Albin, C., 1993, *The Disengagment Negotiations*, Johns Hopkins University Foreign Policy Institute, Washington, DC, USA.;

Sawyerr, A., 1989, Techniques of negotiating with transnational corporations: Tips for the table, in P. Coughlin, ed., *Negotiations Management: Preparation, Strategy and Tactics*, Chapter 4, Commonwealth Secretariat, London, UK.

Sawyerr, A., 1990, Some legal issues arising from the negotiation of the VALCO agreement, in F.S. Tsikata, ed., *Essays from the Ghana-VALCO Renegotiations, 1982–85*, Chapter 4, Ghana Publishing Corporation, Accra, Ghana.

Schelling, T., 1960, *The Strategy of Conflict*, Harvard University Press, Cambridge, MA, USA.

Schelling, T., 1966, *Arms and Influence*, Yale University Press, New Haven, CT, USA.

Schoppa, L.J., 1993, Two-level games and bargaining outcomes: Why gaiatsu succeeds in Japan in some cases but not others, *International Organization*, **47**:353–386.

Schuenemann, M., 1995, GUS: Zwischen Nachlaßverwaltung und Reintegration, *Blätter für deutsche und internationale Politik*, No. 3, pp. 298–308.

Scitovsky, T., 1941, A note on welfare propositions in economics, *Review of Economic Studies*, **9**.

Sebenius, J.K., 1991, Negotiation analysis, in V. Kremenyuk, ed., *International Negotiation: Analysis, Approaches, Issues*, Jossey-Bass, San Francisco, CA, USA, pp. 203–215.

Sebenius, J.K., 1992, Negotiation analysis: A characterization and review, *Management Science*, **38**(1):18–38.

Senti, R., 1996, NAFTA: Die nordamerikanische Freihandelszone: Entstehung – Vertragsinhalt – Auswirkungen, Schultess, Zürich, Switzerland.

Shapiro, J., Behrman, J., Fisher, W., and Powell, S., 1991, *Direct Investment and Joint Ventures in China*, Quorum Books, New York, NY, USA.

Shishkov, Y.V., 1994, V.R. Evstigneev, Reintegratsia Postsovetskogo Ekonomicheskogo Prostranstva I Opyt Zapadnoi Evropy, Moscow, Russia, p. 26.

Shubik, M., 1971, Games of status, *Behavioral Science*, 16 March:117–129.

Simon, H., 1953, Notes on the observation and measurement of power, *Journal of Politics*, **15**(3):500–516.

Sims, R., and Casely-Hayford, L., 1990, Renegotiating the price and availability of energy for an aluminium smelter: The VALCO renegotiations, in F.S. Tsikata, ed., *Essays from the Ghana-VALCO Renegotiations, 1982–85*, Chapter 4, Ghana Publishing Corporation, Accra, Ghana.

Sjöstedt, G., 1991, Trade talks, in V. Kremenyuk, ed., *International Negotiation: Analysis, Approaches, Issues*, Jossey-Bass, San Francisco, CA, USA, pp. 315–330.

Sjöstedt, G., 1994, Issue clarification and the role of consensual knowledge in the UNCED process, in B. Spector, G. Sjöstedt, and I.W. Zartman, eds, *Negotiating International Regimes: Lessons Learned from the United Nations Conference on Environment and Development (UNCED)*, Graham and Trotman/Martinus Nijhoff, London, UK.

Sloss, L., and Davis, M.S., 1987, The pursuit of power and influence through negotiation, in H. Binnendijk, ed., *National Negotiating Styles*, Foreign Service Institute, US Department of State, Washington, DC, USA, pp. 17–41.

Snidal, D., 1985, The limits of hegemonic stability theory, *International Organization*, **39**(4):579–614.

Snyder, R.C., and Robinson, J.A., 1960, National and international decision making in institute for international order, *Problems of Research*, No. 4, pp. 118–121.

Stein, J., ed., 1992, *Getting to the Table: The Processes of International Prenegotiation*, Johns Hopkins University Press, Baltimore, MD, USA.

Stein, J., and Pauly, L., eds, 1993, *Choosing to Cooperate*, Johns Hopkins University Press, Baltimore, MD, USA.

Stewart, S., and Carver, A., eds, 1997, *Advances in Chinese Industrial Studies*, 5, JAI Press, Greenwich, CT, USA.

Stiles, K.W., 1991, *Negotiating Debt: The IMF Lending Process*, Westview Press, Boulder, CO, USA.

Strang, D., and Chang, P.M.Y., 1993, The International Labor Organization and the welfare state: Institutional effects on national welfare spending, 1960–1980, *International Organization*, **47**:235-262.

Strange, S., 1992, States, firms, and diplomacy, *International Affairs*, **68**(1):1–15.

Summers, L., 1993, Statement before the Senate Committee on Banking, Housing and Urban Affairs, Washington, DC, USA, 26 October, p. 2.

Supply and Management Services, 1985, Macdonald Commission Report on Economic Policy, Report of the Royal Commission on the Economic Union and Development Prospects for Canada, 3 volumes, Ottawa, Canada.

Susskind, L., Dolin, E., and Breslin, W., eds, 1991, International Environmental Treaty Making, Program on Negotiation at Harvard Law School, Harvard Law School, Cambridge, MA, USA.

Synge, R., 1983, Ghana prepares to break VALCO stalemate, *African Economic Digest*, 15 July, pp. 2–3.

Tarzi, S., 1991, Third world governments and multinational corporations: Dynamics of host's bargaining power, *International Relations*, **10**(3):237–249.

Tawney, R., 1931, *Equality*, Unwin, London, UK.

Tay, G., 1995, The joint venture contract, in D. Lewis, ed., *The Life and the Death of a Joint Venture in China*, Asia Law and Practice, Hong Kong, China.

Thibaut, J., and Kelley, H., 1959, *The Social Psychology of Groups*, Wiley, New York, NY, USA.

Thomas, K., 1976, Conflict and conflict management, in M.D. Dunnette, ed., *Handbook of Industrial and Organisational Psychology*, Rand McNally, Chicago, IL, USA.

Tilton, M., 1994, Informal market governance in Japan's basic materials industries, *International Organization*, **48**:663–685.

Tracy, B., 1978, Bargaining as trial and error, in I.W. Zartman, ed., *The Negotiation Process: Theories and Applications*, Sage Publications, Beverly Hills, CA, USA.

Tsikata, F.S., ed., 1990, *Essays from the Ghana-VALCO Renegotiations, 1982–85*, Ghana Publishing Corporation, Accra, Ghana.

Tumlir, J., 1985, *Protectionism: Trade Policy in Democratic Societies*, American Enterprise Institute for Public Policy Research Washington, DC, USA.

Tung, R.L., 1982, *US–China Negotiations*, Pergamon, New York, NY, USA.

Umesh, U.N., 1994, The value of trademarks and patents, in R.A. Peterson, ed., *Technology Knowledge Activities*, **2**(1), Summer 1994, The IC^2 Institute, The University of Texas, Austin, TX, USA.

UN Economic Commission for Africa (UNECA), 1989, *African Alternative Framework to Structural Adjustment Programs for Socioeconomic Recovery and Transformation*, UNECA, Addis Ababa, Ethiopia.

Underdal, A., 1992, The concept of regime effectiveness, *Cooperation and Conflict*, **27**:227–240.

Ury, W., 1991, *Getting Past No*, Bantam, New York, NY, USA.

Ury, W., 1992, New safety net in the CIS, *State of World Conflict Report 1991–1992*, Carter Center of Emory University, Atlanta, GA, USA.

US House of Representatives, Committee on Banking and Currency, 1973, *To Amend the Par Value Modification Act of 1972: Hearings*, 93rd Congress, First Session.

US Senate, Committee on Finance, 1971, *Foreign Trade: Hearings*, 92nd Congress, First Session.

Valavanis, S., 1958, The resolution of conflict when utilities interact, *Journal of Conflict Resolution*, **2**(2):156-169.

Victor, D., 1996, The Early Operation of the Montreal Protocol's Non-compliance Procedure, ER-96-002, International Institute for Applied Systems Analysis, Laxenburg, Austria.

Viner, J., 1950, *The Customs Union Issue*, Carnegie Endowment for International Peace, Chapter 4, New York, NY, USA.

Vlasova, M., 1996, Basic models of CIS negotiations, *International Negotiation*, **1**(3):423–443.

Volcker, P., and Gyohten, T., 1992, *Changing Fortunes: The World's Money and the Threat to American Leadership*, Times Books, New York, NY, USA.

Wagner, C., 1993, Perceived correlates of successful joint ventures negotiations in China, *International Journal of Management*, **10**(4).

Wagner, L., 1998, *Problem-Solving and Convergent Bargaining*, PhD Dissertation, Johns Hopkins University, Baltimore, MD, USA.

Wall, J., and Blum, M., 1991, Community mediation in the People's Republic of China, *The Journal of Conflict Resolution*, **35**:1.

Waller, M., 1992, France stands by to spring the Mickey Mouse tourist trap, *Times*, 9 April.

Walt Disney Company, 1993, Annual Report, Burbank, CA, USA.

Walton, R.E., and McKersie, R.B., 1965/1991, *A Behavioral Theory of Labor Negotiations: An Analysis of a Social Interaction System*, McGraw-Hill, New York, NY, USA.

Waltz, K.N., 1979, *Theory of International Politics*, Addison-Wesley, Reading, MA, USA.

Webber, A., 1989, The case of the Chinese diary, *Harvard Business Review*, **89**:6.

Weil, J., 1992, *United Press International*, 12 April.

Weiss, S., 1987, Creating the GM-Toyota joint venture: A case of complex negotiation, *Columbia Journal of World Business*, Summer.

Wells, R., 1993, Tolerance of arrearages: How IMF loan policy can effect debt reduction, *American Economic Review*, **83**(3):621–633.

West Africa, 1983, June 6, p. 1362.

Whitcher, T., 1992, The Trojan mouse is throwing a party, *Daily Telegraph*, 10 April, p. 21.

Williamson, O.E., 1979, Transaction costs economics: The governance of contractual relations, *Journal of Law and Economics*, **2**.

Williamson, O.E., 1981, The economics of organization: The transaction costs approach, *American Journal of Sociology*, **87**.

Winham, G.R., 1977, Negotiation as a management process, *World Politics*, **30**:87–114.

Winham, G.R., 1986, *International Trade and the Tokyo Round Negotiation*, Princeton University Press, Princeton, NJ, USA.

Winham, G.R., 1988, Why Canada acted, in W. Diebold, ed., *Bilateralism, Multilateralism, and Canada in U.S. Trade Policy*, Ballinger, Cambridge, MA, USA, pp. 37–54.

Winham, G.R., 1994, NAFTA and the trade policy revolution of the 1980s: A Canadian perspective, *International Journal*, **XLIX**:472–479.

Winham, G.R., and Grant, H., 1994, Antidumping and countervailing duties in regional trade agreements: Canada–US FTA, NAFTA and beyond, *Minnesota Journal of Global Trade*, **3**:1–34.

Winters, A., 1987, Reciprocity, in M. Finger and A. Olechowski, eds, *The Uruguay Round: A Handbook on the Multilateral Trade Negotiations*, World Bank, Washington, DC, USA, p. 46.

Wonnacott, R.J., 1990, *Canada and the U.S.–Mexico Free Trade Negotiations*, Commentary 21, C.D. Howe Institute, Toronto, Canada, September.

Woodyard, C., 1992, Resort in Europe to test Disney's magic touch, *Los Angeles Times*, 5 April, Part D, p. 1.

World Bank, 1994, *Adjustment in Africa: Reforms, Results, and the Road Ahead*, Oxford University Press, Oxford, UK.

World Bank, *World Debt Tables*, various issues, Washington, DC, USA.

Wriggins, W.H., 1976, Up for auction: Malta bargains with Great Britain, 1971, in I.W. Zartman, ed., *The 50% Solution*, Anchor Press/Doubleday, Garden City, NY, USA, pp. 208–234.

Young, O.R., ed., 1975, *Bargaining: Formal Theories of Negotiation*, University of Illinois Press, Urbana, IL, USA.

Young, O.R., 1989, The politics of international regime formation, *International Organization*, **33**(3).

Young, O.R., 1991, Political leadership and regime formation: On the development of institutions in international society, *International Organization*, **45**(3):281–308.

Zartman, I.W., ed., 1978, *The Negotiation Process: Theories and Applications*, Sage Publications, Beverly Hills, CA, USA.

Zartman, I.W., ed., 1986, *Positive Sum: Improving North-South Relations*, Transaction Books, New Brunswick, NJ, USA.

Zartman, I.W., ed., 1987a, *The 50% Solution: How to Bargain Successfully with Hijackers, Strikers, Bosses, Oil Magnates, Arabs, Russians, and Other Worthy Opponents in this Modern World*, Yale University Press, New Haven, CT, USA.

Zartman, I.W., ed., 1987b, *Positive Sum: Improving North-South Negotiations*, Transaction Books, New Brunswick, NJ, USA.

Zartman, I.W., 1991, The structure of negotiation, in V.A. Kremenyuk, ed., *International Negotiation: Analysis, Approaches, Issues*, Jossey-Bass, San Francisco, CA, USA, pp. 65–77 (especially p. 69).

Zartman, I.W., ed., 1994, *International Multilateral Negotiation: Approaches to the Management of Complexity*, Jossey-Bass, San Francisco, CA, USA.

Zartman, I.W., 1997, Conflict and order: Justice in negotiations, *International Political Science Review*, **18**(2):121–138.

Zartman, I.W., 1997, Explaining Oslo, *International Negotiation*, **2**(2):195–215.

Zartman, I.W., and Bassani, A., 1987, *The Algerian Gas Negotiations*, Pew Case Studies in International Affairs, No. 103, Institute for the Study of Diplomacy, Georgetown University, Washington, DC, USA.

Zartman, I.W., and Berman, M., 1982, *The Practical Negotiator*, Yale University Press, New Haven, CT, USA.

Zartman, I.W., and Rubin, J.Z., eds, 1999, *Power and Negotiation*, University of Michigan Press, Ann Arbor, MI, USA.

Zartman, I.W., Druckman, D., Jensen, L., Pruitt, D.G., and Young, H.P., 1996, Negotiation as a search for justice, *International Negotiation*, **1**(1):79–98.

Zeuthen, F., 1930, *Problems of Monopoly and Economic Warfare*, Routledge & Kegan Paul, London, UK.

Zloch-Christy, I., 1987, *Debt Problems of Eastern Europe*, Cambridge University Press, Cambridge, UK.

Zloch-Christy, I., 1991, *East-West Financial Relations: Current Problems and Future Prospects*, Cambridge University Press, Cambridge, UK.

Index